THRONE
OF
GRACE

THRONE
OF
GRACE

A Mountain Man,
an Epic Adventure,
and the Bloody Conquest
of the American West

BOB DRURY AND TOM CLAVIN

ST. MARTIN'S PRESS
NEW YORK

First published in the United States by St. Martin's Press,
an imprint of St. Martin's Publishing Group

www.stmartins.com

Frontispiece courtesy of the University of the Pacific

Endpaper credits: United States of America North West Map © Science History
Images/Alamy Stock Photo; United States of America South West Map © Hum Historical/
Alamy Stock Photo; *Cliffs of Green River* by Thomas Moran, 1874 © Ian Dagnall
Computing/Alamy Stock Photo; *The Lake Her Lone Bosom Expands to the Sky*
by Alfred Jacob Miller, 1850 © Ian Dagnall Computing/Alamy Stock Photo

Maps by David Lindroth

Book design by Michelle McMillian

The Library of Congress Cataloging-in-Publication Data is available upon request.

ISBN 978-1-250-28583-6 (hardcover)
ISBN 978-1-250-28584-3 (ebook)

Our books may be purchased in bulk for promotional, educational, or business use.
Please contact your local bookseller or the Macmillan Corporate and
Premium Sales Department at 1-800-221-7945, extension 5442, or by email
at MacmillanSpecialMarkets@macmillan.com.

First Edition: 2024

10 9 8 7 6 5 4 3 2 1

Again, and as ever, for the Divine Ms. D.
rfxd

To Maureen Tompkins: For her support and generosity
and especially her friendship.
T.C.

CONTENTS

PART III: THE ODYSSEY

EPILOGUE

A NOTE TO READERS

The English spelling and pronunciation of nineteenth-century Native American tribes was, in the era, notoriously diffuse. This was particularly true among the dialects of European Americans, who, to take just one example, often referred to the Indian nation cited here as the Arikara as the Arickaree, Ricara, Racari, Rees, and dozens of other appellations. For narrative sake, throughout the following text, we have attempted to present readers with the most standardized tribal designations recognized and acknowledged today. Moreover, for the sake of clarity, we have accepted the European American names of such tribes; thus, as another example, we refer to the Indians who call themselves Chatiks si Chatiks—"Men of Men"—as the Pawnee, as early French, British, and Americans usually referred to them.

Further, regarding the term *Indian*: as two white authors chronicling an epoch so crucial to the fate of North America's Indigenous peoples, we relied on historical context. *Indian* not only was in common usage during the decades we write about but also is nearly as customary today. For several previous books we went to pains to check with our Indigenous sources regarding the word. No less a personage than the late Maka Luta Win— who also went by the Anglicized name Mary Ann Red Cloud and was the great-great-granddaughter of the legendary Lakota warrior-chief known to whites as Red Cloud—personally suggested to us that *Native American*, *American Indian*, and *Indian* were all accepted descriptive terms, as were the nouns *warrior* and *brave*.

Similarly, although the etymology of the English word *chief* traces to French and, before that, to Latin, it has since taken on a culturally specific usage among a majority of America's Indigenous peoples—"the hereditary chief who has the power passed down from one generation to the next along bloodlines," explains the Indigenous Corporate Training website, "and the elected chief who is chosen by band members." Herein we thus use the word interchangeably with its synonym *headman*.

Finally, nineteenth-century written English is notoriously cluttered with confounding punctuation, capitalized nouns erupting in the middle of sentences, and multiple spellings of the same word, all of which did not become standardized until comparatively recently. Throughout the following text we present to readers the voluminous writings of our characters precisely as they themselves put those words to paper in letters, journals, periodicals, and military reports from the time period.

PROLOGUE

The hole was dry. Jed Smith was discouraged, not surprised. He had been warned about this stretch of the Santa Fe Trail. The old timers called it "The Water Scrape." For good reason. Smith and his lead scout, the Irish-born Thomas Fitzpatrick, dismounted and ran their fingers through the clumpy alluvium at the bottom of the wash. The granules were cool, damp. Fitzpatrick unsheathed his long-handled fleshing knife and began scraping for an underground spring. Smith, climbing back to the lip, raised his spyglass and swept the horizon.

It was late May 1831, and months of severe drought had rendered the entire Southwest parched and brown. Even the Arkansas River, where their wagon train had topped off its water barrels before crossing into Mexican territory, had been but hip deep. Those casks, lashed beneath the twenty-two Murphy freight wagons laden with trade goods, had been empty going on four days. By the time Smith and Fitzpatrick plunged ahead in their search, the swollen tongues of the wagon mules were lolling out of their mouths. Even Smith's and Fitzpatrick's mounts, sturdy mustangs evolved to ride for days without water, had begun to wobble, close to staggering.

Smith reckoned they were perhaps twelve miles out ahead of the caravan. Over the nearly ten years in which he had traversed the far west's mountains and deserts, its prairies and forests, he had developed an innate sense of direction. Especially distances. Whether covered or yet to be traveled. He knew the Cimarron River had to be near. He squinted through his spyglass. A scraggly yucca, a purple bloom of sage, a sagging cottonwood, would mean they were close. But no vegetation appeared for as far as he could see. All was empty; the only movement came from the ever-shifting sand piles, the eerie "walking hills," carried on their never-ending journey by the blistering south wind.

A stretch of broken ground, twisted and faulted and seeming to snake through a series of knobby rises, finally caught Smith's attention. Some three miles distant, nearly due south. Rocks? Like the subterranean Mojave he knew all too well, the Cimarron was a dry river, its flow disappearing beneath a gravelly bed for months at a time only to resurface after heavy rains. Or when forced upward by an immovable impediment. Like nonpermeable rock.

Smith, saving his saliva, tossed a pebble to catch Fitzpatrick's attention. He swung his chin toward the craggy heights. The Irishman, hard as hickory bark, understood. The two had been boon companions since their initial trip up the Missouri and into the mountains during what seemed a lifetime ago. Words were not needed. Fitzpatrick would continue to dig, awaiting the arrival of the desperate wagon train. Smith would ride south. Fitzpatrick watched through his own spyglass until his friend's silhouette vanished beneath the rim of a distant arroyo.

* * *

Despite having risked a good third of his life breaking mountain trail, trapping and trading beaver pelts, fording ice-strewn rivers, and battling hostile tribes, the vast and rugged territory west of the Mississippi River remained a country of myth to the deeply religious Jedediah Smith—a parable, in a sense, meant to illustrate God's munificence to any man willing to keep the Christian faith through the many trials the Almighty set before him.

Smith had kept his faith; if anything, it had sustained him during his time with heathens and apostates both red and white. It was said that he made the mountaintop his confessional, the forest glade his altar. The high-country outfits he had piloted were sprawling amalgamations of licentiousness and vice, yet he himself touched alcohol sparingly, shied away from tobacco, and—despite myriad opportunities—had never "womaned up." "With his ears constantly filled with the language of the profane and dissolute," a contemporary chronicler wrote, "no evil communication proceeded out of his mouth."

Up to this point, Smith's Lord had indeed placed many trials in his path, few if any more hazardous than at present. The buffalo tracks crisscrossing The Water Scrape, headed in all directions, formed a crazy quilt. The freshest hoof marks, however, appeared to lead to and from the rock outcropping he had spotted, now close enough to make out without his spyglass.

He was within a half mile of the rounded bluffs when the riders showed themselves. Through the shimmering heat haze, Smith counted fifteen, maybe twenty. Comanche or Kiowa, he could not be certain. It was said that a veteran plainsman could tell the difference by studying the ornate stitching adorning their buckskin leggings and moccasins. Smith's attention was more focused on the sunlight glinting off the metallic blue barrels of their rifles and the steel-tipped points of their buffalo lances.

In his time on the borderlands, Jed Smith had absorbed an irrefutable truth foreign to most easterners—that there was no single, amorphous mass of "Indians" inhabiting the North American West. Each of the scores if not hundreds of tribes and moieties scattered across the continent had its own customs, its own ritual beliefs, its own often violent views toward outsiders, particularly whites. And each expected to be dealt with on its own terms. In this case, however, any difference was moot. The Comanche and Kiowa had long ago formed a military alliance that had evolved into the most feared and powerful entity across the Southern Plains. Riding and fighting as one, they had cowed first the Spanish and then the Mexicans and had even driven off the mighty Apache. Presently, with wagon traffic increasing on the thin ribbon of trail connecting St. Louis to Santa Fe that bisected their lands, they had begun to wage war on the trespassing Americans.

Jed Smith had sharpened his battle instincts to a fine edge in lethal confrontations with peoples as disparate as the Arikara and Blackfeet, the Mojave and Arapaho. He recognized when it was time to flee, time to fight, time to negotiate. The band he now studied sat atop stout, well-watered ponies that would easily overtake his own hobbling horse. To run would be futile. And given their number, combat, even if he could find cover, appeared equally bootless. Which left talk.

Jed Smith drew his long-barreled Creamer rifle from its elk-skin scabbard, balanced it across the rise behind his saddle horn, and spurred his mount forward. It was his only play.

PART I

THE HUNTER

Bring me men to match my mountains,
Bring me men to match my plains,
Men with empires in their purpose,
And new era in their brains.

—SAM WALTER FOSS, *THE COMING AMERICAN*

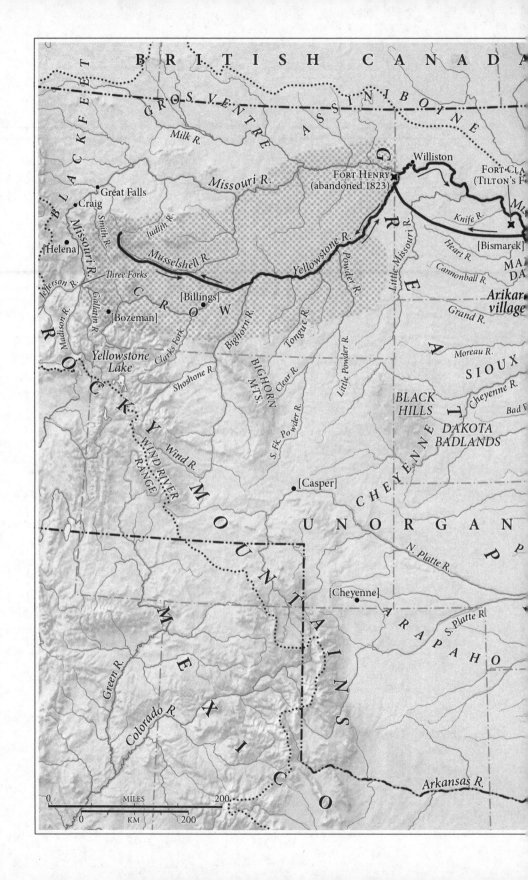

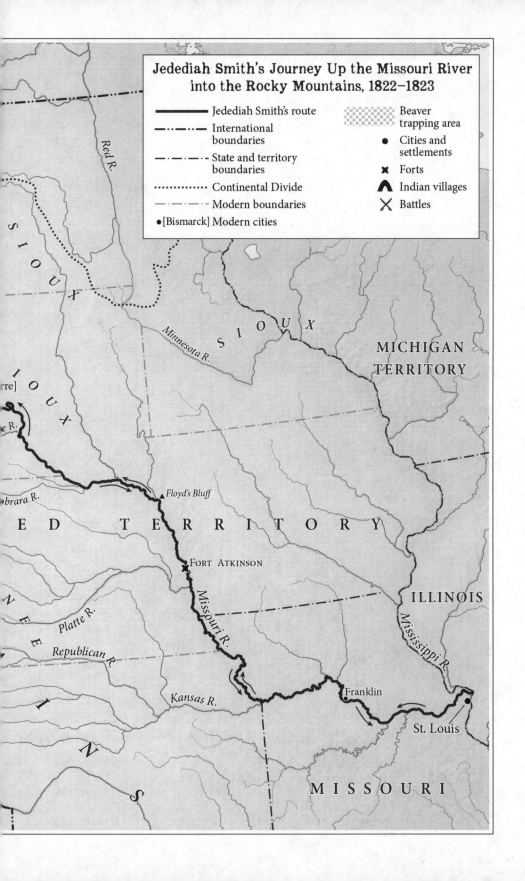

Jedediah Smith's Journey Up the Missouri River into the Rocky Mountains, 1822–1823

——————— Jedediah Smith's route	▦ Beaver trapping area
—··—··— International boundaries	● Cities and settlements
—·—·—· State and territory boundaries	✖ Forts
············· Continental Divide	⋀ Indian villages
—··—··— Modern boundaries	✕ Battles
●[Bismarck] Modern cities	

Red R.

SIOUX

Minnesota R.

SIOUX

MICHIGAN TERRITORY

[Pierre]

SIOUX

e R.

brara R.

Floyd's Bluff

ED TERRITORY

Niobrara R.

FORT ATKINSON

Missouri R.

ILLINOIS

Platte R.

Republican R.

Mississippi R.

Kansas R.

P A W N E E

Franklin

St. Louis

I N D I A N S

MISSOURI

CHAPTER 1

———— • ————

"ENTERPRISING YOUNG MEN"

It must surely have seemed a sight to the tall, young northerner. A hunter by trade, he had passed through a variety of hamlets, villages, and even blossoming boomtowns in his twenty-three years of meandering west. But nothing had prepared Jedediah Strong Smith for the bustling city of St. Louis, a virtual metropolis looming high over the western bank of the Mississippi River.

It was a chilly April morning in 1822 when Smith, likely alighting from a packet that had ferried him from the green fields of northern Illinois, traversed the narrow riverside boulevard the locals referred to as "Under the Hill." The street, slippery with mud and horse shit, was teeming with a cross section of humanity—shallow-shaft Ozark lead miners in greasy overalls cashing in company scrip for kegs of rum; restive Indiana farmers bound for the loamy fields opening up along the Boone's Lick Road abutting Osage Indian territory; peddlers and storekeepers clad in colorful broadcloth frock coats beckoning customers to inspect their wares; and quarrelsome former soldiers of the Republic still wearing their patched and tattered uniforms as they poured to and from the chockablock taverns and bordellos.

Smith passed weathered wooden stalls and narrow storefronts stocked with imports craved by those the fur trade had newly made rich—shimmering cut glassware, handcrafted leather shoes and boots, casks of cognac and wine. There was also a plethora of Black slaves, surely more people of color than he had ever seen, wearing coarse homespun and conversing in pidgin French as they loaded their owners' carts with bar iron and plow molds.

The river itself was clogged with pirogues and keelboats and even the occasional paddle steamer—an invention so newfangled that children and even some adults flocked to the mud flats to watch the wide-bodied vessels labor through the swirling ochre currents. Between and around the larger craft, rough and weather-browned men maneuvered simpler dugout canoes, constructed from hollowed-out cottonwoods disgorged into the Mississippi from its confluence with the Missouri River twelve miles to the north. The canoes rode low in the water, piled with bundles of beaver pelts and buffalo hides, which their wild-eyed pilots were eager to exchange for powder and lead, for tobacco and smoked pork and flour, and especially for the whiskey and rum carried west down the Ohio River or borne north from Natchez and New Orleans.*

Jed Smith was no stranger to water, having grown up along the shores of both Pennsylvania's Lake Erie and Ohio's Sandusky Bay. At the age of thirteen he had signed on as an apprentice seaman on a Lake Erie freighter hauling trade goods between Montreal and what were then the western American borderlands. Yet the sight of the Creole rivermen gracefully steering their sleek vessels to transport hotheaded duelists out to the sandbar in the middle of the river doubtlessly remained a marvel to a naïve country boy. It was on that "neutral" spit of sand nicknamed "Bloody Island," allegedly subject to neither Missouri nor Illinois law, where aggrieved combatants—prone to quarreling over the affections of the soiled

---

* The British and, later, the American use of the word *buffalo* was a bastardization of the immense herds of *boeufs* first encountered by French trappers on the North American Plains in the 1630s. In 1774 the animals were officially classified as "American bison" in order to taxonomically distinguish them from Asian and African buffalo species. However, because the American bison were universally referred to as buffalo across the Old West, that is the designation we have chosen for this narrative.

doves of the local sporting houses—would attempt to blow each other's brains out with their finely crafted Wogdon and Barton flintlock pistols.

Such doings made small sense to Smith, who was descended from a family that had arrived in New England not long after the Pilgrims alighted near Plymouth Rock. Across the generations, his forebears—farmers and artisans—had retained the pious, God-fearing traditions of those early English religious dissidents. One distant relative had earned eighteen shillings a year using his trumpet to summon his New Hampshire neighbors to church each Sunday. And family lore had it that another had praised the Lord for his miraculous survival after a freak eddy had pulled his canoe over Niagara Falls. Like his ancestors, Smith believed that only those whom God elected would receive His grace, and that his righteous deity watched closely to determine who would be saved and who would be damned come Judgment Day. The young man would live his life accordingly.

So it occurred that in the wake of the American Revolution, Smith's father, also named Jedediah, married the Connecticut-born Sally Strong. The newlyweds moved to the Susquehanna Valley village of Jericho in southern New York State. There the elder Smith and his brother-in-law opened a general store that catered to the river folk settling farmsteads along the long watercourse for which the green vale was named.* Jed Smith was the fourth child, and second son, born to Jedediah Sr. and Sally in January 1799; his mother, a dutiful wife of the era, fulfilled her primary obligation by giving birth to five more sons over the ensuing fifteen years.†

Young "Diah," as his family called him, spent his childhood exploring and hunting squirrel, wild turkey, and whitetail deer through the long, green valley's thick stands of soaring oak, boxelder, and fragrant sassafras, which lent the rolling hills a year-round scent of sweet lemon and cinnamon. The

---

* Jericho was renamed Bainbridge in 1814 in honor of the U.S. Navy commodore William Bainbridge, hero of both Barbary Coast Wars as well as the War of 1812.

† The Smiths had three other children who either did not survive childbirth or died in infancy. The Smiths fared better than many families: 46 percent of children born in the United States in 1800 did not live to celebrate their fifth birthday.

Iroquois had long since abandoned the Susquehanna woodlands, but a fascination with the Indians who decades earlier had called the land their home fired the boy's imagination. His ears perked whenever Jedediah Sr. told the story of his great-great-uncle being killed by the Narragansetts during King Philip's War. And as young boys of the era were wont to do, he no doubt scoured the pea vine and clover that carpeted the forest floor, searching for old arrowheads and shards of the clay pots in which the tribe's women had boiled the venerated "three sisters" of the earth—corn, squash, and beans.

When Jed was twelve his father again caught the westering fever and relocated his growing clan to Pennsylvania's Erie County, hard by the eponymous lake. It was here that Jed not only honed his hunter's and boatman's skills but also met a family that would have a lasting effect on his life. The Simons of Erie County's North East Township were what passed for aristocracy on the nascent United States' western frontier. When Jed's favorite sister, Eunice, married Solomon Simons, the son of the pioneer physician Dr. Titus Gordon Vespasian Simons, a bond between the families was formed. It grew even stronger when Dr. Simons's daughter Louisa wed Jed's older brother, Ralph, such that the two families moved as one farther west into northern Ohio.

Dr. Simons had taken an avuncular shine to young Jed, and he began complementing the schooling the boy received from a succession of Methodist circuit riders in reading, writing, and ciphering, as arithmetic was called. He also added a smattering of Latin to the curriculum. When the doctor thought Jed was ready—around the time that British troops were setting fire to the White House during the War of 1812—he gifted him with a newly published leather-bound book detailing the adventures of Meriwether Lewis and William Clark during their momentous twenty-eight-month cross-country expedition to and from the Pacific.

Jed Smith cherished the chronicle, studying the narrative by candlelight, and came to recognize that his treks through the Susquehanna woods and along the craggy shore-scree of Lake Erie and Sandusky Bay were but toddler's steps compared to the epic accomplishments Lewis, Clark, and their Corps of Discovery achieved. Legend has it that along with a family Bible, Smith carried that book with him for the rest of his life in his kit bag, called a "possible sack," as it contained everything a hunter or trapper could possibly need.

Now, a decade later and with that possible sack slung over his shoulder, he found himself hiking up from the St. Louis waterfront to the heights of the city proper, where the capacious municipality rivaled only his brief visit to New Orleans two years earlier.

* * *

Although dubbed the "Mound City," the chain of ancient Native American temple hills and knolls that had once occupied the path Jed Smith now trod through St. Louis were mostly gone, leveled by the New Orleans–born half brothers Auguste and Pierre Chouteau when they laid out the town's grid. It was Auguste Chouteau's father, the French explorer Pierre Laclède Liguest, who in 1764 had selected St. Louis—which he named in honor of France's King Louis IX—as the flood-proof high ground for his fur-trading post. Where feather- and bead-clad members of the Illini Confederacy, a loose affiliation of a dozen or so Native American tribes, had once met to hold religious ceremonies and trade marts, Smith now shared street space with women in flamboyant sun bonnets promenading before finely built houses, many of them constructed of the famed St. Louis clay pressed and kilned into red bricks that were already being exported to Boston and New York.

The ubiquitous brick buildings, such as the new Catholic Cathedral on Church Street with its paintings by Rubens and Raphael and its gold embroideries donated by European coreligionists, were rapidly replacing the old French *poteaux-en-terre* dwellings—essentially roof-bearing grooved elm logs planted perpendicular into the ground. And at the instigation of the Chouteau brothers, whose ornate homes at the crest of the city's tallest hill were the town's jewels, several of the main avenues had even lately been paved. This was much to the consternation of the Gallic traditionalists whose rough-hewn wooden wagon wheels, lacking iron bands, were prone to shattering on the granite cobblestones.

Smith walked west, past the offices of General William Clark, who, in the wake of his epic partnership with Meriwether Lewis, had held several political posts under presidential appointment and was currently President James Monroe's superintendent of Indian affairs. It has never been ascertained if Smith still carried in his pocket the yellowing newspaper clipping he had torn from the *Missouri Gazette & Public Advertiser* months earlier. Nestled among the personal notices on page three of the broadsheet— warnings to local merchants against extending credit to spendthrift wives; shopkeepers' advertisements heralding the recent arrival of barrels of salted mackerel, kegs of Madeira wine, and aromatic "Spanish Segars"— was posted a fifty-seven-word announcement. It was addressed:

TO

Enterprising Young Men

The subscriber wishes to engage ONE HUNDRED MEN, to ascend the River Missouri to its source, there to be employed for one, two or three years.—For particulars enquire of Major Andrew Henry, near the Lead Mines, in the county of Washington, (who will ascend with, and command the party) or to the subscriber at St. Louis.*

The subscriber in question was the lieutenant governor of the newly minted state of Missouri, General William Henry Ashley. Ashley had served as an officer in a territorial militia during the War of 1812 and had subsequently risen to the rank of brigadier general. He saw little need to delineate the tasks awaiting the men he and his business partner and fellow former soldier, the Pennsylvania-born Major Andrew Henry, planned to

---

* The portentous want ad, which ran from February 13 to March 6, 1822, in the *Missouri Gazette & Public Advertiser*, would also appear two weeks later in the *St. Louis Enquirer* and a month after that in the *Missouri Republican*.

take upriver. The western fur trade that had swelled St. Louis's population ninefold to more than five thousand people in the nineteen years since the Louisiana Purchase had also transformed the town into the most thriving "jumping-off point" for the "new" American borderlands—"the Ur-country of the trans-Mississippi frontier," in the words of the Kit Carson biographer Hampton Sides.*

Missouri in general and St. Louis in particular "had long been the portal of American expansion," Sides continues, "the pad where great expectations were outfitted and adventures launched, the place where westering fever burned at its highest pitch." And for weeks now gossip along both the rough quay-side grogshops and in the city's gentrified upper quarter had coalesced around one item: the beaver-trapping expedition that would culminate with the forty-four-year-old Gen. Ashley and Maj. Henry, three years Ashley's senior, re-establishing a fort at the mouth of the Yellowstone River.

It had been years since any company had outfitted up for the mountains. Yet now there were four separate firms racing up the Missouri River. Their managing partners had decided that it was time. Time to re-establish the lucrative beaver trade.

*   *   *

Through much of the eighteenth and nineteenth centuries, the soft felt coat of the semiaquatic North American rodent classified as *Castor canadensis* dominated the European clothing market. Though beaver fur occasionally provided the material for collars, jackets, and even full-length parkas popular in China and Russia, it was predominantly craved by European hatmakers who had long understood that the waxlike lanolin contained in the animal's wool rendered the headgear, whether tricornered

---

* As part of the 1763 Treaty of Paris ending the Seven Years' War—known as the French and Indian War in North America—all French holdings west of the Mississippi were transferred to Spain. In 1795, with Spain weakened by yet another war, the Spanish King Charles III gave the Americans perpetual rights to navigation on the Mississippi. Napoleon Bonaparte won back the western territory in 1801, and President Thomas Jefferson negotiated the Louisiana Purchase two years later.

or high-crowned, water resistant.* Such was the popularity that between 1700 and the outset of the Henry-Ashley expedition in 1822, markets in continental Europe had purchased nearly forty million pieces of beaver headwear from British milliners.

But even earlier in the colonial period the beaver pelt had, from New England to Virginia, been the veritable equivalent of gold as a unit of barter. In December 1621, only a year after the first Pilgrim settlement was founded in Plymouth, Massachusetts, an initial shipment of American beaver furs left for England aboard the fifty-five-ton schooner *Fortune* as payment for needed supplies. Within a few years, the Plymouth colonists had virtually abandoned their original plan to sustain themselves through hunting and cod fishing and instead concentrated their economy almost entirely on the fur trade with Native Americans from the north.

Inevitably, by the time Jed Smith arrived in St. Louis, the beaver population east of the Mississippi had, like the Eurasian species, *Castor fiber*, been hunted nearly to extinction. This left the western United States and Canada as the center of the world's beaver-pelt trade. The cordilleras dividing the North American continent were ideally suited to the construction of beaver dens, or "lodges," and early western fur brokers, known as factors, rarely had to travel farther than the Black Hills in present-day South Dakota—some three hundred miles east of the Rocky Mountains—to traffic in Indian catch. By the turn of the nineteenth century, however, this was no longer the case, and yearslong beaver-hunting expeditions into the ruthless Rockies had been necessary since the first decade of the 1800s. This was the tradition that Gen. Ashley planned to revive.

* * *

---

* Hatters scraped the lanolin-rich short, wooly hairs from a beaver hide, worked them into felt, and combined this with a mixture called mash, which helped mold the concoction into the shape of a hat. Mercury, a toxic metal, was also mixed into this mash, and the symptoms of mercury poisoning—often associated with those of insanity—ran so rampant throughout the industry as to introduce the phrase "mad as a hatter."

The widowed William Ashley had never been west of St. Louis. He had, however, partnered up well, as his joint venture with Andrew Henry would constitute Maj. Henry's return to the granite crags and ridges scraping the western sky. Fourteen years earlier, in 1808, Henry—whose contemporaneous portraits depict a thick-set, slope-chinned countenance with a boyish thousand-yard stare from dark eyes—had signed on with one of the initial outfits venturing into the mountains. That firm, incorporated as the Missouri Fur Company, was the brainchild of Manuel Lisa, a New Orleans–born Spanish American who, in 1802, was granted a contract by French officials to act as the sole trading agent between the Osage Indians and the Mississippi's downriver merchants.

President Jefferson's purchase of the Louisiana Territory from Napoleon Bonaparte's First French Republic the following year eliminated Lisa's monopoly on America's western fur trade, and Lisa found himself searching for new streams of revenue. This proved difficult. Missouri's territorial governor—posthumously discovered to have been a spy for the Spanish Crown—denied Lisa's application to establish trade routes with Santa Fe, then still under Spain's colonial rule. Lisa pivoted and instead looked northwest. Recruiting two members of Lewis and Clark's Corps of Discovery as guides, he ventured up the Missouri River in the spring of 1807 with a party of forty-two men. Reaching the Yellowstone River, Lisa's outfit ascended the watercourse 170 miles to establish a trading post at the mouth of the Yellowstone's confluence with the Bighorn. He named his post Fort Raymond, in honor of his oldest son.

If, as the historian Harrison Clifford Dale proposes, "Lewis and Clark were the trail makers [and] Lisa the trade maker," the news of Lisa's presence on the Upper Missouri was received with jubilation in the nation's capital. For it was there in the mountains that Lisa's venture planted the implicit flag for President Thomas Jefferson's strategic geopolitical design for the North American continent.

For all his agrarian tendencies, Jefferson was far from a shortsighted statesman. He had sanctioned the Lewis and Clark expedition ostensibly to gain a more accurate assessment of the new lands acquired in the Louisiana Purchase, with a secondary goal of gauging the viability of future oceangoing trade with Asia. The true, underlying objective of the undertaking, however, was to counter festering American concerns over British thirst for the territory northwest of the Rocky Mountains. Sensing that war-torn France and Spain were gradually losing their purchase on the New World, Jefferson feared that England was ready to fill this vacuum. As he presciently had written some two decades earlier in his Christmas greeting to Clark's brother, George Rogers Clark, "We shall to the American union add a barrier against the dangerous extension of the British Province of Canada and add to the Empire of liberty an extensive and fertile Country."

Jefferson had cause to worry. Just over one hundred years earlier, in 1670, the English King Charles II had granted a monopolistic royal charter ceding what was then known as Rupert's Land—the 2.5 million square miles west of Ontario, comprising about one-third of modern-day Canada—to the joint-stock corporation Hudson's Bay Company. Moreover, the American president was also casting a watchful eye over an upstart fur-trapping outfit called the North West Fur Company, a Montreal-based consortium of predominantly Scottish Canadians whose hunter-trappers were already blatantly poaching on the Hudson's Bay Company's western territory.

As the Canada–America border west of the Rocky Mountains remained in dispute, the region that would become known as the Oregon Territory—encompassing the current states of Washington, Oregon, and Idaho, as well as parts of western Montana and Wyoming—was nominally up for grabs. The United States, having just flung the Redcoats back across the Atlantic in its War for Independence, was haunted by the specter that England would now attempt to re-enter North America from the Pacific. It was a British person, after all, who had coined the axiom that possession is nine-tenths of the law.

Moreover, the enemy had a geographic jump. In May 1793, six months after George Washington was unanimously re-elected to his second presidential term, the flame-bearded Scottish explorer Alexander Mackenzie set off from what is today the northern section of Canada's Alberta province to seek a route to the Pacific Ocean. Thirteen weeks later he reached the shores of British Columbia, becoming the first European north of Spanish Mexico to traverse the breadth of the continent. Eight years later, Mackenzie published the exploratory journals of his trans-Canadian trek. It had a galvanizing effect on President Jefferson and his political circle.

In reaction, Jefferson alternately bullied and cajoled Congress into funding an expedition to explore the far northwest beyond the Rocky Mountains. He appointed his personal secretary, the former army officer and robust outdoorsman Meriwether Lewis, as its commanding officer. The autodidactic Jefferson personally taught Lewis how to calculate longitude and latitude. He also ensured, at the government's expense, that Lewis was trained by mathematicians, scientists, and geographers in the use of the chronometer and sextant as well as in cartography, botany, and geology. Lewis in turn selected his former U.S. Army commander William Clark, four years his senior, to co-lead the forty-man expedition.

The Corps of Discovery reports regarding the fauna, flora, terrain, and Indigenous tribes it encountered may have held a passing interest for entrepreneurs like Manuel Lisa. But it was the tales of the thousands of mountain streams and ponds aswarm with fat beavers that drove Lisa and others west in 1808. Lisa had turned a sound profit on his first journey into the Rockies. This enabled him to form an even larger trapping expedition the following spring, returning to the mountains with thirteen barges and keelboats crewed by 350 men. These included both the future major Andrew Henry and the well-traveled George Drouillard, the son of a French Canadian father and a Shawnee mother who had served as an interpreter for Lewis and Clark.

During this foray, Henry, acting as his trapping team's *Booshway*, or captain, led a small contingent across the Continental Divide in western Montana before dropping down into Wyoming's Snake River country.* This was the deepest penetration into the Oregon Country that any American outfit had ever made. But the presence of so many white men from the States encroaching on their territory stirred the ire of the Blackfeet, who had forged a tenuous alliance with the Canadians, trading their beaver pelts for British muskets, shot, and powder. Two years earlier the tribe had clashed with a small scouting party from the Corps of Discovery, with Meriwether Lewis personally killing a Blackfeet brave who attempted to steal his rifle and horse.

George Drouillard had been among Lewis's company that day and now during Lisa's second foray into the territory—in a pointed reminder that the tribe had long memories—Drouillard's mutilated and beheaded corpse was discovered in a clearing, its entrails ritually arranged about the desecrated body. Drouillard, esteemed for the number of grizzly bears he had taken down under Lewis and Clark, had not gone down without a fight. Blood trails and tracks on the ground indicated that the surrounded Drouillard, still mounted and using his horse as a shield, ridden in smaller and smaller concentric circles, emptying his rifle and pistols before leaping from his mount and wielding his tomahawk and skinning knife to the end.

Within the year, the Blackfeet had driven those early, outnumbered Americans from the mountains, with the Indians claiming the scalps of twenty trappers. Their success, however, may have been moot. For though men like Manuel Lisa and Andrew Henry had spent years braving the dangers of the Rocky Mountain high country, the naval blockade thrown up by the British during the War of 1812 was to depress the American beaver market for a decade. The trade curve was only just bending up once again when Jed Smith arrived in St. Louis to call on William Ashley.

---

* The term *Booshway*—a bastardized version of the French *bourgeois* picked up by the Americans from the pidgin French-speaking voyageurs—was applied to any acknowledged leader of a trapping party.

CHAPTER 2

—•—

ASTOR'S FOLLY

There were scores of candidates already roaming St. Louis when Gen. Ashley placed his extensive newspaper advertisements seeking hands for his mountain enterprise. Not least of these were the Creole coxswains whom Jed Smith had observed on his arrival. Most of these well-muscled rivermen were as skilled in the wild woods as they were on the water. But Ashley, a born Virginian who had journeyed west following the Louisiana Purchase, remained a slaveholder whose racial prejudices were emblematic of the era. He simply did not trust the mixed-race sailors.

An ardent proponent of the Missouri Compromise, which had brought Missouri into the United States as a slave state to balance Maine's free-state status, Ashley judged the Creoles capable of serving as voyageurs—polemen, oar men, and, in swift-running currents, cable men discharged to the riverbank to lug a vessel upstream by a thick cordelle tied to the mast. But from his point of view, their complexions and fondness for whiskey left them too unreliable in an armed standoff. For he and his partner, Andrew Henry, were preparing not only to trap beaver but, if diplomacy or bribery failed to mollify the Indigenous tribes, to battle for the right to harvest the pelts. Ashley had his eye on the Missouri governor's seat in the election two years hence, and burnishing his bona fides with a victorious gunfight here and there could only animate his campaign.

The expedition's first hurdle would be the two fixed Arikara villages located side by side, overlooking the Missouri some sixteen hundred miles upriver, in what is now northern South Dakota. The Rees, as the whites called them, had once been receptive to Americans passing through their territory. Lewis, Clark, and their regiment had spent five welcoming and peaceful days at the Arikara villages, with Meriwether Lewis noting in his journal that the Indians "were all friendly & Glad to See us." But over the ensuing decades, circumstances had much changed. The turning point occurred in 1807, when word reached the Indians of the mysterious death in Washington, DC, of an Arikara headman who had been convinced to accompany Lewis there. Later that year, Arikara arrows and musket balls had turned back a U.S. Army keelboat escorting home a Mandan chief who had also visited the American capital. The Bluecoats, under the command of Ensign Nathaniel Pryor, took nineteen casualties.*

In a subsequent development that the Arikara took as an egregious insult, the flow of American manufactured goods that the tribe had once facilitated as middlemen between the whites and the more westerly Indian bands had been redirected to market posts located on sites controlled by their hated enemy, the Sioux, who now supervised the distribution of the iron kettles and steel knives, the trade of wool and mirrors, and most especially the rifles and ammunition shipped across the Plains. Ironically, it was the Sioux, factions of whom camped below the Arikara, who had unsuccessfully attempted to forestall the Lewis and Clark expedition. Now, in the run-up to the grand Henry-Ashley undertaking, Arikara attitudes toward the Americans were laden with ambiguity. The eminent Native American historian Roger L. Nichols notes that their perspective toward whites in the early nineteenth century "varied from vicious attacks, through strained relationships, to enthusiastic

---

* The U.S. Army rank of ensign, roughly equal to a second lieutenant, was abolished in 1815.

friendship depending on internal social pressures . . . and the success or failure of their dealings with the Sioux." For the moment, the Sioux were ascendant.

Beyond the Sioux holdings and the Arikara villages, Ashley also expected to encounter the fair-skinned, blue-eyed Mandan inhabiting the far reaches of the Upper Missouri Valley; Cheyenne, Arapahoe, and Pawnee roaming the tributaries of the Platte River; Blackfeet and Gros Ventre prowling the mountain corridors of modern-day western Montana; Shoshone residing deeper in the vast granite basins of the Rockies; and the stately Crows, already being pushed west by the Sioux and now assiduously protecting their new holdings along the buckling Yellowstone and Bighorn bluffs.*

An earlier era of good feeling between infrequent European explorers and traders and the Indigenous peoples of the West—a brief epoch when pragmatic Indians were eager to take advantage of the white intruder's superior technology and manufactured goods—was rapidly devolving into a power struggle over territory and natural resources. The social disorder and diseases introduced by the newcomers only hastened the animosity. Some tribes, like the sedentary and dwindling Mandan population living above the Arikara, lacked the means to carry out guerrilla warfare and instead—with a sexual diplomacy that scandalized prudish easterners— offered their wives and sisters as bedfellows to the "hairy white men" in exchange for gifts. But given the unpredictable temperament of the Arikara—in William Ashley's eyes an inscrutable and inherently malicious people—no one knew what other tribal dispositions toward his and Andrew Henry's party might prove problematic. Eleven years earlier, Henry had barely made it out of the mountains alive after a string of Blackfeet attacks that included the dismemberment of George Drouillard. And only

---

* The European-like physical features and coloring of the Mandan peoples sparked early speculation that the tribespeople were either the descendants of the folkloric "Welsh Indians" said to have emigrated to North America from Wales sometime in the late twelfth century or the result of interbreeding with Scandinavian explorers shipwrecked in North America a century later. Archeologists discount both theories as myth.

recently word had reached St. Louis that the same tribe was beginning to turn on the increasing number of British Canadian trappers flowing through their territory.*

To this purpose, the forty-four-year-old Ashley preferred that a good portion of his expedition be manned by easterners. He recruited the physical elite, flinty Kentuckians and Virginians, Pennsylvanians, New Yorkers, and New Englanders; men who, he assumed, knew their way around a long rifle. Having already made a minor fortune with Andrew Henry in the lead shot and gunpowder business dealing with rough-hewn miners, Ashley knew precisely what type of hands he wanted on this journey. Jedediah Smith considered himself just such a man. As he recalled with a typically laconic entry into his journal, "In the spring [of 1822] I came down to St. Louis and hearing of an expedition that was fitting out for the prosecution of the fur trade I called on Gen. Ashley to make an engagement to go with him as a hunter. I found no difficulty in making a bargain on as good terms as I had reason to expect."

From Ashley's point of view the feeling was mutual. Upon escorting Smith into the parlor of his residence on South B Street not far from the river, the lieutenant governor could not help but be impressed with the lean and lank young job seeker's poise and demeanor. At six feet tall, with a broad upper body, Smith towered over the short and slight Ashley. And with his thick straw-colored hair combed back off his wide forehead, Smith's intense blue eyes highlighted a hawklike nose, tight smile, and a prominent, clean-shaven chin that appeared to have been carved out of quartzite.

Contemporaneous accounts describe Ashley as a peripatetic raconteur, words barking out of his mouth as if he were bumping along in a wagon with broken springs. Smith was apparently unruffled by this tic, and Ashley later wrote that over the hour or so the two conversed, he recognized in the gangly easterner a self-possession rare in a man of his age who might

---

* To the whites in the mountains, all three linguistically related subsets of the Niitsitapi tribe—the Siksika, or Blackfeet proper, the Piegans, and the Bloods—fell under the generic umbrella term *Blackfeet*.

provide a deep keel in rough seas. He also surmised that Smith's enthusiasm for the trapping venture would prove contagious to the entire party. Included in the bargain was the young man's fervent religiosity; in Smith's readings and rereadings of the journals of Lewis and Clark, he saw God's hand in the haunting bugle of the Rocky Mountain elk, in the golden and purple blooms of grape flowers carpeting the valleys of the Northwest, in the rays of the sun refracting through beads of moisture to create rainbows. Ashley hoped that Smith's disdain for profanity and hard liquor as well as his reverence for the Bible he carried might set some sort of example. This was wishful thinking.

For his part, Smith admitted to Ashley that his greatest desire was to learn. He was indeed a fine shot with a rifle, but he had never killed a man. If it came to that, however, he was prepared. He was also curious to study the mores of the western Indigenous peoples who inhabited the lands the Henry-Ashley outfit would soon be penetrating. Would their customs be similar to those of the Eastern Woodlands tribes—the Iroquois, Shawnee, and Delaware—whose sagas had so enthralled him as a boy? More importantly, Smith longed to test his woodsman skills in the mountains and whatever lay beyond. He told Ashley about the book Dr. Simons had gifted him and how his esteem for the feats of Lewis and Clark had sparked a dream to perhaps one day follow in their footsteps down the Columbia River all the way to the Pacific.

The beaver-trade profits to be taken were not trifling to the hundreds of uprooted easterners seeking new beginnings on the far side of the Mississippi, and Jed Smith was not immune to their allure. But Ashley surely sensed in the golden-haired tyro standing before him something besides financial incentive. Smith fairly brimmed with a zeal for adventure and, more explicitly, for exploration. It was as if Lewis and Clark's Corps of Discovery had only just broached the possibilities of what lay past the western peaks, and Smith yearned to complete the job there for the taking.

The early nineteenth century was an epoch in which exploration, politics, and commerce often found common cause in America. The twenty-three states of the union in 1820 contained just shy of ten million people (of whom 15 percent were slaves), while covering a landmass of fewer than two million square miles. Within three decades those numbers would close to triple and double, respectively.* William Ashley, of course, could not have envisioned that the ardent inquisitiveness of the visitor pacing his St. Louis parlor would nearly single-handedly break the trails that would hasten that expansion, much less blaze paths that would limn the borders of the entirety of the future United States. But given Smith's hunger for new vistas, the diminutive general must have had an inkling of Smith's potential for just such a feat.

Smith's physical presence, his comportment, and his profound powers of observation were enough to convince Ashley to hire him on the spot as a hunter-trapper. The contract was more than generous. The company would provide Smith with powder and lead and he and the other hunter-trappers—but not the salaried voyageurs—would be entitled to divvy up a share of the company's eventual profits from peltry.

Smith was well aware that the value of beaver fur had surged in the previous two years from its nadir during the war with England. With British ships blockading American ports for thirty-two months, the price of a pelt had fallen to $2.50 per pound. When the December 1814 Treaty of Ghent ended hostilities, the rates began a slow rebound only to plummet again with the Panic of 1819, the first widespread and enduring financial crisis of the young United States. Now, however, with the American economy finally climbing out of its rut and skins selling for an average of $6 per pound on the fluctuating St. Louis market—about $150 in current, inflation-adjusted dollars—Smith foresaw the profit to be had.

Moreover, the compensation method Ashley and Henry had devised for their hunter-trappers was innovative. The western beaver trade had begun on a simple premise—the exploitation of the Native Americans.

---

* From a population of 9,638,453 inhabiting 1,749,462 square miles in 1820 to 23,191,876 people living on 2,940,042 square miles in 1850.

Men such as Pierre Laclède Liguest, the British brokers on the shores of Hudson's Bay, and the young Manuel Lisa would simply erect a fort and await the arrival of curious Indians. The European Americans would then ply them with cheap trade goods and cheaper liquor, on which the tribes became dependent, and wait for their return with pelts to barter for more. The company factors and hunters might do some trapping as they traveled, but for the most part it was a transactional business.

Competition, however, had altered the old equations, and the Canadian operators of the Hudson's Bay Company and the North West Fur Company, as well as Americans such as Manuel Lisa, had come to realize that their industry was mired in a kind of institutional sclerosis. White hunters in small teams of twos and threes could trap a stream or pond more efficiently than entire Indian hunting parties. On a darker note, William Ashley and Andrew Henry had also absorbed the lessons of the disastrously brief tenure of the now-defunct Pacific Fur Company.

* * *

The Pacific Fur Company was the brainchild of the wealthy New York City merchant, real estate mogul, and fur trader John Jacob Astor, the United States' first multimillionaire. In 1810, Astor dispatched two trapping parties to the Pacific coast. One departed New York by sea, journeying around Cape Horn on the three-masted merchant barque *Tonquin*. The other traveled overland, skirting south of the Rocky Mountain route taken by Lewis and Clark. Their mission was to construct a trading post, christened Fort Astoria, on the narrow littoral between present-day Oregon's coastal mountain range and the mouth of the Columbia River. Fort Astoria, in Astor's vision, would become the base for a chain of fur-trading posts stretching from the Pacific to the Rockies and beyond—"an emporium of the west."

The venture began dismally when in March 1811, eight of the *Tonquin*'s crew were washed overboard and lost while negotiating the Columbia's treacherous sandbar, dubbed "Cape Disappointment" by one eighteenth-century sea captain.* When the *Tonquin's* navigator finally located the channel winding through the rocky shoals battered by thirty-foot waves, the ship sailed seventeen miles upriver, dropping anchor on the south bank not far from where Lewis and Clark had made winter camp six years earlier.

The site could not have offered more of a construction challenge. Studded with huge boulders, nearly impenetrable growths of willow scrub, and several millennia's worth of mammoth fallen conifers, the greatest hurdles to establishing a camp were the giant Sitka spruce. Some measured close to fifty feet in girth and in places were packed so tightly that a man could barely squeeze between them. It took Astor's oceangoing party nearly two months to clear and level but an acre of ground.

Finally, after a small log stockade was erected in mid-June—the first American colony on the West Coast of North America—the *Tonquin* and her crew sailed off to initiate trade with the Indigenous tribes of Vancouver Island. Ill fortune continued to follow the vessel. Anchored in Clayoquot Sound off the west coast of the island, her captain, the former U.S. naval officer and notorious martinet aptly named Jonathan Thorn, invited members of the local Tia-o-qui-aht tribe aboard to inspect his trade goods.

A row ensued when the short-tempered Thorn, frustrated at the asking price for local furs, slapped an elder sachem in the face with a beaver pelt. The Indians feigned remorse and lowered their asking price—with a caveat. In addition to the wool blankets and trinkets proffered by the Americans, each brave asked to receive a steel blade. The deal was struck. Armed with their new knives, the Tia-o-qui-aht turned on the *Tonquin's* crew and killed all but two—a sailor who hid himself in the powder magazine and a Quinalt Indian interpreter called Joseachal, who was only spared because of his marital connections to the powerful Chinookan tribes to the south.

---

* By modest count, over the last two centuries some two thousand ships and boats have sunk or been bashed apart near the confluence of the Columbia and the sea, taking some seven hundred sailors down with them. This has earned Cape Disappointment the sobriquet the "Graveyard of the Pacific" (Johnson, "In Fraught Corner of Washington, Classroom with Forty-Foot Waves," A14).

The next morning, when the Tia-o-qui-aht returned to plunder the ship, the lone survivor detonated the magazine and blew the *Tonquin* to pieces. According to Joseachal, who made his way back to Fort Astoria to relate the particulars of the encounter, "a thunderous roar rolled across the water, echoing for miles along the wooded coast. Torsos, heads, limbs, and pieces of flesh arced over the cover. Shattered bits of wood from the *Tonquin*'s thick hull and cedar canoes rained down upon the sea." Between one hundred and two hundred Tia-o-qui-ahts perished.

The loss of Astor's ship and its surfeit of trade goods was compounded by the onerous deal he was forced to cut to placate the state-sponsored Russian outfits already trapping in western Canada under a charter from the late Emperor Paul I, son of Catherine the Great. To keep the peace with Paul's successor, Alexander I, Astor agreed to supply oceangoing merchant vessels to the Russians to carry their furs to China's Manchu Qing dynasty in exchange for porcelain, tea, and bolts of the coveted Nanking cotton cloth.*

Despite these serial calamities, the Astorians, as they had come to be known, soldiered on. Over the winter they expanded their little outpost to include a blacksmith's shop, a storage shed for pelts, and even a bark-roofed dormitory of sorts. Perhaps more significantly, they also ringed their fort with cannons. The guns were not only to deter hostile Indians, particularly the suspicious Chinookans, but also to serve as a warning to the brash hunter-trappers from the rogue North West Fur Company. As Thomas Jefferson had feared, these Nor'Westers, as they were called, were already infiltrating down the Columbia River from its headwaters in British Columbia and opening trading centers in what would become Washington State and upper Oregon.

In early 1812, the seagoing Astorians were finally joined by Astor's overland company of thirty men (plus the wife and two children of their

---

* Astor's sea captains were already familiar with the routes to Chinese ports, as a part of Astor's fortune stemmed from his smuggling of opium from India into China.

Indian interpreter). This was about half the number with which their captain, Wilson Price Hunt, had begun his two-thousand-mile trek from St. Louis. When inland hunting operations, such as they were, finally commenced, it was soon apparent that the New Jersey–born Hunt had no business leading a wilderness expedition. His parties, woefully unprepared for the rigors of winter mountain survival, faced a dearth of game, snowed-in passes, and canoe-smashing rapids along the wild tributaries of the Columbia, especially the Snake and Salmon Rivers. Forced to take shelter in a makeshift wooden way station some 350 miles northeast of Fort Astoria, their number slowly dwindled from exposure, stealth Indian raids, rattlesnake bites, and bear attacks. They managed to collect or trade for about 2,500 pelts, a paltry first year's take considering the expense and hardship.

That summer, another of Astor's merchant ships arrived at Fort Astoria, bringing not only badly needed foodstuffs and trade provisions but also a contingent of reinforcements for the isolated and depleted outfit. Buoyed by the influx of men and material, come fall, three separate companies totaling sixty trappers set off south for Oregon's Willamette Valley, west toward Montana's Bitterroot Mountains, and north along the trading grounds of British Columbia. Simultaneously, a small party of six men under the Scottish-born Booshway Robert Stuart, a defecting Nor'Wester, rode for St. Louis with progress reports, including the fate of the *Tonquin*, to be carried on to Astor in New York.

World events, of course, soon overtook the Astorians' ambitions. Several months before this second inland foray, the U.S. Congress voted to declare war on Great Britain. The news did not reach Fort Astoria until January 1813. Around the same time, the Astorians learned from North West Fur Company envoys that the eighteen-gun British sloop HMS *Racoon* was en route to the mouth of the Columbia with orders to seize all American assets in the Oregon Country.

As Wilson Price Hunt, who had assumed overall command of the outpost, was away on an exploratory mission to Alaska, the remaining Astorians hastily convened a council. They voted overwhelmingly to sell all their stores, pelts, and the fort itself—estimated to be worth some $200,000 ($3.7 million today)—to the Nor'Westers for $80,500. Astor never saw any of this money; the Astorians divvied it up among themselves and disappeared into the fog of war. On October 23, 1813, the Stars and Stripes was lowered over Fort Astoria and the Union Jack was raised above the renamed Fort George.

John Jacob Astor's dream of fulfilling Thomas Jefferson's historic quest for a transcontinental economic nexus had indeed been realized. It was his foreign competitors, however, who appeared to have completed the monumental undertaking.

*　*　*

The lesson of Astor's Folly, as it came to be known, was that modern trapping outfits venturing into the wilderness required guile, nimble minds, and self-motivation as opposed to merely laying up in stockades waiting for Indians to arrive with pelts. William Ashley recognized what his American rivals had yet to learn. That afternoon in his St. Louis parlor he told Jed Smith that the old ways of recompensing trappers were outdated. His competitors were still following the customary regimen of paying their beaver hunters as they would wage-working clerks, horse wranglers, and camp tenders. These men—*engagés* in the vernacular—were hired for a set amount of time, usually a year, on the condition that if they should take any furs outside their specific duties, they would be the property of the company.

Ashley and Andrew Henry, on the other hand, planned to compensate their trappers at an amount just below market value once travel and provision costs were factored in. The two wagered that under this new method of payment, the free trappers, as they were called, would have greater incentive to increase their catch. Ashley and Henry would still hire engagés, and Jed Smith would straddle this line—receiving a salary for his hunting skills as the outfit made its way to and from the mountains but paid as a free trapper once the real work began.

In the end, the distinction between engagé and trapper was to become

so blurred as to be opaque. Although some Mountain Men—skilled blacksmiths, for example—continued to be hired on the strength of a certain
expertise, most any high-country adventurer could, in a pinch, shoe a
horse, carve a canoe from the trunk of a cottonwood, or sew a new shirt
from a bolt of cloth. Life in the mountains required a panoply of talents
in order to survive, and former flatlanders who signed up for trapping
expeditions soon found themselves becoming competent wheelwrights,
gunsmiths, farriers, coopers, fishermen, butchers, and teamsters. Any beaver hunter who could not repair a broken thermometer or barometer with
glue concocted from a boiled buffalo hoof was not a trapper long for the
mountains.

As Ashley concluded his business with Smith, he informed the young
man that at least four competing organizations were currently forming up
to reoccupy the heaving high granite—a reconstitution of Manuel Lisa's
old Missouri Fur Company; an organization simply referred to as the
"French Fur Company" because one of its managing partners was Pierre
Chouteau Jr.; the American Fur Company, representing the Astor interests
since the fall of Fort Astoria; and the Columbia Fur Company, planning to
penetrate the Upper Missouri overland from Minnesota. Between his own
organizational skills and political connections, Ashley said, he was confident they could outrace all of these challengers to the Continental Divide.

As they sealed their deal, William Ashley apprised Jed Smith to prepare
to leave within a few days. Andrew Henry had already departed upriver
on April 3 with more than one hundred men divided among a keelboat
crew and a mounted shore party. Smith would sail aboard a second vessel, named the *Enterprize*. If and when the subject of hostile Indians arose
during their conversation, it is not recorded if either man expressed a
recognition that neither Smith's family Bible nor Dr. Simons's gifted book
were likely to stop an arrow or rifle ball.

CHAPTER 3

THE HORSE AND THE GUN

By the time of Jed Smith's journey up the Missouri River, warfare across the North American West had evolved dramatically. The changes did not bode well for white men planning to encroach on Indian territory.

Historians have well documented how intertribal confrontations on either side of the Mississippi River—the "Father of Waters" to many Native Americans—was decidedly dissimilar. Prior to the arrival of Europeans on the continent, the skirmishes and raids among the more densely populated societies of the Eastern Woodlands consisted primarily of "mourning wars" fought to take captives in order to repopulate clans, moieties, and villages ravaged by deaths from disease or famine. Showing individual boldness and daring during these lightning raids was also a way for young braves to acquire prestige to elevate their tribal status. Lust for land or conflict over commercial routes, however, was rarely a factor in these fights.

The hostilities across the vast tracts west of the Mississippi, on the other hand, had for millennia been undertaken for control of territorial game reserves, most notably the migratory routes of the tens of millions of buffalo feeding on the grassy prairie. Land was gold, and tribes who controlled it were golden. This Plains Indians' philosophy of security through aggression naturally filtered down to individual warriors, for whom battlefield honors, as in the east, became pathways to Indigenous leadership. To that effect, western warriors had honed a rigid martial ethos since their itinerant Asian ancestors first began crossing the Bering Land Bridge in various migrations around 16,500 BCE and, some four thousand years later, struck south into the great prairies and timbered heights of what is now the western United States.

These lance-wielding hunter-gatherers, stalking the great herds of woolly mammoths, mastodons, and a giant form of the bison long since extinct, crafted their first bows and arrows around the time that Jesus of Nazareth was performing miracles at Cana and the Sea of Galilee. And like bands of hominins from time immemorial, they inevitably turned those weapons against each other. To paraphrase the sociologist Charles Tilly's famous dictum, war made the tribe and the tribe made war.

Further, their martial mindset was accepted by all combatants without challenge—no quarter asked, none given; to each enemy only death, the more excruciating the more gratifying. A captured Crow, Arikara, Cheyenne, Sioux, or Blackfeet would be subjected to ritual tortures—amputations, flayings, disembowelments, burnings—for as long as he could withstand the agonies. Captive women, unless truly needed to replenish a tribe's gene pool, were not exempt from this treatment. Mewling babies, a hardship on the trail, were summarily disposed of by spear, tomahawk, or war club, or their soft skulls were simply smashed against the nearest rock or tree. An arrow was never wasted on them. The mutilations that would later strike white soldiers and settlers as the very essence of inchoate heathenism, however, actually served a purpose beyond inflicting searing pain.*

The preponderance of the western tribes believed that upon death all

---

* Of course, white atrocities could be equally merciless. The Spanish conquistadors were renowned for their cruelty toward the peoples they colonized, and across the Ohio Valley an eighteenth-century confrontation between Indians and European Americans, known as Lord Dunmore's War, was precipitated by a group of Pennsylvania vigilantes murdering a Mingo tribal leader's family in cold blood before partaking in an orgy of debasements of the corpses, including ripping a fetus from the womb of the headman's dead wife and scalping the developing infant.

Indians ascended to an idyllic afterlife in the same physical condition in which their lives had ended. This bucolic paradise, teeming with game and inhabited by fetching maidens, was the Happy Hunting Ground. But if the slain warrior's spirit had no eyes with which to gaze upon this arcadia, no fingers or hands with which to draw back a bowstring, no feet with which to chase the game, no tongue with which to savor the fatty meat, no penis with which to make love, then one man's heaven had become his enemy's eternal hell. Thus did pre-Columbian warriors across the vast western grasslands marching on foot to attack enemy villages know precisely what awaited either side in defeat.

Paradoxically, if the mourning wars in the East produced relatively little bloodshed with their raid, feint, and parry approach, the western sieges against permanent tribal abodes protected by rivers, earthen walls, and wooden palisades could last for days, with casualties sometimes climbing into the hundreds. These bleeding confrontations, primarily but not exclusively between nomadic and evolving horticulturists, often ended in an uneasy détente, with the attackers from the former destroying the croplands of the latter but rarely able to penetrate a village's defenses. It was not unusual for the nomad hunters, after an appropriate cooling-off period, to return to barter dried venison, antelope, and buffalo meat for the agronomists' regrown crops, particularly if tribal leadership had changed hands in the interim.

The appearance of the European Americans altered this ancient western dynamic by introducing two groundbreaking factors into the military equation—the horse and the gun.

*　*　*

Archeological excavations throughout the twentieth century uncovered fossil remains attesting to the presence of two species of prehistoric proto-horses ranging across North America's high plains as late as the waning days of the Pleistocene era, ten thousand years ago. The initial iterations of these animals, with toes instead of hooves, were about the size of foxes;

succeeding generations grew to a bit larger than today's Great Danes. But like the mammoths and mastodons, these mammals also went extinct. Thus—contrary to the tropes seared into our subconscious from countless Hollywood westerns—for most of their history all Indigenous North Americans, from Inuit to Cree to Iroquois to Navajo, were foot-bound.

So it was that with no large beasts of burden available to the Indigenous population, animal husbandry across the New World lagged about four millennia behind the rest of the planet.* Moreover, while their distant eastern relations on the far side of the Mississippi predominantly relied for subsistence on the dense herds of whitetail deer overfilling the forests, tracking and killing buffalo, moose, and elk on foot was an arduous and dangerous undertaking for western tribesmen. It was for this reason that so many Great Plains peoples—again, contra Hollywood—supplemented their nutritional needs by settling in permanent villages and cultivating annual crops.

Yet with the introduction of the modern horse to the Western Hemisphere, the balance of power shifted to those societies most adept at procuring and domesticating the animals. In one of the most serendipitous quirks of history, the breed transported to the Americas by Spanish explorers was uniquely suited to its new environment. Unlike the hulking, grain-fed steeds hitched to carts and plows across the middle and upper regions of Europe or the stout and agile destrier warhorses ridden into clashes from the Battle of Hastings to Bosworth Field, the fleet Spanish mustang traced its lineage to animals that had once roamed the arid steppes of Central Asia. It had reached Iberia via the eighth-century Moorish invasions, culminating a centuries-long journey during which the species had interbred with similar desert horses from the Middle East and North Africa. The result was a self-sufficient and intelligent animal quite at home

---

* As opposed to the horse, mule, donkey, water buffalo, camel, oxen, or even the llama utilized by the Incas, the American bison, like the African zebra, could not be bred to be harnessed or yoked.

in the dry, dusty climates of Spain's Andalusian Plain and, later, the North American West.

The smallish mustang, typically no taller than five feet from hoof to shoulder, was easy to break and able to travel great distances without water. It prospered in the high, dry flatlands of Mexico, feeding on spare clumps of grass, shrubs, tree bark, and even weeds. It was also prolific. Within two decades of Hernán Cortés's conquest of Montezuma's Aztec empire in 1519, the governor of New Spain's northwest frontier territory, Francisco Vásquez de Coronado, rode north as far as present-day Kansas with a *caballada* of more than one thousand horses in search of the fabled Seven Golden Cities of Cíbola.

The coal-eyed Coronado led a cavalry brigade encased head to toe in armor of tempered Toledo steel. They appeared gigantic beneath the flared and crested heavy-metal morions that shaded their faces. The Spanish realized full well the mystique their horses held over the Indigenous tribes. Given the barbarity of their treatment toward the men, women, and children they virtually enslaved in the name of gold and conversion to Catholicism—Christian imperialism riding beneath cross and sword—the Spanish authorities also recognized the consequences of allowing their sullen subjects to literally get their hands on the reins. Thus, whenever Indians did resist or even threaten to rise, retribution was swift and brutal, with severed feet a favorite punishment. It is little wonder the Indians lived in abject fear of the horse and its merciless riders.

Although Coronado never discovered his cities of gold, along his trek north he encountered numerous North American Plains Indians. His descriptions of these resourceful, dexterous peoples hint at future white foreboding regarding what the Spaniard viewed as their quite literal bloodthirstiness. Describing a buffalo hunt, Coronado wrote, "They cut the hide open at the back and pull it off at the joints, using a flint as large as a finger . . . with as much ease as if working with a good iron tool. They eat raw flesh and drink blood. When they kill a cow they empty a large gut and fill it with blood, and carry this around the neck to drink when they are thirsty. When they open the belly of a cow they squeeze out the chewed grass and drink the juice that remains behind because they say it contains the essence of the stomach." More so than Aztecs or Pueblos, Coronado recognized that these Plains Indians would constitute New Spain's greatest peril should they ever acquire mounts. Yet as hard as the Spanish tried, they could not completely fence off their proliferating mustang stock. Southwestern Apaches, in the course of raiding isolated haciendas, ran off horses and later trapped them in box canyons and at water holes. The Apaches ate most of the animals they captured but spared the hardiest to equip with crude tack fashioned from buffalo hide. They then used them as transportation for even more distant sweeps. The early Apaches never mastered the art of breeding these semibroken mustangs. When they needed to replenish their herds, they merely organized more raids. Nonetheless, as the most mobile tribe on the continent, the ambit of Apache attacks across New Spain fell hardest on their ancient enemies, the broken and servile Pueblos.

The Spanish had made one halfhearted concession before consigning the Pueblos to forced labor in farm fields and a desultory conversion to Catholicism. The colonizers vowed to protect them from Apache attacks. With the Apache now mounted, however, this proved impossible. Apache warriors falling on Pueblo communities would vanish like wraiths into the Rembrandt gloom of the territory's arroyos and spectacular rock formations before any punitive Spanish expeditions could even get under way.

In 1680, as Apache attacks on the Pueblos increased exponentially, the Pueblos rebelled, roused by a visionary medicine man known as Juan de Popé. In the fighting that ensued, the Pueblos, seething from the memories of a century of cruelty, plundered ranchos, destroyed government buildings, and burned Spanish missions with a particular zeal. In one case, twenty Franciscan priests captured cowering in a churchyard were gleefully tortured to death before their bodies were heaved back into their flaming *iglesia*. The few Spanish who survived the uprising abandoned their livestock during disorganized flights south to Mexico proper.

Once New Mexico had been cleared of all the hated foreigners, the shaman Popé ordered his people to renounce the language, religion, and even the crops of the colonizers. The Pueblos burned Spanish fields of barley and wheat and slaughtered and ate the Spanish sheep and cattle—"spotted buffalo" to the Indians. But as they had never developed the Apache taste for horseflesh, they merely flung open the corrals and allowed thousands of mustangs to run free across the Southern Plains. Considering that the animal had brought them nothing but pain and hardship—from conquering Europeans to bloodthirsty Apaches—this act of good riddance makes a fundamental sort of sense. But it had one great unintended consequence.

In the wake of this massive mustang exodus, a combination of raiding and trading between tribes spread horse culture across the West. The heretofore dissolute Comanches, barely scratching out an existence in the harsh Wind River country of west-central Wyoming, were drawn south to West Texas by the lure of the feral herds. They were the first tribe to perfect horse-breeding techniques, including gelding, which had eluded the Apaches. Thereafter the flow of horses followed the age-old northerly trade routes that veined the dun-colored prairie. Soon the Wichitas of Oklahoma were mounted, followed by the Kiowas of Kansas and the Pawnees of Nebraska; Utes, Arapahoes, and Arikaras all obtained stock. The mustang rapidly became the most prized commodity on the Plains.

In ways small and great, these acquisitions began to alter the character of life across the prairie, including prompting a raft of societal dislocations and forced migrations. For some traditionally sedentary tribes, such as the Pawnee and Arikara, the arrival of the horse merely meant that hunting parties could now range farther afield after game to stockpile in order to prevent winter shortfalls and ease the threat of famine. Arikara hunters in particular—supplementing their supple ash and juniper longbows with shorter versions more conducive to mounted pursuit of buffalo—used this new means of conveyance to travel as far as the Black Hills, over two hundred miles distant from their villages. And little remarked on by most early chroniclers of Native American mores is the fact that Indian women and girls also benefited from the new equine culture, as packhorses took over for the physical burdens that had previously stunted or damaged, among other body parts, their ovaries and wombs.

On a grander scale, the glut of horsepower persuaded several horticulturist societies, the Cheyenne and Crow among them, to abandon their semiagricultural lifestyles in favor of nomadic, long-distance sorties against both the buffalo and their neighbors. As portable tipis replaced permanent lodges across the Plains, the presence of the horse also drew west such parvenus as the Lakota Sioux, who eagerly departed forested Minnesota to take advantage of the opportunities this new mobility promised.

What historians now refer to as North America's "Great Horse Dispersal" planted the seed of the transformation of the culture of the American West. The arrival of the gun germinated the conceit into full blossom.

* * *

The Spanish in New Mexico may have lost their horses, but they never relinquished their muskets. It was left to British, French, and Dutch traders to arm the continent, tribe by tribe. And if the European lust for deer skins, beaver pelts, and, later, buffalo robes provided the first opportunities for the North American Indians to obtain firearms, the Indigenous peoples' desire for those guns and ammunition reshaped the nature of intertribal confrontations and, in time, warfare against the white man.* The metamorphosis may well have begun on the shores of Lake Champlain on a still morning in July 1609.

It was on that day—while, an ocean away, a London publisher issued the first quarto of Shakespeare's sonnets and Galileo Galilei prepared to

---

* From nearly the first moment European emigrants set foot on the New World's fatal shores, white men and red men had engaged in constant, bloody, and, thanks to superior European weaponry, usually one-sided combat. It was no coincidence that in 1607 the directors of Virginia's Jamestown Company named the soldier of fortune John Smith as one of the expedition's leaders. Similarly, when English pilgrims dropped anchor near Plymouth Rock thirteen years later, they looked to an experienced military officer named Miles Standish for direction.

demonstrate his invention of the telescope to the doges of Venice—that the explorer Samuel de Champlain, having claimed for the Kingdom of France what was destined to become the state of Vermont, opted to take up the cause of a Huron war party marching on their Mohawk archenemies.

The combatant tribes were faced off along the lake that now bears the Frenchman's name. As they readied their shaved and sanded maplewood war clubs and chiseled stone tomahawks, Champlain stepped from the Huron scrum and strode alone to within thirty yards of the Mohawk lines. He loaded his matchlock, or fuse-lit, arquebus with four lead balls, shouldered its long stock, took aim at the Mohawk headman, and fired. The Mohawk leader fell dead, as did the warriors standing to either side of him. The event so astonished the Mohawks, Champlain wrote in his journal, "that, seeing their chiefs dead they lost courage and took to flight, abandoning the field and their fort."

In the decades following Champlain's fatal shot, Indians across the continent never completely abandoned the arrow, lance, tomahawk, and war club as they acquired guns and ammunition through trade. Nonetheless, European-made firearms gradually took pride of place in every warrior's lodge. For good reason. In the southeast, mourning wars among the Cherokee, Creek, and Choctaw intensified as the intrusion of whites with their gleaming steel weapons deeper and deeper into their territories began to decimate tribal numbers through diseases to which they had no immunity, particularly smallpox, typhoid, measles, and cholera. More insidious, Indian-on-Indian confrontations for commercial motives, previously so rare in the east, also surged.

In a series of seventeenth-century "Beaver Wars" fought around the Great Lakes and across the Ohio River Valley, musket-bearing Iroquois decimated their Algonquin rivals. In one typical clash in southeastern Ohio, the Shawnees, the southernmost of the Algonquin peoples, formed a skirmish line against an invading Iroquois army supplied with Dutch guns. The confident Shawnees, whom the earliest French explorers considered the fiercest Eastern Woodlands tribe, wielded longbows and powerful maplewood arrows that could take down a rampaging elk or stun a charging black bear. They naively expected to stop musket balls with tree-bark body armor and shin greaves fashioned from animal hides. The battle was over within moments, the Shawnees routed. But the Iroquois had no intention of living on Shawnee land. Having trapped out the beaver in their own holdings, they saw the rich watercourses of the Old Northwest Territory as fertile ground for the pelts so coveted by white traders.

Not long after, a similar drama played out in the deep forests of what is now Minnesota. There, the loosely bound septet of tribes who called themselves the Otchenti Chakowin—the People of the Seven Council Fires—had once so dominated their pre-Columbian Algonquin neighbors that the Chippewas had grimly dubbed them the Nadowe-Is-Iw-Ug, "Little Adders" or "Little Snakes." The French mispronounced the Chippewa appellation as Nadewisoou and shortened it to Sioux.

The territory's balance of power, however, was abruptly upended around 1660, when ships flying the Union Jack dropped anchor off the shores of Hudson's Bay. The vessels carried British merchants offering muzzle-loading, smooth-bore flintlock muskets, crates of powder and ball, and steel knives in exchange for furs. As Hudson's Bay bordered the homeland of the Algonquin Cree, they were the first to obtain this new weaponry. The Cree, in turn, shared their bounty with their kinsmen the Chippewa. The Cree and Chippewa proceeded to take bloody revenge on the hated People of the Seven Council Fires who had terrorized them for generations.

Exploiting their new edge in firepower, the Algonquins and their allies drove the Sioux from their forested hunting grounds and into swampy wastelands where they were forced to grub for acorns, roots, and wild rice. And still they were stalked like small game. During his epic trans-Canadian journey in 1793, Alexander Mackenzie—soon to be knighted for being the first white man to traverse Canada to the Pacific Ocean—remarked that the pitiable Sioux were so skittish that even the sight of spires of smoke from distant campfires would panic them deeper into the swamps and marshes.

Actions, of course, have consequential, if sometimes long-range, reactions. In this case, such was the collapse of centuries-old Sioux martial traditions that the Lakota branches of the tribe were compelled to forsake their timbered homeland and take their first tentative steps out onto the vast prairie. There they would have to learn once again to adapt. For nowhere was the Indigenous arms race more impactful than across the plains and mountains of the American West.

* * *

The year 1719 would prove one of several fateful forks in the history of the continental United States. It was in the late summer of that year when the little-remembered French soldier and explorer Claude du Tisne, leading a party of voyageurs down the Mississippi, broke west to travel up the Missouri and Arkansas Rivers to establish trading posts among the Osage and Pawnee. Both tribes, dwelling in large, bark-covered longhouses along the respective watercourses, were anxious to acquire firearms to ward off continuous raids by their most ferocious adversaries, the Plains Apache. Du Tisne was amenable to accommodate them in exchange for nearly more buffalo robes than his fleet of pirogues could haul. And so began the western gun trade.

Within five years of du Tisne's voyage, French traders were bartering with Comanches farther to the southwest, and by 1744 they had procured one hundred thousand furs and hides from the tribes in exchange for guns, powder, flints, lead, bullet molds, and sundry items such as steel daggers, cutlasses, and iron cookpots. The going exchange rate, according to the western historians Donald Worcester and Thomas Schilz, "was one gun for twenty medium or ten large pelts." An additional beaver skin bought twenty rounds of shot and, within time, a large keg of rotgut alcohol mixed with water secured thirty additional furs.

Meanwhile, the weapons trade pulsating throughout the middle and southwestern quadrants of what would become the Louisiana Territory was already pushing north. In the late 1730s, the French Canadian explorer Pierre de La Verendrye, dropping down into the present-day Dakotas from Saskatchewan via the Assiniboine River Valley, became the first known European to reach the Upper Missouri River beyond its Big Bend. La Verendrye—whose numerous contemporary portraits suggest he shed his hooded capote coat and woolen pantaloons in favor of Indian-style buckskins—reported that "the upper part of the River of the West is inhabited by wandering savages—very numerous, without firearms, but possessing axes, knives, and cloth like ourselves."*

The mystery of this absence of guns was solved by the Arikara, who informed La Verendrye that the steel tools and cloth serapes had made their way north from Mexico along the old trade routes, but Spanish law prohibited the exchange of muskets for buffalo hides.

Within a few years, however, the peripatetic La Verendrye was reporting that the Cree who had driven the Sioux from Minnesota as well as the Assiniboin—the latter a Siouwan-speaking breakaway band—had themselves migrated to the Northern Plains and were acting as brokers for the Hudson's Bay Company, transporting trade guns to the Missouri River peoples. Before long the Arikara, Mandan, and Gros Ventre were armed. A pivotal point in the western gun trade occurred around the turn of the eighteenth century, when English agents from the Hudson's Bay Company began moving south to the confluence of the Minnesota and Mississippi Rivers, near modern-day St. Paul. There they hosted annual trade fairs, bartering directly with any Plains warriors willing to make the trek east.

As the Arikara villages on the Upper Missouri were natural market centers, that tribe usurped the role of weapons subcontractors from the Cree and Assiniboin. Their most eager buyers were the horse-rich Cheyenne, Arapaho, and Crow, who, despite warnings from the Arikara against dealing with their enemies, in turn armed farther-flung nomadic peoples such

---

* The English word *savage*, derived from the French *sauvage*, has its roots in the Latin *silva*, meaning "wood." It was used by allegedly civilized Europeans to describe black Africans, brown Indians populating the Asian subcontinent, and even the forest-dwelling clans of northwest Ireland. In sixteenth- and seventeenth-century North America, it was taken for granted that the continent's interior teemed with "savage" entities lusting to maim or kill: bears and wolves, poisonous snakes and panthers, and feral humans whose mode of dress, clannish culture, and incomprehensible languages were to European ears barely a step up from the grunts and chirps of animals.

as the Utes, the Bannocks, and the Nez Perce. Most ominously, the flow of weapons west re-empowered the once-forlorn bands of Lakota Sioux, who were proving themselves equal to the Comanche in horse husbandry.

As in the eastern forests, gun possession on the prairie naturally exacerbated centuries-old rivalries and blood feuds. To white eyes, the Native Americans may have been at one with nature, but they were at sixes and sevens with each other. Yet fighting Cree who hated Sioux, Sioux who hated Pawnee, Pawnee who hated Cheyenne, and Cheyenne who hated Blackfeet had once had to weigh the costs of footsore military marches across great distances against the value of potential spoils. Now, in warrior-society counsel lodges dotting the Plains, the preponderance of both horses and firearms made decisions to raid, to fight, to accrue battle honors so much more feasible.

The glorious haul in furs and skins that white traders took from their gun sales blinded them to recriminations they would inevitably face. The warning signs were there. As early as the mid-1790s, the Gros Ventre, whose territory straddled the Montana-Canada border, laid siege to and destroyed a string of British forts in the Saskatchewan valley in retaliation for intrusions into their hunting grounds by Cree armed with English weapons. Not long after, Blackfeet raiding parties began to fall on British and American supply trains hauling weapons to their sworn enemies the Shoshone and Flathead. As smoked bacon was a staple of whites traveling the frontier, a favorite Blackfeet tactic following a successful ambush was to lash captured teamsters to their wagon wheels, pile their uncrated rashers about them, and flame the meat to a sizzle. Relief parties, if they arrived at all, were barely able to differentiate the seared human flesh from the hogback.

Unlike the trials faced by Samuel de Champlain centuries earlier or even Lewis and Clark a mere two decades previous, this was the combustible matrix into which the Henry-Ashley fur-trapping expedition planned to venture in the spring of 1822. The company's eager new hunter Jedediah Smith had admitted to William Ashley that he had never killed a man. This was unlikely to remain the case.

——— · ———

CHAPTER 4

SHIPWRECK

Despite the raucous sendoff, it was far from an auspicious debut. On the morning of May 8, 1822, thousands of St. Louis residents lined the Mississippi riverbank to cheer the departure of the one-hundred-foot by twenty-foot keelboat *Enterprize* carrying some eighty men in the employ of the Henry-Ashley Company. Their destination, the mouth of the Yellowstone River on the present-day North Dakota–Montana border, lay nearly twelve hundred miles miles distant. Three weeks later the vessel, less than a quarter of the way into its voyage, capsized amid seething whitewater while battling downriver currents powered by untold volumes of snowmelt. No crewmen were lost. But $10,000 worth of supplies—the equivalent of a quarter of a million in today's dollars—now rested on the bottom of the Missouri River.

William Ashley, however, was nothing if not ambitious. He immediately set about securing another keelboat to resupply his grounded expedition. Within two weeks Ashley had purchased a second flatbottom and hired an additional one hundred men, about equally divided between crew and mounted shore party. Meanwhile, as Jedediah Smith scoured the broken bluffs of upland Missouri for game to feed the beached party awaiting the replacement craft, he had time to ponder the wonders he had already witnessed on the aborted voyage. To the young man who had grown up in the eastern forests of New York and Ohio, it was if he had entered an alien world.

* * *

Jed Smith and his companions had been stranded on the fringe of a barely charted expanse of close to eight hundred thousand square miles, stretching south from the Canadian border to the Gulf of Mexico. The Louisiana Purchase had doubled the size of the United States, and though bisected by over a dozen major rivers and innumerable creeks and streams flowing east out of the cloud-shrouded Rocky Mountains, the watercourses cleaving the Great Plains supported few aquifers and no natural lakes. These sunbaked tablelands and undulating savannas blanketed by acres of wheat grass and fox sledge were thus prone to vast dust storms and prairie fires in summer and howling winter blizzards beyond the imaginations of most Americans. All told, the area accounted for close to one-fifth of what would one day become the contiguous United States.

In his classic narrative *The Great Plains*, Walter Prescott Webb observed that east of the Mississippi, America was supported by three legs—land, water, and timber. West of the big river, he warned, two of those legs were for the most part absent. Smith was now discovering this. Yet notwithstanding that for the greater portion of the nineteenth century the name Jed Smith would be synonymous with the opening of the intermountain and tramontane American West, for the moment he felt small. Entering this unmapped territory with little more than the rifle he carried and the buckskins on his back, he was as yet unaware that he was not only breaking trail ahead of a rapidly advancing frontier, but, in the words of the distinguished western historian Robert Utley, "No mountain man in his time held more potential for enriching the world's understanding of the North American West than Jedediah Strong Smith."

As one of the company's designated hunters, Smith spent more time away from the star-crossed *Enterprize* than aboard, walking the riverbank ahead of the boat and taking down, as he wrote, "Black Bear, Deer, Elk, Racoon, and Turkeys in abundance." He would leave the dressed game strung from tree branches along the banks to be picked up by the trailing vessel. Smith was still within the recently fixed borders of the fecund state of Missouri as the watercourse wended west before turning north, and as he noted in his journal, "As the country was well stocked with Bees we frequently had a plentiful supply of honey." Most of the competing fur companies relied for sustenance solely on what their hunters could take down, supplemented by whatever wild pawpaws, persimmons, elderberries, mushrooms, and watercress the outfits could forage. But William Ashley left little to chance, and Smith knew that the lean venison and stringy fowl he hung just out of the reach of wolves and coyotes would be complemented by the hardtack and fatty bacon with which Ashley had stocked the boat's larders.

Once beyond the dense screen of burr oak, walnut, and ash that lined the banks of the lower section of the river, the sky above Smith formed a vast blue dome unlike anything he had ever seen back east. He wrote that he was surprised to find few flowers amid the grasshoppers chirping among the shoots of tall grass. And then there was the birdsong or, rather, the near absence of it aside from the peals of burrowing prairie owls and the shrill squawks from the flocks of multicolored parakeets who launched themselves across the turbulent river like flights of green, yellow, and red arrows.*

Come sundown, Smith—like any good hunter—would scan the terrain for the ubiquitous rattlesnake dens pocking the prairie before spreading his bedroll across the highest ground he could find, staring at the night sky as if seeing the stars for the first time and hoping that a breeze would deter the swarms of mosquitos that followed him like a black cloud. A

---

* The Carolina parakeet (*Conuropsis carolinensis*) that multiple early western explorers recorded seeing in their journals and diaries have, like the passenger pigeon, since gone extinct. A few western museums still exhibit stuffed versions of the bird.

brisk wind might indeed alleviate that scourge, but there was nothing to daunt the wood ticks that tunneled beneath his skin and burned like lit match heads.

Smith had been surprised when the *Enterprize* cast off from St. Louis without William Ashley, who remained behind awaiting a delayed shipment of long rifles. In his absence, Ashley had commissioned a veteran boatman named Daniel Moore as ship's master, or, in the French Canadian patois, the vessel's patroon. The voyage had been brutal from the onset. Although the keelboat was outfitted with a tall canvas sail, the contour of the river shaped the captain's course, and the sail was never of much use due to the fickle winds that raked the snaking trajectory of the Missouri. Instead, raw manpower propelled the vessel upstream.

In deep waters, strokers manned twelve long oars, six to a side, projecting from the bow. In more shallow passages, polemen—whose bulging forearms and stout deltoids attested to their physical exertions—lined up port and starboard on the pine running boards that flanked the long wooden cargo box that ran the length of the vessel. They "set" their metal-tipped poles into the riverbed, shouldered the long staffs, and heaved the boat forward as they trudged toward the stern. At a command from the patroon they loped back to the prow to begin the process anew.

But by far the most backbreaking burden fell to the voyageurs who worked the cordelle, a stout towline of thick hemp attached to the mast. The Missouri was in spate. And when swirling rapids made stroking or poling impossible, these crewmen were put ashore to pull the keelboat against the formidable waterflow. It was enervating work, not only fighting the strength of the current but trudging foot by foot, sometimes inch by inch, along the sloping banks through muddy bogs, through tangled and thorny underbrush that tore at buckskin leggings, and around downed trees that littered the riverbank like enormous jackstraws. Sometimes the roaring waters would crumble an embankment beneath the cablemen's feet, pitching them into the river as they scrambled to maintain a grip on the rope. When the boat grounded on a hidden shoal, the entire crew leaped from the deck to put their backs into the effort to dislodge it. Smith was spared much of these onerous struggles due to his hunting duties, although he noted the "slow, Laborious and dangerous" pace of the passage. On a good day the craft might make nine miles.

Several days before the *Enterprize* went under, an enclave of rough cabins on the north bank of the river hove into view. This was Boonville, where twenty-three years earlier the iconic pioneer Daniel Boone had accepted a grant of 850 acres of fertile bottomland from the Spanish authorities then controlling the territory. The great American pathfinder, on the run from U.S. tax collectors, had died in 1820 at the age of eighty-five, but the salt lick bearing his name was still operated by his sons Daniel Morgan and Nathan.* Across the gray water from Boonville the keelboat had briefly put in at the hamlet of Franklin, the most western "town" in the United States, which the few intrepid residents had named in honor of Pennsylvania's most famous founding father.

Though but a cluster of ramshackle wooden cabins and shacks, Franklin was already gaining a seminal reputation. A year earlier, it was from this dusty outpost that the transplanted Virginian William Becknell—who had served as a mounted Ranger under Daniel Morgan Boone in the War of 1812—organized an overland hunting and trading expedition into the newly sovereign nation of Mexico. Becknell intuited correctly that, unlike the recently deposed Spanish colonizers, the Mexicans would be open to commerce with the United States, not least because of the tariffs that could be levied against imported American goods. He was correct. An amateur surveyor, he also discovered a route speckled with water holes that was passable for wagons pulled by draft teams of mules or oxen. It was thus Becknell who was credited with opening what was to become known as the Santa Fe Trail.

---

* Sketchy and unverifiable rumors persist to this day that, while traveling with his son-in-law during parts of 1808 and 1809, Boone joined a trapping party heading upriver when he was in his midseventies. It is said that Boone's final long hunt took him as far as the Yellowstone River and perhaps even across the Continental Divide.

Becknell was not in Franklin when Jed Smith and the crew of the *Enterprize* passed through, but the adventurers did encounter Ezekiel Williams, who had trapped the Rockies with Andrew Henry prior to the War of 1812.* Williams was apparently a natural-born storyteller, and Smith and his crewmates listened in rapt fascination as the old Mountain Man yarned about fighting off monstrous grizzly bears, fording ice-clogged rivers that froze the legs off his packhorses, and ascending gale-scoured crags that even eagles dared not attempt. But they paid scant heed when Williams warned them that they were risking their scalps by proceeding into Indian country. Williams said that he had seen Andrew Henry's party passing upriver a month or so earlier and would not be surprised if Henry and what was left of his outfit were not already being driven downstream by the hostiles. As the historian Dale Morgan blithely describes Smith's reaction to Williams's dark counsel, "Jedediah was not prepared to concede the same authority to village seers that he accorded to the prophets of his Bible." The *Enterprize* plugged on.

Moving upstream and hugging the riverbanks to avoid the swift mid-channel current, the polemen pulled double duty fending off the great pieces of driftwood careening down the watercourse. These included large and gnarled pieces of hidden timber called "planters" that had snagged on the riverbed and were susceptible to breaking loose at any moment to impede the vessel's path. But what the crew feared most were the "sawyers," entire trees ripped from their roots by the current's surge and capable of gashing the keelboat's shallow-draft hull from bow to stern. It was just such a looming disaster that indirectly led to the demise of the craft.

Since departing Franklin, high winds had been buffeting the *Enterprize* for days when, on the afternoon of May 8, the boat's forward lookout cried out. A raft of sawyers arrayed as if in a cavalry charge were hurtling downriver. The shipmaster Daniel Moore ordered the boat heeled as close to

---

* It is not recorded if Smith and his party happened upon a fourteen-year-old apprentice saddler then working in Franklin named Christopher "Kit" Carson. Carson, of course, would go on to become a frontier legend as a trapper, wilderness guide, and U.S. Army officer most associated with the Santa Fe Trail.

the bank as possible. But as the vessel closed tight to land, a whistling gust blew the top of the mast into a tangle of branches from a spinney of overhanging cottonwood. The torque of the collision wheeled the keelboat broadside into the current, where the wooden legion hit it full force. It was awash and swept under in an instant.

That vessels had been sinking for the tens of thousands of years that humans had been a seafaring species did not lighten the party's glum spirits. The hunter-trappers and voyageurs, with Smith at their head, began staking out a spot on a high embankment to begin construction of a makeshift camp from the flotsam that could be hauled out of the water by the outfit's strongest swimmers. Meanwhile, the patroon Moore set off downriver on foot. His aim was Franklin, seventy-five miles away, where he hoped to purchase a horse and ride for St. Louis.

* * *

Daniel Moore did not accompany William Ashley when Ashley and his new flatboat and crew dropped anchor at the castoffs' encampment on June 21. It is not recorded whether the general had relieved Moore of his duties or if the snakebitten former patroon was reluctant to brave a second go at the river. Yet with the additional men to power the flatbottom, the upstream journey became somewhat swifter as the craft passed a succession of Missouri River tributaries, including the sandy mouth of the Platte—a course rippling with carp but too shallow to be navigable for more than a few weeks each spring as it surged with heavy snow runoff. Unbeknownst to any at the time, the Platte was destined to limn the first stage of the Oregon Trail.

Sometime in late summer Ashley's party alighted on the scree below Fort Atkinson, a cantonment built atop the future state of Nebraska's imposing thousand-foot Council Bluff.* Three years earlier, President James

---

* The fort at Council Bluff—not to be confused with Iowa's Council Bluffs across the river and twenty miles to the south—was named for the post's first commander, Colonel Henry Atkinson. It was originally slated to be the first of a string of permanent American military outposts stretching all the way to the mouth of the

Monroe had dispatched a military expedition to the site as, like his predecessor Thomas Jefferson, he feared the burgeoning British influence creeping southeast from the Oregon Country. The best means to counter that
threat, Monroe felt, was the construction of what was then the most western army post in the United States. Compared to Boonville and Franklin,
Fort Atkinson was a veritable hive of activity. Nearly five hundred Bluecoats
mixed easily with various traders, sutlers, and visiting Indians, primarily
agriculturalist Omahas and Poncas, the withers and polls of their packhorses buckling under the weight of buffalo hides and willow-reed baskets
bursting with corn.

The site had history. It was here, in 1804, that Lewis and Clark convened
a gift-giving council among local Native American headmen to smooth
their passage. Eight years later and about five miles distant, Manuel Lisa
had established a now-abandoned fort as a base to trade furs and horses
while also acting as a semiofficial federal Indian agent during the War of
1812. Now the Indians were drawn to the fort not least because both the
reconstructed Missouri Fur Company and Pierre Chouteau Jr.'s so-called
French Fur Company had already established trading posts within the
garrison's whitewashed walls. Ashley's keelboat did not linger long at Fort
Atkinson, but the western neophyte Jed Smith found time to record his
awed impressions.

There was, for instance, Blackbird's Hill, rising some forty miles beyond
Fort Atkinson on a steep rise of sandstone said to be the burial place of
a sinister if crafty Omaha chieftain. The eponymous Blackbird, rumored
to have obtained a supply of arsenic from French traders in the late eighteenth century, not only began slowly poisoning his rivals but claimed
magical powers by predicting their deaths. When smallpox swept through
the Omaha Nation and killed Blackbird sometime around 1800, he was

---

Yellowstone. In 1819 the rifle regiments intended to man these forts got no farther than Nebraska's eastern
midsection before winter storms halted their progress. The following spring, the plan to continue on was
abandoned.

interred on the knoll seated on his favorite horse—which was still alive at the time.

Another forty miles upriver, Ashley and his crew passed the next major landmark known to experienced boatmen. Floyd's Bluff was named in honor of Sergeant Charles Floyd, the only member of Lewis and Clark's Corps of Discovery to die, felled by a ruptured appendix. Looking like nothing so much as a giant medieval French hennin, or princess hat, dropped from the sky onto the prairie, the conical hill had taken on the vestiges of a sacred site. Lewis and Clark had buried Sgt. Floyd with full military honors on the crest of the bluff, planting atop his gravesite a cedar post bearing his name and the date of his death—August 20, 1804. That original cenotaph had been consumed by a prairie fire, as had several replacements. But veteran voyageurs told Jed Smith that if travelers passing on the river noticed no marker and failed to stop to erect a new one, their journey would be plagued by bad juju. The latest wooden monument was standing tall when Ashley's keelboat moved on below.

Stroking, poling, and tugging into present-day South Dakota, Smith noticed an unmistakable change in the terrain. Gone were the low rolling knolls of upper Missouri and eastern Nebraska and Iowa, replaced, he recorded, "by one extensive prairiae interrupted only by a narrow fringe of timber along the rivers, the surface gently undulating and covered with grass. No mountains." More pertinent, this was Jed Smith's introduction to the vast herds of buffalo darkening the flaxen Plains.[*] Thus far he had killed the occasional solitary bull or cow, but of this day he was later to remember, "Perhaps since that time I have frequently seen as many or more Buffalo than were in view . . . but they never made that strong impression that was made by the ten thousands that seemed sufficiently numerous to eat everything like vegetation from the face of the country in a single week."

---

[*] By the turn of the nineteenth century there were an estimated sixty million buffalo migrating across America's western prairies—more than eleven times the number of white people living in the United States, according to the 1800 census.

He also observed that these and untold generations of the humped and horned beasts had left the grasslands speckled with bowls in the dirt called wallows, some as large as ten feet across, where the two-thousand-pound animals had tossed themselves to the ground and rolled to rid their hides of ticks and flies. In the spring the dusty wallows had collected water, providing breeding grounds for frogs and salamanders across a landscape largely bereft of ponds. Now Smith spotted tall bluebells, yellow-flowered yarrow, and the soft, hairy leaves of arnica sprouting from the ubiquitous dips in the earth.

* * *

By July the Ashley entourage had entered Lakota Sioux country. From a distance it appeared as if the tribe's eighteen-foot-tall tipis had blossomed from the flats like prairie chickweed. The Americans, of course, and Jed Smith in particular, had no way of knowing how far Sioux culture had progressed since the Lakota bands had migrated onto the Plains. Early European explorers reported that, back in their Minnesota homelands, the tribe had exhibited no artistic tendencies other than the frightening designs that warriors had painted on their faces and bodies in preparation for battle. Those eastern Sioux did not weave baskets or fabrics, bake pottery, or make jewelry. They lived to fight, and the fires of their blood-feud memories were banked and stoked until the day they died. They still reveled in warfare, but now the white trappers observed that tribal artists using pigments made from various combinations of blood, sap, ground-up roots, dead insects, and even urine had decorated their elk-skin lodges with depictions of the sun, the moon, stars, buffalo, and, of course, horses.

The naïve Smith was fascinated. This was his first encounter with an Indigenous people yet to be tainted by white "civilization." In his journals he described the Sioux as "above the common stature . . . than most Indians, with the intelligent countenances of the generally good looking men, whose appearance in the moral scale would indicate they rank above the mass of Indians." His admiration may have been swayed by the rather surprising convention the Lakota had adopted of seeing to a prized horse's end days. Smith, whose journals at this point reflect a burgeoning appreciation for the value of a good mount, found that instead of slaughtering a dying pony for food, leather, and tools—the custom among most western tribes—old and infirm mustangs who had served their masters well were set loose in secluded pasturages adjacent to water to die a dignified death. The Sioux referred to this parting gesture as a horse being "given to the moon." If not particularly humane in a territory teeming with wolves, mountain lions, and grizzly bears, it was certainly in keeping with the Sioux kill-or-be-killed nature.

By this time the Sioux had temporarily overcome their hostility toward the American intruders and had so reconciled themselves to the white parties passing through their territory that, at Manuel Lisa's urging, they had even allied with the United States against the British in the War of 1812. It was not lost on the tribe that they still depended on eastern weapons traders to continue their domination of the many enemies arrayed against them across the Plains. This last point was driven home when Ashley's party came upon a newly built wooden stockade manned by brokers from the reconstructed Missouri Fur Company. Despite the delay caused by the sinking of the *Enterprize*, the two men who had reanimated Lisa's old outfit, the veteran trappers Robert Jones and Michael Immell, had still not managed to get their own keelboat expedition this far upriver before Henry and Ashley. One of their overland parties, however, had managed to beat Ashley to this spot, and the little general needed to remedy that leg up.

Ashley spent several days parleying with Sioux headmen, who dressed for the occasions in their finest ceremonial bighorn sheepskins and elk hides, their headdresses adorned with various feathers according to their station and wealth in horses. Their vermillion-daubed faces added a gaudy dash of color to the dusty flats as they passed an ochre pipestone fastened to a two-foot-long stem. The smoking rite was accompanied by elaborate hand signals serving a dual purpose—to pay homage to the Great Spirit and to attest that the heart of each man who inhaled the concoction known as kinnikinnick had forsworn any act of deceit. During these conclaves Ashley distributed presents of tobacco plugs and twists, blankets, coffee, and, most craved as a delicacy, refined sugar. On Andrew Henry's advice he also dispensed thin sheets of brass, as the vain Sioux warriors were overly fond of cutting them into ovals the size of silver dollars to weave through their hair.

The pungent odor of the smoldering kinnikinnick—an admixture of wild plains tobacco, dried herbal bark, bearberry, and sumac leaves—did not sit well with Smith, who abhorred tobacco smoke. Further, at the feasts thrown in honor of Ashley's arrival he was hard-pressed to force down the boiled dog that the Indians considered a delicacy.* But Jed Smith could not otherwise help but admire the nomadic culture of the Sioux, particularly their men, who aside from hunting and making war left all other chores to the women and girls.

Given the ethos of the era, young America's viewpoints regarding Native Americans and their lifestyles typically fell into two categories. Some considered the Indigenous tribes as so many wayward children, primitive naïfs similar to Thomas Gainsborough's British "rusties" in need of civilizing Bibles and plows. At the other end of the spectrum were those whose answer to the so-called Indian Problem consisted of one idea: extermination. And though Jed Smith was generally free of the casual racism that infected most of his fellow whites, he was nonetheless a man of his times. Thus his initial observations of Sioux tribal society, conveyed in apparent admiration, can only be construed by modern ears as a backhanded compliment. Their free-spirited culture, he wrote, "could almost persuade a man to renounce the world, take [to] the lodge, and live the careless, Lazy life of an Indian."

William Ashley had no time for such metaphysical musings. He knew

---

* As the peripatetic, Belgian-born Jesuit missionary Father Pierre de Smet was to observe along his many nineteenth-century travels among the Sioux, "No epoch in Indian annals shows a greater massacre of the canine race" (Robinson, "The Education of Red Cloud," 162).

well that he was walking a fine line by engaging so warmly with the Sioux. The next Indian settlements he and his party would encounter on their river journey belonged to the Arikara, who would be keenly aware of his friendly dalliance with their bitter nemeses. For despite its oceanic distances, the American prairie had many ears.

CHAPTER 5

HIVERNANTS

On September 8, 1823, the keelboat bearing William Ashley and his company dropped anchor just past the mouth of the Grand River in northern South Dakota. Five miles upstream, looming above the Missouri's eastern riverbank, were the twin Arikara villages. The settlements were composed of scores of round earthen lodges—"potato holes," the whites called them—roofed with split timbers chocked with hardened sod.

The river, bisected by a large sandbar closer to the Indian towns, afforded the abodes a natural protection to their rear. The leeward precincts, facing the vast prairie stretching beyond the horizon, had been fortified by timber palisades constructed from driftwood and willow branches interspersed with thorny brush. Beyond these pickets lay farm fields holding acres of corn, squash, beans, pumpkins, and sunflowers. Arikara women had perfected the art of parching the sunflower seeds in clay pots and grinding the resultant meal into fist-size globules. When wrapped in buffalo-heart membrane, this easily portable concoction provided their warriors with sustenance on hunting and raiding sorties.*

---

* Prior to the Great Horse Dispersal, it was Arikara hunters, foot-slogging into the South Dakota Badlands over 160 miles away, who had initiated the *pishkun,* or buffalo jump—the technique of harvesting the animals by spooking and stampeding the herds over the terrain's steep, moonscape cliffs.

Gen. Ashley knew there was no way to slip past the Arikara settlements, even in the dead of night. Moreover, the loss of the *Enterprize* and the slow going upriver had forced him to alter his original plans. He had anticipated joining Andrew Henry on the Yellowstone by summer's end. This was now impossible. Instead, given his extra hands, he decided to lead a small party overland toward the Yellowstone, with the keelboat keeping up as best it could behind him. For that Ashley needed horses. Arikara horses. To this end he cautiously led a small trading party, including Jed Smith, toward the more downstream of the villages. He made certain to ostentatiously expose the gifts he planned to distribute among the tribal chiefs and religious leaders.

Every white man on the river was aware of the animosity that existed between the Arikara and the Sioux, with whom Ashley had just pow-wowed. None, however, could have understood the grudge the Arikara carried over the turn of fortune the tribe had borne in relation to their lethal rivals.

* * *

As best modern historians, ethnologists, and paleoanthropologists can surmise, the Indians who were to eventually become known as the Lakota Sioux separated from their Dakota cousins and abandoned the forests of Minnesota for the high prairie sometime around 1700.* Led by factions calling themselves the Oglala—"to scatter one's own"—and the Brule, or "burnt thighs nation," these as yet unhorsed peoples managed to acquire muskets, powder, and balls from renegade English traders. By the late 1720s and early 1730s, reports from French traders indicated that the domiciliary Iowas, Otoes, and Omahas—farming communities still wielding mostly arrows, lances, and tomahawks—were retreating north from their fixed

---

* European Americans, slowly intruding west from the Atlantic coast into the green, forested land east of the Mississippi River, assumed the continent an unending Eden. They would be shocked when such terrain ceased to exist around the ninety-fifth meridian west—a line running a rough southerly course from just west of modern-day Minneapolis to San Antonio. The sere, harsh, and timberless prairie that stretched to the Rocky Mountains appeared as great a barrier as an ocean; even the grasses undulating uniformly before the winds left an impression of waves rolling onto a seashore.

locations in the fertile bottomland of Nebraska and migrating up into the inhospitable wastes of the northern Dakota Territory. Although the reason for this removal remains unclear, historians reasonably speculate that they were fleeing the westering—and gun-wielding—Sioux.

By the mid-eighteenth century, the Lakota Sioux had tracked the wending buffalo herds up onto the grassy, windswept flatiron plateau known to early French explorers as the Coteau des Prairies. This one-hundred-by-two-hundred-mile pipestone escarpment, its edges carved by retreating glaciers and rising gradually to nine hundred feet, is sharply defined on modern satellite imaging maps. Shaped like an arrowhead pointing north, its fins fan south from North Dakota through South Dakota, Minnesota, and into northern Iowa. Although the Sioux progress was slow, perhaps five to six miles a day, they managed to transport their smallish lodge poles and tipi skins across these rocky highlands on the backs of their women and children—including girls as young as six or seven—and particularly their dogs. A strong dog could drag a load of about seventy-five pounds on an A-shaped wooden travois; that is, six to eight buffalo hides that even the most fit women could not heft.

Moreover, during its exodus west, the Lakota branch of the tribe—adhering to ancient council-fire traditions—had broken into seven bands. Intermarriage among these groupings was constant, as was the baffling swiftness with which each clan might change its name.* As the bloody French and Indian War raged along the Atlantic seaboard, the Plains Sioux—now well armed by constant forays back east to the Minnesota gun fairs—made their first contact with mounted Indians, the Arikara.

The Arikara, or People of the Horns, trace their name to the ancient tribal custom of headmen and warriors plaiting their coarse black hair around the wing bones of eagles as a sign of propriety and elegance.

---

* Thus, what Lewis and Clark chronicled in their journals as the Teton Saone, most likely a collective name they bestowed on all Lakota, turn up as the Hunkpapa two decades later. Most historians, for clarity's sake, have since settled on the seven Lakota bands as the Oglala, Brule, Miniconjou, Sans Arc, Two Kettle, Hunkpapa, and Blackfeet-Sioux.

Originally a prehistoric Central American peoples, archeological evidence supports the tribe's oral histories regarding their migration north through present-day Texas and Louisiana with their Pawnee cousins before settling throughout the Missouri River Valley. The Sioux first encountered the Arikara while they were living much farther south of where William Ashley and Jed Smith found them in 1822. They had likely acquired their mounts as well as some Spanish-made sabers in trade with the southern Kiowa, who prized the tribe's corn, squash, and beans.

Despite the haughty Sioux disdain for the agricultural "dirt eaters," to the Arikara the newcomers from the east appeared to pose little threat. The "Rees" had numbers on their side; their total population of perhaps twenty thousand, including four thousand warriors, was nearly double that of all the wandering bands of Sioux put together. Sensing nothing to fear from these emaciated strangers adrift on the windswept high Plains with their dog travois and burdened children, the Arikara initially took pity on the Sioux. After all, they had horses with which to not only ride down buffalo but also overwhelm slow, foot-bound adversaries. The Spanish steel blades attached to the tips of their heavy, fourteen-foot-long buffalo lances were no match for a lice-ridden band of itinerants. This overconfidence led them to accept some Brule and Oglala into their villages and, in effect, provide them with handouts of corn, dried pumpkins, and even a few old worm-ridden nags. This was a mistake. The Sioux never forgave the kindness.

For despite their strong mounts and steel-tipped lances, the Arikara were severely outgunned. And though their fortifications were too strong for the Sioux to storm on foot, raiding parties of Lakota began prowling the edges of Arikara territory, burning their cornfields and slithering on their bellies through saltbush and silver sage to ambush and scalp any man, woman, or child who ventured beyond their picket walls.

In the end, however, it was smallpox that doomed the People of the Horns. Three great epidemics, believed to have been introduced by tainted European blankets, swept through their settlements toward the end of the eighteenth century. The tribe was weakened to the point where, by 1795, even their protected dwellings afforded little security against the marauding Sioux, who by this time had begun breeding captured feral mustangs. What remained of the broken Arikara, still reeling from the pox, fled even farther north, hoping to thwart the proliferating Sioux by allying with the Mandan. The partnership came to naught, as the Mandan, also bereft of horses and more or less acting as Arikara infantry, were ridden down and slaughtered by the score.

So it was that the Arikara abandoned the entirety of the Missouri watershed below the river's Big Bend, near present day Pierre, virtually beckoning someone to claim the land. The Sioux happily complied. The natural horsemanship of the Sioux—equaled only by the outnumbered Crow and, far to the southwest, the Comanche—was in fact fast changing the face of America's Northern Plains. Much as the invention of the stirrup had once turned yurt-dwelling Mongols into the scourge of Eurasia, by 1803, mounted Sioux braves had cleared the Northern Kiowa from their traditional hunting grounds around the Black Hills and crushed a counteroffensive by the Omaha, who, having obtained horses and rifles, attempted to retake their lost Nebraska territory.

William Ashley, of course, knew nothing of this Indigenous history as he bartered for mustangs with the sullen Arikara headmen. As Ashley smoked the peace pipe, Jed Smith wandered the Arikara village. Most Native Americans could differentiate tribal affinities from a moccasin print, a piece of clothing, the style of bow or arrow, and a score of other distinguishing hints. The observant Smith was determined to learn these secrets, surely intuiting that identifying one "Indian" from another at a glance could mean the difference between life and death. This was the beginning of his education.

As such, he noted that the lithe and wiry Arikara men—sullen and suspicious of the white men roaming their village—were shorter than the Sioux. Further, though the Sioux invariably wore their long tresses parted in the middle, with either loose or braided strands falling to either shoulder, the Arikara preferred a hair-lifting effect above their foreheads. Though they had abandoned eagle bones in favor of eagle feathers to achieve this style—with some opting for hide caps from which sprouted buffalo horns—it seemed to most whites that the design was an effort to make themselves appear taller. The Arikara also eschewed the bone breastplates worn by nearly all Sioux braves in favor of bleached buckskin blouses.

Moreover, though Smith had not thought it possible to keep more dogs than he had seen in the Sioux camp, each Arikara lodge seemed to possess dozens of the animals, their jaws snapping like wolves at the approach of a stranger. Unlike the hordes of near-naked children who followed Smith everywhere, the women, clad in long buckskin smocks decorated with elk's teeth, porcupine quills, and river shells, seemed to pay him no heed while they tanned their buffalo hides.

As has been well documented, Native Americans across the Plains wasted no part of the buffalo. Spiritual formalities, including the chanting of psalm-like paeans to the animal's sacrifice, accompanied the butchering of each section of the beast. The ambrosial liver and tongue—the latter boiled in salt water with wild onions until the skin slid off—were awarded to the most successful hunters. The remaining fatty meat, particularly the hump, was meted out in accordance to tribal seniority. Any hides not set aside for trade robes were sewn into leggings, moccasins, and even tack and saddles. The horns were used to carry crushed herbal medicines, and the bones were honed into tools ranging from war clubs to sewing needles. The animal's thick strands of hair were twisted into ropes, and the bladders were set aside for water storage or filled with a pounded mixture of marrow grease, jerked meat, and berries, which was then coated with suet to make a portable and nourishing pemmican. The sinews were fashioned into bowstrings, and the inch-thick skin from the side of the buffalo's neck was set out to bake in the sun before being cut into shields that could stop an arrow and deflect a bullet. In a final celebratory feast, the animal's savory bone marrow was roasted over cook fires fueled by dried buffalo

dung—*bois de vache*, or "wood of cow" in the French Canadian terminol-
ogy of the era—and devoured by the entire tribe.

But it was for its hide that the buffalo was, and is, best known. The
tanning process of creating the iconic buffalo robes—always performed
by women, singing their own buffalo song often with infants in portable
cradleboards strapped to their backs—was grueling. First the acrid skins
were pinned taut to the ground and abraded with a fleshing knife. Then a
mixture of jellied buffalo brains and organs was rubbed into the fleshy side
of the coat until the concoction penetrated the pores, making the leather
stronger. After several days left drying in the sun, the hides were carried
to water and washed until somewhat pliable. They were then tied to poles
with rawhide thongs and stretched taut again. Any stray fleck of meat
still attached was eliminated, and more jellied brains were applied. After
several more days, when the goo had sunk in sufficiently, women or girls
would take up either end of the robe and draw it back and forth around a
small tree for hours, as if operating a large handsaw. When the end product was soft enough to fold, it was a buffalo blanket destined to warm the
laps of thousands of midwesterners and New Englanders through snowy
winters.

Smith was observing these final stages of the procedure when Ashley
approached leading a string of Indian ponies. He had convinced the Arikara to part with the horses on the promise that he would open a trading
post near their villages on his next trip upriver. This, he told the Indians,
would offset the markets the rival fur companies were operating in Sioux
territory. Yet even after the deal had been struck, records Smith, "[We]
moved with great care, being somewhat apprehensive of danger from the
Arikara."

Smith was among the men selected to ride overland with Ashley. Heeling
close to the Missouri on their initial leg, they came upon the fixed Mandan villages in present-day North Dakota and, a bit farther on, the earthen
dwellings of their neighbors the Gros Ventre, distant relations, but now antagonists, of the Crow. Ashley paused briefly at both settlements to pass the

pipe and present token gifts. Then, breaking west, the party rode over and through rolling buttes that folded and buckled as far as the eye could see. The easterners accustomed themselves to the headaches and the wheezes of their lungs as they ascended the Laurentian Divide.* Fording the muddy Little Missouri, they arrived at the confluence of the Yellowstone and Missouri in far-western North Dakota on October 1. Andrew Henry's completed fort awaited them; they were welcomed by a blast of cannon fire.

The semiarid terrain along the North Dakota–Montana border, though technically still a part of the Great Plains, was generally agreed to be the beginning of the Rocky Mountains. Andrew Henry had constructed his outpost, dubbed Fort Henry, between the two watercourses on an elevated tongue of land twinkling with fireweed, big bluestem, and prairie dropseed. The redoubt was essentially a large, square stockade of spiky cottonwood pickets with log blockhouses at each corner. The small cannons, called swivel guns and capable of sweeping all fields of fire, sat atop two of these towerlike structures. The smell of fresh-cut white willows pervaded the air and the rich, tangled timber on the far shores of both rivers hinted at the forested cordillera to the west. There was beaver country. And Blackfeet country.

* * *

Unlike his partner William Ashley, the gruff Andrew Henry did not believe in wasting keelboat storage space on amenities such as bacon and sea bread when it could instead be used to haul beaver traps. His parsimony had backfired, however, when game proved scarce once past the buffalo flats. What began as mere grumbling among his voyageurs reached a point where they had begun deserting by ones and twos under cover of darkness. Unbeknownst to Henry, his partner William Ashley's trailing flatboat was already swooping up some of these stragglers.

---

* The Laurentian, or Northern, Divide—known locally as the "height of land"—is the drainage divide that marks the watershed boundaries between Hudson's Bay, the Great Lakes–St. Lawrence River, and the Gulf of Mexico.

After conferring with Henry, Ashley secured a large pirogue dugout and enough supplies to pack out to St. Louis the bundles of beaver pelts Henry's trappers had already taken. There Ashley would remain, arranging for a second expedition upriver the following spring. In the meanwhile, Jed Smith and the outfit's hunters were immediately mobilized. Putting in on cottonwood dugouts, Henry led one hunting party of twenty or so men farther up the Missouri while Smith fell in with a smaller group heading up the Yellowstone, making for the mouth of the Powder River. Smith would not travel as far as that, as he and another hunter had orders to return to Fort Henry as soon as possible with as much game as their horses could carry in order to salt, smoke, and stockpile the meat for winter.

Smith and his companion were back in Fort Henry within a week, laden with an abundance of dressed deer and antelope meat. By this time Ashley's keelboat had arrived at Fort Henry. Its appearance was in turn followed by the approach of another vessel carrying a crew of forty-three. This was Robert Jones and Michael Immell's Missouri Fur Company expedition. They hauled in briefly at Fort Henry before resuming up the Yellowstone with the intention of trapping and wintering over somewhere near the mouth of the Bighorn.

Jed Smith's intelligence and courage, his integrity and sense of humor, his capacity for endurance, and even what some saw as his grace—"a mild man and a Christian," they called him—had already elevated him into a leadership position among the Henry-Ashley party. He now took it upon himself to warn Andrew Henry of the rival fur company's presence in Montana. He and several mounted companions started up the Missouri, but within a few days they were met by Maj. Henry leading a waterborne party of eight men carrying provisions back to his eponymous fort. Smith informed Henry of the presence of Jones and Immell. Henry was alarmed, worried that they would beat him to the Three Forks of the Missouri by spring.*

---

* The Three Forks, where the Jefferson, Madison, and Gallatin Rivers converge—named by Lewis and Clark in 1805 as an homage to, respectively, the United States' president, secretary of state, and secretary of the treasury—is considered the birthplace of the Missouri River.

The fall hunt that Henry and his forward outfit had undertaken had advanced some four hundred miles to the mouth of the Mussellshell in northwest Montana—a river named by Lewis and Clark for the freshwater mussels lining its banks. Henry had left a dozen or so men at the site to winter over, and he now instructed Smith and his company to continue upriver. They were to assist in setting up camp and stocking in as much meat as possible. Come spring, Henry said, he would return with further instructions. Jedediah Smith was about to earn his Mountain Man credentials.

* * *

The rough-hewn Mountain Men, sniffed at as "French Indians" by flatlanders, had developed a language all their own. No word in this crazy-quilt patois of English, French, Spanish, and a variety of Indian dialects garnered as much respect as *hivernant*, adopted from the Gallic *hibernation* and worn as a badge of honor by anyone who had endured the hunger, freezing streams, hostile tribes, and furiously cold latitudes of an upper Rocky Mountain winter. As such, Smith's journal from this period reads like a hivernant primer. His notes touch on cabin construction, the art of starting a fire in a snowstorm, the intricacies of dressing elk, and even equine food management—once gently fed the shaved, sweet bark of the round-leaf cottonwood, *populus angulate*, a mustang would learn to add winter fat by seeking the bark from downed trees. But what jumps from the pages of his diary is his awe at the natural wonderment of a Montana winter, not least his observations regarding the perambulations of the migrating buffalo.

"We were generally good hunters," Smith wrote, "but at the time unacquainted with the habits of the buffalo. Seeing none in the vicinity we supposed that they had abandoned the country for the winter. We therefore became somewhat apprehensive that we should suffer for want of provisions." Once the Musselshell had completely frozen over, however, Smith was astonished "to see the buffalo come pouring from all sides into the valley of the Missouri and particularly the vast Bands that came from the north and crossed over to the south side on the ice. We there fore had them in thousands around us and nothing more required of us than to select and kill the best for our use whenever we might choose."

Although primarily concerned with laying in meat for the trappers, Smith notes that Andrew Henry had also issued orders to his hunters "to take what beaver we could conveniently." Oddly, in all the *recovered* pages of Smith's copious writings—there are weekslong, monthslong, and even yearslong lacunae—there is no mention of one infamous trapper who wintered over on the Musselshell that season. This was the legendary Ohio River boatman and brawler known as Mike Fink.

Already nearing fifty years old—born at some point in the 1770s to French Canadian parents; Miche Phinke's precise date of birth has never been determined—Fink had acquired a lifetime's worth of nicknames by the time he signed on with the Henry-Ashley expedition. As a sharpshooting teenaged scout during the Shawnee Wars of the late eighteenth century, the militiamen defending Fort Pitt had dubbed him "Bangall" for his uncanny accuracy in taking down hostiles from great distances. And after drifting into the nascent riverboat trade plying the Ohio and Mississippi in the 1790s, he earned the sobriquet "the snapping turtle" for his proclivity toward igniting knock-down rum-shack melees. But the one tag that seemed to stick like a tick to Fink was "King of the Keelboaters."* The everready pugilist was most proud of that.

At six-foot-three and 180 pounds, Fink was a tall man for his era, if not quite a wide-bodied bruiser. Yet he boasted—quite accurately, by all accounts—that he could down a gallon of whiskey and still raise his rifle to shoot the tail off a pig at ninety paces. Just for practice, he and his cohort were known to blast jars of hard liquor off each other's heads from 150 feet. It did not take much urging for Fink, who described himself as half horse

---

* Readers of a certain age may recall the character "Big Mike" Fink, played by the veteran character actor Jeff York, from appearances on the 1955 Disney television series *Davy Crockett, King of the Wild Frontier* and the 1956 Disney movie *Davy Crockett and the River Pirates*. In both roles, Fink was the hard-drinking captain of the keelboat *Gullywhumper*.

and half alligator, to proclaim to anyone listening that he could "out-run, out-hop, out-jump, throw-down, drag out, and lick any man in this country." Despite his bombast, Fink was not a bad hand to have around to help set the heavy iron beaver traps baited with a twig dipped in a mixture of cloves and an oily yellow substance called castoreum, the thick and musky "medicine" secreted from the rodent's sex glands. The traps were then anchored to the creekbank by a five-foot length of steel chain. The trick to trapping, writes the western historian Dale Morgan, was "to catch a beaver by the paw and drown him before he could gnaw the paw off." He might have added that a trapper had best be sure the animal was indeed dead, as a bite from the magnificent teeth of a forty- to sixty-pound adult could penetrate all the way through a man's hand.

The lodges the beaver inhabited in the ponds their dams formed were not hard to find. Following tree-drag ruts to beaver slides—where the animal slithered into the water—the traps were set at dusk and raised at dawn, with the catch skinned on the spot. The pelts, or *plews* in the jargon, were hauled back to camp to be flesh-scraped and stretched and hung to dry on a willow-wood frame while the flat slab of succulent tail—which had once served the animal as a rudder, a communications paddle, and a finely tuned water-pressure detection device that could sense breaches in its dams—was roasted over flaming charcoal.

This is where the innate curiosity that William Ashley had observed in Smith back in his St. Louis parlor expressed itself. He was a font of questions. How long did it take a beaver to drown? Why grab the animal by its five-fingered front paw and not the nape of the neck? Was there a way to tell old beaver slides from newer ones?*

As beaver pelts grew their most luxurious in cold weather, wading into freezing mountain waters in parfleche moccasins to set and raise multiple five-pound traps—a trapper usually carried between five and ten—more or

---

* Respectively: approximately thirty-five minutes; their thick, slippery necks are hard to clasp and hold; a slide whose top had turned to a muddy crust was no longer in use.

less guaranteed the early onset of rheumatoid arthritis so prevalent among Mountain Men. Many, like Daniel Boone himself, who had trapped for decades along the Appalachians, spent the final years of their lives barely able to walk, much less mount and ride a horse. Mike Fink needn't have fretted over this.

At some point over that winter of 1822–1823, the temperamental Fink fell into a simmering argument, reportedly over a St. Louis woman, with a longtime comrade listed on Andrew Henry's roster only as "Carpenter." Feigning a rapprochement, Fink suggested they reconcile their difference in the old Ohio River style—shooting a tin cup of whiskey off each other's heads. Carpenter lost the coin toss to see who would fire first. He had barely placed the cup on his head before Fink shot him between the eyes. Fink claimed it was a rare misfire. But weeks later, during a heavy drinking session, he admitted that he was glad that he had killed the man. At that, a friend of Carpenter's drew the flintlock pistol he had confiscated from Carpenter's cold body and shot Fink dead. No one in the party saw any reason to report the matter to the authorities. Mike Fink died as he lived, and not a few men felt that he had improved the world by taking leave of it.

*   *   *

With Montana's river currents flowing under four feet of ice and Mike Fink and his unlucky nemesis Carpenter resting in shallow hard-dirt graves, Jed Smith and his surviving comrades passed a quiet winter on the Musselshell. Winter ice-trapping was negligible as beavers rarely left their watery lodges during the frozen months, instead mating furiously to produce late-spring litters of two to four kits and surviving on stored provisions of moldering water lilies, cattail roots, and particularly layers of tender inner bark, twigs, and buds from their preferred aspen, willow, and birch trees.

Come the spring of 1823, the first green shoots on the branches of the ubiquitous cottonwoods and box elders were harbingers that the most profitable beaver-trapping season had arrived. Well aware that pelts taken just after the first April thaw brought top dollar, eleven of the Musselshell hivernants decided to push some one hundred miles northwest to the mouth of the Judith River, named by William Clark after a particularly comely cousin.* Smith was not among them. He sensed that his presence might be of better use at Fort Henry, and he rode east. He judged correctly. Andrew Henry needed a trusted hand to relay an urgent directive to William Ashley in St. Louis. Smith was that man. Henry's message was simple: his outfit needed packhorses.

Over the winter, Henry's trappers had lost several mounts in a skirmish with the Bloods, the most aggressive band of the Blackfeet, and a hunting party of Assiniboin had made off with another portion of his herd. He had sent emissaries to barter for horses among the River Crow, as the band along the Yellowstone was called to differentiate them from the Mountain Crow higher up the Wind River valley. But the Crow were not sellers; they were buyers in the sense that they increased their stock almost exponentially by constant raids on enemy tribes. A Crow brave was considered poor if he owned fewer than twenty mustangs, and, having been driven from their territory around the Black Hills by the more populous and powerful Sioux, both Crow factions divined that only superior horsemanship could keep the tribe viable.† To that end, the tribe's infants were tied to saddles as soon as they could sit; by the age of four, male children were riding alone.

A mounted Crow raiding party was capable of covering forty miles nonstop in twenty-four hours even while carrying captives, perfecting the art of escape from their many enemies—including the Blackfeet and the Cheyenne, the latter of whom had allied with the Sioux. Further, as infant mortality was particularly severe among the rugged mountain tribes, their populations were in continuous jeopardy. The Crow, along with their cous-

---

* The Judith lends its name to a group, or wedge, of geologic formations dating to the late Cretaceous period known as the Judith River Group. The formation, running from Montana into Alberta and Saskatchewan, is particularly rich in dinosaur fossils, including Tyrannosaurus bones.

† A Sioux headman, by way of comparison, was considered abundantly prosperous if he owned thirty mounts.

ins the Gros Ventre, had remedied this existential threat to their bloodlines by becoming the only tribes who did not routinely slay women and child prisoners, opting instead for intermarriage and adoption.

The Crow were also unique in another sense. "Thieving," writes the historian Morgan, "was the Crow pride." As such, there was no little irony in Andrew Henry's desperate attempt to secure horses from the tribe. Experienced high-country veterans like Henry were well aware that the Crow were equal-opportunity bandits, stealing horses from trapping expeditions as well as from their fellow Indigenous antagonists. Lewis and Clark had lost mounts to the Crow, as had several of Manual Lisa's expeditions. The difference was, the Crow had no compunction about killing Sioux or Blackfeet or Cheyenne on their raids but rarely harmed the whites. They were casually nonchalant about what at first appears an odd double standard. As one white explorer recalled, "They frankly explain [this] by telling us that if they killed [us], we would not come back and they would lose the chance of stealing from us [again]."

The Crow, when in a certain mood, were known to sometimes trade horses to the whites. Unfortunately for Henry, this was not one of those occasions. And with the rival trappers Jones and Immell in the mountains, he now planned to temporarily abandon his fort and lead his entire party southwest toward the major Yellowstone tributaries. His company would take what beaver it could along the Powder, the Tongue, and the Bighorn before crossing the Rockies above the bend of the Yellowstone and making for the Three Forks. With luck he would outrace Immell and Jones to the area that Lewis and Clark had described as so inundated with beaver dams that the connecting ponds formed a virtual inland sea. There was, however, a singular obstacle thwarting his path. For the higher up he traveled along the tributaries, the less accessible they became to pirogues and canoes. He could cache any pelts taken east of the Continental Divide. But they would only molder in the ground without horses to pack them out come April.

Such did Andrew Henry describe his dilemma to Jed Smith. With that

Smith turned his pony over to the major, fitted out a small cottonwood dugout, and, in April 1823, launched himself down the Missouri. Notwithstanding his encounter with the petulant Arikara, he had yet to meet a hostile Indian. He was due.

CHAPTER 6

A BLOODSTAINED BEACH

William Ashley, with Jed Smith by his side, well understood that he was approaching an inflection point. He was far from certain, however, precisely what lay beyond.

It was the second to last day of May 1823, six weeks after his departure from St. Louis in command of the keelboats *Yellow Stone Packet* and *The Rocky Mountains*. While he and his new crew of some one hundred manjacks made their way upriver, unsettling news flowed downstream. An Arikara war party had only recently intercepted, robbed, and beaten senseless a small contingent of rival Missouri Fur Company factors laden with hides and pelts obtained from the Sioux. This led to a subsequent skirmish between the Arikara and the firm's vengeful white traders that left two braves dead—including the son of one of the tribe's headmen, known by his anglicized name of Grey Eyes. It was against this backdrop, with Grey Eyes's wife having barely concluded the shrill, ululating tremolos of her son's death song, that the Arikara villages hove into view.

* * *

Neither Smith's journals nor Ashley's papers record precisely when or where Smith's pirogue had intercepted the brace of keelboats. It can be reasonably inferred that it was after Ashley's craft had departed Sioux territory. For if Smith had delivered Andrew Henry's desperate plea for horses before then, Ashley surely would have bargained with the friendlier Lakota. Instead, in lieu of the unthinkable gambit of turning back toward the Sioux camp, he would have to attempt a trade with the Arikara.

Over the winter Ashley had hired a battle-scarred Indian fighter named Jim Clyman to recruit enough bodies to man his boats. Like most of Ashley's hunter-trappers, the thirty-one-year-old Clyman was long and lank—there were no fat Mountain Men—with a hawklike face dominated by a pair of deep-set, rheumy eyes that resembled turquoise beads. Described by one acquaintance as sporting a "heavy beard surrounded by hair the color of dried grass that fell upon his shoulders," a photograph taken in Clyman's later years reveals a small, twisted hollow on the left side of his mouth, as if he had lost several teeth. But in 1823, he was certainly hale enough to spend several weeks combing St. Louis's riverfront grogshops and brothels under the hill seeking to hire hands. Clyman, a man whose aphoristic eloquence reflected the schooling he'd received as a child growing up in northern Virginia on land his parents leased from George Washington, had signed on what he considered a few capable men, including several destined to go down in the annals of legendary Mountain Man chronicles. But, like his employer, Clyman had grave doubts that the majority of the "Falstaff's Battalion" he had dredged up would hold together once shots were fired in earnest.

Now, as the two flatbottoms rounded the horseshoe bend beneath the Arikara settlements, Ashley could sense a charge in the atmosphere. A breastwork of driftwood had risen on the midstream sandbar fronting the villages. Rifle loopholes had been bored into the rampart. More ominous, Indian women and girls were out on the bar filling dozens of bladder skins with water, as if preparing for a siege. Ashley scanned the opposite bank. Though it appeared deserted, the crest of the broken high ground, shaded by groves of willows, was riven with craggy gullies where any number of warriors might be hidden. Anchoring his vessels in the middle of the channel about ninety feet from either shore, he and a small party including Smith and the redoubtable interpreter Edward Rose rowed a small skiff to the pebbly beach.

The fortysomething Rose was of mixed-race origins—said to be part Cherokee, part Black, and part white. Years earlier he had signed on with the original overland party of Astorians making for Oregon but quit the outfit in the Rockies to live for a time with the Crow. The multiple scars on his face, including a ghastly cut that had permanently disfigured his nose, attested to a hard life, and it was suspected that during a stint working for Manuel Lisa he had stolen trade goods to ingratiate himself with the various Indigenous bands with which he subsequently went to reside. There were also sketchy reports that Rose was wanted by authorities in New Orleans for piracy and in Louisville for murder and robbery. But because of his tribal experiences, Rose knew Plains and Mountain Indian culture as well as a multitude of their languages, having even hunted with an Arikara band for a brief period.

It was the Crow who had dubbed Rose "Five Scalps" after, leading a buffalo hunt, he had single-handedly charged a large war party of Gros Ventre with only two buffalo-hide shields, an ax, and his skinning knife. With bullets bouncing off his shields, Rose killed three Gros Ventre with his ax and two more with his blade, all the while condescendingly berating the Crow braves for their cowardice. Rose's African American complexion and fierce, mutilated countenance may have made for frightening descriptions on wanted posters. But outstanding warrants irrespective, he was a good man to have about in a fight.

Ashley, Smith, Rose, and the others were met on the beach that spring afternoon by a heavily armed Arikara entourage that included two of the tribe's principal chiefs. One was named Little Soldier; the other was the grieving Grey Eyes. Ashley invited both onto the skiff. Little Soldier declined, but Grey Eyes stepped aboard. This was a start.

Ashley avoided the subject of his previous commitment to open a trading post near the settlements. Instead, he plied Grey Eyes with presents of tobacco, coffee, and refined sugar while, through the interpreter Rose, making his case for peace. Not every white man on the Missouri River, he told Grey Eyes, particularly those in his own party, could be held responsible for the death of his son. Grey Eyes accepted the gifts but merely nodded at Ashley's protests of innocence. At this Ashley got to the point. He required fifty mounts, and he had knives, iron pots, woolen blankets, and an assortment of trinkets including steel fish hooks, flints, glass beads, hand mirrors, and mother-of-pearl combs to bargain with. Grey Eyes nodded yet again before wordlessly returning to the villages. He reappeared at dusk with news that the Arikara would trade. He motioned Ashley to pitch his tent on the beach. The horses would arrive in the morning.

Grey Eyes was true to his word. Shortly after dawn, the headman himself led nineteen mustangs down from the heights. He promised more to come. Ashley, still suspicious, declined to move his keelboats from midchannel. Instead he ordered the transfer of trade goods to the beach via his two skiffs. All seemed fine until, toward late afternoon, the negotiations abruptly ended when another Arikara chieftain demanded rifles and ammunition before the tribe produced any more ponies. Grey Eyes called for a tribal council and the Indians departed.

Ashley was not keen on his outfit spending a second night under Arikara guns. But he had no choice. He returned to the boats with his trade stock and left Jed Smith in charge of a squad of about forty riflemen to protect the hobbled horses. Among these were two new hands to whom Smith had immediately warmed.

One was the twenty-four-year-old Thomas Fitzpatrick, who, like Smith and Jim Clyman, was that rare westering adventurer who had received a formal education. Whereas Smith's and Clyman's teachers had been Methodist circuit riders, Fitzpatrick's schoolmasters were Roman Catholic priests in Ireland's County Cavan. The rawboned gossoon, sporting a thick nimbus of prematurely graying hair, had left home seven years earlier and enlisted as a mate on a commercial frigate bound for New Orleans. From there he had made his way up the Mississippi to St. Louis, where the recruiter Clyman judged him suitable high-country material. This was wise. Born and raised on a small, green island whose highest peaks, MacGillycuddy's Reeks, barely scraped the sky at just over three thousand feet, Fitzpatrick was drawn to the wild and free-spirited fraternity of the Rocky Mountain explorers whose steely edges lent them the air of the ancient bands who flocked to the legendary Cu Chulainn, "The Hound of Ulster," and Ireland's most mythical warrior-hero.

Yet if Fitzpatrick's fanciful tales of ancient Eire and his command of letters were already impressing his largely illiterate American compatriots, it would be his flint and cunning that was to catch the attention of Indians across the west. Soon to be known as "Broken Hand" among the tribes, Fitzpatrick would earn the nickname in a running battle with the Blackfeet during which he killed several of his pursuers before plunging his mount off a forty-foot cliff overlooking the Yellowstone River, shattering his left wrist in the process. Conversely, if Fitzpatrick had already proven his mettle on the high seas, Jed Smith saw in another Jim Clyman recruit, the apple-cheeked Jim Bridger, something of a younger brother in need of a wing to be taken under.

James Felix Bridger was the eldest boy of a Virginia surveyor who relocated his family to St. Louis with the onset of the War of 1812. The rough river town had taken its toll; by Bridger's fourteenth birthday both his parents and two siblings were dead. An autodidact who spoke passable French and Spanish yet could neither read nor write English, Bridger had been apprenticed to a local blacksmith, where he gradually became proficient in the handling of guns and horses as well as acquiring a rough sense of a boatman's duties. These were credentials enough for Clyman, who hired him as a hunter-trapper, at nineteen the youngest of the group.

At six feet, two inches, Bridger's most striking features were a set of keen gray eyes set over protruding cheekbones wide enough to catch falling snow. He wore his mop of long brown hair parted in the middle and became known for a "kind and agreeable manner," which he would project for the rest of his life. Smith was so impressed by the teenager's poise that he playfully nicknamed him "Old Gabe" after the Archangel Gabriel, the youngest of the Bible's four seraphim. If Gabriel's fierceness in battle with Satan in the Book of Daniel is to be believed, it was a prescient appellation.

Though the names of Jedediah Smith, Thomas Fitzpatrick, and Jim Bridger are largely forgotten today, the three would, taken together, form a trinity upon which the myth of America's western expansion would become reality. Throughout their lifetimes these trail-breaking explorers and mountaineers, men with no scientific training, would be only dimly cognizant, if aware at all, that the charts they compiled and the landmarks they recorded on their wanderings were to become the roadmaps by which the carbonated forces of American commerce and government plotted to create a coast-to-coast empire.

For the moment, however, there were hostile Arikara to deal with on the plains of South Dakota. The next thirty-six hours would offer a profound study in perfidy and power politics, gamesmanship and stupidity, heroism and tragedy.

* * *

Gale-force winds blew in from the west as Jed Smith's complement of riflemen spent a second restless night on the beach. William Ashley had received no communication from the Indians since they had stalked off, and by early the next morning a fierce thunderstorm was roiling the river. If Ashley was even contemplating having his vessels make an upriver run for it, the heavy squall made the decision for him. There was also the matter of the nineteen horses he had already acquired. They would never be able to swim across the turbulent water. Loath to abandon the mounts, Ashley could only sit and wait.

By late afternoon the storm had spent itself, and Ashley was invited up to the Indian villages to palaver with an Arikara headman known as Bear. He was instructed to come with only his interpreter, Edward Rose. Rose, his antenna quivering, warned Ashley that something was amiss. Ashley replied that he refused to show the Indians any fear. The Arikara must be made to understand that he and his company were representatives of the all-powerful Great White Father in Washington.

When the two arrived at Bear's lodge, the headman Little Soldier was also there. After the pipe was passed and formal introductions made, it was Little Soldier who spoke. He struck an avuncular tone; a tare, Rose suspected, amid the wheat. After assuring the white men of their friendship, Little Soldier suddenly switched to a broken English that he said Bear could not understand. He told his visitors that, against his will, the tribe's warriors were preparing an attack. He advised Ashley that with the storm winds lulled and the river calmed, he should swim the horses he had already gathered across the Missouri as soon as possible and make his escape. Ashley was perplexed at the Indian's apparent comity. He nonetheless thanked Little Soldier, saying he would take his suggestion under consideration. Edward Rose bit his tongue.

Once back on the beach, Ashley relayed the gist of the conversation to Jed Smith and the others. It was nearing dark and most, including Ashley, agreed that their best course was to wait out yet another night to see if the Indians changed their minds about delivering more mounts. If not, they would chance a move up the river in the morning. By now Rose was near apoplectic. He argued that Little Soldier's seeming friendliness was a ploy; he was merely trying to save the Indian horses from the hail of bullets and arrows sure to soon engulf them. He pointed to the Indian braves now moving furtively among the willows atop the rise on the far bank of the river. Swim the horses, Rose said, and those warriors will be the ones collecting them. That the sanest voice at the conclave appeared to belong to a borderline psychotic known as "Five Scalps" did not bode well. From there the bleak circumstances only grew darker.

* * *

As Edward Rose was a known quantity among the Arikara, he felt no compunction about returning to the lower village that evening in search of a woman to sleep with. An apparently mindless trapper named Aaron Stephens, pocketing several trade trinkets, decided to follow him for the same purpose. Why Stephens thought this was a good idea will never be known. Stephens's departure was soon followed by howling cries and the thumps of war drums. The din grew as Rose raced down to Smith's cohort on the beach.

The randy Stephens was dead, Rose said, his limbs severed and the eyes gouged from his decapitated head. The Rees were out for more blood. As there was no other cover on the strand, Smith did his best to arrange his now squabbling riflemen into huddled defensive positions behind the increasingly skittish horses. Some men wanted to retreat to the keelboat. Others vowed to make a last stand on the gravelly sands. Still others argued to charge the settlement to recover what was left of Stephens's corpse. The indecisiveness lasted until sunrise—which was accompanied by the first fusillade from the heights above.

Jed Smith's party took the brunt of the initial salvo, although the keelboats proved easy targets for the Arikara on the far shore wielding both British muskets and bows. Ashley's entire detachment was soon caught in a three-way crossfire—from the heights above both riverbanks and from a band of warriors who had secreted themselves behind the sandbar's breastworks. Smith, firing and reloading as he ran, scrambled from position to position to steel his charges and do what he could for the wounded. He also kept a weather eye on the stalwart young Bridger as men began to scream for either reinforcements or extrication. Ashley attempted to rally his voyageurs on the *Yellow Stone Packet* to weigh anchor and pole for the beach in a rescue attempt. His efforts went for naught; the creole boatmen were frozen in fear.

Within moments most of the horses on the beach were either dead or dying, as were a fair number of men. As far as Smith could tell, the Arikara, lofting arrows over their picket ramparts or firing their London fusils through the loopholes in their stout palisades, were taking few casualties. Before it became a complete slaughter, Ashley managed to launch his two skiffs. When an oarsman on the first was blown overboard by a rifle ball, the craft spun downstream. The second, however, reached the beach. But Smith's riflemen, using the prostrate horses as makeshift cover, had resigned themselves. Most were greenhorns to Indian fights. Either from a deranged overestimation of their own firepower or a racially inspired ferocity to go down fighting in a do-or-die battle to avenge the life of their comrade Stephens, most stood their ground. The skiff returned to Ashley's keelboat with only four men, two of whom were wounded.

Yet almost immediately the gallants on the beach, including Smith, Fitzpatrick, Bridger, and Clyman, recognized their error. Arikara warriors by the hundreds began spilling down the slope at right angles toward their position. Men still standing thrust the muzzles of their rifles into their belts and plunged into the swift Missouri current under a shower of arrows and shot. Smith, covering the retreat by himself, was the last to splash into the cold, murky water after ascertaining that no living companion was left behind. As one survivor described it, "Some of them made it. Others were shot down before they got well into the water. Some who appeared to be badly wounded sank."

The entire engagement had lasted less than twenty minutes. It was not over.

* * *

Simultaneous to Smith's flight from the beach, one of the keelboats finally weighed anchor while Ashley took an ax to the anchor cable of the second. The current carried the two vessels downriver at about the same speed as the escapees from the beach. Small vignettes played out across the battle front.

When Edward Rose made the river, he swam not for the keelboats but for the southern end of the sandbar. Digging in beneath the bloated belly of a dead horse, he waited patiently for an Indian to show himself between the slats of the deadwood breastwork before firing, picking off brave after brave. Such was his "excitement of a scene so congenial to his feeling" that only the roar of Gen. Ashley's voice ordering him aboard the *Yellow Stone Packet* snapped him out of his killing frenzy.

Farther downstream, Jim Clyman had shed his rifle and pistol, his ammunition pouch, and his thick buckskin blouse to stay afloat. He considered himself a "tolerable strong swimmer" yet still found himself floundering in the swirling current. Suddenly a hand gipped his belt and hauled him into a skiff. His rescuer was the trapper Reed Gibson, who had recovered the dinghy that had drifted downstream and snagged on a bar. As Clyman coughed up water, Gibson fell forward, struck by a ball. Clyman implored him to hang on. Incredibly, Gibson sat up and dipped his oar for several more strokes before falling over again, faint from loss of blood.

Clyman, his breath returned, grabbed the lone oar to use as a paddle and veritably willed the craft through the current to the river's far shore a bit downriver. Leaving Gibson in the boat, he climbed a few steps up the riverbank for better vantage. He spotted three Arikara swimming after him. By this time Gibson, shot through the bowels, had somehow dragged himself out of the skiff and up the bank. He exhorted Clyman to hie—"Save yourself, as I am already dead and they can get nothing off me but my scalp." Clyman ran for his life onto the open prairie while Gibson half-crawled, half-rolled back down to the riverside and buried himself in brush.

The warriors, who had not spotted Gibson, chased Clyman for three miles before he eluded them along a hitch of broken high ground. He later claimed that as the spent Indians panted at the base of a hillock, he climbed the highest rise, turned, "and made them a low bow with both my hands." This is unlikely.

Clyman had been lucky. He was hundreds of miles from any friendly settlement. But the chase had taken him across the tongue of land where the river horseshoed. Spotting the water's glint, he had just entered a thick spinney of timber along the bank when the keelboat carrying Ashley rounded the meander. Heeling to port, the crew scooped him up. Clyman found Gibson bleeding out in the stern. Gibson died within the hour as Clyman wept over the body of the man who had saved his life.

After floating for a distance, William Ashley ordered anchors dropped at an island some five or six miles below the hostile encampments, not far from where the Grand emptied into the Missouri. He counted heads. Twelve men dead. Twelve more wounded, two of them mortally. A quarter of his force. He was of a mind to increase the percentage by shooting the cowardly creole voyageurs. Instead, thinking more clearly, he offered a proposal. If the company timbered up the exposed flanks of the keelboats, how many were willing to try to slip past the Arikara village by night? Thirty loud and scratchy "Ayes" pierced the air, including several from the wounded. Not near enough.

Nearby, two graves had been dug to hold the remains of Reed Gibson and another slain trapper named John Gardner. In lieu of a cleric, Jed Smith stepped forward to give the invocation. He had apparently retrieved his Bible from his possible bag on the keelboat, and, bowing his head, he intoned several pertinent verses. In his final, extemporaneous remarks, Smith spoke of a stern God whose stringency was leavened by His compassion. Given the circumstances, the former celestial emotion appeared much more apparent than the latter. The graves were left unmarked, lest the Indians disinter the bodies for ritual mutilation.

* * *

The following morning, Ashley called for a volunteer to set out on foot to carry news of the disaster to Andrew Henry on the Yellowstone. Smith stepped forward, as did a French Canadian hunter known only as Baptiste. Ashley calculated the odds. Two runners had a better chance of getting through than a man alone.

Bidding the messengers Godspeed as they settled into the bow of the skiff rowing them to the river's western bank, Ashley set about stocking the smaller of the keelboats, *The Rocky Mountains*, with guns, ammunition, and the remaining supply of hardtack and bacon. He then transferred what remained of his trading stock and beaver traps to the *Yellow Stone Packet*. On this larger craft he would send his worthless boatmen 450 miles down-river with the wounded and equipage to get word of the disaster to Colonel Henry Leavenworth, the new commanding officer of Fort Atkinson. In the meanwhile, he and the two dozen or so hardies who had agreed to stand with him, including Clyman, Bridger, and Fitzpatrick, would sail to the mouth of the Cheyenne River, about seventy-five miles south of the Arikara settlements. This was near enough to Sioux lands to deter any trailing hostiles. There they would await reinforcements.

CHAPTER 7

THE MISSOURI LEGION

The sun had barely broached the eastern horizon when, on June 3, 1823, Jed Smith and his fellow courier shouldered their rifles, hitched their possible sacks to their belts, and struck due west on foot. Avoiding Arikara territory along the wending Missouri River Valley, they followed the route of the Grand River as far as the Little Missouri, where they veered northwest toward the North Dakota–Montana border and the mouth of the Yellowstone. The slog to Fort Henry should have taken over a month. But loping at a brisk pace for sixteen to twenty hours a day, pausing only to bring down game and sear the meat over discreet fires, the two reached their destination in less than three weeks.

Andrew Henry had only just returned to the stockade from a trapping expedition, and Smith related all that had occurred at the Arikara villages. The major sat silent for a moment, absorbing the news before passing on information that was equally grim. The Arikara, he said, were but a piece of a larger, darker puzzle. In the mountains, the three bands of the Blackfeet had risen as one. He added that the small company with whom Smith had wintered over on the Musselshell was effectively no more. The eleven trappers had been ambushed by Bloods along the Judith in mid-May. Four men were killed in the skirmish. The surviving seven had fled back down the river in two canoes. The Indians had chased for days. It was as if a scene out of Fenimore Cooper's *Leatherstocking Tales* had come to life.*

Smith also learned that a separate hunting party of Blackfeet had virtually wiped out the Missouri Fur Company expedition led by Michael Immell and Robert Jones. The previous autumn, that outfit had taken some fifteen hundred pelts before spending the winter among the Crow. Immell and Jones had cached the plews and, come spring, led their diminished company northwest, as desertions had reduced the party to thirty men. Not far from Smith's old Musselshell encampment the troop had stumbled across a hunting party of Blackfeet. In the ensuing clash, four trappers were killed. Immell and Jones—who boasted of beating back Blackfeet while trapping with Manuel Lisa thirteen years earlier—were not deterred.

They rallied their party to continue on by dangling the prospect of the fortune in furs that awaited each man at the Three Forks. Several days later they reached the fabled triple confluence of rivers only to find that the Indians had purposely trapped out the entire area as a warning to the whites.† Unfazed, the hunters slogged on, following the Jefferson River up into the Centennial Mountains of northwest Montana. There they found rich beaver country and took more than one thousand plush spring pelts.

Immell and Jones, delighted by their haul, turned back for the Yellowstone sometime in mid-May. Slowed by the pace of their packhorses carrying not only peltry but also the outfit's traps, they were tracking the banks of the Jefferson on a narrow and twisting mountain trail when, rounding a particularly treacherous curve, war whoops rent the air. A party of Bloods burst from behind the thick understory of snowberry and mallow nine-

---

* James Fenimore Cooper, who would publish his *Last of the Mohicans* three years later, in 1826, was known to incorporate sketches from real life into his fiction, as when he used Daniel Boone's rescue of his kidnapped daughter as the basis for the key scene in his most famous narrative.

† To add insult to injury, during a lull in their raids on the Americans, the Blackfeet traded the furs they took from the Three Forks region to Hudson's Bay Company factors in exchange for rifles and alcohol.

bark obscuring the trunks of the towering ponderosa pines. There was no room on the path for the trappers to form a defensive circle.

The Blackfeet reeled in among the whites, scything with battle axes and bludgeoning with war clubs. Immell and Jones were among the first to die. Five more men soon joined them, while four others fell wounded. Some Indians set about mutilating the living and dead while others ran down the company's horses.* The survivors, fifteen in all, benefited from a quirk in Indian warfighting. Native Americans across the western mountains and plains rarely followed up rapid military triumphs with what today would be called mop-up operations. Thus while the braves trilled their victory songs, the rump of the Immell-Jones party managed to reach the rafts they had used to cross the Yellowstone, put in, and make for the Crow encampment.

In these two confrontations alone, the Missouri Fur Company had lost more men than its Henry-Ashley rival had during the fight at the Arikara villages. Taken together, the death toll constituted the most lethal to date in the history of the fur trade. A small saving grace for the survivors from the Missouri Fur Company was the packs of pelts taken the previous autumn. Two of the outfit's trappers dug up the cache, loaded the furs into canoes, and started off down the Yellowstone toward the Missouri and St. Louis beyond. If they had a plan to slip their cargo past the Arikara, they did not say.

Within days Andrew Henry was also on the move, with Jed Smith in tow. Leading a convoy of canoes carrying just over twenty men to the rescue of his partner William Ashley, he left another twenty anxious trappers behind to safeguard his fort.

* * *

It was mid-June by the time the voyageurs crewing the *Yellow Stone Packet* dropped anchor at Fort Atkinson and delivered William Ashley's commu-

---

* As more whites encountered the Indian way of war, they took to carrying lengths of leather thongs—or, in the case of soldiers, spare bootlaces—looped at each end precisely to avoid the fate of the wounded of the Immell-Jones party. When it seemed as if all was lost in an Indian fight, a man would remove his moccasin or boot, loop one end of the thong around his big toe and the other around the trigger of his long rifle, and turn the gun on himself.

niqué to Col. Henry Leavenworth. Leavenworth shared its contents with
Benjamin O'Fallon. O'Fallon, the post's subagent for the Upper Missouri's
Indian Affairs Bureau, had been appointed to the position by his uncle, the
famed General William Clark. Ashley's letter was blunt. He beseeched Leavenworth "to make these [Arikara] people account to the government for
the outrage committed." He also volunteered his small force of twenty-three
men as auxiliary militia. Ashley added that he had sent couriers to alert his
partner Andrew Henry of his predicament. When and if Maj. Henry arrived
with reinforcements, he wrote, they too would take the militiaman's oath.

Col. Leavenworth was torn. The military chain of command dictated
that he report William Ashley's situation and his request for assistance to
the since-promoted General Henry Atkinson in St. Louis. Notwithstanding the 1807 gunfight between the Arikara and the Bluecoats escorting
the Mandan chief home from Washington, DC, never before had the U.S.
Army formally issued battle orders against a western Indian tribe. Leavenworth recognized that if he decided to muster and march, he might be
taking a career-defining risk.

On the other hand, awaiting orders from Gen. Atkinson could take
weeks. Goaded by the Indian-hating O'Fallon, and perhaps weighing the
political implications of ignoring the entreaties of the lieutenant governor
of the state of Missouri, Leavenworth decided to act on his own. He mobilized six companies of his Sixth Infantry into the field. And thus was initiated the phenomenon of the American West's cyclical festivals of violence
against its native inhabitants.

* * *

Eager to join Leavenworth's punitive expedition was the Missouri Fur Company's acting general partner Joshua Pilcher, who was still seething over the
Arikara attack on his brokers the previous spring. The thirty-year-old Pilcher
had replaced Manuel Lisa as the company's chief field officer upon Lisa's
death three years earlier. If Lisa's approach to the Plains and Mountain Indians had been conciliatory wherever possible, Pilcher's took the opposite tack.

Pilcher's childhood in western Virginia had coincided with the blood-drenched Shawnee Wars of the late eighteenth century, and he shared the Indian agent Benjamin O'Fallon's long-held dream of grinding the western tribes into submission by force of arms. O'Fallon's uncle William Clark may have held some fond memories of the Native Americans whose guidance and goodwill had allowed he and Meriwether Lewis to survive their historic trek. The bigoted O'Fallon fostered no such sympathies. O'Fallon believed that the irreversible subjugation, if not the eradication, of the continent's Indigenous peoples could only be achieved by the massive firepower of the U.S. government.

O'Fallon's reply to Ashley's letter, which had specifically cited the headman Grey Eyes as the instigator of the confrontation at the Arikara settlements, left no doubt as to his intentions. "It is not only an individual, but the whole A'rickara nation that owes us blood," O'Fallon wrote to Col. Leavenworth. "I am in hopes that no true American will tamely stand by and witness the reception or even recognize a white flag, so long as the [lodge] of an A'rickara is decorated with the scalp of our people."

Needless to say, O'Fallon's sentiments fell on sympathetic ears in Joshua Pilcher. If contemporary portraits are accurate, O'Fallon and Pilcher could have been born brothers. Both had a proclivity for posing in black frock coats that matched their wide, black cravats; both sported thick manes of black hair brushed back fiercely from broad foreheads into raptors' crests—birds of prey sharing a fraternal mindset not only in their loathing of Indians but also in their mutual detestation of the British. The future prosperity of Pilcher's Missouri Fur Company, of course, depended on the fulfillment of O'Fallon's view that once the tribes were eliminated and the Hudson's Bay Company and Nor'Wester trappers were driven back over the Canadian border, the American fur trade would constitute the singular agent of U.S. hegemony along the Upper Missouri and beyond. Thus Pilcher was particularly gratified to read O'Fallon's short coda in his letter to Col. Leavenworth. With the Arikara cowed into submission by U.S. firepower, O'Fallon wrote, "the Blackfeet will hear and tremble."

From O'Fallon's and Pilcher's points of view, the major stumbling block to this means to an end was Col. Leavenworth. In formal portraits, the clean-shaven, Connecticut-born Leavenworth exuded the air of an eastern patrician, not least because of his habit of striking Napoleonic, hand-in-tunic poses. Though Leavenworth had distinguished himself in multiple engagements during the War of 1812, since his posting to Fort Atkinson he had exhibited what civilians like Pilcher and O'Fallon considered an irrational empathy toward the plight of the tribes whose lands the Americans wanted. O'Fallon in particular doubted that the colonel had the crimson temperament required to fight, and annihilate, entire swaths of Indigenous peoples. The Indian agent viewed Leavenworth's attitude toward Native Americans as naïve at best, idiotic at worst. Pilcher, in concurrence, added that he feared the "imbecility" of Leavenworth's romantic notions. As Leavenworth had ordered O'Fallon to remain at Fort Atkinson while his expedition marched north, it fell to Pilcher to maintain focus on not merely victory over the Arikara but, if possible, their extermination.

For all the civilian suspicions about Leavenworth, he was in fact a competent military tactician. He immediately recognized that without a complement of mounted dragoons, the Arikara would likely disappear into the boundless prairie during the month or so it would take his troops to march on the villages.* There, hidden among the wrinkled plains, the hostiles would remain until either the weather turned or the American supply lines ran dry. To remedy this quandary, the colonel dispatched emissaries to disparate Lakota bands entreating them to join his expedition as flying columns. The Sioux horsemen, riding ahead of Leavenworth's foot soldiers, would serve the dual purpose of sweeping away any Arikara scouts who might spot his footbound columns as well as lulling the hostiles into believing that William Ashley's "bleeding traders" had merely enlisted Indian mercenaries to avenge their pride.

---

* The word *dragoon* is derived from the dragon guns—shortened version of blunderbusses—carried by legendary French mounted forces.

The Sioux—envisioning plunder and the destruction of their enemy's permanent camps—readily accepted Leavenworth's invitation and, as it happened, upheld their end of the bargain. Streaming north astride their finest warhorses—the animals' manes sporting ribbons and feathers; their flanks dusted and painted with red ochre symbols delineating enemies killed, scalps taken, mounts stolen—more than seven hundred Lakota warriors, perhaps a third of them wielding firearms, cleared the path of any Arikara lookouts. It was Leavenworth who would waver.

* * *

The riotous swirls of dust kicked up by the 230 officers and enlisted men of the U.S. Army's Sixth Infantry Regiment were near blinding. The force, supported by close to fifty riflemen from Joshua Pilcher's Missouri Fur Company, departed Fort Atkinson on June 22, 1823. Three keelboats, one manned by Pilcher's trappers, sailed abreast of the foot soldiers. The vessels hauled not only emergency rations and surplus ammunition but also two six-pound cannons and a medium howitzer. William Ashley's *Yellow Stone Packet* was among the flotilla. Benjamin O'Fallon had bullyragged twenty or so of its crew into returning upriver to atone for their faint hearts during the fight below the Arikara settlements.

The excursion had just passed Council Bluff when one of the boats snagged on a planter, foundered, and went under, taking seven soldiers with her. To Leavenworth's relief, none of the artillery pieces were aboard. Less than a week later a violent storm wracked the river and nearly sank the *Yellow Stone Packet*. She was only saved by a fortuitous sandbar but lost her mast and most of her deck. While her voyageurs scrambled to refit the craft, a mounted messenger arrived informing Leavenworth and Pilcher of the Blackfeet "massacre" in the mountains.* Immell dead. Jones dead. One thousand spring pelts lost. The news only stoked Pilcher's already flaming ire.

---

* In the long epoch of martial engagements between European Americans and the continent's Indigenous peoples, it should be noted that whites have always been keener to affix the label *massacre* to successful Indian attacks while preferring to designate their own such victories as *battles*.

* * *

William Ashley had spent the better part of June traversing the Lower Missouri in search of horses. Though revenge on the Arikara was never far from his mind, he also sensed that his organization's creditors in St. Louis were becoming anxious, and the coming fall trapping season also consumed his thoughts. He had initially entertained the idea of bulling past the Arikara settlements aboard a timbered-up *The Rocky Mountains* once Andrew Henry and his reinforcements arrived. After obtaining mounts from the Sioux, he changed his mind. He now felt it more advantageous for his hunter-trappers to make their way overland to the mountains and avoid the Arikara altogether.

It was during one of Ashley's downriver trading sorties that he learned of Col. Leavenworth's expedition. The enterprise, ballyhooed up and down the lower section of the river as "The Missouri Legion," was, as noted, the first American Army unit to officially strike out to engage western Indians. The citizens of St. Louis threw parades.

By early July, Ashley had stepped back onto the deck of *The Rocky Mountains*, berthed on an island across from the mouth of the Cheyenne River in north-central South Dakota. Maj. Henry and his company were awaiting. The canoeists who had preceded Henry downriver hauling what was left of Immell and Jones's peltry had been subjected to a guantlet of rifle fire and arrows as they rode the swift current past the Arikara villages. Yet, oddly, when Henry's larger outfit gained the settlements, the Indians streamed onto the beach flapping buffalo robes, the traditional invitation to stop and parley. Ruse? Peace offering? It did not matter. Henry had paid them no heed.

Poling upstream to the mouth of the Teton River in anticipation of Col. Leavenworth's arrival, Gen. Ashley and Maj. Henry dispatched their keelboat to Council Bluff with a skeleton crew to ride out the winter and set about dividing their eighty-odd remaining men into two rifle companies to append to the so-called Missouri Legion. Thomas Fitzpatrick was made quartermaster of the entire battalion while Jed Smith was tapped to lead one detachment, with Jim Clyman as his second-in-command. A hunter named Hiram Scott headed the other. Although it is not recorded to which outfit Jim Bridger was assigned, it seems likely that Smith requested his presence by his side.

Leavenworth's troops and keelboats arrived at Ashley's new camp on July 30. A week later, having folded their trappers into his soldiery, the colonel resumed his march. By August 8 the entire column had forded the Grand. The next morning Leavenworth sent his Sioux horseman, adorned with white muslin headbands to differentiate them from the Arikara, ahead of his infantrymen onto the plain before the enemy villages. Seven hundred Arikara warriors poured out of the settlements to meet them. Their black war paint glistened in the midsummer sunlight.

* * *

The relentless Jim Clyman, having volunteered to take point for Jed Smith's battalion of trappers, was among the first of the foot soldiers lagging behind the mounted Sioux to arrive on the scene. His initial reaction to the scrum, as he wrote with his typical lack of punctuation, struck him as "more like a swarm of bees than a battle field they going in all possible directions the Rees having mounted." In fact, so haphazard was the fray that when Col. Leavenworth reached the scene he ordered his companies to hold fire lest they cut down their Indian allies. In retrospect, this was the turning point of the engagement; it was virtually over before it even began.

At the sight of the Bluecoats, the Arikara broke and raced back behind their battlements. Leavenworth, waiting for the vessels hauling his artillery, had his regiment halt just shy of rifle range. The soldiers watched as the victorious Sioux, having lost but two braves, savaged the bodies of the dozen or so Arikara splayed across the prairie. It is more than disheartening that Jed Smith's journals for this period have never been recovered. In the aftermath of witnessing his first true Indian fight, what must Smith's thoughts have been at the spectacle recorded by men like Clyman?

Clyman watched as Sioux horsemen dragged the severed and scalped heads of their enemies across the plain on cords while others dismounted to lop off the arms, legs, hands, and feet of the dead Arikara. The severed limbs were impaled on lances or sharpened sticks and paraded about the battle-field in victory celebrations. Next, he spotted a behemoth Lakota warrior leap from his mustang and, mimicking the grunts and snuffles of a bear, move on his hands and knees toward a dead Arikara brave. Settling over the corpse, the Indian lowered his head again and again over the body's bare breast, each time gnawing away great chunks of flesh with his teeth. The other Sioux turned their heads and implored the whites not to look. This, they said, would negate the power, in Clyman's words, of "the grizzle Bear medicine." Near simultaneously, an ancient Sioux headman summoned one of his wives to the field and guided her to a fallen Arikara brave who lay within gunshot dis-tance of the picketed lower village. He handed her a war club. The old woman bashed the brains out of the dead man while the old chief taunted the Arikara as cowards for permitting a woman to strike their warrior.

Such ritual displays continued until dusk, when Col. Leavenworth's ar-tillery pieces were finally hauled from the keelboats. The planned bom-bardment of the settlements would have to wait until daybreak. No one slept much that night. Even Clyman, who bore scars from his battles with the Shawnee and Cherokee during the War of 1812, was unnerved by what he recalled as the unrestrained chaos of the "waling [sic] of squaws and children the Screams and yelling of men the firing of guns the awful howl-ing of dogs the neighing and braying of hosses and mules . . . intermingled with the stench of dead men and horses."

* * *

The shelling began at sunup. One six-pounder was dragged to within range of the upper Arikara village by a company of riflemen while the other can-non and the howitzer concentrated on the lower settlement. The initial cannonball sallies tore through the Indian palisades and earthen lodges like steel rivets punching holes in papier-mâché, although the exploding

shells of the howitzer merely arced over their targets and splashed harm-
lessly into the river beyond. Yet even after adjusting the latter's gunsights,
the impact of the artillery barrage did not produce Leavenworth's desired
effect—to either force an unconditional surrender or bring the Arikara
back out onto the field of battle. On toward noon the colonel was forced to
adjust his strategy, convening a council of his officers to discuss a frontal
infantry assault. Some felt he was buckling under the strain of command.
For Col. Leavenworth now faced the possibility of annihilating an entire
Indian tribe without official sanction from any superior officer or, worse,
taking heavy losses in bloody lodge-to-lodge fighting.

By this time, the famished Sioux, their mission complete, had dispersed
into the Arikara croplands, where they gorged themselves on corn, pumpkins, and squash. Their banquet was interrupted by a messenger from
Leavenworth. The colonel was still debating whether to mass his forces to
storm the lower village, but his clumsily worded communiqué to the Sioux
chiefs—"to save their stragglers from the tomahawks of the Aricara"—was
interpreted by the Indians as a sign of American weakness. Moments later
Leavenworth was mortified to see several Sioux headmen conferring with
their Arikara counterparts in front of the lower village. He and Joshua
Pilcher rushed to join them.

Before Leavenworth even reached the parley, one of the Arikara war
chiefs ran to him. The Indian begged the colonel to take pity on the tribe's
women and children. Grey Eyes, he said, the very chief who had instigated
the entire episode, was dead, cleaved asunder by a cannonball. Was that
not enough? To Joshua Pilcher's visible disgust, Leavenworth appeared to
agree. With that the Arikara headman Little Soldier and several clan leaders
joined Leavenworth and his officer corps, taking seats on buffalo robes laid
out in a circle on the switchgrass grass to discuss the terms of surrender.

Leavenworth told Little Soldier and his peers that in order to save
themselves from complete annihilation, they must comply with three
conditions. They were to return any property confiscated from William
Ashley's company after the battle on the beach two months earlier; they

must vow to refrain from attacking any keelboats plying the Missouri in the future, and, as a show of good faith, they were to surrender five hostages, all respected warriors, to be transported back to Fort Atkinson. To drive home his points, the colonel, an imposing sight in his blue-and-buff uniform, stood to make a grand speech detailing the overwhelming strength of the U.S. Army's infantry companies. As the historian Dale Morgan wryly notes, "The Rees might have been more impressed had they witnessed some striking evidence of [this]." Nonetheless, after a brief conference, Little Soldier and his fellow chiefs acceded to Leavenworth's demands.

It is impossible to say who was more repulsed by the outcome of this pantomime, Joshua Pilcher or the Sioux. The latter, who had done the only real fighting, rode away disgusted, suspicious, and angry—in the process stealing six army mules and seven of the mustangs they had sold to William Ashley only weeks earlier. Pilcher, in the meanwhile, merely glowered at the colonel. When it came time to smoke the calumet, Pilcher initially refused, warning the Arikara that he and his trappers were not finished with them. At Leavenworth's barked command Pilcher finally put the pipe stem to his lips. He had, after all, formally signed the official oath of a militiaman, which bound him to obey the colonel's orders. However, it was clear to all, not least the Indians, that Pilcher's was an empty gesture. How empty would soon become apparent.

* * *

For all of Colonel Henry Leavenworth's tactical expertise, he proved a poor strategist. Or, perhaps, as Pilcher and the Indian agent Bernard O'Fallon might have put it, an effete Indian-lover. For if the purported premise for the entire Missouri Legion's expedition had not already run off the rails, one last hitch in the treaty negotiations showed Leavenworth to also be a vacillating negotiator.

It was nearing dusk when Little Soldier, in accordance with the demand to return William Ashley's property, trudged from his village leading a single horse buckling under the weight of eighteen buffalo robes and three rifles. When Little Soldier insisted that this was all he could gather from the ruins of the bombarded settlement, Leavenworth ordered his men into assault positions. Platoon and company commanders were still mustering their troops when Edward Rose galloped up to the colonel. Rose had been exploring the damage to the settlements done by the artillery. In addition to reporting thirty freshly dug graves, he told Leavenworth that at the sight of the Bluecoat skirmish lines, the Indians were preparing to abandon both villages for the prairie. There, Rose suggested, the colonel's detachment might waste weeks if not months chasing them hither and yon.

Col. Leavenworth called another meeting of his officers. The talk was heated. His subordinates, hungry for battlefield honors and promotions, pressed for an immediate assault. But Leavenworth, as he later reported to Gen. Atkinson, felt that the Arikara had been "sufficiently humbled." Again summoning Little Soldier, the colonel dropped his stipulation to recompense William Ashley for everything he had lost. The buffalo robes and rifles that the Indians had produced, he said, would suffice. He instructed his adjutant to draw up formal peace proceedings to which the Arikara headmen would be expected to, in the vernacular, "touch the pen" the following morning.*

This decision was too little, too late. Even in this relatively early western stage of negotiations between the two races, the shrewdest of the Plains Indians were beginning to realize—as their eastern counterparts had long ago learned—that however many concessions to which they acquiesced, the duplicitous American newcomers ultimately took what they wanted. Real power, they recognized, flowed not from an inkwell but from an

---

* As the overwhelming majority of American Indians could neither read nor write, the U.S. government had obligingly worked out a practice wherein a tribal headman would step up to a table holding the terms of a treaty binding his people, as in this case, to pledges of amity. Sometimes these agreements included licensed and regulated trade practices with the United States. The pact was then read aloud in English and translated by an interpreter—as if the words "licensed" and "regulated" carried any meaning in Native American culture. Finally, a clerk or scribe seated at the table would extend a fountain pen, which the Indian would touch with one or two fingers before the scribe added his name to the document.

otter-skin arrow quiver or, better yet, from the muzzle of a long rifle. That night the entire Arikara tribe slipped past the American sentries and disappeared into the northland, leaving their villages deserted.

Disconsolate and humiliated, the next morning Col. Leavenworth divided his troops into marching regiments and keelboat crews for the unhappy trip back to Fort Atkinson. The latter included two slightly wounded Bluecoats, his only casualties. The abashed Missouri Legion had traveled but several miles when Leavenworth climbed a rise to turn for one final look at his "battlefield." Thick clouds of black smoke rose over the abandoned Indian settlements. Pilcher and his men had fired the lodges.

Leavenworth was incensed; Pilcher unapologetic. Writing to the colonel—and, later, to William Clark, to War Department officials, to several congressmen, and to a bevy of newspaper editors—Pilcher accused Leavenworth of demonstrating to the Upper Missouri tribes "the greatest possible contempt for the American character." Leavenworth, he charged, had created "impassable barriers" to any future commerce along the Missouri River. In his defense, Leavenworth argued that the Arikara had been "fully convinced of our ability to punish any injury . . . and that they would have behaved well in the future if we left them undisturbed." Pilcher's burning of the villages, he charged, had undone his diplomacy.

By the time the U.S. Army's Col. Henry Leavenworth and the Missouri Fur Company's head field agent Joshua Pilcher took their feud public, Andrew Henry, Jed Smith, and the rest of the hunter-trappers from the Henry-Ashley outfit were halfway to the mountains. Unaware of the scorching war of words echoing through the halls of Congress and filling flatlander newspaper columns, few of the men on that dusty trail put much faith in the fantasy that their struggles with the Arikara were over. But, in the end, a line had been drawn and crossed.

Despite its anticlimactic denouement, what historians now label the "Arikara War" constituted the first time that the U.S. Army officially took up arms, however halfheartedly, against Plains Indians. It would, of course, be far from the last.

PART II

THE PASS

I defy the annals of chivalry to furnish the record of a life more wild and perilous than those of a Rocky Mountain trapper.

—Francis Parkman

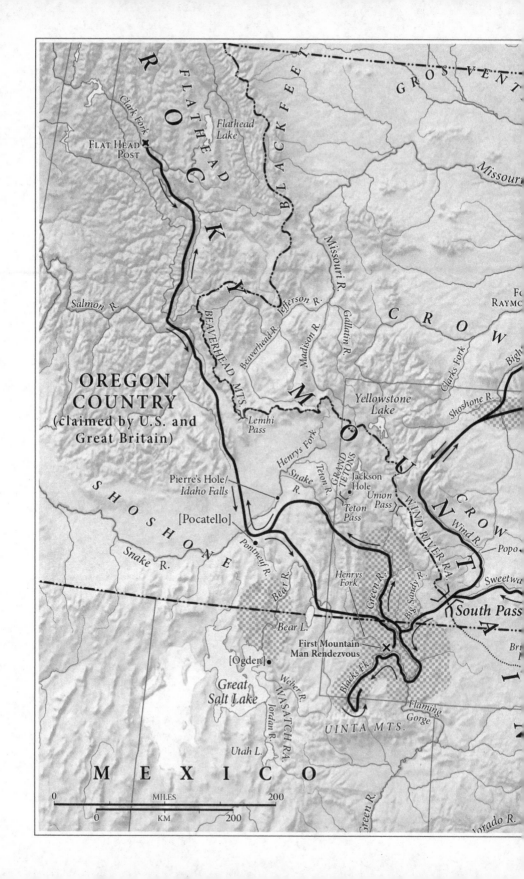

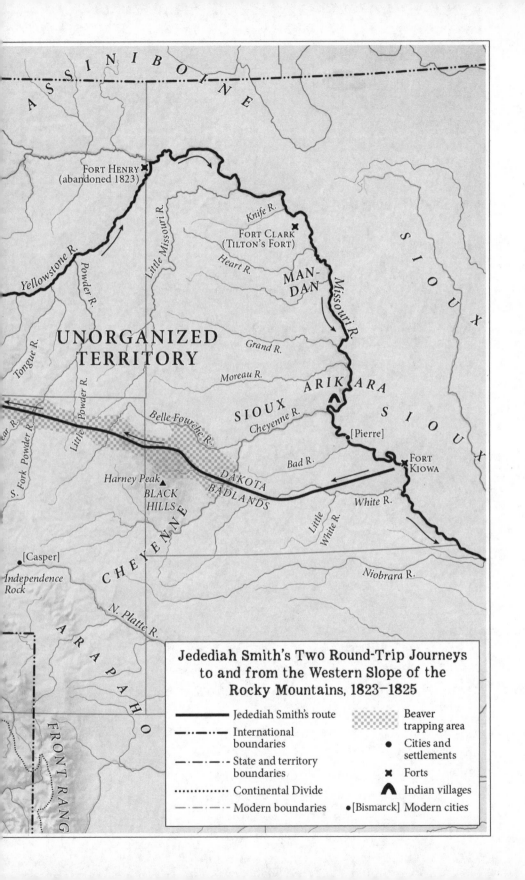

ASSINIBOINE

FORT HENRY
(abandoned 1823)

Yellowstone R.

Powder R.

Tongue R.

Little Powder R.

S. Fork Powder R.

ar R.

UNORGANIZED
TERRITORY

Little Missouri R.

Knife R.

FORT CLARK
(TILTON'S FORT)

Heart R.

MAN-
DAN

Missouri R.

SIOUX

Grand R.

Moreau R.

ARIKARA

SIOUX

Belle Fourche R.

SIOUX

Cheyenne R.

[Pierre]

FORT
KIOWA

Harney Peak
BLACK
HILLS

DAKOTA
BADLANDS

Bad R.

White R.

Little
White R.

CHEYENNE

[Casper]

Independence
Rock

Niobrara R.

N. Platte R.

ARAPAHO

FRONT RANG

Jedediah Smith's Two Round-Trip Journeys to and from the Western Slope of the Rocky Mountains, 1823–1825

—— Jedediah Smith's route	▦ Beaver trapping area
—··—··— International boundaries	• Cities and settlements
—·—·— State and territory boundaries	✗ Forts
·········· Continental Divide	⋀ Indian villages
—·—·— Modern boundaries	•[Bismarck] Modern cities

CHAPTER 8

LES MAUVAIS TERRES

Word of Col. Henry Leavenworth's desultory showing against the Arikara spread rapidly throughout the West. The Indian agent Benjamin O'Fallon's grand scheme to make the Native Americans "tremble" at the might of the U.S. Army had the nearly opposite effect. Tribes already ill-disposed toward the encroaching whites became more emboldened, while the Bluecoats' tepid response to the Arikara belligerence began to sow doubts among peoples, from the Mandan to the Sioux, who had managed to survive, if not thrive, in the shadow of American expansion.

These shifts in attitude were not lost on William Ashley and Andrew Henry, the latter slowly making his way back toward Blackfeet country. Following their dismissal from Col. Leavenworth's regiment with honorable discharges—Joshua Pilcher's company received dishonorable discharges from the furious Leavenworth—the partners settled accounts with their remaining voyageurs and ordered *The Rocky Mountains* keelboat sailed back downriver. They had acquired enough packhorses in trade with the Sioux for Henry to lead the bulk of the company overland to the Yellowstone along the familiar Grand River passage. A rump party of perhaps fifteen trappers under Jed Smith's command was dispatched on a more southerly route across central South Dakota. Smith's ultimate destination was the western slope of the Continental Divide.

Fortune may have momentarily frowned on the Henry-Ashley enterprise to this point—Maj. Henry's paltry plew take in 1822 was exacerbated by the Arikara debacle, which, all told, had cost the firm what today would be the equivalent of nearly $60,000. But Gen. Ashley, his Missouri political ambitions still very much alive, saw in the apparent fiasco what the old-school Gallic business elites of St. Louis—a powerful investor class—might term an unexpected *lagniappe*. With the aggrieved and combative Arikara prowling the Upper Missouri, all of the rival fur companies had abandoned plans to trap the Rockies in 1823. Andrew Henry and Jed Smith thus had a monopoly on prime beaver locations.

Maj. Henry's larger outfit included the now-blooded Jim Bridger and a mysterious and taciturn hunter named Hugh Glass whose close-set eyes, long corvine nose, and down-turned mustache created the appearance of a perpetual frown. Glass, an experienced trapper, had taken a bullet through his thigh during the fight on the Arikara beach and had been one of the mourners at the subsequent impromptu funeral service for the two men presided over by Smith. Depending on the opaque sourcing of the era, Glass may or may not have hailed from Pennsylvania and may or may not have been the son of either Irish or Scots Irish immigrants. As it was, the fantastical stories surrounding his early life were already approaching legend.

Prior to signing on with the Henry-Ashley company, Glass was said to have been shanghaied by the New Orleans pirate Jean Lafitte, only to escape after two years on the high seas by jumping ship and swimming to Galveston Island off Texas. Later, he and a hunting partner were rumored to have been taken captive by the Pawnee while hunting buffalo somewhere in present-day Kansas. Glass allegedly was forced to watch his companion burn at the stake while he was inexplicably adopted into the tribe. He supposedly lived with the Pawnee for a period of years before making his way to St. Louis. None of these tales are verifiable. In any case, the fact remained that despite his dour persona, Glass had proven himself a handy man with a long rifle and hunting knife.

In the meanwhile, William Ashley had a final piece of business to settle prior to returning to St. Louis to calm the nerves of his creditors. He had managed to acquire temporary juments for Jed Smith's party from a veteran factor manning Pierre Chouteau's trading post, dubbed Fort Kiowa, some eighty miles southeast of South Dakota's present-day capital of Pierre. Per Ashley's arrangement, the broker lent Smith and his outfit the horses to carry their traps, chains, trade goods, and sundry equipage in accordance with a uniquely early-frontier accord—we'll do for you now and you'll do for us later. The animals, it was agreed, would be returned when Smith obtained replacements from the more remote tribes nearer to the mountains. To ensure the handshake contract, the factor also provided a French Canadian guide to lead Smith and his men, walking beside their packhorses, across the daunting Dakota Territory.

Because Andrew Henry planned on westering along the presumably less perilous Grand River route, Smith was allowed to siphon some of the company's most trusted hands. Among his train were the frightening interpreter Edward Rose, the Irishman Thomas Fitzpatrick, the proven Jim Clyman, and a slim and lank former Missouri constable named William "Bill" Sublette—said to be so skinny that he could hide behind a cottonwood sapling. Whatever the twenty-four-year-old Sublette's physical anomalies, he had fought like a panther during the shootout with the Arikara.

Smith and his men were but a few days out from Fort Kiowa when they forded their first river. Their French Canadian guide warned them against gulping the water; more than a few small sips, he said, and their innards would be knotted for days. The trappers, having just completed a long, dry march across the desolate Dakota highlands, ignored him and plunged into the cream-colored White River. They swallowed great mouthfuls of what Clyman described as the "sweetish, pungent" liquid. They paid the price. The river was infused with a dangerous amount of alkaline silt, and over the next few days stomach cramps wracked the outfit. Some may have considered it worthwhile; it would be some time before they saw water again.

Striking west from the White River, forty-eight hours passed as Smith's company, their water horns sucked dry and their eyes darting helplessly into the monotype distance, began to suffer from hallucinatory dehydration. Slogging across the arid high plains through thick stands of prickly pear whose needlelike thorns tore at the flanks of both men and beasts, they gradually diverged from the straight column they had held since the start of their journey. With their mounted guide having vanished over the western horizon in search of a rumored tributary of the White, Clyman—like the others, nearly dragging his stumbling packhorses behind him—had drifted so far to the north that he feared "we ware not onley long but wide and it appeared like we might never all collect together again." Suddenly, nearing dusk, Clyman's mustang, its breath rasping, took off at a halting lope. It had smelled water. Clyman panted after the animal and splashed into the spring-fed waterhole alongside his horse. He drank his fill before firing off a rifle round to alert the others.

One by one his compatriots and their horses reached the oasis in varying states of distress. They filled their gullets and fired off more shots. By nightfall all but three had found the spring. The moon was high when Jed Smith finally appeared leading three mounts. The two missing men were still alive, he said, if only barely. They had both collapsed and he had buried them in sand up to their necks to help retain what moisture was left in their bodies. Filling several water horns and saddling a trio of the most refreshed horses, Smith disappeared into the darkness to either rescue them or complete their internment. It was close to midnight when he returned with the bedraggled trappers in tow. The legend of Captain Jedediah Smith the Booshway was growing.

Over the next several days Smith and his party struck two separate Sioux camps along the Cheyenne River, one Brule and one Oglala. They managed to trade for thirty-some horses, enough for each man to now ride alongside his jument. Finally mounted, they sent the guide back to Fort

Kiowa with the borrowed mustangs and again set a course due west. For a time both men and animals were well fed and watered as they followed the clear-running Cheyenne over a landscape home to over sixty varieties of short grasses. These were prime fodder for buffalo, pronghorn antelope, and mule deer, not to mention the millions of prairie dogs that provided food for wolves, foxes, coyotes, black-footed ferrets, hawks, and eagles. And though bighorn sheep weighing up to forty pounds were hunted to extermination in this area of South Dakota by the mid-1920s, they were plentiful enough roaming the knobs and mesas a century earlier. The outfit ate well.

Each man knew that from here on their uncharted course would take them over the Black Hills and into the Powder River Valley toward the Bighorn where it met the Wind River at the "Wedding of the Waters." There, if they survived the journey, they would winter over after caching any pelts they trapped along the way. Come spring they would strike for the Divide and, beyond, the fabled beaver-rich creeks of the western slopes of the Rockies. Before any of this could occur, however, they would have to negotiate a stretch of the most inhospitable terrain on earth.

So it was that when the game vanished, the grasses thinned, and the loamy brown soil gave way to an ashy, pearl-colored dust that powdered the flanks of their mounts, Smith and his crew realized that they had entered what early French explorers, the first whites to set eyes on the landscape, aptly christened *les mauvais terres*. The Badlands. The huge piles of sun-bleached buffalo bones littering cliffside canyons—the result of the buffalo jumps that the horseless Arikara had initiated and other tribes soon emulated—only heightened the eerie atmosphere. These were indeed bad lands.

* * *

Encompassing 380 square miles of territory in present-day southwestern South Dakota, the austere and treeless patchwork of crazy-quilt buttes, slate-gray gullies, towering hoodoos, and winding canyons known as the

Badlands was once the westernmost bed of North America's Great Inland Sea. This shallow body of water, formed during the late-Cretaceous period between eighty million and sixty-five million years ago, connected the Arctic Ocean to the Gulf of Mexico. To the west was what archeologists have named the demi-continent of "Laramidia," effectively severed from the "Appalachia" landmass to the east. Countless millennia later, a dome of molten rock ruptured the earth's crust on the water's western shore and gave rise to the towering granite outcroppings of the Rocky Mountains and Black Hills. The earth to the east of these surging ranges crumpled and folded in on itself in a chain reaction, and the Inland Sea drained.

For a time after the salt water's disappearance, rivers and streams flowing out of the mountains spread mud, gravel, and sand across the area, which was slowly transformed from a lush, semitropical ecosystem into a dry, geological wasteland containing no potable standing water. Northern winds combined with flash floods and feathery hoarfrost to further erode the soft sedimentary rock and volcanic ash, leaving exposed in the terrain's sharp ridges and cliff faces the fossil remains of the Inland Sea's spectral creatures—proto-alligators, giant sharks, and predatory marine reptiles such as the toothy, snakelike mosasaur, which grew up to fifty feet long.

What Jed Smith and his riders made of the petrified bones of these fantastical aquatic carnivores protruding from canyon walls is not recorded, although Jim Clyman, returning from a scouting mission, did file one strange report. Clyman claimed to have discovered an ancient orchard of "petrifid timber" from whose tree branches, long since turned to stone, dangled "petrifid" fruit that had transformed into rubies.*

Smith and his parched trappers were likely hewing close to the "Badlands Wall," a steep, chalky precipice that runs sixty miles on a rough east-

---

* Several years later, a St. Louis newspaperman caught wind of Clyman's alleged discovery and in true tabloid fashion proceeded to adorn the petrified trees with "wild cherries peetrified into rubies of reddest hue, and peetrified birds a-sittin' on the branches a-singin' peetrified songs" (Morgan, *Jedediah Smith and the Opening of the American West*, 85).

west line and delineates North America's Upper and Lower Prairies. One day a distant thunderclap precluded the shadow of a rare storm cloud that momentarily darkened the cerulean sky. The muzzling rain likely saved their lives. Men caught what drops they could in their mouths and water horns while their horses pawed at the damp mudholes to drink. Finally riding out of the western terminus of the scabby territory and back onto prairie highlands, the group caught its first sight of the Black Hills some forty miles distant. The Oglala Sioux author Luther Standing Bear once described the outline of those dark heights as "a reclining female figure from whose breasts flowed life-giving forces." After days spent crossing the desiccated Badlands, it is doubtful that anyone in Smith's party would have argued.

Within a week the company was ascending the gentle rises that formed the eastern slope of the range. Traveling through thick stands of spruce and ponderosa pines, the little outfit feasted on elk steaks, hazelnuts, and wild plums. Before settling in each night, they set their beaver traps in the clear, cool streams that fed the Cheyenne and Belle Fourche Rivers. Reaching the massif's dividing ridge not far from Harney Peak, at 7,242 feet its highest summit, they found the descent on the steeper western slope more hazardous despite the beauty of the winding ravines studded with black-eyed Susan and whose granite flanks were nearly invisible behind thick tufts of bull thistle, yellow arrowleaf balsamroot, and mats of evergreen kinnikinnick.* One morning, searching for easier passage for the horses, Smith led his group down just such a defile.

Smith was riding several paces ahead of the train when a hulking grizzly bear entered the gorge from the far end. His horse reared, throwing him to the ground, and the bear charged. Before anyone could get off a

---

* It was Smith's alleged sighting of great veins of gold in the rugged and rocky country, reportedly related to Jim Bridger, that led to George Armstrong Custer's Black Hills gold expedition half a century later. Custer's expedition did indeed discover gold on the western slope of the range in 1874, inciting yet another war with the Sioux, which precipitated his death at the Battle of Little Big Horn. Yet, like Jim Clyman forgoing plucking the rubies from the branches of the "petrifid" orchard, Smith's indifference to this great treasure lends the story, and Bridger's retelling of it, more than a hint of fable.

shot, the animal was atop Smith. Its pounce broke several of his ribs (as well as his butcher's knife), and with its human prey dazed and supine, the bear went for the kill. It clamped its jaws around Smith's head and tore into flesh.

At this point several of the company had closed enough to get off careful shots. They may have wounded the grizzly, but they did not kill it, and it sped into the underbrush never to be seen again. Smith's compatriots were momentarily at a loss. The scene confronting them was gruesome. The crown of Smith's skull had been laid bare by the bear's claws, his left eyebrow and the skin around it had been either slashed or bitten off, and his right ear was hanging by a few mangled ligaments. As Clyman recounts, "None of us had any surgical Knowledge what was to be done."

Splayed in a welter of his own blood yet somehow still conscious, Smith directed several men to ride ahead to locate a campsite near water. He then told Clyman to fetch a needle and thread to sew him back together. Clyman numbly complied. After washing Smith's wounds and cutting back what was left of his sandy mop of hair, Clyman stitched every rip and tear as best he could, leaving the dangling ear for last. "I told him I could do nothing for his Eare," Clyman writes. "O you must try to stitch [me] up some way or other said he then I put my needle stitching it through and through and over and over laying the lacerated parts together as nice as I could."

Incredibly, Smith managed to lift himself onto his saddle and ride to a creek-side camp the scouts had located about a mile away. There a few men pitched the outfit's only tent and helped their captain, his energy finally spent, into his bedroll.[*]

Ten days passed before Jed Smith was able to again mount a horse. Why his wounds did not become infected may or may not have been due to an aphorism attributed to Jim Bridger—"Meat don't spoil in the moun-

---

[*] Though far from being as disfigured as, say, Edward Rose, Smith was nonetheless self-conscious enough about his appearance to thereafter wear his hair long enough to cover much of the hideous scarring.

tains." Nevertheless, as the late October nights were growing colder and the trappers had already lost close to two weeks traveling time, Smith ordered camp broken. The company resumed their trek west, slower along this leg, as Smith's cracked ribs precluded any hard, prolonged riding. He could only hope to soon meet up with Edward Rose, who, prior to the bear attack, had ridden ahead to make contact with the Mountain Crow high up on the Wind River in northwestern Wyoming.

Smith's troop was now traveling through the Powder River country. Even this late in the season it brimmed with quail, grouse, and fat prairie chickens; with herds of mule deer, elk, and pronghorn, and especially with buffalo, untold millions of which migrated through the territory. Smith had heard reports of earlier frontiersmen riding from sunup to sundown through grazing droves measuring thirty by seventy miles. Now here they were.

Some days after passing just such a throng, the troop was overtaken by a pair of Missouri Fur Company men. These were factors, not trappers. Joshua Pilcher—hearing of Smith's overland trek and attempting to make the best he could of his thwarted beaver-hunting season—had sent them to follow Smith's trail in the hope of trading for plews among the Mountain Crow. Together the group pushed up into high country through thick stands of Douglas fir, western hemlock, and white pine, their needles glistening in the crisp November light. Smith could not help but notice that the red alder and dwarf mountain dogwood had already shed their leaves, their blossoming drupes providing winter fodder for flocks of northern cardinals, hermit thrushes, and dark-eyed Juncos.

One evening, as snow dusted the valleys below and crowned the high peaks, "Five Scalps" Rose and an entourage of whooping and yipping Crow hunters—Clyman's journal records fifteen or sixteen—galloped into the trappers' camp on the Powder. This was Smith's first encounter with the tribe, and he was taken aback. If he had found the Sioux a stately people, the tall, handsome Crow struck him as virtually statuesque.

Proud of their thick, long hair to the point of narcissism, the men of the tribe wore their black tresses piled high atop their heads, styled into pom-padours from which two braids beginning above the ears fell below their waists nearly to the ground. Most sported a version of a looping necklace constructed of multicolored beads, wolf teeth, and bear claws that wrapped tight just beneath their jaws, like a choker, before descending loosely in swirling patterns to mid-chest. Moreover, in what the Bible-toting Smith could only assume to be a blessing from the Creator—Charles Darwin's science of genetics being still some quarter century in the future—the braves displayed a physical trait that distinguished them from just about all other Plains and Mountain Indians. Due to a varied combination of diet and lifestyle, the dentition of most adult Native Americans of the epoch resembled a broken and abandoned picket fence. Yet plentiful contempo-raneous descriptions of the Crow describe their teeth as straight, gleaming white, and remaining intact in their mouths well into old age.

Over the next few days Smith and his outfit were also surprised to see the Indians wade into the Powder to cleanse themselves each morning. Where most western tribes, perhaps out of geographical necessity, prac-ticed what might generously be termed a casual hygiene regimen, Crow males invariably bathed daily, even if the effort meant hacking through a foot of river ice. Their ablutions made it all the more disconcerting when the trappers reached the Crow winter encampment and found a great many of the women—busy repairing damage to tipis and tapping into the soft wood of box elders to collect sap to make sugar—to be, as the chival-rous Smith might have put it, less handsomely endowed by the Almighty.*

Smith and his men had ridden into the Crow camp after sunset, and the next morning the scalpel sharpness of the mountain light illuminated

---

* Three decades later, the caddish fur trader Edmund Denig, a lifelong employee of John Jacob Astor's American Fur Company, would churlishly—or perhaps drunkenly, as Denig was a prodigious imbiber of rye whiskey—attribute to "course-featured" Crow females everything from "bad features" to "filthy habits" to "red eyelids caused by the venereal diseases" (Denig, *Five Indian Tribes of the Upper Missouri*, 155–156). It should be noted that Denig may have been employing what Sigmund Freud would later label *projection*, for in portraits of the man, his beady eyes and pinched face resemble nothing so much as Dickens's description of the evil dwarf Daniel Quilp from *The Old Curiosity Shop*.

an otherworldly realm of clear, cold streams winding through effervescent green timberland. To the white men, the thick stands of lodgepole pine and blue spruce seemed to cower beneath jagged towers of snow-streaked granite. The Crow had raised their lodges in a narrow valley in the shadow of the prodigious Wind River Mountain Range, dominated by a soaring, wolflike fang tearing at the brooding sky—the Star Watcher, the Indians called the mountain. At nearly fourteen thousand feet, this was Wyoming's third-highest peak, destined to be formally named after the explorer John Fremont.

For Jed Smith—who, in Jim Clyman's charming turn of phrase, had already seen hills that would be called mountains in other countries—this was his introduction to the true majesty of the Rockies, what the earliest French explorers had called *dont la pierre brillait jour et nuit*—the heights "whose stone shone day and night."

It did not disappoint. Nor did the company. Awaiting Smith's party was a small troop of men dispatched by Andrew Henry from his new fort on the Bighorn. They, like Smith's outfit, planned to commence trapping west of the Continental Divide come spring. Smith found one of them, a hunter named Daniel Potts, in the expansive lodge of a Crow headman, being nursed back to health after losing two blackened toes to frostbite while traversing the aptly named Bad Pass through the Bighorn Mountains. Potts had kept a journal, and he had tales to tell. Disturbing tales.

CHAPTER 9

GLASS

Jed Smith and his men crammed into the Crow chief's lodge to listen to Daniel Potts relate his account of Andrew Henry's ill-starred journey from the flatlands. In the shadows of the tipi sat the stoic leader of Potts's outfit, a Danish-born former oceangoing sea captain who had Americanized his name to John Henry Weber. Like the Irishman Fitzpatrick, the forty-four-year-old Weber had washed up in New Orleans during the Napoleonic Wars and worked his way north to the Missouri Territory. When William Ashley and Andrew Henry began their joint lead-and-powder business in Missouri's old Sainte Genevieve district, Weber—a man with "the nose of a Roman emperor and eye as regal and piercing as that of an American eagle"—befriended and went to work for the two. Eventually he signed on to their first mountain expedition.

Weber, his bulging seaman's forearms discernable even beneath his buckskin blouse, was a listener. He let Potts do the talking, interjecting the occasional grunt for narrative emphasis. Potts's story began several days out from Fort Kiowa, with Maj. Henry at the head of the train of packhorses following the Grand River. That morning, Potts said, the major directed two men to forge ahead in search of game. A third man, the "self-willed and insubordinate" Hugh Glass, took this as an affront. Glass, who considered himself the best tracker in the outfit, insisted on joining them. It was almost as if Glass was daring anyone, particularly the man for whom he ostensibly worked, to challenge his defiance. Andrew Henry let it pass.

As the three hunters fanned out, a giant she-grizzly sprang from the brush fringing the river. The huge silverback, seven hundred pounds by one estimate, literally enveloped Glass. Shots from his companions eventually brought the animal down on top of Glass. But not before he had been mauled beyond recognition. Unlike the bear attack on Jed Smith, not only was Glass's head bitten and clawed but the gray-tipped behemoth had nearly severed his throat. It was said that Glass's arms, legs, chest, and back were barely recognizable as belonging to a human being.

When Maj. Henry reached the scene, he called a halt to the march. Glass would die soon, he surmised, and despite the man's sour disposition he deserved a proper interment. But Glass refused to "go under." Going under, they called the passing, that or going over or going across; it made no sense to some, but quick or slow, it was a hazard of the trade. Henry—fearing that Arikara might be lurking—promised half a year's wages to any two volunteers who would stay with Glass and bury him when the time came. The first to step forward was a veteran mountaineer named John Fitzgerald. He was followed by the young Jim Bridger. The next morning Henry and his company bade them both farewell.

Not long after, Henry's outfit had bedded down for the night when a fusillade of gunshots rent their camp. Two men were killed, two more wounded, and two horses that had taken rifle balls had to be put down. The company fired volley upon volley in the direction of the unseen attackers. At dawn they found one dead Indian in the underbrush. He was fair-skinned, with sandy hair and blue eyes. Mandan. It was more than unnerving to contemplate the idea that even the formerly docile Mandan had taken to the warpath. The trappers could only hope that the brave might have been a renegade riding with the Rees.

Henry and his troop reached the mouth of the Yellowstone without further incident, where the small force he had left behind to safeguard his fort reported more distressing news. In his absence close to thirty horses had been stolen by reivers, presumably Blackfeet or Assiniboin. Henry was still contemplating his options when, five days later, Fitzgerald and Bridger straggled in. They reported Hugh Glass dead and buried. They brandished his rifle and knife as proof. Henry allowed Fitzgerald to keep the rifle and awarded the knife to Bridger.

In the end, Henry saw no reason to maintain his headquarters so far from the trappers he planned to send over the Continental Divide. With that he cached a portion of his powder and shot, hollowed out a small flotilla of cottonwood pirogues, and abandoned the fort to move farther up the Yellowstone. Before leaving he carved a message on a plank as to his whereabouts and nailed it to the stockade gate.

Within a week his convoy had reached the confluence of the Powder and the Yellowstone, where long skeins of whitewater compelled strictly overland travel. By chance the Americans crossed paths with a large hunting party of River Crow, who on this occasion were amenable to horse trading. Henry acquired close to fifty mounts as well as two large bundles of beaver plews taken high in the mountains. "Crow pelts," as they were called, with their longer and thicker fur, were the most prized on the St. Louis market.

The Crow also warned Henry that the three branches of the Blackfeet had again held council, and all had reiterated their vows to wage constant warfare against the Americans wherever they found them in the mountains. Henry took the news with equanimity—there was no turning back now—and pushed farther up the Yellowstone, past the Tongue, and to the mouth of the Bighorn. It was from there, while putting the majority of his men to work building a new stockade, that he had dispatched John Henry Weber, Daniel Potts, and several others to find Jedediah Smith.

Potts concluded his tale as far as he knew it. Yet while he and Weber had wended their way up the Bighorn to the Wind River, there remained several missing scenes of the drama Potts had crafted. They resonate to this day.

* * *

Hugh Glass remembered awakening with a start. Swaths of big bluestem prairie grass covered his face and body, like wreaths laid on a grave. He was alone. He instinctively reached for his rifle. It was gone, as was his skinning knife. He later told the fur trapper–turned–California rancher George Yount that he vaguely recalled Andrew Henry leaving two men to watch over him.

Glass felt a parcel beneath his throbbing head. It was his kit bag—his possible sack—containing his steel razor and a shard of flintstone. He heard a burbling sound, a spring. With every muscle and tendon in his body afire, he inched toward the water and drank. A portion passed through his esophagus into his stomach. The rest dribbled out from the gash in his neck. Wild cherries hung thick from branches over the pool, with a patch of tart buffalo berries within slithering distance. The fruit and water sustained him for ten days, until he felt strong enough to half-walk, half-crawl toward the bank of the Grand.

It was the buffalo calving season, and not far from the riverbank a wolfpack had brought down a baby cow. The wolves ignored Glass until he struck fire to the dry grass with his razor and flint. The snarling pack reluctantly retreated from the flames. Glass seared the meat and gorged. The carcass lasted days. When he was not eating and sleeping, he passed the time picking insects from his half-closed wounds.

As best Glass could remember, he survived on berries, roots, and the haws, or fruits, of wild dog rose. Occasionally he would stumble across the remains of a decaying buffalo. Sweeping away the maggots, this supplied him with what little protein he ingested. As he staggered across the prairie following the Grand River east, at some point he reached its confluence with the Missouri.

Here Glass's story diverges into several narrative streams, albeit each running southeast with the river. Some contemporary accounts say Glass made it to Fort Kiowa under his own power—limping, sometimes crawling, over two hundred miles in six to eight weeks. Others have it that he was rescued by a band of Sioux who had ridden up the Missouri to pick over the abandoned Arikara corn fields. A third chronicle puts him reeling into contact with the French Canadian trapper Antoine Citoleux, known by his second surname Langevin, who was leading a tiny expedition upriver from Fort Kiowa. Glass, likely delusional toward the end of his trek, never set the record straight.

What is certain is that Glass, either at Fort Kiowa or farther upstream, fell in with Langevin's six-man outfit. Langevin's party had been contracted by the French Fur Company factor Joseph Brazeau to test the mood of the Arikara, who had erected a new village next to the Mandan in North Dakota. Brazeau, known as "Old Cayewa," had long traded among the tribe, and he convinced Langevin that his name alone would ensure them safe passage. The farther up the Missouri they traveled, however, the stronger became Langevin's doubts. At one point, berthed for the night at an island camp below the now-neighboring Arikara-Mandan settlements, Langevin drew up his last will and testament.

Whether the emaciated Glass's decision to join Langevin's upriver trek was made out of a lust for vengeance toward the men who left him for dead, a sense of duty, or a desire for past payment—or a combination of all three—is not recorded. By an eerie coincidence in Glass's already fantastical journey, before reaching the Indian villages Langevin and his squad spotted a canoe heading downriver carrying three white men. The two parties did not stop to parley. If they had, Glass might have recognized John Fitzgerald, one of his betrayers. Fitzgerald and the two others, after hearing the Crow tales of Blackfeet on the warpath, had quit Andrew Henry's company on the Powder and were making for Fort Atkinson to enlist in the army.

Just shy of the Arikara-Mandan settlements, Glass was put ashore to hunt. He had not walked far before a mounted party of Arikara spotted him. In no shape to run, he shouldered his rifle and counted what moments remained of his life. Suddenly, whether for sport or antipathy toward the

Rees, two Mandans appeared from nowhere and one swung Glass up onto his horse. The Mandan mounts were stout, and they outraced the Arikara to Tilton's Fort, a stockaded trading post on Mandan land recently opened by the Columbia Fur Company's William Tilton, a former North West Fur Company trapper who had journeyed overland from Minnesota with a small crew of brokers.

There were some, not least the Indian-hating government agent Benjamin O'Fallon, who accused former Nor'Westers like Tilton of still secretly working for the Canadian company, fomenting tribal reprisals against the Americans to advance British aims. It was widely believed that these double agents supplied the tribes with whiskey—"the water that makes men crazy," as the Sioux called it—in exchange for their allegiance.* Whatever the case, Tilton treated Glass well, just as he had another of Langevin's crew who had asked to be released from service after, he told Glass, a black premonition had washed over him. Perhaps the man was a seer. Word soon reached the post that Langevin and his remaining quartet of traders had been slaughtered by the Arikara.

Upon learning the news of Antoine Langevin's unfortunate endeavor to reforge trading ties with the Arikara, Tilton and his men abandoned their fort while Hugh Glass, undaunted, set out on foot for the Yellowstone. Two weeks later he reached the derelict Fort Henry, read Andrew Henry's note, and started up toward the Bighorn. It was New Year's Eve 1823 when he made out the strains of fiddles over the thrash and thrum of the rushing river water. This was an era of omens and witching spells, of mysticism and prophetic visions—an age when men, even hard men, believed in ghosts. When Glass pushed open the stockade gate, his former fellow trappers were well into tipping their kegs in celebration of the holiday.

At the sight of Glass—"Features sunken, arms and hands wasted, all skeleton and skin," writes one chronicler—the revelers froze. It was not

---

* In fact, what was known as "whiskey" along the frontier was in reality a frightful amalgam of various amounts of crushed red pepper, tobacco, and molasses stirred into diluted grain alcohol.

until Glass invited them to touch his emaciated body to prove that he was not a specter that all resumed what had now become a double commemoration. All, that is, except Jim Bridger.

Glass spotted Bridger lurking in the shadows. Having learned of Fitzgerald's departure, he approached the panic-stricken teenager and spoke in what witnesses recalled as a severe monotone. "Young man, it is Glass that is before you," he said. "The same that, not content with leaving, you thought, to a cruel death upon the prairie, you robbed helpless as he was, of his rifle, his knife, of all with which he could hope to defend or save himself."

Bridger awaited the death blow. He knew he deserved it. Abandoning a wounded comrade ranked equal to murder and horse theft among the unwritten rules of the frontier.

But Glass's voice softened. "I swore an oath that I would be revenged on you and the wretch who was with you," he said. "And I ever thought to have kept it. For this meeting I have braved the dangers of a long journey. But I can not take your life; you have nothing to fear from me; go—you are free—for your youth, I forgive you."*

Bridger never spoke of the matter again. Some speculate that on that fateful day when he and Fitzgerald departed, Glass may have fallen into a coma and that the two mistook the gurgling breath escaping his neck wound for a death rattle. Others surmise that the older Fitzgerald, fearing lurking Indians, talked the impressionable Bridger into leaving. As it was, for the rest of his long and adventuresome life, none held Jim Bridger's immature misstep against him.

* * *

---

* Glass's dramatic nineteenth-century adventures were reincarnated in verse—John G. Niehardt's 1915 poem *The Song of Hugh Glass*—and in film, in both the twentieth and twenty-first centuries, albeit with the usual Hollywood liberties. He was played by the actor Richard Harris in 1971's *Man in the Wilderness*. Leonardo DiCaprio took on the role in *The Revenent*, released in 2015, for which DiCaprio was awarded the Academy Award for Best Actor.

Of course, neither Daniel Potts, John Henry Weber, nor any of the trappers enjoying the winter hospitality of the Mountain Crow were yet aware of Hugh Glass's odyssey and its dramatic denouement. Moreover, as the venerated Edward Rose was a member of Jed Smith's party, over the next month or so the Americans were treated as honored guests. This included invitations to observe several winter buffalo runs. It is not clear if any of the whites had ever witnessed an Indian buffalo hunt. Considering the wonderment Jim Clyman exhibits in describing the proceedings, it is doubtful.

Skittish Indian ponies were not inherently adapted to chasing down snorting, horned beasts that could weigh up to three thousand pounds, stand six feet at the shoulder, and measure twelve feet from nose to tail. A good buffalo horse, often selected at birth if born under a propitious sign such as a rainbow or a meteor shower, was instead groomed for the task. First the young colt was accustomed to the scent of its prey by smearing it with buffalo fat and swaddling it in buffalo robes. When old enough to be broken, a buffalo-hair cord was fitted over the mount's tapered muzzle and attached to leather reins made from buffalo sinews. As both rider and horse required agility, stamina, and above all complementary reactive instincts only acquired by countless hours of instruction and practice, a horse's owner would spend years training his animal to charge by continually riding at full gallop in and among the tribe's remuda, running as close astern to ill-tempered stallions as possible.

At first glance the hunt itself struck the white observers as just another ill-disciplined, barely controlled Native American exhibition of chaos—"getting behind a large herd and [driving] them pell mell down the valley," wrote Clyman. But American eyes had not been trained to detect the ceremony's controlled, formal structure.

In the case of the Crow, this commenced with two columns of horsemen arraying themselves on either side of a narrow valley or gorge. Once the buffalo had passed, the riders followed, at first at a walk, then at a trot, and finally at a canter. During intertribal battles, a warrior might break ranks for the self-seeking glory of counting coup. No such ill-discipline was allowed during the buffalo hunt; the fear of being whipped and shunned by elders kept all in line. Spooking the herd farther into the defile by waving blankets and howling like wolves, the hunters at last broke into a gallop and flung their spears. Any buffalo that turned to stand and fight— and there were many—would be lanced below the hump or, if possible, through the soft underbelly. The head of the drove, in the meanwhile, was stalled by prepositioned hunters to either side of the vale—usually all the camp's older men and younger boys—decimating the animals with arrow and ball.

At the conclusion of the display, the punctuation-averse Clyman records, "Squaws old men and children following and Buchering and securing meat and skins as fast as possible the night after this grand hunt not more than half the people came in to camp they remaining out to watch the wolves from the meat until they could get it packed and dr(y)-ing." When Clyman asked a headman how many animals had been taken down on a particular hunt, he was told upward of one thousand. Again because of Rose, the Americans were served the best cuts of buffalo meat and marrow. Clyman notes that they were even presented the ultimate delicacy—the still-steaming liver extracted from the dying animals and seasoned with bile dripped from its punctured gall bladder. An all-night feast followed, after which, Clyman hints, the white men were offered a choice of the tribe's widows to warm their winter beds.

Unlike their Crow hosts, the trappers weren't much for bathing in frozen river waters or meticulously cleaning their butts after a bowel movement. The dried corn husks, bundled tufts of hay, or even the odd mussel shell that flatlanders used to wipe their asses were a luxury in the mountains. Moreover, after months of rubbing their filthy hands on their clothing to cleanse them of putrid castor bait and game grease and beaver blood, their ubiquitous buckskin shirts and leggings—golden-hued when freshly tanned—were soon unrecognizable. The western novelist Don Berry, foraying into nonfiction in his Mountain Man history *A Majority of Scoundrels*, paints a vivid description. Each man, Berry writes, looked as if he had dressed in "black. Dirty black, greasy black, shiny black, bloody black, stinky black." It remains unknown what their Crow female companions made of this.

In any case, the white men's lack of sanitary formalities did not seem to faze the Crow men, particularly as Smith directed Rose to employ a lavish hand while distributing gifts to chiefs, warriors, and religious sachems. In the meanwhile, Smith spent much of his time trying to learn as much as he could about the beaver lands to the west—territory that, unbeknownst to him, in his State of the Union address President James Monroe had only just declared off-limits to the European powers in his famous Doctrine of December 1823.

Initially the Crow were confused by Smith's queries regarding the far side of the Wind River Mountains. Were not the beaver pelts they put forward for trade enough to satisfy these hunters? Further, what man in his right mind would voluntarily choose to leave the paradise the tribe called home, with its magnificent vistas, sparkling waters, and plentiful game? It took some time for the interpreter Rose to adjust their thinking. When the Crow finally came around to the idea that the Americans were truly moving on, they informed Smith—now uniformly addressed as Captain Smith—that the western slopes of the Rockies held beaver so thick that his traps would not be necessary. He and his men need only walk the banks of the creeks and ponds with clubs to secure more pelts than they could carry.

In his inquisitions, Smith also invariably inquired about an elusive watercourse called the Rio Buenaventura, rumored to flow all the way from the Rocky Mountains to the Pacific. The Indians were nonplussed.

*   *   *

Some myths die hard. Ponce de Leon's Fountain of Youth. The Northwest Passage. The Seven Cities of Gold. Such was the case of the Rio Buenaventura—the River of Good Fortune.

Throughout his two-term presidency, Thomas Jefferson had been a fervent believer in this fabled mother of all western American waterways and was disappointed that Lewis and Clark had never found it during their expedition. Jefferson envisioned the river as the highway from which would spring all manner of American commercial opportunity on its journey from somewhere in the western mountains to the Pacific Ocean. In the view of not only the former president but also a bevy of explorers, politicians, businessmen, and potential settlers, this magical headwater would truly consolidate a continental United States.

The multiple adherents to the legend of this grand river were heavily influenced by a plethora of eighteenth-century Spanish maps delineating this "Western Mississippi." In reality, the wellspring of the fantasy of the Rio Buenaventura was the result of a sign language miscommunication between a party of Spanish monks and a band of Ute Indians fifty years earlier. It was in 1776, the very year that the American colonists declared their independence from Great Britain, when an adventurous party of Franciscans—searching for heathen souls to convert across the territory between Neuevo Mexico and Alta California—ran across the Indigenous hunting party. The Indians informed the priests of a great river that flowed into a large, salty body of water. The Ute, whose tribal dominions at the time encompassed most of present-day Utah and parts of western Colorado, were undoubtedly referring to one of the three rivers—the Bear, the Weber, or the Jordan—that empty into the Great Salt Lake. But the myth of a watercourse to the Pacific persisted, and the error would not be corrected by either American or European cartographers for well over another half a century.

And so it was that even as Jed Smith prepared to depart from the Crow encampment, the current president, Monroe, as well as a host of Americans throughout the east remained hopeful if not optimistic that the Rio Buenaventura would be the fountainhead upon which the western expansion of the United States would blossom. There is no little irony in the fact that it would not be a watercourse but a wide land gap in the Rocky Mountains that would eventually secure what the Washington-based writer and editor John Louis O'Sullivan would in the near future describe as America's "Manifest Destiny."

CHAPTER 10

SOUTH PASS

It would be another twenty-six years before the narrow cleft in the Wind River Mountains was officially dubbed Union Pass.* Designated or not, however, Jed Smith knew it was there. As far back as the winter of 1807–1808, the explorer John Colter had traversed the gap to cross the Continental Divide. Smith knew well the legendary stories of Colter and his travels, which had begun under the aegis of Lewis and Clark. A key member of the Corps of Discovery, "Private Colter" was cited often in Meriwether Lewis's reports for his superior scouting skills and, like the unfortunate George Drouillard, for his uncanny ability to communicate in sign language with the Indigenous tribes the expedition encountered.

Although no contemporaneous images of Colter exist, given his incredible adventures it is likely he was a man of significant physical strength, keen mental acuity, and a wellspring of luck, a quality valued in a wild country where the slightest misstep could end in a grisly death. Further, there were unconfirmed rumors that prior to enlisting with Lewis and

---

* In 1860, the gap through the Rocky Mountains was officially designated "Union Pass" by the U.S. Army captain William Raynolds. Raynolds—employing the fifty-six-year-old Jim Bridger as his guide—was leading an expedition of the Army Corps of Topographical Engineers through the pass while exploring the Yellowstone region.

Clark, the Virginia-born Colter had acquired his sharpshooter's eye and his gift as a pathfinder while fighting in the Shawnee Wars under the Kentucky militia commander Simon Kenton, Daniel Boone's best friend.

As it was, Colter was already in his late twenties by the time he joined the Corps of Discovery, an advanced age for the epoch that makes his decision to re-enter the wild high country time after time all the more incredible. What one might describe as Colter's second career as a civilian mountaineer began in August 1806 when, returning from the Pacific with Lewis and Clark, he encountered two trappers ascending the Missouri River in a large, flat-bottomed pirogue. Colter requested permission to join them, and Meriwether Lewis granted him an honorable discharge nearly two months shy of his term of service. It was both a show of thanks and a sign of respect. Having just spent twenty-eight hard months journeying thousands of miles to and from the Pacific Coast, Colter literally hopped from one boat to another in order to wend upstream back toward the mountains. This would prove a significant milestone, a demarcation of the American journeys of pure exploration melding into voyages of commerce.

The trapping partnership Colter had entered into did not work out for reasons unexplained, and by the following spring of 1807 he was again canoeing down the Missouri when, near the mouth of the Platte, he crossed paths with Manuel Lisa's outfit making its way toward the confluence of the Yellowstone and the Bighorn. Lisa's company included the young Andrew Henry and, to Colter's delight, his old Corps of Discovery compatriots George Drouillard and John Potts.[*] For a second time Colter turned around, signing on to guide Lisa through the Upper Missouri country and help him establish Fort Raymond at the meeting of the two rivers.

Once the stockade was completed, Lisa prevailed on Colter to act as his trading emissary with the various bands of Crow and Shoshone spread about the mountains. He would also encounter the eastern branch of the

---

[*] As best as can be discerned, John Potts was no relation to the journal-keeping, story-telling Daniel Potts whom Jed Smith had found at the Mountain Crow camp.

Salish peoples known as the Flathead, who lived in the northern plateau region between the Rockies and the far-western coastal cordillera.* All three tribes, hereditary enemies of the Blackfeet, were known to hunger for the white man's rifles, shot, and powder to counter the territorial stranglehold the better-armed Blackfeet had enjoyed for generations.

The Blackfeet, one of the few Algonquin-speaking tribes to venture west out of the eastern timberlands, had emigrated into the mountains from their home around the Great Lakes well before the *Niña*, the *Pinta*, and the *Santa María* weighed anchors at the Spanish port of Palos de la Frontera. The self-styled Niitsitapi, or "Real People," were soon dubbed the *pied noir* by the French, allegedly a reference to the darkened condition of their moccasins after the long trek across the prairie.

Settling into a crescent of territory ranging from northern Montana into parts of southern Alberta and Saskatchewan, the tribe immediately clashed with the Shoshone, and a centuries-long standoff between the antagonists ensued. Then, sometime in the 1730s, a Shoshone raiding party fell on a Blackfeet village riding giant four-footed animals. The Blackfeet had never seen horses. Frightened and alarmed, they dispatched runners east to their Cree and Assiniboin cousins pleading for help. Their relatives not only sent warriors as reinforcements, but they carried curious hollow metal sticks that hurled tiny if deadly missiles with such velocity as to be invisible. Acquiring rifles marked the onset of Blackfeet hegemony across the area.

As Blackfeet war parties, now mounted, prowled farther afield, the Shoshone were pushed back across the Continental Divide and both the Crow and Flathead, still wielding but arrows, clubs, and spears against musket balls, were hunted like game. John Colter explained this imbalance of power to Manuel Lisa, who sensed, correctly, that the trod-upon tribes would pay dearly in beaver pelts for modern weaponry. Lisa hired

---

* Early European explorers, misinterpreting a sign language parley, had named these Indians the Flathead, conflating them with their western cousins the Chinook, who practiced head-flattening of their infants as a mark of status.

Colter to spend the winter of 1807–1808 traveling over five hundred miles by birchbark canoe and on foot through the snow-choked wilderness to spread word among distant Native American camps that Lisa's trading post was open for business.

Colter's journey took him from the Bighorn Basin to the upper reaches of the Wind River range, where he traversed Union Gap to become the first white man to lay eyes on the trio of soaring peaks that French explorers would rather unsubtly name the Grand Tetons. Ascending Teton Pass and dropping into Pierre's Hole, he then limned the northern edge of Yellowstone Lake—another first for a white man—and temporarily lent his name, "Colter's Hell," to the stinking sulfurous river later renamed the Shoshone. By the summer of 1808, Colter had fallen in with a small band of Flathead buffalo hunters whom he was escorting to Fort Raymond when they were ambushed near the Three Forks by a party of Blackfeet numbering near one thousand. Colter had already taken a ball to his leg and all looked lost until, at what appeared the fight's most dire moment, an even larger force of Crow fell on and routed the Blackfeet.

That fall, having recovered from his wound, Colter and his old Corps of Discovery companion John Potts set off in two canoes to trap the same Three Forks region. They were paddling north on the Jefferson when a painted band of Blackfeet appeared on the east bank and motioned them ashore. Colter slipped his traps into the shallow water and complied. Potts refused, even after he was shot and wounded. Watching the Indians disarm and strip Colter naked, Potts managed to level his rifle and fire, knocking one of the Blackfeet from his horse. A cloud of arrows perforated Potts and his canoe. Colter saw great daubs of his friend's blood stain the river red as both Potts and his foundering craft slipped beneath the surface. Indian swimmers dived into the river to recover Potts's body and drag it onto the bank. Colter watched as the corpse was hacked to pieces and beheaded.

Bracing for a similar fate, Colter was surprised when, after a short council, a headman stepped forward and ordered him to run. Given a small head start, Colter soon heard whoops and trills. Turning, he saw scores of warriors chasing. Over several miles Colter gradually outpaced the mass of Indians except for one dogged brave brandishing a lance. The Blackfeet had closed to within twenty paces when Colter, nearing exhaustion, his feet cut to pieces, and spurting gouts of blood from his nose and mouth, suddenly halted. He turned and spread his arms. The warrior, whether from surprise or exhaustion, tripped as he launched his spear. The weapon struck the ground between the two. Colter pounced, snatching the flint-tipped lance and driving it through the Blackfeet's chest, nailing the warrior to the ground like a pinned butterfly. Then he ran on, the shouts of the rest of his pursuers echoing through the granite canyons.

Three more miles of chase led Colter to the banks of the Madison, where he spotted a beaver slide. Slithering atop the animal's trail into the water, he ducked beneath a mass of tangled driftwood, keeping his face above water. There he hid, listening to the moccasin squelch of the frustrated Blackfeet searching the muddy riverbank for his footprints. That night he slipped away. Fort Raymond lay more than two hundred miles distant.

Naked, surviving on roots and tree bark, eleven days later John Colter lurched through the stockade gate. Historians have long contended that if Meriwether Lewis's early confrontation with the Blackfeet laid the fuse for the white man's decades-long war with the tribe, it was John Colter's intent to arm their hated enemies that lit the match.

Not long after what came to be known as "Colter's Run," Colter understandably retired from the beaver trade following the gruesome killing of his old trail mate George Drouillard. Sometime in late 1810, he made his way back to St. Louis after six years in the mountains. Now, a decade later, Jed Smith was determined to follow in Colter's footsteps through Union Pass and across the Divide. It is not recorded if Smith expected to face the same hardships overcome by what some consider to be America's first Mountain Man.

* * *

Sometime during the second week of February 1824, Smith set off from the Crow encampment with eleven men leading packhorses in single file. Edward Rose had opted to winter over with the Indians after reportedly trading his favorite rifle for a wife, and three or four others who had come west with Smith fell in with John Henry Weber's outfit.

Smith's ascent to the 9,210-foot-high Union Pass was doomed from the start. Snow had been falling in the high peaks for days, and barely halfway up the trail the massive drifts were breaching the withers of the company's juments. Further progress proved impossible. Forced back to the Crow lodges, the old surveyor Jim Clyman took the initiative. Spreading a buffalo robe across the ground of a headman's tipi, Clyman covered it with sand and proceeded to pile the granules into heaps representing the mountains to the west. How, he asked, do we get to the other side?

An Indian spoke, and Edward Rose gouged a rut in the sand leading almost due south from their present position. The line was the Popo Agie River, a tributary of the Wind. The Crow advised Smith to stay with the Middle Fork of the frozen stream some fifty-five miles to its source at the southern end of the Wind River range. From there they would cross the ridge near the river's headwaters and drop down to yet another watercourse called the Sweetwater. Follow the Sweetwater upstream, Rose's translation continued, and the white men would find a route across the mountains. Once on the western slope, they would encounter what the Crow called the Seeds-ka-day and the Spanish the Rio Verde—the Green River.

What the Indian was describing was a gap in the Rocky Mountains that would come to be known as South Pass, a twenty-mile-wide breach in the wall of granite at over eight thousand feet in elevation. Clyman's crude sand hills would lead to one of the most pivotal moments in the history of the United States.

*　*　*

Considering that South Pass had been used for millennia by Native Americans, the term *discovery* is naturally laced with a fair amount of hyperbole.

In fact, the little party that Robert Stuart had led overland from Fort Astoria to St. Louis thirteen years earlier had likely traversed the pass west to east when hostile Blackfeet blocked their path farther north. Why Stuart never ballyhooed this gateway to the Pacific has been lost in the fog of history, but his near silence on the matter has been a centuries-long bounty for conspiracy theorists. One hypothesis has it that since Stuart had been a Scottish Canadian Nor'Wester before defecting to the Astorians, he was hording the geographic knowledge for the British authorities. This is evocative of Daniel Boone's "discovery" of the Indian trail known as the Cumberland Gap through the Appalachians in 1769. Unknown to Boone at the time of his explorations, nineteen years earlier a secret British-funded expedition had documented the same mountain cut. But the gap's location had been locked away by the then-British colonial governor of Virginia as a state secret.

The late western historian Dale Morgan, however, believed the answer to the Stuart conundrum to be more prosaic. "In American exploration," he wrote, "discoveries have to be made and remade." It was thus Smith's "destiny," Morgan continued, "to walk unknowing in the footsteps of many great wilderness adventurers."

There is little argument that traversing South Pass was indeed the stuff of "destiny." This integral, wagon-friendly corridor of grassy plains bisecting the Rockies at the southern terminus of the Wind River range was to become the geographic key to the mass American migration of hundreds of thousands of westering pioneers along the Oregon Trail and its two land tributaries, the Mormon Trail and the California Trail. It would indeed change the face of the nation. But Morgan's use of the word *walk* is carrying a heavy load. In Jed Smith's case, the verbs *shuffle*, *wobble*, or perhaps even *stumble* might be more appropriate.

In late February, Smith's party again set out for the Divide despite the onset of a raging blizzard. Following the Crow directions, the trappers hugged the eastern salient of the Wind River Mountains as they broke trail through the pitted country, the lone sounds the creak of their frozen tack and the brittle whistle of the north wind as it bent the branches of the stunted scrub oak and cottonwood girding the banks of the Popo Agie. Jim Clyman and Bill Sublette, their beards iced over, nearly froze to death literally running down and killing a lone buffalo cow after their horses gave out. In the meanwhile, their compatriots—hats pulled low and collars high, their mittened fingers barely able to feel their reins—were left to wonder if the snowfall would ever cease.

As they negotiated the ridge at the headwaters of the Popo Agie, the ferocity of the biting *poudrerie* funneling down from the Canadian plains scoured all game from the area and left the tops of the surrounding heights bald and brown. The gale-force winds—"a hericane direct," wrote Clyman—also prevented the outfit from making a fire. It was nearing dusk on the day they found the Sweetwater, and that night the little party took refuge on the lee side of a spinney of willow trees. They huddled together clutching their buffalo robes close to keep them from blowing away. There they remained for thirty-six hours waiting for the storm to abate.

Come sunrise on their second morning in the willow grove, Clyman and a trapper named Francis Ziba Branch—like Jed Smith a former Great Lakes sailor who had drifted west to try his hand in the mountains—volunteered to venture down the Sweetwater in search of food. Following the watercourse east, they had not traveled far when they came upon a gulch so narrow that the only way forward included multiple crossings over the river ice.* While traversing the tight canyon, Branch looked up, spotted a bighorn, and brought the sheep down with a single shot. The two lugged the choicest cuts of the animal back to the clump of willows. But the wind again blew away all attempts at a fire.

Sometime in the middle of the night Clyman was awakened by what he did not hear—howling wind. Snow was still falling but the gales had

---

* Clyman and Branch had entered what in decades hence would become famous as the Three Crossings of the Oregon Trail. So steep and tight were the cliffs to either side of the Sweetwater here that thousands upon thousands of wagons carrying those who would become scientists, settlers, missionaries, and gold seekers west on the great thoroughfare of nineteenth-century North America were forced to ford the river three times over a two-mile span.

lulled, and this time the sagebrush and kindling fired. The gray tang of cottonwood smoke and the aroma of broiling sheep roused the others. As the troop, in Clyman's words, "talked cooked eat the remainder of the night," Clyman again offered to scout farther downriver. Just beyond the narrow canyon, he entered a sheltered valley rife with dry aspen and, more important, an abundance of sheep. Smith decided to move the camp into the glade, and his company remained there for at least a week riding out the blow while culling most of the bighorn herd.

It was sometime in mid-March when Smith climbed one of the bare, rounded hills protecting the aspen valley and determined that it was time to move on. Before departing, he instructed his men that should they separate, either by intent or in error, they were all to rendezvous back at this site in the first week of June. Their dried mutton long gone, the group trekked west for fourteen days through a steady snowfall until Clyman and Bill Sublette, again riding point, spotted another lone buffalo. They killed it with simultaneous rifle shots. So hungry was the outfit that they did not bother with a cookfire. Falling on the animal, they tore at the carcass with their butcher knives and wolfed down the raw flesh. The trappers did not know it, but they and the wayward beast had just traversed South Pass.

CHAPTER 11

———— • ————

THE SURVIVOR

The snowfall had finally eased. Through scattered flurries Jed Smith puzzled over the lay of the dry gullies and paused often to read the direction of the water running beneath iced-over streams. It finally struck him. He and his party had crossed the Continental Divide.

Smith's small troop soon struck the frozen Big Sandy, a tributary of the Green. A few days later they made the Green itself, its slushy spillover feeding thick spinneys of western river birch standing athwart the waterway like sentries. The Spaniards far to the south had named the river after the narrow ribbons of spiky grasses and windblown trees and shrubs that lined its banks as it snaked through the rocky wastes of eastern Utah before emptying into the Colorado. But even at this latitude the shales that made up its bed reflected a mossy hue.

The valley of the Green River may have been unknown to Smith's party, but it was far from virgin trapping country. Ute, Crow, and Arapaho hunting parties had taken furs from the hundreds of beaver ponds dotting the western slope of the Rockies. And when Andrew Henry, then working for Manuel Lisa, traversed the Divide in Montana near the Three Forks of the Missouri in 1811, he likely skirted the Green's upper watershed near the southern spur of the Gros Ventre Mountains.

More definitively, three North West Fur Company expeditions led by the Scottish-born Canadian Donald McKenzie recorded roaming south out of the Snake River country and trapping the creeks flowing into the Green's headwaters between 1816 and 1819.* McKenzie's three forays into the Snake, Green, and Bear River valleys proved prodigious, responsible for about half of the entire firm's annual haul of pelts taken over that period. Not least of these were acquired at an 1819 gathering that McKenzie organized along the north shore of Bear Lake, when nearly ten thousand Native Americans from various tribes arrived to trade with the Canadians. Now, however, five years later, Smith still saw more than enough beaver sign to be encouraged.

As the Americans waited for the ice to break up and their weary horses to fatten on the early spring cordgrass and sedges peeking through the snow cover, Smith laid out his campaign plan. Fitzpatrick, Clyman, Francis Ziba Branch, and another man listed on the Henry-Ashley manifest simply as "Stone" would trap the northern waters of the Green. The six others, with Bill Sublette as Booshway, would comb the lower branches. Smith would accompany Sublette's party as far as the Black Forks River, then break off by himself to trap the 175-mile tributary that flows north out of Utah's Uinta Mountains and into southwestern Wyoming.† With Smith's journal for this solitary expedition either missing or nonexistent, historians again rely here on the writings of Clyman for perspective. He does not disappoint.

Clyman relates that as he, Fitzpatrick, and the others rode north they took beaver pelts aplenty. They also encountered a band of Shoshone, the tribe who had remained in the mountains to wage everlasting war with the Blackfeet when their Comanche cousins migrated to West Texas nearly a century

---

* The blood ties between Donald McKenzie and Sir Alexander Mackenzie remain murky. Some Scottish records show them as cousins, although it is generally assumed that Donald's mother, Catherine, was a sister to Alexander Mackenzie's father, Kenneth.

† The Black Forks of the Green River was destined to become the point where the Oregon, California, and Mormon Trails diverged into three separate paths.

earlier. Clyman recognized them as "Diggers," as he called them after their fashion of grubbing for edible roots, from the intricate porcupine quillwork adorning their buckskin blouses. They were on foot and accompanied the trappers for a spell.* It had been barely more than a decade since any Shoshone outside of Sacagawea and her clan had first laid eyes on white men, specifically the overland party of Astorians led by Wilson Price Hunt. At first they had taken these strange beings with hairy faces and lupine blue eyes to be animal spirits in human form. When one young warrior finally screwed up the courage to approach the Astorians, Hunt's journal reports that "his fear was so great that I could not get him to show me, by sign language, the route that I should take [toward Oregon]. His only concern was that I not take away his fish and meat and that I commend him to the great spirit."

In the interim, however, the Shoshone had grown accustomed to the Hudson's Bay Company's trappers and traders flowing through their country, and Clyman's group was happy to share with the Indians their overabundance of beaver meat as well as the bountiful snow geese shot from the sky as they migrated to their seasonal breeding grounds in western Wyoming. But then one warm morning the last of the snow cover disappeared and so too did the Shoshone—stealing the outfit's twenty-odd mounts and packhorses in the bargain. This was no mean loss. A good horse on the frontier would sell for between $150 and $300, with the smartest and sturdiest costing as much as $500. As it was, Fitzpatrick's party had no choice but to continue trapping on foot until it came time to begin the return journey to rejoin Jed Smith and Bill Sublette at the aspen grove on the Sweetwater.

Clyman and his men cached their pelts, traps, and chains and hung their saddles and tack on tree branches before heading downriver. They had only walked several miles when they surprised a small hunting party of five or six Shoshone mounted bareback on several of the pilfered horses.

---

* Clyman's nickname for the Shoshone was the exception, as most whites—taking their cue from Plains tribes—referred to them as the "Snakes" after their habit of painting intimidating snake heads on their spears and lances.

The outgunned Indians surrendered the animals and, having little recourse, led the whites to their camp a mile or so up into the mountains. There, to Clyman's delight, he found "our old acquaintances that we had fed with the fat of beaver while the earth was thickly covered with snow." With Fitzpatrick holding his pistol to their chief's head, the remainder of the horses were produced. The company returned to their cache site, dug up the pelts and gear, saddled up, and rode day and night until they felt they were out of Shoshone territory.

Following an unremarkable return through the gentle grade of the now snow-free South Pass, Clyman's company found no sign of the others in the little aspen valley. The herd of bighorn sheep, however, had somehow replenished itself and had been joined by a small drove of buffalo. Days of feasting followed. The Sweetwater was broad at this location but as yet still too shallow to be navigable. As a fur trapper was always happier to transport his peltry by water rather than overland, Fitzpatrick and Clyman, their bellies full, rode downstream to see where the river might be deep enough to put in skin boats. Fitzpatrick turned back after fifteen miles, leaving Clyman to search on.

Jed Smith arrived at the meeting site not long after, his horses laden with pelts. It had only been a few days since Fitzpatrick and Clyman had parted company, but already the snowmelt from higher elevations was deepening the Sweetwater. This meant the North Platte and the Platte would likely also be navigable for perhaps several weeks. Smith directed Fitzpatrick, Branch, and Stone to begin constructing a large bullboat, or coracle, with which to transport their furs to the flatlands. The round craft was built from several bull buffalo hides sewn together with rawhide cord and fitted over a rude wooden wattle, in this case made from the plentiful aspens. The vessel's seams were caulked with animal tallow mixed with ashes, creating a waterproof shell. Meanwhile, Smith followed the river east with the intention of finding and returning with Jim Clyman.

Smith rode until he encountered the Sweetwater's confluence with the North Platte. There, in a thick copse of willow, he found a lean-to constructed of driftwood as well as recently cut firewood, but no ashes. He guessed that the little camp belonged to Clyman. He also saw Indian sign. This was both Cheyenne and Arapaho territory, two tribes—like the Blackfeet and now the Arikara—fiercely opposed to white trespass. From the number of hoof prints, he judged that a score or more braves had ridden through the vicinity. War party? Hunting party? He had no way of knowing. He searched the area for Clyman's body, or at least for the suggestion of a fight. He found no blood trails, nor even the hint of a struggle.

Smith returned upriver to find that Bill Sublette's outfit had arrived with a grand haul of plews. This did not assuage the bitter news he shared—Clyman had likely gone under. The next morning, with the bullboat complete, the entire take of peltry was bundled and heaped into the coracle. Smith judged he packed up some $8,000 worth of furs, a little over $200,000 today. The water was by now running high, and he was confident that Fitzpatrick and his two hands could crew the unwieldy vessel down the Sweetwater to the North Platte, and thence to the Missouri and a waiting William Ashley in St. Louis. While Fitzpatrick and his crew floated east, Smith, Sublette, and the five others would backtrack through South Pass and, come autumn, trap the Green's tributaries even farther north and west.

As Jed Smith rode toward the sunset, one cannot help but wonder at his feelings regarding Jim Clyman. Clyman had become a stout friend, and Smith likely shuddered at the idea of what the Indians had either already done to, or would do to, their captive. As it happened, quite similar thoughts were running through Clyman's mind.

*　*　*

The little camp Smith had discovered in the willows along the river was indeed Jim Clyman's. But he was very much not a prisoner. Yet.

When Clyman and Fitzpatrick separated days earlier, the former had made his way to the banks of the North Platte below what is today Casper, Wyoming. There, expecting Smith, Fitzpatrick, and the rest to soon catch up, he erected his crude shelter beneath the willow canopy and cut branches for a fire. Before he could strike flint to steel, however, he heard voices on the far bank of the river. Indian voices. Crawling through the brush, he could see that the band was painted for battle. But as it was dusk and the North Platte was a good sixty-five feet wide at this point, he could not make out to which tribe they belonged. He was not foolhardy enough to inquire. Scraping a small trench into the prairie as silently as he could, he buried his saddle and tack and swatted his horse into the night lest it give away his hidey-hole.

Clyman remained concealed in the willow brake while the painted hostiles, he wrote, "soon raised 4 or 5 fires turned loose or tithered all their horses their being 22 Indians and 30 horses I did not feel myself perfectly safe with so large number a war party." Watching a near-full moon rise and "recoclecting" that the terrain behind him was so "bare and sandy [that] I could be trased as easily as if it had been snow," he nonetheless decided to chance an escape.

Clyman waited until most of the hostiles had bedded down. The rest appeared to be too busy tending their fires to notice him as he crept toward a rocky ridge about two hundred yards to his rear. Climbing the granite esker, he settled in between two high boulders overlooking the confluence of the Sweetwater and North Platte. Around midnight, as far as he could tell, his "disagreeable neighbors" doused their fires and broke camp. But as they rounded up their grazing horses, two of the mounts spooked and splashed across the North Platte. Several braves chased them on foot while eight to ten more mounted up and spread out to surround the runaways. The moon was high, and from his perch atop the ridge Clyman could clearly see the footprints he had left in the sand. The Indians were more intent on running down their ponies, however, and failed to notice the telltale sign. Finally, with their horses reined, they rode north.

Clyman, still expecting his party of fellow trappers to arrive at any moment, spent the next day exploring a deep rock canyon that the Sweetwater had carved over the millennia directly through the granite ridge.

The long gorge, known to the Indians as Devil's Gate—a name carried over by westering white settlers—is three hundred feet wide at its entrance but measures just thirty feet across at its base. The ever-narrowing cut turns the placid river into a turbulent, unnavigable waterway as the current squeezes through the crevice, the noise of the whitewater near deafening. Clyman, who had diverted around the ridge on his journey downstream, wondered how he had not heard the roaring waters. He made a mental note to warn Smith and the others not to put in any bullboats until well below this vessel-killer.

Toward early afternoon he watched from above as another party of some twenty Indians, this time all afoot, crossed the Sweetwater on drift-wood rafts above Devil's Gate. Scurrying for cover amid the high cliffs, he did not see Jed Smith searching for him near where the mounted war party had made camp on the North Platte.

Jim Clyman, over seven hundred miles west of the closest American settlement or army post, waited eleven days near the confluence of the two rivers for his companions. When they had not appeared by the morning of the twelfth, he made his decision. Rather than retrace his steps, he would follow the curve of the North Platte north and then east toward the Missouri. He had eleven balls in his ammunition pouch. At one point during his journey he lay prone in the tall switchgrass after spotting Indians in the distance running buffalo. After they moved on, he stumbled across a dilapidated bullboat snagged on a sandbar. He rode the river until the craft fell apart, then continued on foot. He managed to take down a buffalo and spent two days in a grove of cottonwoods searing the animal's meat, soothed by the songs of a flock of purple martins.

On his second afternoon among the cottonwoods, he eyed a herd of wild horses on the horizon approaching the river to drink. After fashioning a crude halter from the buffalo's rawhide, he loaded one of his last rifle balls and waited. Eventually a great black stallion reached the riverbank. If Clyman could nick the mustang's neck and momentarily stun him—what hunters call "creasing" a wild horse—he might rush him, fit the halter, and mount him. His aim was not true. His shot shattered several of the animal's cervical vertebrae and killed it. At the sound of the gunshot the rest of the herd scattered.

Moving on, ever eastward, the dazed and fatigued Clyman failed to notice an Indian encampment before they spotted him. He saw no other choice and walked into their midst. He recognized the braves as Pawnee, distinguishable by their unique scalp-locks stiffened with buffalo tallow to resemble a buffalo's horn. They were the only tribe on the Plains to wear their hair as such. The Indians robbed Clyman of his rifle, knife, the remainder of his black powder, and the few balls he had left. They also took his blanket and flint. Smirking with disdain, the Pawnee made it clear through hand signals that they only took the scalps of living white men, not the half dead. Clyman did, however, lose his long hair to one memento-seeking Indian who gathered it into a ponytail and cut it at the nape with Clyman's own knife. He recalled, "I bearly saved my scalp but lost my hair." As the Pawnee rode south, the brave who had barbered him tossed Clyman a leather pouch containing a few grains of parched corn.

Days later, near starving, Clyman snuck up on two fighting badgers. He killed them both with the bleached thigh bone of a long-dead animal— "horse brobly" he guessed. Fighting off mosquitos and black flies, he bit off what fur he could from their backs to stuff into his threadbare moccasins and tore open their bellies with his fingernails to eat the raw meat. He puked most of it back up, but still he kept moving, swimming several wide streams pouring into the Platte. Weak and, he presumed, dying, he often awoke in the tallgrass not remembering for how long he had been passed out. On one of these occasions, after eighty days out, he lifted his head with great effort and spotted what he at first took to be a mirage. It was not. The American flag was waving from a tall staff.

"I swoned emmediatly how long I lay unconscious I do not know I was so overpowered with joy The stars and stripes came so unexpected I was completely overcome."

Clyman, summoning the last dregs of his strength, eventually slumped toward Fort Atkinson's main gate. When he awoke two days later, he was stunned to see Hugh Glass sitting by his bedside. Glass looked almost as bad as Clyman felt. With good reason. The man who was rapidly becoming known as the luckiest frontiersman along the borderlands had just survived yet another death-defying journey.

CHAPTER 12

———— · ————

DEAD MEN WALKING

The ghost now proffering a tin cup of hot coffee to Jim Clyman in that summer of 1824 had twice within a span of ten months been presumed dead. Clyman well remembered the story Daniel Potts had told at the Crow encampment about the "demise" of Hugh Glass after the grizzly mauling; he peppered Glass with questions about how he had survived. Glass was less interested in talking about the bear attack, about his abandonment by Jim Bridger and John Fitzgerald. He was more focused on the tale of his latest *via dolorosa*.

Seven months earlier, he said—at just about the time that Clyman, Jed Smith, and the others had started down the Popo Agie—Glass had been camped with Andrew Henry on the Bighorn when the major called for a volunteer. Henry needed someone to carry a message to William Ashley in St. Louis. Five men stepped forward, Glass among them.* He had ulterior motives—lethal affairs to settle with Fitzgerald.

Maj. Henry, fearing attacks by Blackfeet, Arikara, or even Mandan

---

* Although Andrew Henry's letter to William Ashley was never recovered, historians speculate that Henry wanted Ashley to know that the Missouri Fur Company had managed to get an overland party to the Mountain Crow camp on the Wind River—that is, the two factors who had traveled part of the way with Smith's company. What makes little sense, however, is a question that endures to this day: Why would Henry deplete his trapping outfit of five healthy bodies entering the height of beaver season?

along the Grand River route, instructed Glass and the others—listed only by their last names of More, Chapman, Dutton, and Marsh—to give the Upper Missouri country a wide berth. Instead, traveling on foot, his couriers took a southeastern course via the south fork of the Powder River. This would lead them to the Platte and thence onto the flatlands.

The Powder was still ice-bound, but by the time the contingent made the Platte the current was in spring spate, running fast and deep enough for a bullboat. They constructed a vessel and had floated over one hundred miles when, at the confluence of the Platte and the Laramie, they were hailed by an Indian hunting party. This was Pawnee country, they knew, and as the United States was formally at peace with the tribe, they dropped their guard when the braves summoned them to shore. The five white men were invited to partake in a feast in the headman's lodge—the largest of the thirty-eight tipis they counted. They accepted. Only Dutton brought his rifle.

The Indians, talking freely, had no idea that Glass understood a few words in the Arikara tongue. The meal had only but commenced when Glass realized that their hosts were not Pawnee but Rees running buffalo much farther south than their traditional hunting grounds. More troubling, Glass divined that they were from the faction once led by the late headman Grey Eyes. Their leader was a warrior named Elk's Tongue, who had served as Grey Eyes's first lieutenant. Glass quickly came to understand that the bonhomie was a ruse. The Indians intended on killing them to avenge their chief's death.

Hoping none of the Indians were fluent in English, Glass spoke fast and in a low tone, pretending to compliment their hospitality while in fact passing his discovery to his horrified companions. On his signal the five trappers burst from the lodge and ran for the bullboat. Their rifles and ammunition were, of course, gone. They jumped into the craft and paddled furiously for the opposite bank. The game afoot, some two dozen Arikara splashed into the waist-deep water and gave chase.

The trappers abandoned the bullboat—the very craft that Jim Clyman was to find weeks later—and scattered across the prairie. As Dutton was armed, the Indians avoided him. Marsh was too fleet to catch, and he later reunited with Dutton to make Fort Atkinson. There they reported their three companions dead. They were nearly correct. The desperate Hugh Glass was still alive.

Glass had out-hared the Arikara on his track, he told Clyman, but survival was no certain thing. It was near dusk by the time he climbed a mesa scarred by a crooked maze of switchback trails veining the granite tableland. He squeezed in between a clutch of rocks and watched. Below him the Indians first overtook Chapman, then More. Both were killed, their deaths followed by the ritual depredations to their corpses. Later that night, with his pursuers having given up the search, Glass crept from his hiding spot and began walking east. He was more than five hundred miles from Fort Atkinson. He had done it once; he could do it again. At least this time he had with him not only his flint and striking steel but his hunting knife as well. This, he said, made him feel "right peart . . . all alone among the painters and the wild varmints."

The coda to Glass's second saga occurred when he came face-to-face with Private John Fitzgerald at the fort. Both men were taken aback—Glass by Fitzgerald's uniform, Fitzgerald by the burning eyes of the man he had left for dead. As Fitzgerald stammered an offer to return Glass's rifle, Col. Leavenworth happened upon the confrontation. Glass was momentarily flummoxed. As one chronicler wryly relates, "It was not the custom of the colonel . . . to permit his privates to be shot up by civilians."

In the end, Glass reluctantly relented. Much as he had addressed Bridger, he told Fitzgerald, "Go, false man & answer to your own conscience & to your God; I have suffered enough by your shameless perfidy and heartless cruelty."

Within days of relating his story to Jim Clyman, Hugh Glass joined a trading company bound for Santa Fe. Given all he had been through, one understands his desire to abandon the Northern Plains. Baring his lyrical soul, Clyman composed a poem in honor of Glass's departure:

Mourn not dear friends to anguish deriven
Thy children now unite in heaven
Mourn not for them who early blest
Have found in Heaven eternal rest
So ends this part of the record

* * *

First High Glass. Then Jim Clyman. Finally, ten days after Clyman's arrival, Thomas Fitzpatrick, Francis Ziba Branch, and the trapper known only as Stone stumbled through the gates of Fort Atkinson. They appeared, in Clyman's description, "in a more pitiable state if possible than myself." The three were the last of a veritable parade of dead men walking to seek assistance from Col. Leavenworth that fall. Portentously, all had traversed the eastern portion of what was to become famous as the Oregon Trail.

As Clyman had feared, Fitzpatrick's bullboat had foundered and capsized in the rapids of Devil's Gate. All their peltry lay at the bottom of the Sweetwater. But the three had the presence of mind to spend several days diving for the furs. After spreading the plews to dry, they hauled them on their backs for five miles before caching them at the base of a great slab of red granite sprouting from the prairie that would soon come to be known as Independence Rock.*

When Fitzpatrick recovered his strength, he composed a letter to William Ashley detailing the wealth of furs accumulated beyond the newly "discovered" South Pass. Taking but a few days of rest to recover from his trials, Fitzpatrick then borrowed horses from a Missouri Fur Company factor and set off with Branch, Stone, and a newcomer to the fort, James "Jim" Beckwourth, to retrieve the buried plews.

---

* A fanciful story has it that Independence Rock, an isolated peak at the southeastern tail of the Granite Mountains and now a national historic landmark, received its name because Fitzpatrick and his crew buried their peltry on July 4. More likely, however, is that the rounded monolith derives its name from its location on the Oregon Trail. Wagon trains assembled on the Missouri River and bound for Oregon and California hoped to reach the rock by Independence Day in order to avoid the first mountain snowfalls.

* * *

According to William Ashley's journal notes, he opened and read Thomas Fitzpatrick's dispatch with not a little trepidation. The summer of 1824 had not been kind to Gen. Ashley. His bid for the Missouri governorship was crushed by his rival Democratic-Republican candidate Frederick Bates, a favorite of the aging former president Thomas Jefferson. And it seemed that at every desultory campaign stop, word reached him from Fort Atkinson of the serial catastrophes suffered by his trappers in the mountains. Worse still, not long after his August electoral defeat, his partner Andrew Henry unexpectedly arrived in St. Louis with such a meager haul of pelts that Ashley contemplated taking advantage of America's recently enacted bankruptcy laws.

Theirs was a dispiriting conversation. Henry reported that he had lost four men in a gunfight with the Gros Ventre on the Yellowstone and two more on his trip down the Missouri to an ambush by the increasingly hostile Sioux. The Mountain Crow, he added, had robbed, beaten, and banished from their territory the two factors from Joshua Pilcher's Missouri Fur Company. Moreover, during his downriver journey he had passed what was left of Tilton's Fort, the Columbia Fur Company trading post on Mandan land. The stockade had been destroyed. Almost as an afterthought, the major also disclosed that during the engagement with the Gros Ventre, the Indians had discovered and made off with the cache of powder, lead, and the entire stock of trade goods—blankets, iron kettles, knives—that he had buried at Fort Henry. As if this weren't enough, Henry saved his biggest news for last. He was quitting the fur-trade business to return to his lead mine. Closing in on his fiftieth birthday, Henry had simply had enough.

The following day Ashley met with the Indian agent Benjamin O'Fallon. The two concurred that the scenario across the Upper Missouri Country was indeed a farrago of bleak tidings. What was left of Ashley's trapping outfits was disheartened and scattered across the west as the Blackfeet, Gros Ventre, and Sioux joined the Arikara in painting for war. The Crow had inexplicably turned belligerent. And judging from the wreckage of Fort Tilton, even the Mandan appeared to be rising. It was all too much for O'Fallon. As he fulminated in a letter to William Clark, "The trappers and hunters are descending from the mountains and are going out of Indian country, leaving the upper Country stained with the innocent blood of the most daring and enterprising portion of our people."

Never far from O'Fallon's mind—and reflecting a growing unease in the seats of power on the Eastern Seaboard—were the geopolitical ramifications of American hunter-trappers abandoning the Rockies. These hard men had doubled as explorers and amateur cartographers, and their retreat was akin to inviting the British to fill the vacuum they left behind. The Oregon Country and its neighbor New Caledonia—present-day British Columbia—was essentially a vast empire of natural resources whose fur, fisheries, and timber holdings were the envy of the world. And the Hudson's Bay Company, having merged with the North West Fur Company three years earlier under political pressure from London, was literally planting Union Jacks across the pathway that Lewis and Clark had marked for a future continental United States.

The previous winter a contingent of fourteen Hudson's Bay deserters had crossed the Continental Divide west to east and almost immediately engaged in a series of gunfights with both the Crow and the Cheyenne. Weeks later they staggered into Fort Atkinson and beseeched Col. Leavenworth to help them retrieve the pelts and traps that the Indians had stolen. Leavenworth's hands were tied, of course, even when the Canadians described a string of satellite stockades in the Oregon Country from which the Hudson's Bay Company was now operating. Aside from the old Fort Astoria, renamed Fort George, Canadian trappers under British administration were also working out of a compound called Flathead Post in northwestern Montana, from the new Fort Nez Perces at the confluence of the Snake and Columbia in Washington State, and from the smaller Spokane House headquarters straddling the Washington-Idaho border.

The frontier had erupted at this news, and residents along the borderlands, not least men like O'Fallon and Pilcher, blamed incompetent Washington politicians for not doing more to secure this precious swath of land. For many Americans, the most risible manifestation of this diplomatic ineptitude was the accord reached between the United States and Great Britain in 1818. Therein, the two nations agreed to a joint occupation of the Oregon Country for ten years while negotiators quarreled over precisely where the northwestern portion of the international border would run.

The U.S. Congress was adamant that the forty-ninth parallel boundary established east of the Rockies be extended beyond the mountains all the way to the Pacific. London countered with a proposal for a partition continuing along the forty-ninth degree only as far as the Columbia River. After reaching the river, British officials insisted, the boundary line must drop down to follow the watercourse to the sea. This would cede to Great Britain most of present-day Washington State, including potential ports on the Puget Sound. It was common knowledge that the United Kingdom was on the cusp of embarking on its "Great Game" against the Russian empire in Central Asia, and wily British politicians in Whitehall appeared to be already playing a practice round literally half a world away.*

Yet with the border negotiations between the two countries scheduled to resume in only four years, William Ashley sensed an opportunity. The former lieutenant governor was not lacking in ego, and it was said that he tended to view himself in the "first person perpendicular" tense. Though he may have failed as a politician, he now calculated that he might still prevail as the statesman who retained the Oregon Country for his nation—and, in the process, resuscitate his fur-trade operation. The latter depended to some extent on Thomas Fitzpatrick recovering the sizeable stockpile of peltry he had cached at the base of Independence Rock. Yet far more important, for both Ashley's ledger books as well as America's future hegemony west of the Rockies, were successful trapping seasons by the two outfits led by Jed Smith

---

* The *Great Game*, a term coined by Rudyard Kipling in his novel *Kim*, was a century-long political and diplomatic standoff that saw the British empire try to expand into Afghanistan and other Central Asian territories and khanates in order to deter a suspected Russian invasion of colonial India.

and John Henry Weber. Thomas Fitzpatrick's letter confirmed that Smith had already pushed past the Continental Divide. Ashley could only hope that Weber had followed suit.

As for the precise location of any of those men at the moment, no one knew. Even Fitzpatrick could only guess that Smith, Bill Sublette, and the others—if they still lived—were somewhere in the vicinity of the Green River Valley. As for Weber, Fitzpatrick recalled him speaking of planning to traverse Union Pass from the Wind River Crow encampment once the snows abated. Whether this actually occurred, and if his journey was successful, Ashley could only hope.

* * *

Eight hundred miles to the west of the fretting and plotting William Ashley, Jed Smith knew nothing of the serial calamities that had befallen his comrades across the mountains and prairies. Nor was he aware of the swelling anger of the Plains tribes gearing for war. An irony nonetheless loomed: Smith, making his way toward the meandering Snake River, would soon encounter a band of Indigenous peoples whose tribe he had only heard stories about. Stories from long ago. Odder still was that they would beseech him for help. The surprise was that they were Iroquois.

CHAPTER 13

FLATHEAD POST

The Snake River Country is a geographic anomaly. Bounded by North America's Great Basin to the south, the Pacific coastal ranges to the west, and the Rocky Mountains to the east, it contains close to forty major rivers and creeks that flow into the meandering, thousand-mile-long Snake River. Yet for all its coursing waterways the river's drainage area—some 110,000 square miles—was, and remains, a semiarid grassland. Modern tree-ring data and archeological pollen studies indicate that the territory was already experiencing higher temperatures and lower rainfall by the early decades of the nineteenth century—that is, by the time Canadian and American trappers arrived. As it was, however, the terrain remained flush with beaver.

It was through this pelt-rich high desert that, by September 1824, Jed Smith and his six companions rode north. As the first Americans in a decade to have ventured across the Continental Divide, his outfit's trapping success along the Green River had merely brushed up against the Hudson's Bay Company's line of demarcation. Now Smith, whether he recognized it or not, was embarking on a full-scale frontal assault. His little troop, in fact, represented the first stirrings of a tentative U.S. occupation of the far

northwest frontier that could weigh heavily on international border negotiations. And the British knew it.

There are discrepancies as to where Smith and his company spent the late
spring and summer of 1824 after Thomas Fitzpatrick descended the Sweetwater. In a letter to Gen. Henry Atkinson years later, William Ashley refer-
ences Smith passing "the three buttes." This leads some to conclude that the
trappers had turned directly northwest toward the Grand Tetons after ranging back through South Pass. But verified reports of Smith taking and caching
an eye-opening eighteen hundred beaver pelts before striking north leaves
others to infer that his party may have retraced its steps down the Green and
up the Black Forks before turning toward the Snake.

In the event, it is definitively recorded that it was along the Portneuf
River in present-day southeastern Idaho where Smith happened upon a
dozen forlorn Iroquois hunter-trappers in the employ of the Hudson's Bay
Company. They were led by a headman known as "Le Grand Pierre" Tivanitagon, whose western legacy redounds to this day in the shallow valley, or
"hole," on the far side of the Tetons to which he has lent his name. When
Smith found him, Tivanitagon and his Iroquois were in acute distress, having barely survived a recent battle with the Shoshone in which they lost
their horses, their traps, and most of their furs. They offered Smith a cache
of pelts they had previously buried, 105 in total, in exchange for an armed
escort back to their Booshway's camp farther west on the Snake. Smith,
perhaps recalling his childhood curiosity about the ways of these eastern
woodland natives, struck the bargain. As he later recalled, the last Indians
he ever expected to meet west of the Rockies were Iroquois.

*　*　*

It was Donald McKenzie who introduced the idea of standing up trapping
brigades manned by Iroquois and Abenaki tribesmen, Indians long familiar with taking beaver from the St. Lawrence area. A further McKenzie
innovation was to expand these brigades to withstand even the most with-
ering hostile attacks. The dark-and-dour-visaged Highlander had roamed

the Northwest for years in various capacities and concluded that though
the smaller outfits from the States may have proven more efficient in terms
of pelts taken per man, the Americans also sustained heavier casualties and
lost product, whether through accidents or Native American raids. As such
he salted his new and larger crews with former Canadian indentured servants whose terms of bond had expired and even teams of Sandwich Island-
ers transported by merchant ships delivering supplies to British factors on
the Pacific Coast.[*]

Prior to the subsummation of the Nor'Westers by the Hudson's Bay
Company in 1821, McKenzie had been sent west by the latter in 1816 to
overhaul the firm's underachieving Columbia Department. He immediately outperformed expectations. Although the vast Columbia Department stretched south from Alberta and British Columbia to the northern
borders of present-day Nevada and Utah, McKenzie's past expeditions for
John Jacob Astor's Pacific Fur Company led him to direct the company's
concentration on the area southeast of the Columbia River.

McKenzie's foresight proved prescient for at least one of his successors
in a fairly momentous encounter. For when he returned to Winnipeg in
1821 to assume the governorship of the Crown's Red River Colony—a
twelve-thousand-square-mile tract of land carved from Hudson's Bay territory—he was succeeded, albeit temporarily, by the burly, brash, and red-
bearded Finan McDonald, whose family had emigrated to Canada from
Scotland when he was a child.[†]

The forty-one-year-old McDonald was an experienced mountain hand,
having descended the Columbia River sixteen years earlier as an assistant
to the London-educated astronomer, mathematician, and cartographer

---

* The Hawaiians, called "Oweyhees" by the phonetically minded British and Americans, lent their bastardized name to a county, a river, and a mountain range in Idaho.

† The brutal evictions euphemistically known as the Highland Clearances involved the removal between
the mid-eighteenth century and the mid-nineteenth century of a vast number of tenants from the Scottish
Highlands by rapacious landlords. Many of these now-homeless crofters emigrated to Canada's Red River
Colony.

David Thompson.* Legend had it that McDonald had acquired his nickname, "Buffalo," for wrestling one of the beasts to the ground in his youth.
But as McDonald now saw it, he was too old to be taking the field and had
only reluctantly agreed to lead one last beaver hunt in the interim between
McKenzie's departure and the arrival of McKenzie's official successor as
head trader, yet another Scots-born adventurer named Alexander Ross.

Riding out of Flathead Post in early 1823, McDonald and his party of six
salaried clerks, or engagés, and forty-five trappers had just ranged over the
Continental Divide at North Pass in the Beaverhead Mountains—the same
route taken by Meriwether Lewis and William Clark.† Suddenly scores of
rifle balls whistled out of a dense thicket of Douglas firs skirting the trail.
Three trappers fell dead, and at McDonald's command the rest arrayed
themselves on either side of the conifer grove and poured volley after volley
of buckshot into the trees. In response came defiant taunts but a steady de-
cline in return fire, signaling to McDonald that his assailants were running
low on ammunition.

McDonald guessed that the hostile war party, who he assumed were
Blackfeet, likely outnumbered his own. He was less than enthusiastic
about the idea of hand-to-hand fighting in the gloomy *baud*. So, with a
breeze rising and three more of his men picked off, he ordered the little forest fired. The wind carried the flames rapidly, and within moments
the Indians, Blackfeet indeed, boiled out of the burning timber. A wall
of gunfire leveled them. Of the seventy-five braves McDonald counted,
seven escaped. Fifty-eight were killed trying to flee and ten more were
found burned to death, left to "remane," McDonald wrote, "as Pray for
the wolves. We Shoe them what war was they will not be so rady to attack
People another time."

---

* Over his long career as a geographer and surveyor, David Thompson, known to the northwestern Indian
tribes as "Koo-Koo-Sint," or Stargazer, would fill seventy-seven field notebooks while mapping some 1.5
million square miles of North American wilderness, or about one-fifth of the continent.

† The pass, at an elevation of 7,373 feet, is known today as Lemhi Pass after Fort Lemhi, a nearby outpost
founded in 1855 by Mormon missionaries.

He was nearly correct. The engagement, the closest thing to a pitched battle ever fought between trappers and Native Americans in the mountains, did leaven Blackfeet raids for a spell, particularly against Hudson's Bay Company brigades. But the tribe, bristling for vengeance, would not stay quiet for long. In the aftermath of the skirmish, McDonald crossed the Salmon Mountains and trapped down the Bear Valley through the spring.* He returned to Flathead Post in the fall by way of the Three Forks and the Missouri River's Great Falls—the farthest into U.S. territory that any Hudson's Bay Company outfit had ever penetrated. McDonald arrived at the station in late autumn with 4,339 pelts, the largest number ever recorded by the Columbia Department and—despite the loss of several mounts to Indian horse thieves—a glowing testament to Donald McKenzie's large-brigade policy. It was also a record that the incoming Alexander Ross was determined to surpass.

Yet for all McKenzie's visionary accomplishments, neither he nor his successors could ever quite instill their notions of adamantine discipline in the rowdy trappers, particularly the Iroquois. To the fastidious Scots Canadians, the eastern Indians were notorious layabouts; in one report McKenzie accused Tivanitagon's followers of being more interested in running buffalo and racing ponies with friendly western tribesmen than in working beaver streams and ponds. And when the Iroquois were not in the field, he wrote, it pained him no end to watch them loiter about the Columbia Department's disparate stockades gorging on food purchased on credit that, McKenzie suspected, would never be repaid.

If anything, Alexander Ross's antipathy toward the Iroquois was even more blistering. Ross was a former Astorian-turned-Nor'Wester who had originally come west on the ill-fated *Tonquin*, and he found the eastern Indians "unruly, ill-tongued villains." For good measure he added that the

---

* At approximately 350 miles, the Bear is the longest river in the United States the waters of which never reach the sea. Rising on the north slope of the Uinta Mountains straddling the Utah-Wyoming border, the Bear courses through southeastern Idaho before bending around the Wasatch Range, bisecting Bear Lake on the Idaho-Utah border, and emptying into the Great Salt Lake.

former indentured servants working beside them—"freemen" as they were known—were little better: "A more discordant, headstrong, ill-designing set of rascals God never permitted together in the fur trade," Ross noted in his journal.

And therein lay the Achilles' heel of the Hudson's Bay Company's enhanced-brigade business model. The officers running the organization viewed their hired help, in the words of the company's imperious colonial governor George Simpson, as "the very scum of the country." As such, a bureaucracy that was essentially feudal in nature set in. The Canadian trappers were reimbursed for pelts at about the same penurious rate of sixty cents a plew that the company paid the western tribes in trade. Conversely, Iroquois and freemen were charged rapacious prices for the supplies and food— including rancid horsemeat—on which company stores held a monopoly. As the historian Dale Morgan observes, "The men were reduced to virtual serfdom; however large their catch, it was swallowed up in their debt."

Unlike their American counterparts, the Canadians had little incentive to increase their beaver take under these stratified social and financial conditions. This was particularly true of the proud Iroquois, whose oral histories were imbued with tales of their former Confederacy controlling great swaths of the North American continent long before the arrival of Europeans. That Governor Simpson and his commissioned "gentlemen" such as Donald McKenzie, Finan McDonald, and Alexander Ross felt that it was only a question of whipping their Indian brigades into shape through stricter management was folly.

There was also another commercial drawback to McKenzie's system that some worried would affect future profit taking. This was the simple equation of men to beaver. American hunting parties were as yet too small to genuinely dent the West's beaver populations. But even Finan McDonald acknowledged that as advantageous as a fifty-man outfit might be against hostile Indians, it could also be "two strong" in terms of taking fur. The more numerous the party, McDonald worried, the richer a river's tributaries and ponds had to be, particularly if the waterways had been trapped in previous seasons. The Canadians, following the millennia-long Indigenous taboo against overhunting, did attempt to trap on a sustained-yield basis, often closing posts in areas that needed to be given time to replenish their beaver stock. But sooner or later, McDonald sensed, the animal population was bound to give out.

Alexander Ross found this theory rich coming from a man who had only just returned to Flathead Post with over four thousand plews. As such he was determined to soldier on, and in February 1824 Ross led a brigade of fifty men and a coterie of camp followers into the Snake River Country. They were barely a month on the trail when Tivanitagon petitioned Ross to allow his dozen or so Indians to break off from the westering company to work the watercourses farther south. Ross, still negotiating the eastern portion of the bow-shaped Snake River Plain, was hesitant. On the face of it, the economics of the request made sense, particularly since to this point his men, as McDonald had predicted, were already taking far fewer pelts than he had expected.

But given Ross's immutable prejudices, he did not trust Tivanitagon's "good for nothings" to trap without his exacting supervision. In the end, however, his commercial imperatives prevailed, and he reluctantly acceded to Tivanitagon's proposal. So as Ross continued west, the Iroquois passed through the "hole" beneath the Tetons that would soon bear "Le Grand Pierre's" name and trapped down the south bank of the Snake all the way to the Blackfoot River in far-western Montana. From there they jumped to the Portneuf—and into their fateful confrontation with the Shoshone.

Alexander Ross's journals are a font of invective, and in them he blamed the Iroquois and their feckless ways for the hardships that befell them. Yet to some extent their misfortune could be laid at Ross's feet. While scouring the western regions of the Snake, several of Ross's traps and chains were stolen by the Shoshone. In retaliation, Ross seized a small remuda of Shoshone ponies. The Indians, valuing their mustangs over the white man's equipage, had little choice but to hand over the traps. But Ross, thinking to teach them a lesson, refused to return all of the horses. The incident naturally left bitter

feelings. Ross's party was too large and well armed for the Shoshone to con-
front. But several days later when they ran across the dozen wandering Iroquois, they took their revenge.

That the outnumbered eastern Indians even came out of the engagement alive was due more to luck than to their fighting prowess. Early in the
attack a Shoshone headman was shot and killed. Following tribal custom,
his followers paused the assault to prepare the chief for his afterlife. It was
during this lull, with the Iroquois expecting a second clash at any moment,
that Jed Smith and his men happened upon the scene. With the Americans
setting a rear guard, all slipped away that night.

* * *

Alexander Ross was aghast when, in the late spring of 1824, the Iroquois
contingent limped into his camp on the Salmon River with Smith and
his little company in train. Not only was "Le Grand Pierre" Tivanitagon's
crew "trapless and beaverless, naked and destitute of almost everything,"
he wrote, but Ross also suspected the Americans were less interested in
trapping than they were in spying on his operation. His intuition was un-
derlined when Smith mentioned that sometime within the year, an even
larger hunting outfit led by Andrew Henry was set to cross the Divide.
Smith naturally had no idea that Maj. Henry had already dissolved his
partnership with William Ashley.

Ross set down his apprehensions in his journal. The taproot of this latest American intrusion, he felt, stemmed from the desertion of the small
party of Hudson's Bay Company freemen two years earlier. He theorized
that the runaways had absconded with their furs to sell to the Americans
forted up on the Yellowstone and Bighorn Rivers for a better price. This
was evidenced, he added, by Jed Smith's refusal of Ross's offer to part with
his eighteen hundred cached furs—not to mention the 105 plews he had
taken from the Iroquois—for anything less than $3 a pound. To the Scots-
man this was an outrageous exorbitance. Smith's argument that each skin
might well fetch three to four times that price in St. Louis fell on deaf ears.

More disconcerting was Smith's stated intention of accompanying Ross back from central Idaho to Flathead Post. It further irked the Canadian that he found in Smith "a very intelligent person." For what other reason would such a savvy American make the decision to visit his stockade other than to learn as much as possible about the Hudson's Bay Company's modus operandi? Given the terms of the Oregon Country's joint-occupation agreement between Great Britain and the United States, there was nothing Ross could do about this short of outright murder. Whether he considered this option, he did not record.

That Ross was completely in error regarding the travails of the defectors who had lurched into Fort Atkinson with barely the clothes on their backs was beside the point. Regarding his second supposition, however, it is not inconceivable that Jed Smith did indeed sense that Gen. Ashley, not to mention the U.S. government, might be curious as to the breadth and depth of the British company's reach. After all, with a successful trapping season already behind him and nearly two thousand cached pelts awaiting his retrieval, he could afford the dalliance.

In the end, however, a small saving grace for Alexander Ross obtained— since the departure of the Iroquois his outfit had accumulated furs beyond their wildest dreams. This good fortune continued on the return journey to Flathead Post as they trapped the Bitterroot and the Clarks Fork Rivers. It was late in November when Ross, Smith riding at his side, triumphantly entered the stockade. The post's factor—who just happened to be Finan McDonald—counted some 4,900 pelts, a good five hundred more than his own record. McDonald, whether jealous or merely Scots obstinate, attributed the haul less to Ross's expertise than to "more luck than I had . . . he had no Batil with the Blackfeet or [horses] stolen by the [Shoshone] he was better furnish in traps than I was the year before."

Jed Smith and his cohort lingered at Flathead Post for three weeks, watching the pelts Ross had taken properly baled and stacked in a row of six booth-like huts linked by a single roof to keep both furs and trade goods dry. The Americans had initially been surprised to discover cohorts, wives, and even children traveling with Ross's brigade, as this was technically forbidden by Hudson's Bay Company regulations. It soon became apparent, however, that the women served an important purpose. The consensus among trappers was that the fastest anyone could accomplish the triple burden of skinning, cleaning, and stretching a beaver pelt was thirty minutes. That this time-consuming labor was taken up by the women in-country undoubtedly influenced the efficiency and effectiveness of the Canadian expeditions by increasing the amount of terrain the brigades could cover.

Now, at Flathead Post, Smith observed a veritable battalion of predominantly Indigenous female partners and wives making moccasins and snowshoes, smoking salmon and venison, collecting fall berries and mixing pemmican, and helping tote supplies and pelts. But most interesting to the Americans was the ritual spectacle of the winter trade fair the British company had established with the local Indigenous population. More than eight hundred Indians were milling about the camp, and beginning on November 30, each tribe was assigned a day to bring in their skins and dried buffalo meat, starting with the Flathead, as this was their territory. The Pend d'Oreille, Kutenai, and smaller contingents of Nez Perce and Spokane followed, in that order.

On the first appointed morning a company of mounted Flathead braves paraded into the fort, chanting peace songs and discharging their guns in salute. Their tribute was returned by the ritual firing of the post's three-pound cannon. Smith later discerned that the brass field piece was largely ceremonial; the Flathead had long been on good terms with the Canadian trappers and the Blackfeet rarely ventured this far northwest. Over the next few days, while the Indian men and the white traders passed the pipe, tribeswomen led packhorses laden with skins and meat to the company's clerks. It was a festive event, and the females had come dressed for the occasion with intricate porcupine quillwork adorning their buckskin dresses, their faces set off by shell-pendant earrings and colored beads woven through their hair.

By December 3, Ross had added close to another twelve hundred Indian plews to his own haul. He had also stocked his larders with eleven thousand pounds of buffalo meat. The Hudson's Bay Company's clerks meticulously provided a further miscellany of peltry gained in trade—the skins of 529 muskrats, fourteen otters, eight fishers, three minks, two foxes, and one marten.

Yet despite his successful hunt and winter jamboree, Ross learned that the Hudson's Bay Company's governor Simpson had already replaced him as head trader with the notoriously ornery Quebecois Peter Skene Ogden. Ogden had in fact arrived at Flathead Post mere hours before Ross and Jed Smith passed through the stockade gate. An irate Simpson considered Ross "empty headed" for allowing Smith and the Americans onto the post. As a sop to his successful hunt, however, he nonetheless promoted Ross to the position of the fort's chief factor, replacing the retiring Finan McDonald.*

Simpson had also entrusted Ogden with a secret directive that the new head trader had no intention of revealing to the Americans. Ogden was to abandon the Hudson's Bay Company's long-held sustained-yield policy in order to intentionally denude the Snake River country of all beaver. Simpson knew that this would probably take years; he felt it worth the wait. For it was the colonial governor's goal to eventually create a barren buffer zone between his firm's rich upper Northwest holdings closer to the northern Pacific coast. If American trappers dared to venture into this high country encompassing parts of present-day Wyoming, Idaho, Utah, Nevada, Oregon, and Washington, he wanted them to find, in his words, nothing but "a fur desert."

---

* As the high-country trappers and traders were generally free of the racism that infected the flatlands, many went native themselves in all but name, "womaning up" with Indigenous wives and siring mixed-race families. Their nondiscriminatory values, however, only went so far, particularly when they returned to so-called civilization. Here Finan McDonald proved the exception. When he departed the Columbia River country for Ontario, he became one of the few Mountain Men to take his Native American wife, Peggy, and their five children with him. Twenty years after his close call with the Blackfeet at North Pass, McDonald was elected as a representative from Ontario's Glengarry County to Canada's provincial Parliament.

CHAPTER 14

"A SLY, CUNNING YANKEY"

In October 1824—one month before Jed Smith rode into Flathead Post with Alexander Ross—the Hudson's Bay Company's governor George Simpson made his way from the organization's command post in Manitoba to the headwaters of the Columbia River. From there Simpson began a personal inspection tour of the enterprise's Columbia Department. The joint-stock corporation's London-based board of directors had installed the thirty-two-year-old Simpson as their Canadian viceroy three years earlier on the strength of the shrewd business acumen he had demonstrated while working at his uncle's sugar brokerage house in the capital city's famed Tower Street. Simpson's primary attraction to the Hudson's Bay board was his ruthless focus on profits over people.

Early portraits and late-in-life photographs typically depict Simpson in a magisterial pose—a diminutive man whose dark, high-collared frock coat and cravat are set off by long and bushy sideburns, perhaps grown to compensate for a hairline prematurely retreating across his domed forehead. Yet despite his less-than-robust countenance, the ambitious young Simpson was renowned for his physical stamina. Now, as he made his way down the Columbia from trading post to trading post, he noted everywhere what he considered mismanagement, extravagance, and outright waste. It was this initial western voyage that led him to slash both the company's western workforce by 50 percent and reduce the wages of those he did retain.

Simpson spared little thought to the men and women, particularly the Indigenous families, he put out of work by ordering stockades shuttered. The bottom line was all that mattered. To Stephen Bown, the Canadian historian and master chronicler of the Hudson's Bay Company, Simpson's employees "were being managed in a way similar to how he managed the beavers." That is, he applied the firm's sustained-yield beaver-trapping policy to its human workforce.

It was along this downriver passage that Simpson learned of Alexander Ross's decision to allow Jed Smith's party onto Flathead Post. He quietly seethed at what he considered trespass by the Americans; this only seemed to justify his earlier decision to replace Ross with the former Nor'Wester Peter Skene Ogden. Meeting with Ogden at the Spokane House post on the present Washington-Idaho border, he instructed Ogden to depart for Montana and relieve Ross of his position as head trader. Ogden was to refit Ross's brigade and plunge back into the Snake River Country for the spring trapping season with the intention of eradicating as many beavers as possible. Even beaver kits mewling for their missing mothers were to be killed. Simpson also added a major wrinkle to the traditional hunt. Instead of returning to any of the company's inland stockades with his peltry to expedite overland delivery to ships waiting in Hudson's Bay, Ogden was to continue west to Fort George via the Umpqua and Willamette Rivers. There he would load his pelts into the hold of a London-bound supply ship scheduled to drop anchor in early summer.

It was an open secret among British politicians, Simpson included, that whatever the outcome of the British-American treaty convention to set the international border, the United States would likely come away with all territory south of the big bend of the Columbia River. Until that boundary was officially recognized, Simpson's greatest fear was that American trappers would consider the region to the northwest of the watercourse a part of the Oregon Country. As such they would incrementally inch ever closer toward the untapped, beaver-rich mountain streams of today's British Columbia, a subsection of Rupert's Land then known as New Caledonia.

New Caledonia was not yet officially a British possession. It was, instead, what was termed an unorganized area of British North America. This meant that instead of the area being governed as a Crown municipality, the Hudson's Bay Company had been granted a royal charter to handle the responsibilities of local administration much as the East India Company ran the Indian subcontinent.

The United Kingdom planned to eventually claim New Caledonia as a Canadian province—not least to sweep away the Siberian trappers already nibbling at its western coasts—and Gov. Simpson's management of this territory was a precondition for the confederation of Atlantic and Pacific Canada. Thus Simpson's twofold strategy—to solidify the Crown's claim to New Caledonia by building and enlarging forts to increase the British presence in the region while simultaneously stripping the Snake River Country of all beaver. American trappers attempting to reach New Caledonia would first have to traverse an expanse of beaver-barren territory larger than Mexico. As he noted in his journal, "For political reasons we should endeavor to destroy the country as fast as possible."

In the thirty-four-year-old Ogden, Simpson had selected precisely the man to carry out his scheme. Ogden had begun his career in the fur business in his midteens as a Montreal-based clerk for John Jacob Astor's American Fur Company. Then, in 1809, he signed on with the North West Fur Company as an apprentice factor. The pugnacious Ogden's stunted, simian-like countenance was matched by his character, which included a detestation of all things American. Much of this likely stemmed from his New York–born father's fierce loyalty to the Crown during the revolution. Such was the elder Ogden's despondency with George Washington's string of military triumphs that prior to his son's birth he emigrated to Quebec.

From the young Ogden's first posting as a Nor'Wester in Saskatchewan he exhibited a knack for intimidation. It was the height of the rogue outfit's rivalry with the Hudson's Bay Company, and Ogden was known to hang about the gate of a nearby stockade operated by Hudson's Bay men showing off his knife-throwing skills and brandishing his single-shot flintlock pistols. Once, when a Hudson's Bay pack train struck east to deliver furs to waiting British ships, Ogden ostentatiously led a party of Nor'Westers just ahead to impede any trading they might do with the Indians.

The most heinous allegation against Ogden occurred in 1816, when he was accused of murdering a Cree Indian who had done business with Hudson's Bay traders. Eyewitnesses reported Ogden slicing up the man's corpse as if he were butchering a buffalo. This of course occurred during an epoch when killing a Native American barely registered with authorities on either side of the border. Nonetheless, the recorded descriptions of Ogden's grisly mutilation proved too much even for his superiors at the North West Fur Company. Contemporaneous reports suggest that the company's officers transferred him farther into the interior as a hedge against law enforcement investigations against *them*.

No one was ever held accountable for the Indian's murder, and Ogden drifted about the far west from camp to camp as a trapper and factor until the North West Fur Company was subsumed into the Hudson's Bay Company in 1821. Which is how Gov. Simpson found him working at the firm's Spokane House.

Now, three years later, Peter Skene Ogden was no less chagrined than Alexander Ross had been to find Jed Smith and his men riding alongside his fifty-nine-man brigade as it departed Flathead Post in late December 1824.* He even assigned his second-in-command, a flinty Canadian officer who had fought for the British during the War of 1812 named William Kittson, to shadow the Americans and, if possible, report on their conversations. Smith in particular aroused Ogden's ire. He wrote that he considered him "a sly, cunning Yankey." For Smith's part, the distrust was mutual. He

---

* Also traveling with Ogden that winter were thirty women and thirty-five children, including Ogden's Nez Perce wife and Kittson's Kutenai wife.

was not unaware that aside from personal and economic competitiveness, he and Ogden each represented contending national interests.

By early January the company had slogged through three feet of snow as far as the Big Hole River, a tributary of the Jefferson. It was not lost on Smith and his men that to reach North Pass, the British were trespassing on land ceded to the United States in the Louisiana Purchase. Given the circumstances—not the least of which was that their small party of seven men was in effect being offered an armed escort through Blackfeet country—they kept their objections to themselves. This proved propitious one starless night when two dozen grazing horses were run off by the Indians. Ogden formed a party to give chase and recovered nine of the animals. Yet to the Canadian trappers this was a bad omen. Their mood blackened further when an Iroquois woman accidentally shot and killed her trapper husband while camped below North Pass.

Still fighting the weather, it took Ogden's brigade another month to cross the Divide and drop down into what is known today as the Lemhi Valley, an arid little vale nestled in the crook of eastern Idaho where Meriwether Lewis had reunited Sacagawea with the Shoshone band led by her brother, the headman Cameahwait. They were only an eight-day ride from the Snake River. But there they were stalled for seven weeks by the perpetually monochrome skies producing shoulder-high snows clogging the trails out of the hollow. Once Ogden had reached the neutral Oregon Country, he unfurled the Hudson's Bay Company flag, a modified ensign of the British Royal Navy featuring the initials "H—B—C" on a red field, with the Union Jack in the upper left corner. The Americans again took sour notice.

Smith and his restless crew were traveling lighter than the Canadians— among the regular trading and trapping equipage being hauled by Ogden's packhorses were several dozen buffalo-hide tipis. Thus, in mid-March, the Americans determined to strike through the mountain drifts on their own. It was a delicate decision. Plowing through thigh-high snow, a rider ran the risk of losing feeling in his feet and legs and gradually succumbing to frostbite. Toes could always be amputated, but gangrenous limbs meant certain death on the frontier. And should Smith and his men dismount and don snowshoes to break trail for their mounts, their buckskin leggings would absorb so much moisture that their clothing might freeze solid soon after they regained the saddle.

Nevertheless, on the night of March 17, Smith judged that the powerful northern gusts had abated enough to chance a breakout. He had learned during his rough journey toward South Pass that gentler winds meant not only fewer snow drifts but also less effort to start wood fires in the wet, leaden air to defrost and dry their buckskins and blankets. Sometime around midnight Smith passed word among his crew that it was time to slip away.

Smith's disappearance stunned Ogden. The next morning he ordered camp broken. There happened to be a drove of some six hundred buffalo also snowbound in the Lemhi Valley, and it was his second-in-command William Kittson's idea to spook the herd with an Indian-style run to force the animals to trample a path up and over a steep defile. It worked. As soon as Ogden's company reached the eastern verge of the Snake River Plain, he broke off thirteen of his men to pursue and "annoy and oppose the Americans" by trapping the same streams and ponds.

Over the next six weeks, the cat-and-mouse game intensified as the two outfits jockeyed for trapping advantage while hopscotching the labyrinth valleys of the Blackfoot, Snake, and Portneuf Rivers. Smith's party, keeping ahead of the Canadians, avoided any run-ins with the implacable Blackfeet. Ogden had less luck. Since their rout by Finan McDonald, the tribe had honed their battle tactics. Unless they severely outgunned their opponents, they were now content to pick off lone trappers one by one. Three of Ogden's men barely escaped ambush with their lives, albeit losing their traps and furs in the process. A fourth was unluckier: his scalped and disemboweled corpse, his penis shoved down his throat, was discovered two days after he failed to return to camp. A few days later the Indians also stole twenty of Ogden's horses. This time none were recovered.

By late April 1825, when Jed Smith reached the upper Bear River where it makes its big turn just southeast of present-day Pocatello, the night croaks of wood frogs awakening from hibernation were already beckoning the coming of spring. It was here that the Americans were intercepted by a small band of Indians looking to trade. The startled Smith, eyeing their pompadoured hairstyles from a distance, must have taken them for Crow straying far from their home grounds. Upon closer inspection the Americans saw the third braid of hair running down their backs, typical of the Shoshone. Smith had few goods worth bartering for, but during the parley the Indians mentioned that far down the river, nearly to its mouth, another American company was trapping the waterway's tributaries and ponds. Smith and his troop, over eighteen months in the wilderness since departing Fort Kiowa, had not seen a fellow countryman since. They rode south that night. Ogden's watchers never saw them go.

CHAPTER 15

"SHETSKEDEE"

Back in St. Louis, it was Thomas Fitzpatrick who ultimately rescued William Ashley from bankruptcy. Fitzpatrick's successful retrieval of the $8,000 worth of cached peltry from beneath the base of Independence Rock translated into the seed money Ashley required to outfit another trapping expedition. More pertinent, the letter Fitzpatrick posted to Ashley from Fort Atkinson contained the Irishman's fulsome descriptions of the veritable beaver paradise that lay beyond South Pass. This information was propellant enough for Ashley to revive his career ambitions.

He reckoned that if Jedediah Smith and, with luck, John Henry Weber represented the vanguard taking the offensive against the British in the Oregon Country, it would damn well be the Missouri Militia's illustrious brigadier general William Henry Ashley whom future Americans would salute for supplying that front line with reinforcements. In the process Ashley would also stake claim as the man whose actions ensured that the far northwest became a permanent part of the United States. Perhaps the governor's seat in the next election was not out of reach after all.

On his receipt of Fitzpatrick's communiqué sometime in September 1824, Ashley immediately applied for a federal license to trade on the far side of the Rockies with the Shoshones, a tribe Fitzpatrick called the "Snakes."

Ashley was well aware that fur *trading* was by this point a distant second to fur *trapping* as a profit-taking venture. It was likely that by seeking an official permit he was merely complying with the outdated bureaucracy of the U.S. Congress, which still required petitioners to designate with which tribes their trading posts would do business. As further evidence that legends are difficult to kill, particularly mythology that might prove financially or politically beneficial, in Ashley's application for his license he mentioned that said "Snakes" inhabited a territory riven by "two large rivers," which he assumed to be branches of the Rio Buenaventura. The two waterways referenced were obviously Fitzpatrick's representations of the Big Sandy and the Green. The Rio Buenaventura, on the other hand, remained purely a figment of Ashley's perfervid imagination.

The little general wasted no time assembling and stocking his expedition. He sensed, correctly, that he was racing against a westering notion beginning to take hold on the far side of the Mississippi. Fitzpatrick's letter had also recounted in detail the "discovery" of South Pass, putting particular emphasis on the ease with which wagons might negotiate the wide gap in the Rockies. The now-retired Andrew Henry had read the dispatch, and he mentioned Fitzpatrick's excitement over the wagon-friendly notch to a friend who happened to own a St. Louis newspaper.* When the story ran, publications across the frontier and beyond reprinted it—including the influential Baltimore-based *Niles' Weekly Register*, at the time America's most widely circulated magazine. Notes the reliably florid Dale Morgan, "Here is the dawn of South Pass on the American consciousness, and two years would not pass before the fact was blazing in the West with noonday brilliance."

Anticipating this "blaze" in the form of migrating missionaries, farmers, miners, and even lumberjacks, Gen. Henry Atkinson informed Ashley that he planned a large army expedition up the Missouri River the follow-

---

* Thomas Fitzpatrick, rightfully famed for the many accomplishments of his oversize life, was also briefly feted for an exploit properly earned by Jed Smith: "Major Fitzpatrick, the Discoverer of the South Pass," read the headline in *The St. Louis Reveille*.

ing spring. The ostensible purpose of the enterprise was to secure treaties of "perpetual friendship" with as many of the northern tribes as possible before the flood of pioneers washed over their land. But the 475 rifle-bearing Bluecoats from the First and Sixth U.S. Infantry regiments whom Atkinson would lead upriver would also serve as a not-so-subtle reminder to the Indians of the consequences of failing to grasp the importance of this "friendship."

That Gen. Atkinson could not intuit the agitated Indian mindset any more clearly than his subordinate Col. Leavenworth was indicative of the long history of European American blunders in their relationships with North America's Indigenous peoples. The more the white race convinced itself that it knew precisely what it was doing in regard to the red race, the more peril it was likely to face.

In any case, William Ashley had neither the time nor patience to wait on Gen. Atkinson's timetable. He immediately went about supplying his company of twenty-five men—now gathered at Fort Atkinson and including Thomas Fitzpatrick and Jim Clyman. He purchased fifty horses and large quantities of sugar, coffee, tobacco, lead, powder, and knives as well as the usual Indian trade fare. Much of this, he wrote, was to be transported by "a wagon and team &c," the first-ever reference to a wheeled vehicle attempting to traverse the plains north of Santa Fe.* Ashley stalled his departure from Fort Atkinson for several days hoping that Andrew Henry would have a last-minute change of heart and join the party as its field captain. This was not to be. And in the first week of November 1824, the caravan headed west with the forty-six-year-old Ashley himself as its Booshway.

The trail was hard going. Below-freezing temperatures measured with one of the German physicist Daniel Gabriel Fahrenheit's newfangled thermometers as well as a string of seemingly endless blizzards limited the

---

* The journals of William Ashley and Jim Clyman reveal nothing more about this supply wagon. Given the nightmare conditions of the winter journey, it likely ended up as firewood not long after rolling out of Fort Atkinson. Still, its purchase signaled the death knell for the cordelled keelboat era of fur trapping.

company's progress to but a few miles a day. With game scarce, the men were reduced to subsisting on the flesh of the horses that succumbed to the weather, abetted by a daily ration of half a pint of flour boiled into a tasteless porridge. One hundred miles out of Fort Atkinson, Ashley turned south toward the Platte, where his outfit crossed paths with a band from the Pawnee Nation known to the whites as the Grand Pawnee, one of the confederation's four tribal subsets. The Grand Pawnee were migrating to their winter camp on the braided Arkansas River, which then defined the border with Mexico. They informed Ashley that he would find firewood for fuel and sweet-bark cottonwoods to feed his horses at the junction of the north and south forks of the river. They also advised him in the strongest terms to make a winter camp at this confluence and wait for the spring thaw; to travel on in the dead of winter would be suicide.

No sooner had the Grand Pawnee disappeared over the southern horizon than the trappers fell in with another Pawnee faction, the Loup, named by French trappers after the wolves that roamed their hunting grounds along the three Loup tributaries that fed the Platte. Jim Clyman, skirting these fellow travelers with his hat pulled low, surreptitiously studied both Indian bands to see if he recognized any of the braves who had robbed him earlier in the year. He did not. And notwithstanding Clyman's suspicions, Ashley managed to trade with the Loup for twenty-three mounts as well as a supply of dried buffalo meat.

At the juncture of the North Platte and South Platte, a Loup headman told Ashley that if he was determined to move on, the swales along the south fork of the river would provide more timber. He appreciated the Indian's counsel and diverged from the northern route taken by Glass, Clyman, and Fitzpatrick on their desperate treks to Fort Atkinson. The Loup Pawnee rode with the trappers up the southern branch of the river for several days, following a path conveniently smashed through the deep snow by a vast buffalo herd also meandering west. The Loup chief had not lied, and on reaching a small island in the frozen waterway thick with cottonwood, Ashley made camp to refresh his horses.

It was here that the Indians departed—but not before warning the white men that the Grand Pawnee were wintering on the Arkansas with a large band of Arikara. This latter was the same clan, led by the headman Elk's Tongue, that had lured Hugh Glass into ambush and killed two of Glass's companions. Ashley naturally recalled the Grand Pawnee headman so strenuously urging him to hole up on the Plains and wait for better weather before heading into the high country. Was his company being set up for ambush? That night he doubled his guard and spent the wee hours of New Year's Day 1825 prowling the periphery of the little isle listening for the sounds of a war party that never materialized.

A month of hard trail-breaking ensued, and the first week of February found the trappers at the base of Colorado's Front Range, which Ashley described as a sheer and imposing "mass of snow and ice." They managed to cross this easternmost spur of the Rockies and move northwest onto Wyoming's arid Laramie Plains, leaving the watershed of the South Platte and entering that of the North Platte. But on reaching the Medicine Bow Range, they were stymied for six weeks by five feet of snow clogging the mountain passes. Tramping still farther north along the eastern flank of the massif, winter's slow wane allowed the men to trap the several streams running out of the peaks when they were not hunting buffalo, antelope, and mountain sheep. In late March—just as Jed Smith was breaking out of the Lemhi Valley—Ashley finally found a notch spanning the Continental Divide between the Medicine Bows and Elk Mountain. His party became the first white men to ride through what was later designated Bridger's Pass.*

It was not until sometime in early April that Ashley spotted a blueish wall of granite scraping the sky at what he guessed was perhaps eighty miles to the north. He fancied that the heights might be the southern

---

* The rather nondescript cleft—at 7,532 feet, about the same elevation as South Pass—was officially named in 1850 when Jim Bridger guided a U.S. Army Corps of Topographical Engineers over the Continental Divide. Given William Ashley's ego, it was probably just as well that he had been dead for twelve years when the pass he had "discovered" was officially commemorated with an underling's name.

terminus of the Wind River Range, the gateway to Fitzpatrick's beaver Eden. Neither Fitzpatrick nor Clyman, however, had seen the mountains from this vantage and could not be certain until Indians struck their camp that night and absconded with seventeen horses. The next morning a scout found a black-gneiss arrowhead at the scene, of the type exclusive to the Shoshone.* The Indian sign was a double-edged sword. If they had indeed wandered into "Snake" country, the cordillera rising in the north meant they were west of the Wind River Mountains. On the other hand, the raiders had left the outfit so bereft of horseflesh that the men had to take turns carrying heavy packs of supplies and equipage on their backs while keeping their eyes peeled for hostiles.

Riding with the company was the novice Jim Beckwourth. A fine horsemen, a crack shot, and even a good hand with a bow and arrow, Beckwourth was already cementing his reputation as the premier "gaudy liar" amid a passel of tall-tale-tellers.† It is unlikely that any of the American hivernants were familiar with the British satirist Samuel Butler's sage adage regarding truth-telling—"Any fool can tell the truth," Butler noted, "but it requires a man of some sense to know how to lie well." Yet it was nonetheless taken as the highest form of flattery along the borderlands to be known as an embellisher extraordinaire, though the reserved and religious Jed Smith proved the exception to this rule. To sit by a roaring winter's fire, sour mash in hand, listening to the likes of Jim Bridger or Jim Clyman or Thomas Fitzpatrick spin tales of taking down an entire sleuth of griz or single-handedly warding off a hostile war party rivaled any tales told around the table at Southwark's Tabard Inn. And Beckwourth, the dark-skinned twentysomething son of a Virginia slaveholder and his mulatto mistress, was fast refining the custom.

Following the horse raid, however, nerves were on edge, and Beck-

---

* Thomas Fitzpatrick was to later learn that the artful, horse-stealing Crow often purposely left arrowheads of rival tribes at the scene of their raids, as they had in this case.

† A chestnut among the yarn spinners was the description of a mountain valley so large that it took an echo eight hours to return. A man could thus yell "Wake up!" before bedding down at night and hear his own voice rousing him in the morning.

wourth's stories about the gruesome tribal tortures his fellow trappers would endure if taken captive were so embroidered with gore that the old hands had to suggest he ratchet down his bullshit. Big loud yarning in a St. Louis saloon or even in the safe confines of the Fort Atkinson sutler's store might be an admired sociable trait; in hostile Indian country it could cost you your edge. This attitude dismayed Beckwourth. As he was later to recall, "No jokes, no fireside stories, no fun."

Finally, after fording the Big Sandy on April 19, the company alighted on the banks of what Ashley happily noted in his journal as the "Shetskedee," mangling the Crow name for the Green River. Three days later, his outfit's bellies full of fresh buffalo meat, he set assignments. Jim Clyman was to lead a party of five men, including the loquacious Jim Beckwourth, north to trap across the same terrain Clyman had covered the previous year; a new hand named Zacharias Ham would take another crew of six to comb the tributaries to the northwest; and Thomas Fitzpatrick, at the head of five others, would follow the Green south toward the Uinta Mountains, much as Jed Smith and Bill Sublette had done the previous spring. A priority, needless to say—although Ashley said it anyway—was for every man to keep a weather eye out for any sign of Jedediah Smith and John Henry Weber.

In the meanwhile, Ashley and another six men began construction on a large bullboat to take them on a voyage of discovery to find what lay below the mouth of the Black Forks. Ashley was not certain whether the Green would empty into the Colorado or the fabulous Rio Buenaventura. But he was determined to find out.

Before each company went its separate way, Ashley contributed to a mythic slice of Americana. He told his hunter-trappers that on his expedition downriver, "at some conspicuous point not less than 40 or 50 miles from this place," he would cache all his supplies and trade goods in expectation of a grand "Rendevoze for all our parties on or before the 10th July next." He would, he said, strip trees of their bark in order to leave a trail to this summer gathering. But if the terrain he chose was timberless, he would construct five-foot cairns whose top rocks would be "made red with vermillion" to distinguish them from the stone pillars that Indians used to warn fellow tribesmen of evil spirits. Beneath each of these mounds, at the northwest corner, would be buried a letter as to the assembly point's precise whereabouts.

And thus was the first Rendezvous, the most famous legacy of the American Mountain Man, birthed on the banks of the Green River in the spring of 1825.

CHAPTER 16

———— • ————

GUNS ALONG THE BEAR

For such a vast and near-barren territory, the northeastern rim of America's Great Basin had suddenly become unusually crowded.*

Not only had Jed Smith located his compatriot John Henry Weber working the lower reaches of the Bear River in early 1825, but Weber had also collected several squads of American free trappers not contracted to any organization. All told, when Smith and his six hunters found the old Danish mariner, they counted close to forty men using his campsites as their mobile headquarters. Unbeknownst to any of them, not far to their south another American-based trapping outfit had streamed up from the white-washed Mexican mountain village of Taos. This hunting party, headed by the veteran trader-trapper Etienne Provost, consisted of perhaps two dozen hivernants. And that did not even count William Ashley's twenty-five-man troop only just entering the quarter. The Hudson's Bay Company's Peter Skene Ogden, who assumed that Smith's tiny crew was his only competition, was in for a shock.

Where and when John Henry Weber had crossed the Continental

---

* The Great Basin, comprising nearly all of Utah and Nevada as well as portions of Wyoming, California, and Oregon, is North America's largest area of contiguous endorheic watersheds; that is, the little water that exists therein never flows to an ocean, sea, or gulf.

Divide the previous year was not recorded by the journal-keeping Daniel Potts. Given Potts's later entries, it seems likely that Weber waited out the snow season in the Mountain Crow camp on the Wind River before negotiating the rugged Union Pass. From there, Potts writes that Weber's party trapped the Green River southwest throughout the spring of 1824. Come autumn they ascended a low ridgeline in the Uinta Mountains and, over the new year, "fell on a considerable river called the Bear." Though Donald McKenzie had roamed the Bear River and its tributaries as early as 1819, the watercourse would not appear on American maps for several years.

Nor does Potts mention when and how Jim Bridger came to join them. The logical conclusion is that Bridger split off from Andrew Henry on the Bighorn and made his way to the Crow encampment sometime after Jed Smith's departure for South Pass. Wintering over with the Crow, Weber and his men had accustomed themselves to the disfiguring facial scars Smith was left with after the grizzly attack. But the still-angry lesions, despite having lost their bright crimson flush, must have taken Bridger aback on first sight of his old mentor.

Smith told Weber, Bridger, and the rest all he had learned about the Hudson's Bay Company's operations during his stay at Flathead Post. It remains unrecorded if he realized at the time that he and his party had squared a circle created by a series of previous isolated explorers. Scaling mountains, traversing ancient lava plains, and penetrating primeval forests, they were the first Americans since Lewis and Clark to cross the Continental Divide north and west of the Three Forks; the first Americans since Andrew Henry fifteen years earlier to trap the Columbia River's drainage along the upper Salmon and Pierre's Hole; and the first Americans since the Astorians to pass through Jackson Hole and the Teton Pass. In the process the Smith-led troop had become the only Americans to range from South Pass to North Pass along the western edge of the continent's high cordilleras. But topography was not at the front of Smith's mind at the moment: he concluded his discourse to Weber's men with a warning about Ogden's oncoming brigade.

At that Bridger surprised Smith with news of his own. Not long before he had accepted a wager and followed the Bear to its mouth. There, sloshing through the forty-five thousand acres of wetlands then forming the river's delta, he dismounted to drink from a lake.* The water he described was so briny—its salinity in places three to eight times higher than any of the earth's oceans—that Bridger was convinced he had reached an arm of the Pacific. At this Smith's mind surely began to churn. Although hardly as single-minded as William Ashley about the existence of the Rio Buenaventura, Smith was well aware of the potential value of such a find.

Even as late as the mid-1820s, the most trusted maps of the western United States were an amalgam of Native American hearsay, Spanish supposition, British guesswork, French fancy, and wishful thinking. A few respected scientific journals even postulated that the Great Salt Lake was drained by a giant whirlpool that connected to the Pacific via a network of underground rivers. In truth, the vast area between the Rocky Mountains and the Spanish missions dotting the Pacific coast—nearly one and a half million square miles—remained terra incognita to all European Americans. East of the Rockies, the valleys of the Missouri River and its tributaries had been heavily explored; to the southwest the Santa Fe Trail had opened similar vistas. And, of course, the northern latitudes west of the mountains had been combed by multiple Canadian explorers and trappers. But few white men had crossed the empty land that lay in between. Moreover, the isolated journeys of those who had slipped along the edges of this Great Basin and lived to tell about it added little to the general stock of geographic knowledge.

Gen. Ashley, for instance, was working off the era's most widely accepted depiction of this territory, John King Robinson's 1819 *Map of Mexico, Louisiana, & the Missouri Territory &c.* Robinson had borrowed details from the charts and drawings of the German geographer Alexander von Humboldt's 1804 explorations into northern New Spain, Zebulon Pike's

---

* Within a century, man-made dams, diversions, and dikes had reduced these wetlands to three thousand acres.

expedition across Colorado two years later, and the subsequent publication of the cartography of Lewis and Clark. So sketchy was true knowledge of the topography of the Great Basin that the mapmaker may as well have added the notation "Here Be Dragons." Further, the hallmark of Robinson's atlas was a large lake just west of the Rocky Mountains from which a river flowed into San Francisco Bay. South of this river ran yet another waterway, nearly paralleling its course, that emptied into the Pacific below Monterey. Not one but two Rio Buenaventuras!

This was, of course, mere self-deception, as William Ashley was presently discovering on his voyage down the Green River. The sheer fantasy of the magical river to the Pacific flowing from the briny lake whose water Jim Bridger had tasted was confirmed by a party of Ute Indians, who made clear to Bridger that the pool had no outlet. Thus the fact that Bridger had become the first white man to lay eyes on Utah's Great Salt Lake was overshadowed by the disappointment of once again not finding even a single Rio Buenaventura.*

As it was, Smith, Bridger, and the other Americans had more immediate concerns than the chimerical watercourse. The British, as the saying went, were coming.

* * *

The hunting season had not begun well for Peter Skene Ogden. First, he had stewed for nearly two months in the snowbound Lemhi Valley. Then he had lost the American Jed Smith's trail. Now, in early May, having crossed the low divide between the south fork of the Snake River and descended into the Bear River Valley, he and his trappers saw much beaver sign but few of the animals themselves. The answer to this mystery was supplied when he encountered a band of Shoshone, the same "Snakes," he deduced,

---

* Donald McKenzie, who never followed the Bear River to its mouth, surmised that the Bear drained into the Colorado River. Had he trapped farther south, he might have been celebrated as the first European American to set eyes on the largest saltwater lake in the Western Hemisphere. As it is, some modern-day historians of the nineteenth-century fur trade, extrapolating from oral histories of Etienne Provost's travels, posit that Provost may have encountered the Great Salt Lake some months before Jim Bridger.

who had attacked Pierre Tivanitagon's Iroquois the previous year. Despite mutual suspicions—"They appeared very doubtful of us & we so equally in regard to them," Ogden noted in his journal—an uneasy parley ensued.

The Indians told Ogden that a large party of American trappers—Weber's men—had already scoured this country clean of plews. The same outfit, they added, was now working the lower Bear. This was the precise direction Ogden had intended taking. Considering this "a fatal blow to our expectations," he instead turned for what the Shoshone called Willow Valley—a north-south-running hollow spanning the border of today's northeastern Utah and southeastern Idaho. The swale was part of a chain of small mountain basins carved by glaciers 120 millennia ago, and to Ogden's delight, the streams flowing down from the surrounding rough hills left by the ice floe's retreat teemed with beaver.

Taking an average of eighty prime pelts a day over the next several weeks, Ogden's spirits rose. At this rate, he calculated, he was well on his way to breaking Alexander Ross's record as well as fulfilling George Simpson's directive to trap the territory clean. Moving down through Willow Valley, he noted in his journal the thousands of gulls flying overhead, indicating that he was close to some large body of water. When his party reached the valley's southern terminus and traversed the Wellsville Mountains, a spur of the Wasatch Range, he dropped down into the lowlands that currently hold the Utah city that today bears Ogden's name. Ogden was now well below the Snake River Country, a mere twenty miles or so east of the Great Salt Lake. Previous Hudson's Bay expeditions had ventured into the Bear River Valley and overstepped the Snake River watershed to hunt northern Nevada, southern Oregon, and even parts of northern California. But this was as far south as any British-Canadian excursion had ever sojourned. And here Ogden's fortunes turned again.

On the evening of May 22, one of his trappers rode into camp accompanied by two white men and a small escort of mounted Ute. To Ogden's astonishment, several of his own freemen greeted the white strangers as old comrades. Which, in fact, they were—these were two of the fourteen

Hudson's Bay Company deserters who had scuffed into Fort Atkinson almost three years earlier. The tale of their relentless roundelay back into the
mountains, told now over a stoking bonfire, beggared belief.

It took but a few weeks on American soil, their tale went, for the stranded
defectors to conclude that the U.S. Army had no intention of redressing the
crimes committed upon them by the Crow and Cheyenne. They also felt
themselves decidedly *de trop* in foreign territory. As such, eight of the men
had enlisted in a trapping concern piloted by Etienne Provost—something
of a borderlands celebrity in the St. Louis environs since emigrating to Missouri from Quebec in the early nineteenth century. Not least of Provost's
notoriety stemmed from the two months he and the venerable August
Chouteau had spent in a Santa Fe *calabozo* ten years earlier as guests of
His Most Christian Majesty Ferdinand VII of Spain. Provost and Chouteau,
heading a surreptitious trapping expedition into Spanish Colorado's upper
Arkansas River, had been arrested by a company of blue-and-gray-clad *sol-
dados* and detained under hellish conditions before being expelled back to
the United States. Over the ensuing decade Provost had dined out so often
on the strength of the dramatic retelling of his jailhouse saga that it was said
that he now so filled his buckskins that his portraitist needed to send out
for extra paint.

In the wake of Mexican independence, Provost and another French
Canadian known to history only as LeClerc spied a main chance.* They
outfitted a trapping company at Fort Atkinson that included the eight Hudson's Bay deserters and, following old William Becknell's Santa Fe Trail,
made for Taos. From there they rode north into Colorado and swept the
serrated Sangre de Cristo range, the "Blood of Christ" mountains that constitute the most southern spur of the American Rockies. Moving inexorably

---

* Provost's surname was pronounced "Provo," the spelling of the Utah city and river that today honor his
heritage. Moreover, as the historian Dale Morgan frustratingly submits, "So many LeClaires, LeCleres, and
LeClercs were scattered all over the [contemporaneous] fur-trade literature that identification of any one of
them at a given time or place is usually an act of faith." Morgan nonetheless takes a stab, guessing that it was
Francois LeClaire, one of the original Astorians, with whom Etienne Provost partnered.

northwest, Provost's company crossed the San Luis Valley and began trapping the headwaters of the Rio Grande in the San Juan Mountains.

Although the mysterious LeClerc had shuttled pack trains to and from Taos to sell and trade plews for supplies, by the time Provost and his trappers reached the pine-blanketed southern slopes of the Uinta Mountains, most of his men had been in the field for two years. Along their travels they had survived lethal blizzards, wolves and grizzlies, avalanches, and even a Shoshone ambush that left seven of their crew dead. Although neither Provost nor LeClerc was aware of it, this meant that while Jed Smith, Thomas Fitzpatrick, Jim Clyman, and Bill Sublette had been combing the upper valley of the Green River in the spring of 1824, Provost and LeClerc were trapping just south across the Uinta Range. Thereafter Provost led his company north, which is how they had come to take advantage of Peter Skene Ogden's hospitality.

The morning after the arrival of Ogden's surprise guests, as the Hudson's Bay Company's Booshway chewed over the repercussions of the burgeoning American presence throughout the area, Provost himself rode into the Canadian camp with several of his trappers. Despite his girth, the fortysomething Provost, sporting the sword-edged black goatee that had become his trademark, remained a dangerous man. And today he was not in an agreeable mood.

With or without proof, it was a matter of faith among Americans, including Provost, that British provocateurs were behind the Shoshone antagonism toward any trappers not flying the Hudson's Bay Company colors. During the brief, contentious meeting between the two Quebecois, Provost blamed Ogden for the Indian skirmish that resulted in the deaths of seven of his men the previous fall. Ogden, rightly, protested that the Shoshone were equal-opportunity plunderers. Provost was not mollified and stormed off. Ogden observed that had Provost's party not been so outgunned, "they would most willingly shoot us if they dared." The day's drama had only just begun.

Later that same afternoon a tattered cavalcade of forty or so mounted men approached Ogden's encampment from the west. They were led by the bull goose free trapper Johnson Gardner, an old Henry-Ashley hand from the early Yellowstone expeditions. Gardner, flying the Stars and Stripes from his saddle's flag boot, had been traveling with John Henry Weber and was incensed over Jed Smith's tales of the Canadians trespassing on American soil on their route to North Pass. Gardner's breaking point was Smith's account of Ogden's column marching under the Hudson's Bay banner that featured the Union Jack.

Outlined against a lambent sunset, Gardner halted his men one hundred yards from Ogden's campsite. Several tense, silent moments ensued during that daunting period that the French-speaking among both crews referred to as *entre Chien et Loup*—between the dog and the wolf, between the known and the unknown. Gardner broke the spell. All of Ogden's trappers, he hollered, were trespassing on U.S. territory. More to the point, he continued, he was prepared to offer $3.50 a pound for their beaver pelts. This was five times the price Ogden was paying. The freemen and the Iroquois, Gardner said, owed the British company nothing. He swept his arm in the direction of his riders. Many of your own compatriots, he said, have already come over to us.

He then turned to Ogden. "You have had these men already too long in your service, and have most shamefully imposed on them, treating them as slaves, selling them goods at high prices and giving them nothing for their skins." Murmurs of assent rose among the Canadians. Ogden surreptitiously signaled Kittson to round up and hobble their horses. As the sun disappeared behind the western peaks, the standoff continued through the night. At daybreak Gardner made his move. Entering Ogden's tent, he demanded that the Canadian produce a license that allowed him to trap this far south. If not, he was to depart immediately. "Remain at your peril," Gardner growled.

The surly Canadian knew this game well. Intimidation had once been his daily bread. He calmly replied that it was for London and Washington to determine to whom this land belonged. When his own government instructed him to withdraw, then and only then would he retreat. The irony that both men were currently south of the forty-second parallel and thus facing off on sovereign Mexican soil appeared to occur to neither man.

With that, Gardener began circulating among the freemen and Iroquois lodges exhorting the Canadian trappers to join him. Ogden, Kittson, and several loyalists raced to secure all the furs they had previously taken. The atmospherics escalated to the point where the two parties leveled guns at each other. Ogden, perhaps more wary than his American antagonist of sparking an international incident, ordered his men to stand down. In the confusion, eleven of the Iroquois under Pierre Tivanitagon and five of Ogden's freemen managed to snatch their plews and cross to the American lines. Many left their Indigenous wives and mixed-race children to the Hudson's Bay Company's tender mercies.

In ways far and wide, Peter Skene Ogden was a hired thug. But he was not stupid. Despite his bravura about standing his ground, he knew when he was beaten. Gardner and his overwhelming posse, now close to sixty men, never lowered their rifles as the Canadians trooped back over the Wellsville pass and into the Willow Valley.

That night, Ogden doubled his guard. He also instructed Kittson to take several men and lay in wait south of the main camp in order to intercept any trappers having second thoughts about joining the Americans—to no avail, as it happened, as three more freemen managed to slip away with their haul of pelts. By candlelight Ogden, contemplating his sudden peripeteia, put pen to paper to vent his frustrations.

"Here I am," his journal entry reads, "Surrounded on all Sides by enemies & our expectations & hopes blasted for returns this year." He added that to continue trapping below the Snake River Country or even along its southern rim would in essence put him in the employ of the Americans for no wage, as he did not trust the freemen who remained with him to forgo the lure of $3.50 a pound as long as they were so near to its source. He was, of course, correct, and by the time he had put enough distance between his outfit and the Americans he had lost a total of twenty-nine men and with them some seven hundred plews.

Nor, from Ogden's point of view, did it now make sense to follow Gov. Simpson's directive to make for the waiting ship at Fort George. The meager packs of furs he'd managed to retain would barely take up space in the vessel's hold. He would be a laughingstock. Instead, he divided his party into two skeleton crews. He would lead the first toward Fort Nez Perces via the beaver hunting grounds of Clark's Fork and the western Missouri. A second column under Kittson would trap its way back to Flathead Post via North Pass. This was technically U.S. territory; he did not care.

The two arrived at their respective trading posts in the autumn of 1825 with just over three thousand plews between them. This was a tolerable haul. But it belied the calamitous nature of the expedition. George Simpson's stratagem of bleeding the Snake River Country dry would have to wait for future seasons. Peter Skene Ogden knew well that the governor was not going to be happy. Indeed, it struck him that if the territory was going to be converted into a fur desert, it just might be the encroaching Americans who would complete the task. His own gloom stood in graphic relief to the jubilation pervading his adversaries' camps.

CHAPTER 17

"RANDAVOUZE CREEK"

Swirling south on the Green River's brawny current, William Ashley sped out of western Wyoming and into present-day Utah. He was more than one hundred miles below the mouth of the Black Forks, Jed Smith's old hunting grounds, when the suspicion set in. He sensed that he and the six men crewing his sizable bullboat were not following anything resembling the Rio Buenaventura toward the Pacific.

The vessel's pilots had expertly navigated the rapids of Utah's Flaming Gorge—which Indigenous canoers had long avoided as the most dangerous on the river.* And Ashley, who could not swim, barely avoided drowning in an eddy along the boulder-strewn falls of Split Mountain Canyon. It was just beyond this drop where they encountered a hunting party of Ute—the "Eutau tribe" Ashley called them in his journal. Distant cousins of the Shoshone, the two tribes were often conflated by trappers. In this case, the Indians' casual demeanors—none seemed even moderately intrigued by the appearance of the hairy strangers—told Ashley that this was not their first encounter with white men.

---

* The Flaming Gorge cataract, whose walls at the time rose to more than one thousand feet on either side, was briefly christened "Ashley's Falls." It is for the moment—dependent on the ongoing western American drought—subsumed by the Flaming Gorge Reservoir.

A cryptic sign-language dialogue ensued. Ashley finally presented two small pennants. One depicted the Stars and Stripes, the other the Union Jack. The Indians pointed to the former, clapped the little general's shoulders, and produced a calumet and hare-skin pouch of kinnikinick. After adding tobacco to the pipe and smoking, Ashley purchased horses from the band. At their urging, he followed them to what he hoped would be the encampment of either Jed Smith or John Henry Weber. Instead, he was led to the main bivouac of Etienne Provost. Provost, having entered the Great Basin from the south, assured Ashley that his intuition was correct. The Green River, far from flowing into the Rio Buenaventura, was but a tributary of the Rio Colorado.

Ashley's disappointment was tempered by Provost's next words—Provost had learned from his own roaming trappers that Jed Smith had recently reunited with John Henry Weber. Both men, he said, were currently working the lower Bear River with a passel of free trappers. Further, they had been joined by a party of defectors from the Hudson's Bay Company. Provost said that the remainder of the Canadians, led by a man named Ogden, had been driven back north. Ashley in turn told Provost of his plans for a summer rendezvous and mentioned that on his downriver journey he had chanced upon the perfect setting.

What Ashley called "Randavouze Creek"—and what was later, albeit briefly, renamed Henry's Fork—is a short, placid affluent that originates in Utah's Uinta Mountains and flows north into Wyoming, where it empties into the Green.* There was much beaver sign on the stream as well as along the smaller brooks that fed it. It was at the sandy mouth of this watercourse, near a pretty grove of willow trees, where Ashley told Provost that he had "made marks indicative of my intention to randavouze here."

Via Provost and his network, word of the gathering site spread rapidly among the trapping crews working the tributaries of the Green and the

---

* Not to be confused with Henry's Fork of the Snake River, nearly four hundred miles to the north in Idaho and named after Maj. Andrew Henry.

Bear. By late June 1825, in parties large and small, the men, greasy as always, began to drift in. Soon there were 120 in all as well as several bands of curious Ute. More's the pity that there are no detailed contemporaneous chronicles of this inaugural Mountain Man Rendezvous. One is left to imagine the surprise and pleasure Jed Smith, Bill Sublette, and the others felt in finding Jim Clyman veritably risen from the grave. And though Smith's most emotional outpourings appear to have been reserved for religious services, he nonetheless possessed a deep warmth for the men he considered friends. Thus his bittersweet reunion with Thomas Fitzpatrick, who only days earlier had lost a man to an Arapaho war party, was surely just as heartfelt.

Many of the free trappers knew each other from having worked the Rockies over the years with sundry outfits. Like Ogden's Canadians happily greeting the long-lost deserters, the yarns that must have been exchanged among these old companions luxuriating beneath blue fugs of tobacco haze issuing from clay pipes were no doubt prodigious. Years later, the loquacious Jim Beckwourth recalled that physical competitions dominated this first assemblage: "hunting, fishing, target shooting, foot racing, gymnastics and sundry other exercises."

Settled behind a makeshift driftwood table off to the side of the revelry, one person was in fact keeping meticulous records. But William Ashley was not recording homecoming scenes or eavesdropping on back-pounding conversations. Awash in beaver skins, he was toting his figures—202 pounds from the free trapper Caleb Greenwood, 189 from Isaac Galbraith, 136 from Thyery Goddin. So it went for days; the free trappers, the former Hudson's Bay men, and Provost's hands lining up to trade their catch for supplies while Ashley's own hivernants handed over pelts by the bale. These included the eighteen hundred that Jed Smith's little troop had cached the previous spring.

By the time the transactions were complete, Ashley had collected 8,829 pounds of fur. This, in his estimation, was worth between $45,000 and $50,000 on the St. Louis market. Today that would make him a millionaire.

In exchange for the plews, he traded coffee and sugar at $1.50 a pound, moccasin awls at $2 per dozen, steel knives at $2.50 apiece, and thick blue cloth blankets at $6 a yard. All this while the cylinders of his mind turned like a set of bank-vault tumblers falling into place.

Ashley's dire financial circumstances as well as the desire for patriotic recognition had compelled him to journey into the mountains during the cruelest winter months. When he had concocted his plan to gather all his company at one site, it was for the sake of safety and convenience. He had no notion that Etienne Provost's outfit was in the vicinity, nor that he would be collecting pelts from free trappers and disaffected Canadians. But the enthusiasm the assorted companies showed for his trade fair planted the seed of an idea. What if he did this annually?

Future summer conclaves could be supplied by packhorses or even wagon trains traversing the gentler grades of South Pass in more suitable weather. This alone would not only shave five hundred miles off the winding Upper Missouri river routes but also eliminate the expense of large crews of voyageurs to man the unwieldy keelboats. Further, unlike the path Jed Smith had blazed through the Badlands, in the spring and summer months the Platte River corridor provided ample water and game, fuel for fires, and forage for wagon teams.

Ashley had also noticed a growing disdain among the trappers for what they considered the constraints of flatlander life. Several told him they would be happy enough never to leave the high country for "the comparative thralldom of civilization," as a Missouri newspaper reporter put it. And if he were to become the conduit between these Mountain Men and the St. Louis merchants, delivering needed provisions in exchange for their peltry, this would make him even wealthier. From a logistical point of view, it all made perfect sense.

As Ashley saw it, the northern passes across the Continental Divide opened by Lewis and Clark, by John Colter, by the hapless Astorians, had served their purpose. They were too towering, too isolated, and as often as not too snowbound to provide a means to a profitable end. They also presented a further risk in that they were continually patrolled by the un-yielding Blackfeet. In addition, just to reach prime beaver lands, trapping outfits need to run a hostile gauntlet of still-seething Arikara, belligerent Nez Perce, horse-thieving Assiniboin, and a Sioux Nation that was increas-ingly turning against the whites. Since the onset of his and Andrew Henry's operations three years earlier, they had lost several scores of men, untold horseflesh, and thousands of dollars in furs, equipage, and provisions to Indian attacks coming and going along the Upper Missouri. The calamities that had befallen the Missouri Fur Company's Immell and Jones on the Musselshell—still fresh in everyone's mind—cut a deep impression.

That threat, however, could now be eliminated by following the Platte River corridor. Despite the presence of Pawnee, Crow, and Shoshone along this new trace, Ashley reckoned that each tribe had proven that they could be dealt with—or bought off—with a deft enough touch. He intuited that the Crow in particular, with their uncompromising animus toward the Blackfeet and the Sioux, might even be turned into stalwart allies. *Amicus meus, inimicus inimici mei.* The enemy of my enemy is my friend. As for this new Arapaho menace? He was confident that, in time, he would con-coct a solution.

Then there was the new approach to the fur business that he and An-drew Henry had pioneered. Despite the government's obsolete regulations, the days of operating out of far-flung trading posts were over. The stockades were hard to defend and harder to maintain and supply. The number of abandoned establishments along the Missouri and its tributaries, begin-ning with Manuel Lisa's old Fort Raymond on the Bighorn, was testament to the futility of forting up. And with the streams and ponds on the eastern slopes of the Rockies becoming progressively trapped out, erecting posts along the remote tramontane regions was a fool's errand. The Hudson's Bay Company, a musclebound, Crown-backed monopoly, had the capital to cover loss-leading outposts. The smaller American outfits did not.

But above all, annual summer trade marts would go far in establishing the vast swaths of land on the windward side of the continent's majestic stone hills as *American* territory. The rendezvous might be William Ash-ley's immediate moneymaking idea, but the expansion of the United States would serve as his legacy.

For his plan to work, however, Ashley needed a new partner, a field captain with intelligence and courage and experience. In short, he needed a vibrant leader like Jedediah Smith, whose stony grit had, in but three years, come to equal the high country he explored. In Smith, Ashley rec-ognized a man whose besetting humors were tensile strength and tung-sten competence—precisely the traits called for in this wild territory while Ashley managed financial affairs as the company's *fonctionnaire* in the still very Francophile St. Louis.

It is not recorded how Ashley posed this proposition to Smith. It is known that he enthusiastically accepted. After the deal was struck, the two men began to devise their next courses of action.

Their first order of business was hauling nearly nine thousand pounds of furs out of the mountains. They agreed that a pack train to the Bighorn was their best option, and from there bullboats down the Yellowstone to the Missouri. With luck, General Atkinson's army expedition and, more crucial, his government keelboats, would still be somewhere in the vicinity. Let the U.S. Army provide not only transportation through Indian Country but a mighty military escort as well. Finally, as someone had to return to the mountains in the fall with winter provisions, it was decided that Smith would descend with Ashley and subsequently handle that chore. They then collected the lists of necessities from both their own men and the free trap-pers: powder and shot and gun locks; tobacco and coffee and soap; kettles and trap springs and brass nails.

At some point Ashley was approached by "Le Grand Pierre" Tivanita-gon. He and his Iroquois, the old headman said, would likely be trapping far to the north when Smith returned to the mountains. But he looked forward to next summer's rendezvous and presented his wish list of sup-plies to be transported for the gathering. Aside from basic trade goods, Tivanitagon asked if Ashley could also pack in several bolts of colored silk and sewing needles as well as assorted earrings, ribbons, and combs for his women. If possible, he also wanted strings of "slay bells" with which to adorn his Indian ponies.

To the white trappers, the request for such Indian "fofarraw," as they termed it, was laughable. Their mocking grins quickly faded when Tiva-nitagon added his last items: whiskey and rum. Much whiskey and rum. Even the teetotaling Jed Smith could not deny that the mountaineers who risked their lives at backbreaking work across hostile tribal lands de-served a keg, or ten, as a reward.

So it was that no future rendezvous were ever conducted without hard liquor to lubricate the proceedings.

*   *   *

Jed Smith and William Ashley departed the little willow grove on Hen-ry's Fork in early July. Their caravan consisted of fifty mounted retainers, including Jim Bridger, Thomas Fitzpatrick, John Henry Weber, Jim Beck-wourth, and an equal number of fur-bearing packhorses acquired from the Ute. The lanky Bill Sublette, who in his short time working with Ash-ley and Smith had burned like a cool flame, was the natural choice to be named Booshway of those remaining in the mountains.

The caravan followed the Green and Big Sandy Rivers before traversing South Pass, where one man was killed by a grizzly when he strayed too far into tangled brush to empty his bowels. Riders often dropped to the rear to screen the trailing packs of gray wolves and coyotes lurking just out of rifle range waiting for a horse to collapse. The troop then retraced Smith's path of two years earlier from the opposite direction—down the Popo Agie to the Wind, down the Wind to the Bighorn, down the Bighorn to the Yel-lowstone, and down the Yellowstone to the Missouri. They took the usual, blood-earned precautions against Indian attack, including scouts flanked out to all four compass points while traveling and nighttime campsites defended by makeshift breastworks. Additional sentries were also posted to attend the hobbled horses.

Despite the safeguards, the train was bushwhacked twice by Indian war parties. What Smith presumed to be a rogue band of horse-stealing Crow attacked one night to no avail, retreating after a gunfight without even recovering two of their dead. Farther north, along the Yellowstone, Blackfeet warriors managed to make off with eighteen horses by so spooking the animals with their screams and gunshots that the mustangs burst their hobbles and stampeded. Though no trappers were killed, one was wounded. It is a measure of the mundanity of the violence that permeated the mountain west that Gen. Ashley could describe his return trip through the Upper Missouri country as "nothing remarkable." This may have had something to do with the fact that he lost no pelts.

Upon reaching the confluence of the Yellowstone and the Missouri, it was almost as if Ashley's meeting with Gen. Atkinson had been prearranged. For there, at noon on August 19, they found the general's expedition encamped at what was left of the old fort established by Andrew Henry. Equally fortuitous, three keelboats were tied up at the water's edge. Atkinson and his troop, accompanied by the Indian Affairs subagent Benjamin O'Fallon, had only just returned from the Three Forks, where they had been unsuccessful in locating, much less proffering treaties to, the Blackfeet.

Atkinson and O'Fallon had what they believed to be more success with the various bands of Sioux, Cheyenne, Crow, Mandan, Otoe, and Pawnee who had met with them to touch the pen to friendship accords. Their would-be successes were mere fool's gold. As the Arikara negotiating with Col. Henry Leavenworth two years earlier had sensed, the peacemaking ceremonies were in truth rather pointless formalities, as the Indians had no real understanding of what they were agreeing to or, as was commonly the case, giving away. Conversely, the government usually had no intention of living up to the transactional terms of most signed bargains.* To that end the Native American participants often treated the performances as jokes,

---

* This was evidenced by plans being hatched in Washington, DC, that very year to forcibly remove large segments of the eastern tribes who had signed treaties to an "Indian Country" in modern-day Oklahoma.

passing off drunks and the mentally unstable as chiefs while accepting gifts of blankets and beads and slyly inquiring if Gen. Atkinson had guns for sale (he did not). Upon Atkinson's departure, the Native Americans would continue to live their lives as if nothing had changed.

As it was, to Atkinson and O'Fallon the sight of Henry Ashley's and Jedediah Smith's bullboats streaming down the Yellowstone piled high with stacks of peltry merely capped what they considered a triumphant voyage. After the trappers stowed their treasure in the vessels' cargo boxes, the remainder of the two-thousand-mile river journey was something of a mobile celebration. Above Council Bluff they found Joshua Pilcher, making plans for his reconstituted Missouri Fur Company's autumn mountain excursion. Pilcher presented Ashley with a gift—an adult grizzly bear shackled by a thick chain around its neck.* Then the trappers were honored with a rolling cannon salute as they approached Fort Atkinson.

Reaching St. Louis on October 4 and dropping anchor "under the hill," the company was feted by thousands of the Mound City's residents, in Jim Beckwourth's recollection, "hail[ing] our landing with shouts that deafened our ears."

Ashley deposited and reweighed his skins at the fur brokers' auction house before scuttling off to settle accounts with his debtors. With an eye toward accruing future political capital, he also ordered Beckwourth to re-gift the grizzly "as a pet" to the vivaciously handsome Major Thomas Biddle, the War of 1812 hero who had married into the wealthiest merchant family in Missouri. Ashley was well aware that Biddle's older brother was president of the Bank of the United States. Beckwourth notes that while chaining the bear to an apple tree on Biddle's property, "he made a furious spring at me; the chain, very fortunately, was a strong one, and held him fast." Such were the times.

---

* Ashley placed Beckwourth in charge of the care and feeding of the *Ursus arctos horribilis* chained to the deck of one of the keelboats. After fortifying himself daily with "a few glasses of 'artificial courage,'" the gaudy liar confesses in his memoir to feeling "exceedingly valorous" in his dealings with the old silverback, "who seemed to think himself Captain of the ship."

Jed Smith spent the next several weeks ricocheting between blacksmiths, horse traders, saddlers, gunsmiths, and shopkeepers to gather supplies for the return trip west. As Smith's now-well-paid compatriots were feted into what Dickens called "gincoherence" in the grogshops and rum shacks of the burgeoning metropolis, Smith celebrated quietly by attending several Methodist services at the city's old courthouse. As he once wrote to his parents, "God only knows, I feel the need of the wach & care of the Christian Church." It was also during his brief St. Louis sojourn that Smith stood as an usher when William Ashley, in a coup de foudre, took one Eliza Christy as his second bride. No doubt many of the reception's guests wondered as to the identity of the young man with the horribly scarred face in the groom's train.

A mere thirty months earlier, Smith had enlisted as one of the Henry-Ashley Company's rawest high-country recruits. Now he was the most traveled American west of the continent's great cordillera as well as a co-owner of the firm. His fund of experience and information was such that when he stopped by Gen. William Clark's office to apply for his permit to re-enter Indian Country, the general pumped him for descriptions of the fantastic and breathtaking lands and peoples beyond the mountains. Clark well knew that Smith's "discoveries" would be of no small interest to the White House, the War Department, and the people of the Union so eager to expand U.S. territory.

* * *

On October 30, 1825, Jed Smith departed St. Louis at the head of a sixty-man company, a mix of trappers and engagés. He led 160 horses and pack mules hauling provisions valued at $20,000. In a fulsome report overbrimming with superlatives, the St. Louis–based *Missouri Republic*—never mentioning Smith by name—noted that "a party of men in the employ of Gen. Ashley [was off] to the bosom of the mountains." The rival *Missouri Advocate* assured its readers that, once through South Pass, these intrepid cavaliers would commence their beaver hunts "down the several rivers which go to the Pacific ocean."

The reference to the nonexistent if abiding idea of multiple tributaries running into the Rio Buenaventura had obviously come from Ashley himself. The man was hopelessly addicted to the irrational notion—the madness of the sane, modern psychoanalysts call it—and clung to a conversation he claimed to have had with a band of Indians during the Rendezvous. The native peoples, he said, had described for him a mighty river flowing out of the "extreme west end" of the Great Salt Lake. Ashley never named the tribesmen who shared this information. They were obviously not the Ute who, plenty familiar with the lake and its environs, had assured Jim Bridger that the great inland sea was self-enclosed.

That Jedediah Strong Smith, at Gen. William Henry Ashley's urgings, would continue the search for these mysterious waterways was a given. Smith had no idea that in the pursuit of this quest he would become the first American to cross and recross the vast unmapped portions of the West that no white man had ever before seen. Nor could he have guessed that it would be five long years before he again set foot in St. Louis.

PART III

THE ODYSSEY

My needle is slow to settle . . . but it always settles between west and south-southwest. The future lies that way to me, and the earth seems more unexhausted and richer on that side.

—Henry David Thoreau, *Walking*

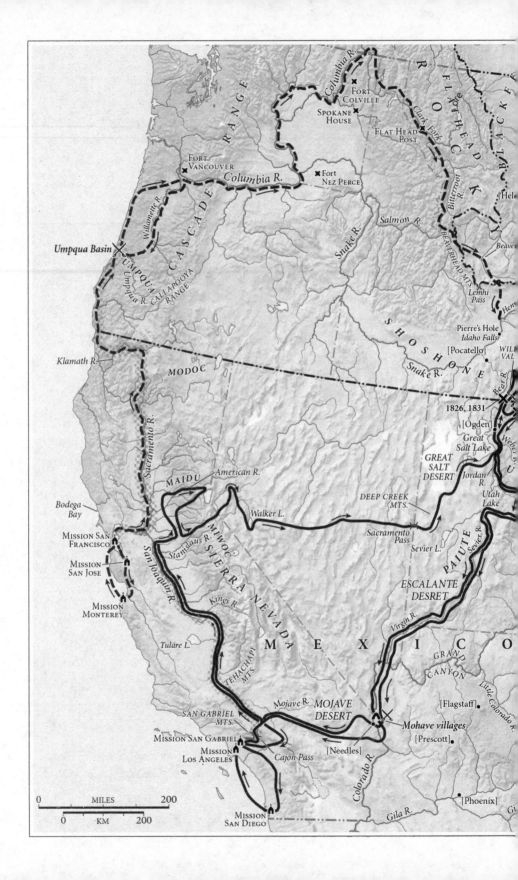

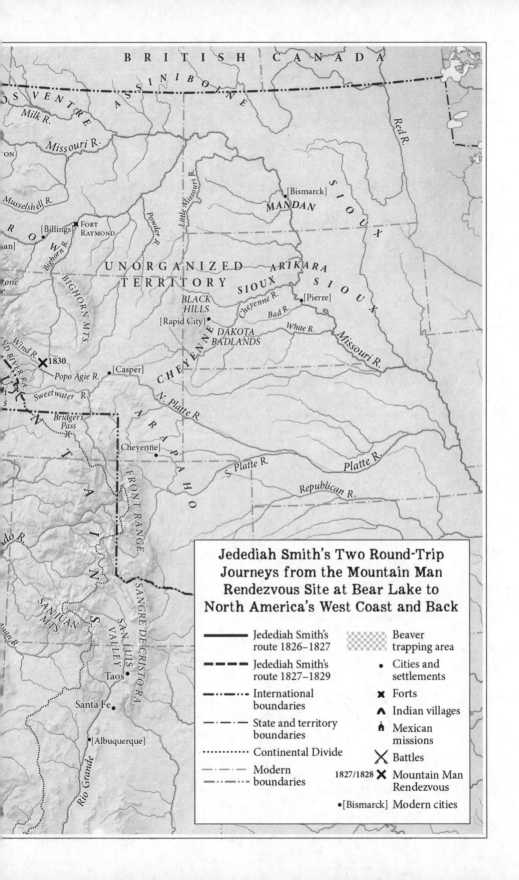

BRITISH CANADA

ASSINIBOINE

GROS VENTRE

Milk R.

Missouri R.

Musselshell R.

Red R.

Little Missouri R.

Powder R.

[Bismarck]

MANDAN

SIOUX

Billings

FORT RAYMOND

Bighorn R.

W. R.

BIGHORN MTS.

UNORGANIZED TERRITORY

ARIKARA

SIOUX

SIOUX

BLACK HILLS

Cheyenne R.

[Pierre]

[Rapid City]

Bad R.

DAKOTA BADLANDS

White R.

Missouri R.

Wind R.

1830

ND RIVER R.

Popo Agie R.

[Casper]

CHEYENNE

Sweetwater R.

N. Platte R.

Bridger's Pass

[Cheyenne]

ARAPAHO

S. Platte R.

Platte R.

Republican R.

FRONT RANGE

SAN JUAN MTS.

SANGRE DE CRISTO

SAN LUIS VALLEY

Taos

Santa Fe

[Albuquerque]

Rio Grande

Colorado R.

Jedediah Smith's Two Round-Trip Journeys from the Mountain Man Rendezvous Site at Bear Lake to North America's West Coast and Back

——— Jedediah Smith's route 1826–1827	▦ Beaver trapping area	
— — — Jedediah Smith's route 1827–1829	• Cities and settlements	
—··— International boundaries	✖ Forts	
—·—· State and territory boundaries	⋀ Indian villages	
·········· Continental Divide	⋔ Mexican missions	
—·—·— Modern boundaries	✕ Battles	
	1827/1828 ✖ Mountain Man Rendezvous	
	•[Bismarck] Modern cities	

CHAPTER 18

EASTERN STIRRINGS

A soft snow swirled from the sky on the morning of November 1, 1825, as Jedediah Smith's pack train, bypassing Fort Atkinson, veered off from the turbid current of the Missouri. Seven hundred miles to the west, along the now-familiar Platte River route, rose the Rocky Mountains. Despite the brisk air and snow cover, the trail soon smelled of sweat and shit and piss, human and animal, that rose to form a sour miasma over the long thread traversing the prairie. Among the trappers traveling with Smith were a veritable pantheon of hard men destined to become high-country legends, including Jim Bridger, Thomas Fitzpatrick, John Henry Weber, Jim Clyman, and Jim Beckwourth. They had been joined by a twenty-two-year-old newcomer to the west named Robert Campbell, with whom Smith immediately struck up so fast a friendship that he would soon designate him the executor of his will.

Campbell, yet another Irish-born adventurer, was the youngest son of a Scottish clan chieftain who had migrated to Ulster's County Tyrone. Sickly as a child, and with no prospect of inheriting his father's land holdings, he decided to seek his fortune in America. Securing a berth on a British barque and alighting in Philadelphia three years earlier, he had drifted west to St. Louis. Campbell still suffered from pulmonary issues, likely a latent form of tuberculosis, and was advised by a Missouri physician that mountain air was the key to restoring his health. Albeit lacking a formal education, Campbell displayed an autodidact's grasp of figures, and Jed Smith and William Ashley hired him as the company's chief clerk. In a sepia-toned photograph taken several years later, the dour-and-dark-visaged Campbell appeared anything but the public's perception of a mousy accountant, with his rooster's comb of thick jet-black hair and a matching tuft of beard dominating a countenance that gazes past the lensman with a lithifying stare.

By a month out, as Smith had undoubtedly foreseen, unrelenting winter storms had set in across the Plains and his mounted party, their kidneys bruised and their hindquarters saddle sore, stopped to spend most of December in an old Pawnee campground on the Republican River. Screened from the blowing snow by a thicket of cottonwood, they used the respite to dry the fresh buffalo meat that hunters brought in and to curry and fatten their horses on tree bark. Come the new year and an unexpected easing of the blizzards, Smith ordered the caravan decamped. Picking up the North Platte, they made for South Pass.

Everyone in Smith's party recognized that this was no mere resupply mission; there were beaver to be taken before the summer Rendezvous. To that end, after traversing South Pass in early 1826, Smith split his company into two platoons. He himself led a larger expedition north toward the Bear River, hoping—fruitlessly, as it occurred—to find Bill Sublette and at least some of the American trappers he had left behind the previous fall. The second troop, with Weber as Booshway and including Bridger, Fitzpatrick, and Beckwourth, pushed west toward the Utah river that now bears Weber's name. It was not long before this company encountered hostiles.

According to Beckwourth, mere days after the two groups separated, a blinding sleet storm forced Weber's trappers to huddle for cover in a rocky box canyon near the present-day site of Ogden, Utah. Such was the miserable weather that the Americans were apparently careless hobbling their horses and mules. They paid for their negligence when a raiding party of Bannock took advantage of the whiteout conditions to run off all eighty of their mounts. For nearly a week Fitzpatrick and Bridger led a small group of men on foot through the rugged Uinta Mountains tracking the Indian sign. When they finally spied the Bannock camp, Fitzpatrick ordered an assault directly into its midst.

The Bannock, cousins to the Northern Shoshone, were known to occasionally roam as far east as western Wyoming, but their tribal lands lay predominantly to the northwest along the current Idaho-Oregon border. As such, their interactions with white men had been limited, and they likely had no idea that these interlopers, lacking mounts no less, could or would follow their trail. Fitzpatrick was well aware of the western adage comparing Indians to wolves—run and they chase; chase and they run. Sure enough, taken aback by Fitzpatrick's audacious charge, most of the Bannock—the semi-reliable Beckwourth puts their number at several hundred—scattered as the Americans whooped and hollered into their midst. The few braves who stood and fought were cut to pieces.

As the triumphant assailants hunted trophies, Bridger and a few men slipped through a thicket of willow and frightened off the Indian boys left to guard the remuda. They not only recovered the stolen stock but also managed to acquire another forty Bannock ponies. When Bridger met Fitzpatrick with his haul of horseflesh, he expected the Irishman to be ecstatic. By now it was well known across the borderlands how much Fitzpatrick hated losing mounts to Native American raids, and how proud he had been to retrieve the eight mustangs pilfered by the hapless Shoshone the previous summer. Instead, Fitzpatrick was disconsolate. He was perfectly willing to kill an Indian for righteous cause, as was the case when he had held his gun to the Shoshone chief's head. But disfigurement was beyond his moral ken, and he had not been able to stop his men—"out for hair" in frontier parlance—from taking six Bannock scalps. Bridger, an avid scalp hunter himself, was nonplussed.

* * *

Meanwhile, thirty miles to the north, Jed Smith had again subdivided his outfit on reaching the Bear River Valley. Caching his Rendezvous supplies, he left a small detachment to trap the streams running into the Bear while he led a group of thirty riders farther west. Traversing the Promontory Mountains—on whose summit the Golden Spike of the transcontinental railroad would be driven forty-three years later—he found the country along the northern shoreline of the Great Salt Lake not only devoid of beaver but the most desolate landscape he had yet to encounter. The dark blue water pouring from the sulfureous springs into the lake proved unpotable, and his horses and chuffing mules—refusing to graze on the tussocks of salt-resistant grasses that barely clung to life along the bleached littoral—began to wither and buckle. Moving farther inland, a chiaroscuro of unending snow fields dotted with gray sagebrush provided meager sustenance for his mounts while the occasional dark and stunted juniper tree beckoned like a medieval rendering of the angel of death. Even the air itself carried the whiff of hellfire, infused as it was with the rotten-egg odor of the hydrogen sulfide emitted from the lake's salt-infested bacteria.

By the time Smith's troop reached the far northwest corner of the briny sheet of water, it was obvious to all that their captain was no longer searching for beaver grounds. Smith was, in fact, determined to either confirm or put to rest the rumor of a river flowing to the Pacific from the western shoreline of the great inland sea. To that end, he instructed Jim Clyman and three others to construct a bullboat and circumnavigate the lake. As the quartet set off in the buffalo-skin vessel, Smith pushed the remainder of his party even farther west toward the high and dry wastelands of northeast Nevada.

It will never be known if Smith expected to somehow miraculously greet Clyman and his waterborne companions on the Rio Buenaventura somewhere along these barrens. As it happened, hugging the southern rim of the Great Salt Desert, he ventured through isolated patches of spiny greasewood and dense shadscale whose leafy bract and tiny fruit flowers managed to barely sustain his horses. His mules, however, refused to browse on the tar-tasting vegetation and took to gnawing on the cracked leather of their pack saddles and even nipping at each other's tails. With his men surviving on stringy rabbit meat and the occasional sage grouse, a desperate Smith finally veered north toward the Snake River Country. As his troop turned, so did its luck.

The area surrounding the confluence of the Snake and Salmon Rivers in today's western Idaho had been trapped extensively as recently as the summer of 1824 by Alexander Ross of the Hudson's Bay Company. But the beaver stock had rebounded remarkably in the intermittent two years, and Smith's hunters took pelts aplenty as they hopscotched east through the river valleys of the Boise, the Payette, the Big Wood, and the Big Lost. With their remaining pack animals staggering under the weight of the oily plews, the Americans finally alighted in southeastern Idaho in June 1826. From there they dropped down into Willow Valley, the designated site for the second great summer Rendezvous. By this time the little basin straddling today's Utah-Idaho border was already acquiring a new name— Cache Valley, indicative of the multiple packs of pelts various teams of trappers had buried in the glacial vale in anticipation of Smith's return with provisions.

To Smith's great good surprise, awaiting him at the Rendezvous site was Jim Clyman, who reported no western river flowing from the Great Salt Lake. Clyman recounted having "coasted the lake" for twenty-four days; he and his three companions—finding no fresh water until reaching its southern extremity—had survived on a diet of tiny brine shrimp and pintail ducks and Canada geese shot from the sky. Clyman, however, did speculate as to a seasonable estuary running through what he took to be a possible, if currently dry, cut in the lake's western bank. In reality, what he had undoubtedly happened upon was an ancient opening in the shoreline through which water had retreated from the Great Salt Desert and into the lake some eleven thousand years earlier.

Smith took in Clyman's report with a stoic silence. He was not all that surprised. But he knew Col. Ashley would be disappointed.

* * *

As the July date for the Rendezvous neared, hundreds of free trappers and Native American traders—including Pierre Tivanitagon and his Iroquois contingent—began trickling into the valley from all compass points. Bill Sublette and his hunters finally made their appearance—they had been working the territories far to the northeast—as did Etienne Provost and his motley crew, trailed by the Canadians who had deserted Peter Skene Ogden's expedition the previous summer. Although grateful for the supplies Jed Smith packed in, it was William Ashley's arrival that received the loudest huzzahs. Ashley and twenty-five men had departed St. Louis in March with a separate train of one hundred horses and pack mules carrying trade goods that included jugs of the much-anticipated rum and real whiskey, as opposed to the near poisonous "spiritous water" distributed to the Indians. As a bonus, and earmarked specifically for Tivanitagon's Iroquois, Ashley also delivered a potent mixture of Mexican wheat liquor laced with laudanum known as Taos Lightning.

What followed was an alcoholic bacchanal, a carnival of sorts that one participant recorded as "an inversion of the conventional order where, for a few days, society's outliers ruled." The sound of celebratory gunfire was constant, and men stayed awake for hours on end arguing over hands of seven-up and euchre and dancing wild fandangos to the strains of bluesy fiddles. One Rendezvous scene was piquantly captured by the only white woman present—the scandalized wife of a wayward missionary who had attached himself to the resupply caravan in the hopes of converting "red heathens."

As the preacher's spouse described it in her journal, "Captain Bridger's company comes in about ten o'clock with drums and firing—an apology for a scalp dance. Fifteen or twenty Mountain Men and Indians come to our tent with drumming, firing, and dancing. I should say they look like emissaries of the devil, worshipping their own master. They had the scalp of a Blackfeet Indian, which they carried for a color, all rejoicing in the fate." The next day, in an act of hungover contrition, Bridger demonstrated for the couple the old Indian trick of ridding their clothing of the ever-present fleas and lice by spreading the garments over ant hills, with one breed of insect devouring the others.

Meanwhile, William Henry Ashley, basking in the adulation for enabling this wild, wet pageant, had one more surprise to spring. It was at what he termed the "grand frolic" that was the Mountain Man convention of 1826 that he offered to transfer all his remaining shares in his company to the triumvirate of Jed Smith, Bill Sublette, and a mysterious frontiersman named David Jackson. Ashley proposed an exclusive arrangement between him and this new company. Each summer thereafter he would arrive at Rendezvous to purchase their furs at $3 worth of supplies per pound—plus what today would be called a service fee of just over $1 a pound for transporting the peltry back to St. Louis.* In exchange, Ashley was to be the sole provider of annual provisions to Smith, Jackson, and Sublette, with the three selling the merchandise to the free trappers for the best price they could obtain.

In essence, William Ashley was reaping the rewards of two straight overwhelming beaver hunts—he would eventually return to St. Louis that fall with more than twelve thousand pounds of pelts. As for his choice of successors, Ashley's nine-month partnership with Jed Smith made the pious easterner a logical choice for the position of senior partner in the new outfit. And Bill Sublette's pluck and tenacity dating back to the battle on the Arikara beach stood him well in both Ashley's and Smith's eyes. Historians, however, have expressed bafflement not only as to David Jackson's inclusion in Ashley's offer but also as to where he fit in the annals of western exploration prior to this moment.

Some speculate that Jackson, like Sublette, had fought on the strand of pebbly sand below the Arikara villages in 1823, although his name does not

---

* Despite a plethora of alliances and ever-shifting business models over the next decade, the wilderness price of pelts—$3 worth of supplies per pound—held until the Rendezvous of 1834, when, under the pressure of competition, it rose to $5 per pound in merchandise or $3.50 in cash.

appear on the company's employee manifest. Others surmise that during the summer of 1825 Jackson had been one of the outriders who accompanied Ashley and Smith through South Pass and down the Popo Agie with their haul of furs. It is guessed—for there is no better verb—that he broke off from the company at the Bighorn River to return to the mountains via Union Pass and Jackson Hole. This conjecture is underpinned by near-unanimous agreement among contemporaneous mountaineers that the now infamous Wyoming hollow in the shadow of the Grand Tetons was christened after Jackson.

As it was, Ashley was now a rich man, and destined to become even wealthier both financially and in political clout. Perhaps intuiting this outcome, before departing Missouri in March he had done his usual proselytizing to St. Louis newspaper reporters regarding the wonders of the far west. Barely mentioning Smith, he emphasized his own outsize role in opening the territory beyond South Pass, albeit deigning to speak briefly of the bit part played by God Almighty. Describing the "discovery" of the gap in the mountains, Ashley—generously sharing foresight with his Christian Lord—told *The St. Louis Enquirer*, "The Great Author of nature [who] in His wisdom has prepared, and individual enterprise has discovered, that so 'broad and easy is the way' thousands may travel it in safety, without meeting with any obstruction deserving the name of a MOUNTAIN." Ashley made certain that the newsmen understood that they were speaking to the earthly entity who was responsible for that "individual enterprise."

Further, in what reads as a thinly veiled valedictory aimed at anxious easterners contemplating a journey to the farthest end of the continent along the route he had made possible—and just possibly sojourning in Missouri long enough to vote—Ashley specifically denigrated "the sterility of the country" immediately west of the Rocky Mountains in favor of the glorious, loamy soil of the Oregon Country. That he had never actually seen these potentially fertile farmlands was a mere bagatelle.

It was left to a more objective writer, the Mountain Man–turned-journalist Charles Keemle, to muse over precisely what Jed Smith's two

The only known contemporary image of the Mountain Man and explorer Jedediah Strong Smith. *Courtesy of the University of the Pacific*

From his New York City headquarters, America's first multimillionaire, John Jacob Astor, looked to increase his wealth by establishing Fort Astoria, a fur-trapping post on the West Coast. *Courtesy of the Library of Congress*

The valuable beaver pelt was pursued by fur trappers from Canada, England, France, and Russia as well as the United States across the mountain ranges of North America. *Courtesy of the State Historical Society of Missouri*

Confronted by Indians, John Colter, who had previously accompanied Lewis and Clark on their legendary expedition, was about to embark on an escape that would go down in history as "Colter's Run." *Courtesy of the Denver Public Library Special Collections*

Pierre Chouteau Sr. was a founder of St. Louis, the burgeoning city from which his sons became early participants in the lucrative fur trade. *Courtesy of the Missouri History Museum*

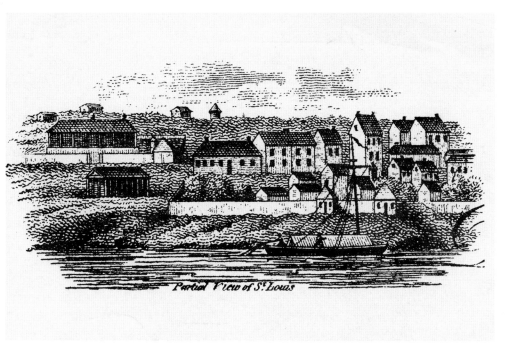

It was from St. Louis, the "Mound City" on the Mississippi, that the earliest keelboat expeditions up the Missouri River commenced. *Courtesy of the Missouri History Museum*

Though crude, bulky, and difficult to navigate, makeshift bullboats such as the one pictured here proved crucial to transporting tons of beaver pelts along the myriad rivers running out of the Rockies. *Courtesy of the Denver Public Library Special Collections*

No longer a nomadic tribe by the 1820s, the Arikara villages featured structures made of baked mud impervious to the arrows and bullets of attacking enemies. *Courtesy of the State Historical Society of North Dakota*

The Indian agent Benjamin O'Fallon, nephew of the legendary General William Clark, did not disguise his hatred of the Upper Missouri tribes. *Courtesy of the State Historical Society of Missouri*

Blackfeet braves, like the warrior depicted here by the Swiss-French artist Karl Bodmer, were to become the fiercest opponents of Mountain Men such as Jed Smith and the white encroachment he represented. *Courtesy of the Denver Public Library Special Collections*

Chieftains of the Gros Ventre tribe, such as the headman illustrated here, allied with the Blackfeet to stem the tide of white intruders across the Upper Rocky Mountains. *Courtesy of the Joslyn Art Museum*

As American expansion crept closer and closer to their territories, even the once-docile Mandan tribe found it necessary to take up arms against the interlopers. *Courtesy of the Denver Public Library Special Collections*

Ancient enmities ran deep among the indigenous tribes of the west, with battles such as this between Sioux and Blackfeet warriors a common occurrence. *Courtesy of the Library of Congress*

In the aftermath of his famous expedition with Meriwether Lewis, William Clark spent decades as a Superintendent of Indian Affairs in a futile attempt to protect and preserve tribal culture by removing Indians from the influences of white society. *Courtesy of the Library of Congress*

Despite being riddled with tall tales, the entertaining recollections of Mountain Men such as James Beckwourth nonetheless provide valuable sources of historical information. *Courtesy of History Colorado*

Jim Bridger is often credited with being the first white man to "discover" the saline waters of the Great Salt Lake. *Courtesy of the Library of Congress*

Mountain Men are depicted here crossing rough, high-altitude terrain in this painting by the famed artist of the American West, Charles Russell. *Courtesy of the Library of Congress*

The Virginia-born James Clyman, boon compatriot of Jed Smith, was one of the few former Mountain Men to enjoy a long life, which ended at age eighty-nine in California. *Courtesy of the Museum of the Mountain Man*

Despite the nickname "Old Gabe" bestowed upon him by Jed Smith, Jim Bridger was still only a teenager when he joined Smith's initial fur-trapping expedition. *Courtesy of the Denver Public Library Special Collections*

Despite his noticeable girth, the French-Canadian trapper and raconteur Etienne Provost proved one of the most skillful, durable, and dangerous of the men who sought their fortunes in the western mountains. *Courtesy of the Utah State Historical Society*

No matter the beaver-hunting trail, the austere peaks of the Rocky Mountains never loomed far. *Courtesy of the Denver Public Library Special Collections*

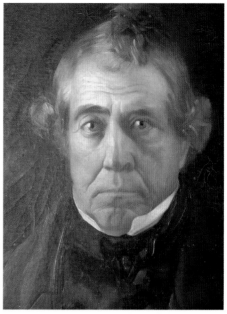

The Londoner George Simpson was to become the powerful and ruthless supervisor of the Hudson's Bay Company's far-ranging operations in North America. *Courtesy of the National Archives of Canada*

As an antidote to Indian attacks, the Scottish-born Donald McKenzie introduced the concept of "brigade trapping" into the Hudson's Bay operations. *Courtesy of the National Archives of Canada*

Jed Smith was one of the first white men to traverse the wagon-friendly South Pass of the Rockies in Wyoming, a so-called "discovery" that opened the Oregon Trail to thousands of westering Americans. *Courtesy of the Library of Congress*

The mid-summer Mountain Man gatherings known as Rendezvous afforded both trappers and local tribes the opportunity to trade and socialize. *Courtesy of the Denver Public Library Special Collections*

The romance of the annual Rendezvous attracted prominent artists such as Alfred Jacob Miller, who created paintings like *Pipe of Peace at the Rendezvous. Courtesy of the Stark Museum of Art*

San Gabriel Mission

The Spanish Mission San Gabriel served as a temporary home to Jed Smith and his company of men during their travels in California. *Courtesy of the Library of Congress*

In 1830, a wagon train funded by Jed Smith and his partners, Bill Sublette and David Jackson, became the first wheeled vehicles to set off on what would become the Oregon Trail. *Courtesy of the Denver Public Library Special Collections*

The relentless Jedediah Smith, expecting to die at any moment, leads his company on the first-ever crossing of the Escalante and Mojave Deserts. *Courtesy of the University of the Pacific*

A view of the interior of Fort Laramie on the Oregon Trail in 1834, as depicted by the painter Alfred Jacob Miller. Seventeen years later, it would be the site of a landmark, if short-lived, treaty between the United States and the western tribes. *Courtesy of the Walters Art Gallery*

successful expeditions to the far side of the cordilleras would mean for the future of the United States. After interviewing Ashley and members of his returning party, Keemle understood that Smith's groundbreaking journeys, because they personified the agenda of a providentially ordained American empire, "were indeed of no small interest to the people of the Union." The abundance of water, game, and firewood along what was to become the Oregon Trail, he reported, was enough to sustain "a thousand men, and often ten thousand [on] overland expeditions to that remote region."

Keemle's articles soon found their way into diplomatic pouches circling the globe. They were of particular interest to authorities in both Mexico City and London. In those capital cities, the implications of the opening of South Pass reverberated like the clang of broadswords. The Mexican president Guadalupe Victoria, midway through his four-year term as the country's first chief executive, was still attempting to stabilize his newly independent republic when news of this chink in the Rocky Mountains reached his Palacio Nacional. Victoria, the insurgent general who had led the revolutionary movement against Spain, was well aware that his fractious country's sparsely populated northern rim—stretching from Texas to California and including the vast, barely charted lands in between—had now instantly become more vulnerable to his powerful northern neighbor's lust for land.

And across the Atlantic, the Hudson's Bay Company's board of directors dispatched an urgent directive to their North American governor, George Simpson. It warned that Missouri trappers traversing South Pass and roaming the Oregon Country's precincts could well constitute the vanguard of a full-scale American hegira. The firm's officers urged Simpson to ratchet up his policy of denuding the Snake River Country of beaver—"to hunt as bare as possible all the Country South of the Columbia and West of the [Rocky] Mountains"—in order to continue to deny the Americans a foothold abutting the company's upper Columbia District. Their orders concluded by noting that "if the American Traders settle near our establishments, they must be opposed, not by violence . . . but by underselling them, which will damp their sanguine expectations of profit."

Charles Keemle's pointed conclusion to his well-sourced reports describing this road west would prove portentous: "Wagons and carriages," he wrote, "could go with ease [along] the whole route through a level and open country."

Needless to say, in contrast to the dread such a gentle pathway into North America's far west inspired in Mexico and Great Britain, those portents were soon stirring imaginations across the United States. Powerful businessmen, investors, and politicians of all stripes recognized that the existence of South Pass would serve as a clarion call to throngs of land-hungry Americans eager to settle the territories on the far side of the once daunting mountains that bisected the continent. Jed Smith, on the other hand, had no intention of waiting for the bugler's summons.

CHAPTER 19

·

"A COUNTRY OF STARVATION"

The engagé's name was Harrison Rogers. Little was known about the twenty-something, not even his precise age, before Jedediah Smith tapped him to be his amanuensis during Smith's 1826 expedition into North America's trackless Southwest. But it was Rogers's subsequent journals that would cast him—and Smith's trailblazing excursion—into the spotlight of American history.

The patchy records of Rogers's past suggest that he hailed from Missouri's Boone's Lick area and that he had been a strong if somewhat diffident trapper employed by the Ashley-Smith partnership for at least one beaver-hunting season, perhaps arriving in the mountains as part of Smith's supply run from St. Louis the previous winter. Sometime in his youth, Rogers's strict Calvinist parents, likely New Englanders who had migrated west around the turn of the century, had ensured that their son received a quality education. It was his writing ability that first caught Jed Smith's eye.

Rogers's eloquently precise prose may have lapped in on gentle waves, but its undercurrents ran deep. Whether compiling to the half ounce the measurements of the gills of rum distributed to the trappers on the final night of Rendezvous, reflecting on a shallow desert lake "touched gold by the morning sun," or describing the physical variations between American and Mexican cattle—the latter, he observed, "broad and handsomely striped, have larger horns, longer legs, and slimmer bodies; the beef [tastes] similar to ours"—the man was a wordsmith with a perceptive eye. The pride-of-place intimations suffusing Rogers's elaborate daybook entries also suggest that he recognized that he was defying the flatlander cliché of the illiterate, half-human Mountain Man gone as savage as a red Indian. He was also considered a bit of a dandy, flaunting moccasins embroidered with the exquisite porcupine quillwork distinctive to the Cheyenne and Arapaho.

More to the point, Rogers's keen interest in geography equaled that which had been drummed into the young "Diah" Smith by his childhood teacher and mentor Dr. Titus Simons. To most early eighteenth-century trappers, territorial knowledge counted for less than little unless it led to the reward of rich beaver holdings. But Smith inherently sensed that the fur trade played a much larger role in national and international affairs than its relatively minor economic significance would suggest. And it was from Rogers's copious journals that he would borrow much of the topographical information he compiled in long letters to American government officials, including Gen. William Clark, regarding "a section of the country which has hitherto been measurably veiled to the citizens of the United States."

That this veiled "section of the country" just happened to belong to Mexico was apparently deemed irrelevant. If beaverless swaths of land held no interest for most Mountain Men, to soldiers and politicians like Gen. Clark, the detailed and descriptive missives sent by Smith opened new vistas for a young nation—"Hercules in a cradle," as Alexander Hamilton had described it—hungry for more territory.

Though Smith expressed few geopolitical opinions in his journals, it is unlikely that during his most recent sojourn to St. Louis he did not sniff the prevailing winds held by a majority of Americans of the epoch— including a growing cadre of statesmen spearheaded by the influential Missouri senator Thomas Hart Benton. Benton's voice was one of the earliest in declaring that expansion toward the Pacific across Mexican territory, whether morally or legally appropriate, was inevitable. As the political, profit-seeking, and burgeoning bureaucratic institutions of the United States crept west, so too did the hard-edged sense of such a certitude. It would be decades before that dream was realized, but the stirrings had begun.

This was particularly evident when Smith inadvertently became the first American to lead an overland party into what Spanish conquistadors had dubbed the oven-hot *caliente fornalia*, and what the newly ascendant Mexican republic claimed as the coastal province of Alta California.

* * *

It was sometime in July 1826, during the final days of the second annual high-country Rendezvous, when Jed Smith and his new partners Bill Sublette and David Jackson devised their strategy. The two junior members of the nascent firm would lead separate hunting parties north from the Cache Valley and into the familiar fur-bearing grounds ranging across the Snake River Country to the western edge of the Rockies. Their objective—to secure a fall catch large enough to settle their debt to William Ashley. A substantial haul would also incentivize Ashley's delivery of provisions the following summer.

Dispersed among Sublette's and Jackson's outfits were the usual reliables—Jim Bridger and Thomas Fitzpatrick, Jim Clyman, and John Henry Weber and Jim Beckwourth. Even Tivanitagon and his Iroquois decided to ride alongside Sublette, although they tended to break off on their own for weeks at a time. The novice Irishman Robert Campbell would keep the books while learning the trapping game.

For his part, Smith would take fourteen men, including the clerk-diarist Rogers, southwest of the Great Salt Lake, where, as the historian Dale Morgan observes, "no white men had ever before explored."* Smith, too, would keep a weather eye out for beaver, but his primary objective

---

* One is here left to ponder Morgan's choice of words, for among Smith's party was the teenage trapper Peter Ranne, who, Harrison Rogers makes clear in his journals, was a free man of color.

remained to determine once and for all the existence or nonexistence of the elusive Rio Buenaventura. He told Sublette and Jackson that should he strike the watercourse he would follow it to its confluence with the Pacific, likely near Monterey or San Francisco Bay. From there he would work his way up the West Coast and, on reaching the mouth of the Columbia, turn east to hunt the tributaries of that river on his return trip to the mountains the following spring.

Thus did late August find Smith's caravan of fifty horses moving south through the valley of the Great Salt Lake, some five hundred square miles of parched bottomland enclosed by the lake itself to the northwest, the Wasatch Range in the east, the Oquirrh Mountains due west, and Traverse Mountain on the south.* A section of this upland hollow, more than four thousand feet above sea level, had once been entirely subsumed by an Ice Age body of water since named after the Parisian-born explorer and U.S. Army geologist Captain Edward Louis de Bonneville—the Bonneville Salt Flats. As Smith's troop pushed through the gap in the Traverse Ridge to drop down into the Utah Valley, they passed the steplike terraces that indicated Lake Bonneville's ancient shorelines. These remain etched into the flanks of the Traverse Range to this day.

Beyond the Valley of the Great Salt Lake, the smaller and greener Utah Valley was the ancestral home of the Ute Nation. On encountering their settlements, Smith presented to the tribe's elders the usual gifts of steel knives, moccasin awls, razors, tobacco, needles, and combs. He also distributed what the meticulous Rogers tabulated as "50 balls; 1 lb. powder," a veritable arsenal to defend themselves against their Navajo and Comanche enemies. Smith, having no idea what manner of game ranged beyond Ute Country—a vast territory marked on contemporary maps as "The Great American Desert"—held tight to the seven hundred pounds of dried buffalo meat burdening his pack animals. This was wise. For though on the

---

* Twenty-one years later, when Brigham Young led his wandering Mormon flock of Latter-day Saints from Nauvoo, Illinois, through a notch in the Wasatch Mountains, he is said to have looked down on the remote valley of the Great Salt Lake and simply remarked, "This is the place."

road ahead he and his men were to take down the occasional antelope or bighorn sheep, they would see no more buffalo.

Splashing up the shallow Sevier River southwest of the Utah Valley, Smith momentarily thought he had chanced upon a tributary of his Rio Buenaventura. But following the thin ribbon of water only led him to its swampy drainage into yet another self-enclosed reservoir, the saline-heavy Sevier Lake. Undaunted, Smith pressed south through the blistering September temperatures of the Escalante Desert, he and his men choking on the tactile clouds of fine loess soil kicked up by the clopping hooves of his hard-pressed mounts. He wrote that the life-leached lands through which they rode constituted "a Country of Starvation—Sandy plains and Rocky hills once every 20 30 or 40 miles a little pond or Spring of water with a little grass."

The outfit spotted the occasional Indian sign—a snuffed campfire, the remains of a skinned black-tail hare. And on occasion one of the hands reported a ghostlike glimpse of human movement in the red-rock western hills that loomed thousands of feet over the prickered plain. But no Indigenous peoples ventured forth to parley until, along a lonely stream since dubbed the Santa Clara River—where today's "Three Corners" of Utah, Nevada, and Arizona converge—the trappers stumbled into a tilled plot of corn and pumpkin.

The kitchen garden was tended by a tribe that Smith called the "Pa-Utches"—the Paiute. These near-naked and forlorn Indians, distant cousins to the Utes, lived in a squalid homeland of the uprooted, having fled the autocratic Spanish priests who would make them into indentured servants on the California missions. As such, the Paiute scratched out a living on hard dirt while complementing their harvest with a diet of anything that crawled, slithered, or hopped. Their village was a rude assemblage of flimsy shelters composed of willow and cottonwood branches caulked with cornstalks, and their poverty was reflected in what Smith regarded as the stunted appearance of the emaciated children clothed in lice- and flea-ridden rabbit skin.

Smith and his men, however, were in no condition to judge. One is left to imagine what the Paiute made of the scrawny train of pale riders entering their territory, nearly as naked as the Indians themselves, dragging along on dilapidated horses whose ribs poked through their withered flesh. By now the exhausted Americans, their supply of buffalo meat long gone, were desperate to trade their dwindling supply of trinkets for whatever comestibles the tribe could offer.

As so often has been demonstrated throughout the course of humanity, it is frequently the most destitute peoples—impoverished in every way except kindness—who are willing to open their meager storehouses to strangers. Thus it was that the Paiute, as generous in spirit as they were lacking in nourishment, fed Smith and his men as best they could. Heaps of boiling corn-and-pumpkin stew were ladled from clay pots as the trappers wolfed down sun-dried cuts of jackrabbit meat and—their hunger overcoming their distaste—skinned iguana.

It was at the Paiute settlement where two of Smith's company called it quits. Rogers's account book records that one Manuel Eustavan and a Canadian Nipissing Indian logged merely as "Nepassing" requisitioned a final supply of knives, chisels, and awls and turned back north. Smith must have watched their retreat with an anxious foreboding, wondering who would be next.

As there was no word for *goodbye* in the Paiute language—a rough linguistic equivalent is the phrase *until we meet again*—upon Smith's departure, he took their winsome smiles and warm hand signals as a heartfelt fare-thee-well. Moving on, he and his company pushed west until striking what is today the Virgin River hard by the Nevada-Utah border. Smith christened it the Adams, in homage to the current president John Quincy Adams. He and his outfit followed the waterway's southwesterly flow for ten days across a chert-flecked landscape untrod by even the old Spanish friars before reaching the banks of the roaring Colorado on October 3, 1826.* The river's muddy, copper-red current was surging in spate.

---

* Today, instead of a confluence with the Colorado River, the ever-diminishing Virgin River flows into the equally shrinking Lake Mead just east of Las Vegas, Nevada.

Smith and his now dozen hardies had ridden nearly six hundred miles in just over ten weeks. They had forty beaver pelts to show for it.

* * *

Jedediah Smith faced a conundrum. At first glance the swirling red rapids of the aptly named Colorado River appeared far too dangerous to attempt a crossing. Yet on the eastern bank of the wide and swollen watercourse his little company could make out a small "Pautch farm" of corn, beans, and musk melon. His emaciated crew, on foot after losing over half of their mounts to starvation and heat stroke, had for days choked down nothing but rancid horse meat as they traversed a wrinkled and mazelike terrain. In the end, Smith decided that their hunger pangs left him no option but to chance a fording of the raging waters. No men drowned, although several more mounts from his diminished remuda were lost.

The Americans, sating themselves on the garden bounty and curious as to its mysterious crop-keepers, followed the river's contour in a south-by-southwest direction for yet another three weeks. Forced from the riverbank by impenetrable jumbles of thorn-brush and jimson weed, they trudged, in Smith's words, through rough country "remarkably barren, rocky, and mountainous." Finally, in late October, they encountered the first of three Mojave Indian villages spread across an expansive valley. To the north, east, and south rose sere, jagged peaks, their crags cloaked in a blue haze. Due west, across the Colorado, lay an enormous sandy desert. This was the eponymous Mojave. Harrison Rogers noted turkey vultures circling in the cornflower sky.

At first glance the broad bowl into which Smith's trappers descended appeared nearly as arid as the terrain to the west. They had no idea that in but a few months the early spring rains would briefly transform the dun valley floor into an Eden-like oasis. Yet something hinted at such an outcome: the Mojave tribe, the most populous of the several Yuma peoples who had settled the area centuries earlier, appeared remarkably hale. They beheld the ragged Americans with astonishment.

White men, even the evangelical Spanish Franciscans, had long avoided what they considered these uninhabitable badlands—not realizing that the seasonal spring showers combined with an annual river overflow to spread layers of fertile alluvial soil conducive to growing crops, including the out-lying vegetable patch Smith's party had feasted on farther north. Upon in-specting his surroundings, Smith's initial skepticism—exacerbated by his experience with the Paiute—fell away. He was particularly struck by the tall and handsome bearing of the Mojave men. Clad only in rough loincloths, with chiseled cheeks seemingly sharp enough to cut falling silk, they were reminiscent of stately Wind River Crow—with one variance: the men and boys worked beside the women and girls in the fields, a custom Smith had never observed in an Indian tribe. And though the usual hardscrabble life of an Indigenous woman in the West seemed to have taken a physical toll on most of the settlement's more mature females, several of the younger girls were comely enough, in the words of the historian Morgan, "to draw even Jedediah Smith's eye."

The Americans were further impressed with the tribe's log-framework lodges, finished with a robust wattle-and-daub as sturdy as any Native American living quarters they had seen along the Missouri River. They were even more taken by the ingenuity with which the peoples who called themselves the 'Aha Makhav had engineered interlacing acequia to redi-rect muddy rivulets of the Colorado to irrigate not only the checkerboards of vegetable plots but also rustling fields of cotton and wheat. It was at the Mojave village where Smith likely experienced what today might be called a psychological benefit afforded by the sight of the vibrant green leaves sprouting from the willow and mesquite trees lining the river. Their ver-dancy also appeared to have a soothing effect on his motley troop, damp-ening the despondency and squabbling that had hung over the company like an illness since the departure of Eustavan and Nepassing.

Smith and his crew, in an attempt to revive what remained of their horses, camped for over two weeks with the Mojave. The days were hot and dry, the nights cool. The Indians, like the less fortunate Paiutes, did not hesitate to share their victuals with the visitors and even bartered a few of their stouter mounts, stolen from Mexicans, in exchange for what was left of Smith's trade goods. Nor were the Mojave shy about sharing geographical details. In a letter to Gen. Clark, Smith was able to confirm that the Colorado River did not empty into either the Gulf of Mexico nor the Pacific Ocean as previously conjectured, but instead flowed into the Gulf of California. If geography is destiny, this was valuable information.

One elder tribesman, who introduced himself in Spanish as Francisco, became particularly friendly with the trapper Abraham LaPlant, who had some of the same language. Using Francisco and LaPlant as dual interpreters, Smith discovered that about 150 miles to the west, beyond the slender series of Cedar Mesa Sandstone spires rising from the desert and later dubbed "The Needles," the San Bernadino Mountains cleaved as a sort of gateway to "the Californias."* Smith, by this point near mystically transformed from Missouri hunter-trapper into America's premier explorer, weighed his options. A return trip north via the route he had taken, if indeed his outfit survived the journey, would be to admit defeat. No beaver pelts. No Rio Buenaventura. No hope.

But who knew what opportunities lay across the Mojave Desert and the rain slope of the San Bernardinos? As Smith would write to the American envoy Joel Poinsett in Mexico City, at his current location he had learned from the Indians that he "was not far from some of the [Spanish] Missions . . . & I detirmined [sic] (as this was the only resort) to go to that place as soon as my men and horses should be able to travel."

Employing two Mojave scouts to guide him across the desert, Smith and his company reforded the Colorado and struck west toward The Needles on the golden morning of November 10, 1826. It was a fraught decision. The wary former colonial authorities of New Spain had once little reason to fear aberrant Americans roaming the continent's great, inhos-

---

* The fabled Route 66, the "Mother Road" running from Chicago to Santa Monica completed in 1926, bisects the downtown area of present-day Needles, California.

pitable southwestern deserts for the simple reason that they would be unlikely to come out alive. And even the young Mexican government—already mobilizing an army to put down a revolt by Anglo settlers on its northeastern fringe in the state of Coahuila de Tejas—had sought to limit its open-trade policies to Pacific ports and a few inland hubs such as Taos and Santa Fe.* But here was an armed American troop seeking to enter the Mexican republic via what some might consider the back door. Alarm bells were certain to sound.

---

* In December 1826, a month after Jed Smith's party ventured into the Mojave Desert and ten years before events at the Alamo, Anglo settlers-turned-insurgents of what came to be known as the Fredonian Rebellion, led by the immigrant speculator, or *empresario*, Haden Edwards, sought to establish the independent Republic of Fredonia in East Texas. The insurrectionists were routed by the Mexican army within weeks.

CHAPTER 20

A SPANISH INQUISITION

Jed Smith's pair of Indian guides, runaways from the California missions, were more than familiar with the mesas and coulees that delineated the ancient trade route across the Mojave Desert. The trail, such as it was, followed the dry, alkaline arroyos of the Mojave River, a stream Smith named the "Inconstant" for its pernicious habit of disappearing underground for interminably long stretches. Native peoples had for millennia transported goods from the Pacific coast to North America's interior along this path, including the seashells that early white explorers had been astonished to find adorning the braided horsehair reins of tribal mounts throughout the Rockies and beyond.

The Mojave pilots warned Smith and his men to keep their horses from feeding on the poisonous red berries of the desert holly and the alluring yellow flowers sprouting from the toxic creosote bushes known as greasewood—the very same plant that Smith's grazing mounts had fed on to such noxious effect a year earlier during his journey through northern Nevada. They also taught the Americans how to extract water from the spiny meat of a barrel cactus and suck dry the juicy stems hewed from prickly pear cacti, although the life-giving nectar was nonetheless strictly rationed. This meant thirsty twelve-hour days in the saddle beneath a near-blinding sun reflecting off the white-salt crystals that in places carpeted the desert's limestone sand. So "complete" were these "barrens," Smith wrote to Gen. Clark, that the sight of the outstretched branches of the occasional Joshua tree—what the Spanish called the *izote de desierto*, or "desert dagger"— must have recalled his childhood religious instructions; through a glare-induced squint the giant yuccas did indeed harken the biblical Joshua extending his arms and keeping them aloft until the twelve tribes of Israel completed their conquest of Canaan.

After fifteen days of grueling travel, the reappearance of the Mojave River flowing out of the bedrock gorges of the east-west-running San Bernadino foothills signaled a milestone—Smith and his company had now completed the first-ever recorded journey from the Missouri River to California. Oddly, neither he nor Harrison Rogers mention this feat in their journals. As the troop followed the river upstream and traversed a low, boxy notch called Cajon Pass, the sparse desert flora was supplanted by towering groves of pine and cedar. And when they descended into the San Bernadino Valley it was as if the easterners had passed through a portal in time and wandered into spring.* Glades of majestic dark oak stood sentry over myriad streams flowing from the San Gabriel Range to the north, and Rogers recorded thousands of the aforementioned Mexican cattle feeding on the lush blue grasses that covered the "handsome bottoms" extending south. "Horses, sheep, hogs, etc. in proportion," he wrote, a fitting complement to the otherworldliness of the environmental transformation.

Encountering an Indian herdsman, the American outfit was guided to a large *asistencia*, or sub-mission, whose two rows of capacious buildings struck Rogers as constructed like "a British Barracks." Here Smith and his entourage were met by friars who ordered a cow butchered for beef-steaks and a hog roasted over a spit. As the meats simmered, the trappers were feted with plates of cornmeal accompanied by wine stomped from grapes harvested from local vineyards and cups of whiskey distilled

---

* It was also here that the teenaged Peter Ranne became the first free Black man to set foot in California.

on site by the Franciscans. The feast concluded with the distribution of bowls of liquid chocolate to wash down the servings of fresh apples and oranges as well as tort-like desserts made from figs and peaches gathered from the mission orchards. When the tablecloths were finally removed, Spanish "sigars" were passed. Such was the American trappers' introduction to "the Californias."

As this hacienda was merely an outlying post, the next morning Smith accompanied one of the priests to the nearby Mission San Gabriel, some five miles to the southwest. Surrendering his rifle and sidearms to the Mexican army's corporal of the guard at the gate of this larger compound, he conferred with the head-of-mission, the forty-eight-year-old Father Jose Bernardo Sanchez. Soon thereafter a rider hied off to San Diego to inform the territorial governor of the singular arrival of a party of mysterious *Americanos* who had managed to negotiate the Mojave Desert.

* * *

Despite the loss of the Spanish Crown's patronage in the wake of the Mexican revolution, Mission San Gabriel—like its twenty counterparts sprawled along coastal California's six-hundred-mile Camino Real as far north as the little village of Mission San Francisco Solano—remained self-sufficient via the sale of cattle hides, tallow, and soap to the American and European merchantmen and whalers who plied the Pacific. The friars and Mexican *soldatos* based at the sites—ostensibly to protect the inhabitants from the 150,000 or so Native Americans roaming farther inland—may have presented an amiable face to visiting fellow whites, as Smith certainly felt. "Old Father Sanchus has been the greatest friend that I have ever met with in all my Travels," he wrote to William Clark. Despite being a "Catholick," he added, "he is worthy of being called a Christian . . . and may God prosper him and all such men."

The plight of the tens of thousands of subjugated Indians from over twenty different tribes who performed the actual work of the missions told a bleaker tale. Forced to convert to Catholicism, these men, women, and children toiled under brutal conditions in virtual slavery. Mission San Gabriel alone housed roughly one thousand of these laborers, and Harrison Rogers records that floggings were near-daily occurrences for even the most minor infractions. More severe punishments were administered for what the priests considered pointedly pronounced acts of defiance, particularly desertion. On re-entering California, for instance, both of the Mojave runaways who had guided Smith and his company across the desert were immediately imprisoned and sentenced to be hanged. One died in a filthy *calabozo* awaiting the rope, while the sentence of the second—pardoned at the last moment after Smith's intercession—was commuted to a life in chains. Such were the mores of Jed Smith's new Christian friends.

In the meantime, Smith, having been joined by the rest of his company at Mission San Gabriel, anxiously awaited news from San Diego concerning his fate. Noting Harrison Rogers's "disapproving eye toward the prevailing theology," Smith set aside his own Protestant antipathy toward the "Popish superstitions" of his hosts and prayed near daily at the compound's ornate chapel. He interspersed these devotions with strolls through the plantation's sumptuous flower gardens, visits to Pueblo de los Angeles about nine miles to the west, and—despite his doctrinal aversion to alcohol and tobacco—gracious samplings of the wines and cigars of which the priests were so proud. He preferred the liquid chocolate.

Having sailed safely past the shoals of papacy, Smith returned this hospitality by drawing maps for Father Sanchez of the route he had followed west, concentrating on what he recalled of the sun-bleached Mojave. Suspecting even at this early date that the charts he had made traversing the rivers, valleys, and even the scrublands across southern Utah, southeastern Nevada, and northern Arizona might be of value to U.S. officials, he purposely left those areas vague to his Spanish host. As a further show of good faith, he directed two of his crew, both able blacksmiths, to forge a bear trap to capture a rogue *oso negro* wreaking havoc on the mission's orchards. That the trap also crippled hungry Indians surreptitiously stealing fruit under cover of darkness goes unremarked in either Smith's or Rogers's journals.

Though disarmed, Smith's men were treated no less obligingly than their captain. The priests continued to ply them with copious meals and steady rations of wine, whiskey, and gin, and at one point issued bolts of cloth to the thirteen threadbare Americans to sew into new shirts. One night the visitors disbursed the last of their trade trinkets to the mission's Indian women and girls. The conscripts returned the favor by serenading them with a concert of "tolerable good music" by a quintet consisting of "two small violins, one bass violin, a trumpet and triangle." This, Harrison Rogers wrote, was merely a prelude to their generosity. For not long after, he was approached in his quarters by a "forward" lass who beseeched him to "make her a *blanco Pickanina*." The rigid Calvinist with New England roots felt "ashamed," and demurred. Rogers does not record if his companions maintained a similar God-fearing discipline.

As nine days passed with no word from San Diego, Smith grew more and more impatient. He and his men, becoming varyingly fluent in pidgin Spanish, were excited by the stories the Indians told of the mountains to the far north—peaks beyond the San Gabriels from which innumerable rivers and streams tumbled into an even more expansive vale. This was the Sierra Nevada high country banking California's vast Central Valley. It was certain, all agreed, that the territory was home to untold beaver lodges. Why else would a community of Russian trappers have erected temporary settlements on Bodega Bay north of San Francisco? To the Americans whose livelihoods depended on the heft of their seasonal catch, the mere notion of such a trove of peltry augured a beguiling denouement to what had been to this point a lengthy, dangerous, and fruitless hunt. They just needed to get there.

Moreover, for all his exploratory zeal, Jed Smith was still a businessman with a fiscal responsibility to his partners and employees and, of equal concern, a substantial debt to pay off to William Ashley. He too chafed to move on.

* * *

Despite their luxe accommodations, Smith was not unaware of the grumblings resurfacing among his anxious troop of detainees. Judging from the tone and content of his journal passages, he also suffered pangs of guilt for the meager beaver catch taken to this point, worrying that he had not held up his end of his new partnership. He naturally had no idea how William Sublette and David Jackson were faring on their separate sweeps through the Snake River Country and northern Rockies, a count on which he need not have fretted.

Albeit constantly harassed by raids and skirmishes with hostiles, particularly the combative Blackfeet, Sublette's and Jackson's combined fall hunt of 1826 proved a tremendous success. By the time they reconvened in the Cache Valley in December, they had accumulated near $23,000 worth of plews—$600,000 today.* This was more than enough to square their account with William Ashley and have a tidy profit left over. Such was Sublette's elation at their good fortune that he took it upon himself to return to St. Louis to inform the general of the bonanza. As riding through the winter snowdrifts would prove impossible, he and the dark-skinned trapper Moses "Black" Harris fashioned snowshoes out of cottonwood branches and buffalo-hair rope, loaded their packs with supplies of dried buffalo meat, and piled fifty pounds of sugar, coffee, and other essentials onto a travois pulled by an Indian-trained dog.† On New Year's Day, they began the thirteen-hundred-mile trek to St. Louis.

The journey of Bill Sublette and "Black" Harris was destined to become

---

* In the process, Sublette and his trappers, following the Yellowstone River to its source, became the first European Americans to lay eyes on the 136 square miles of Yellowstone Lake, the largest body of water in what is today's Yellowstone National Park. Accompanying Sublette, the diarist Daniel Potts—who had lost toes to frostbite on his 1823 journey to join Smith and company at the Wind River Crow encampment—recorded for the unbelieving the daily eruptions of Old Faithful and its surrounding paint pots.

† As with so many early high-country adventurers, little is known of the coffee-skinned Moses Harris's background. Rumored to be either a mulatto or a free Black and said to hail from either South Carolina or Kentucky, he was feted upon his death from cholera in 1849 in a poem written by his compatriot Jim Clyman, which included the lines, "and for the freedom of equal rights, he crossed the snowy heights."

lore across the West, not least because at one point they faced the distressing choice of starving to death or eating their dog.* But it was the unwelcome surprise that awaited Sublette in St. Louis that may have had the greater immediate effect. For upon reaching the city, Sublette was to discover that Gen. Ashley had exploited a loophole in the contract he had signed to exclusively supply the firm of Smith, Jackson, and Sublette at that summer's Rendezvous. Specifically, the terms of the deal he had made stated that Ashley would "furnish no other company or Individual with Merchandise." But he had added a codicil, apparently overlooked by the young partners, allowing a new trapping outfit to form up under his auspices. To this end, Ashley was currently in negotiations with the reconfigured French Fur Company's managing partner Auguste Chouteau—the son of the venerable Pierre Chouteau—to collaborate on a separate beaver-hunting expedition that would compete with the three men who had bought him out.

In retrospect, Ashley's was a sound, if somewhat perfidious, business decision. After all, if he were to underwrite a large company to provision Smith, Jackson, and Sublette come summer, why should the men he engaged for the journey simply turn around with the furs they had collected in exchange for the supplies? Remaining in-country to trap for a year under Ashley's banner not only made financial sense but also, from the general's point of view, certainly didn't cut into anyone's profit, as he felt that there were more than enough pelts to go around.

Needless to say, Bill Sublette would not quite see it that way.

* * *

Jed Smith of course had no knowledge of these high adventures and low machinations taking place far to the east when, on December 8, 1826—as the friars at Mission San Gabriel gathered their congregants to celebrate

---

* Their harrowing winter trek across the snow-packed mountains and plains sparked stories in newspapers and magazines from St. Louis to Boston, the most famous of which—the journalist Matt Field's "The Death of a Dog"—was published to much acclaim in *The New Orleans Daily Picayune*.

the Dia de la Immaculada Conception—a uniformed courier arrived at the compound. He carried a written message from Alta California's governor-general Jose Maria de Echeandia, who was requesting Captain Smith's presence in San Diego. The invitation was veiled in the usual florid diplomatic language. But Smith inferred an underpinning of Toledo steel.

Smith, escorted by a brace of soldiers, reached the governor's sunbaked headquarters four days later. He was initially taken aback. Gov. Echeandia looked to be in the foothills of his twenties, too young and untried for a man invested with such wide-ranging authority.* Smith was also surprised by the man's physical stature. Having grown accustomed to the portly mission padres, including the "fair and fat" Father Sanchez, he had not expected to be standing before such a tall and slender official. Echeandia loomed a good four inches over the six-foot Smith and peered down at the wayward American with a long, vulpine face. The governor, of whom no images exist, has been described by contemporaries as a suave if "juiceless" administrator; the only hint of the responsibilities he bore was the leathery skin around his ravaged brown eyes, prematurely creased with age lines resembling parentheses. "Very much of a Gentleman," Smith was later to note, "but very Suspicious."

Further, and more than baffling, Echeandia, a former lieutenant colonel with the Mexican army's corps of engineers, professed to have no idea what a beaver was, much less why men trapped them. In his official report he thus categorized Smith and his company as *pescadors*, or fishermen. This of course begged a more crucial question: Just what were American fishermen doing wandering about the arid Mojave Desert? Smith's presentation of his trading license from Gen. Clark only exacerbated the governor's mistrust. The permit enumerated hunting passports for the fifty-seven men whom Smith had led from St. Louis. Where were the other forty-five? Was Smith's little band merely a scouting party for some guerilla military movement into sovereign Mexican territory?

---

* Governor-General Echeandia's birthdate has never been established.

Smith parried these inquiries as best he could, attempting to convince Echeandia "of the truth that I was only a hunter & that Dire necessity had driven me here." Yet by their third meeting the governor left Smith with the impression that he might have to confer with his superiors in Mexico City before sorting through this vexing predicament. Given the travel time between San Diego and the Mexican capital, that could mean months of detention. Uppermost in Smith's mind was the prospect of losing the spring hunting season while he and his men sat under a protracted house arrest, even one so comfortable as Mission San Gabriel.

As a final gambit Smith received permission to send a courier to Harrison Rogers exhorting Rogers to select the outfit's best eight beaver skins and have them shipped to San Diego at once. Although he had neither the mercury nor the mash to mold a beaver hat, he hoped to show the governor how to "face," or attach, a pelt to an officer's cloak as a collar or hood, thereby demonstrating not only the animal's worth but his own good faith. Echeandia was unimpressed.

From the young Mexican governor's point of view, the American company's arrival in Alta California represented a double-edged sword. As both the *jefe politico* and *jefe militar* of the territory, Echeandia was well aware of the colonial fragmentations still generating political tremors across the North American West. There was, he well understood, a veritable cold war being waged along the Canadian border between the United States and the British Crown, the latter employing the Hudson's Bay Company as its proxy. And in his own backyard he was dancing a pas de deux with the pesky Russian trappers and sea otter hunters north of San Francisco Bay who had been issued licenses by his predecessor. Sorting through the emotional temperature of the era's geopolitics left him at sixes and sevens.

If this Captain Smith was, as Echeandia suspected, a Washington spy, the repercussions of simply allowing him to be on his way would be ruinous to the governor's career. On the other hand, the man's travel license had been signed by one famous American general in William Clark, and he had only recently been partnered with yet another American general in

William Ashley. It was not lost on Echeandia that general officers, no matter their nationalities, tended to have friends in high places that spanned international borders. His superiors in Mexico City might look equally askance at the detention of a man with such influential colleagues.

Gov. Echeandia was on the verge of washing his hands of the entire affair and shipping Jed Smith off to Mexico City to allow the capital's bureaucrats to sort through this dilemma when a deus ex machina appeared in the form of a sea captain out of Boston named William Cunningham. Cunningham, whose merchant brig the *Courier* had been trading up and down the California coast for several months, was currently berthed in San Diego. The seaman was a known entity to the governor, a reliable interlocutor whose word could be trusted. When Cunningham and several other American shipmasters vouchsafed the authenticity of Smith's permits and passports, Echeandia relented and agreed to free Smith and his men. He would even supply them for their journey home—with one ironclad condition. The trappers were to return to the United States via the same Mojave Desert route through which they had entered Mexican territory.

Despite visions of thousands of California beaver eluding his traps flitting through Jed Smith's mind, he acceded to the terms.

*　*　*

Mid-January 1827. Cajon Pass. Inflection points were becoming too common in Jed Smith's travels. He had reached one with William Ashley that long-ago morning on the Missouri River beneath the Arikara settlements. He had confronted another with his decision to trail the Hudson's Bay Company's Alexander Ross to Flathead Post. A third had arisen at the Mojave villages when he had forgone the option of retracing his path back to Utah and instead journeyed west into California.

Now he faced yet another on the slopes of the San Bernadino Mountains. Forge back into the blistering Mojave Desert, as Gov. Echeandia demanded? Or turn north toward the Sierra Nevada's lush beaver holdings?

His mood was further fouled by thoughts of the trapper who had deserted the company the previous night.

Smith, as he had pledged, led his outfit through the pass. The landscape altered dramatically, as it had three months earlier. A shimmering wave of heat haze rose from the salt flats in the distance. The trickling Mojave River was already beginning to disappear beneath the sands. With a wave of his hand, Smith halted his train at the edge of the desert. He turned in his saddle. Eleven pairs of eyes stared back at him. Anxious. Beseeching. No one spoke. The late-afternoon light, Harrison Rogers recorded, threw sharp-edged shadows. Smith spurred his mount and rode north.

CHAPTER 21

DREAMS OF COOLING CASCADES

The breathtaking San Joaquin Valley was more prodigal than even its most fervent Indian enthusiasts at Mission San Gabriel had described.* Herds of tule elk, blacktail deer, and pronghorn antelope fed off the verdant grasses, sedges, and the carpet of acorns that crunched underhoof. Jed Smith's skittish mounts, sixty-eight in all, most supplied by Gov. Echeandia, bucked at the scent of grizzly bears and mountain lions. And always, rising in the east, loomed the snow-capped Sierra Nevada. Creeks too numerous to count rushed down from the heights, the cold, torrential waters bounded on either bank by thick stands of oak and sycamore. In the valley proper, the streams converged to form Kings River, a 132-mile watercourse that in turn flowed into the wild San Joaquin and thence into San Francisco Bay. It was here that Smith and his trappers commenced their spring hunt.

To Americans of the epoch, California was a nebulous territory narrowly defined by its Spanish-speaking coastal communities, an errant province with but nominal ties to distant Mexico City. Ten weeks earlier,

---

* California's four-hundred-mile-long Central Valley is roughly divided into two parts, with the southern two-thirds called the San Joaquin Valley and the northern third known as the Sacramento Valley. Bounded by the Pacific Coast Range to the west and the Sierra Nevada in the east, the Central Valley stretches south from the Cascade Mountains to the Tehachapi Range in today's northwestern Los Angeles County.

when Smith's troop had cut back west through a gap in the low-crested Tehachapi Mountains—the southernmost range of the Sierra Nevada—he may very well have believed that he had obeyed Echeandia's edict simply by abandoning the San Bernadino Valley. Of course, this was far from what the provincial governor had in mind.

Sovereign Mexico, by dint of the Adams-Onis Treaty of 1819, extended from the Pacific coast to the Sierra Nevada and beyond. And the land grants that Mexican authorities were only just beginning to contemplate issuing to American settlers should they pledge fealty to the Mexican republic and convert to Catholicism were quite distinct from an armed foreign posse traversing Alta California's interior. It is not recorded if by this date Gov. Echeandia's reports on the presence of Smith and his trappers had reached President Victoria in Mexico City. In either case, Victoria's apprehensions over the ramifications of the existence of South Pass were already manifesting themselves.

By April 1827, Smith and his party had covered nearly two hundred miles unmolested, working their way north along the Sierra Nevada's windward slope as far as the Sacramento River (which today forms the western border of California's capital city). Mistaking that roiling waterway for the outflow of William Ashley's mystical river, Smith dubbed the Sacramento Valley the "Valley of the Bonadventure." Peculiarly, after searching for this legendary watercourse for years, instead of following its path into the eastern foothills, Smith—his horses by now packing more than fifteen hundred pounds of plews—continued north, searching for a break in the high, snow-covered ramparts through which he and his men could transport their peltry back to the Utah Rendezvous.

At one point Smith suspected that he had found just such a pass in the dry, winding canyon through which the American River snaked down from the peaks. But even in May, the six-foot wall of snow frosting the high Sierra proved too daunting. Five of his horses starved to death during the attempt to push through the drifts. With the remainder of his mounts floundering and his men near frozen, Smith retreated to the verdant grasses and blue gentian of the glacial meadows that led back down to the Central Valley. Retracing their path south, the outfit backtracked nearly seventy-five miles to the banks of yet another tributary of the San Joaquin in the north-central quarter of the province—the waterway known today as the Stanislaus River. There Smith pondered his options.

Despite purposefully keeping his distance from the coastal missions and their attached garrisons—"150 miles to 200 miles from the sea," Smith reckoned in his journal, overestimating his distance from the military presidios by double—it was only a matter of time before news reached Mexican authorities of the expelled American trappers once again ranging through the district. This occurred in May, when the Franciscan head of Mission San Jose wrote to Gov. Echeandia denouncing their presence. The priest accused the foreigners of conspiring with the San Joaquin Valley's wild, forest-dwelling Miwok Indians to foment the desertion of nearly four hundred of their tribal brethren from his compound straddling the eastern shore of San Francisco Bay.*

Echeandia, at the time visiting the Monterey church founded half a century earlier by the venerated Father Junipero Sera, doubted that Smith had anything to do with the escaped Indians. The allegation did not fit with the measure of the man he had taken in San Diego. He nevertheless dispatched a company of soldiers to take Capt. Smith into custody. By the time the patrol arrived at the camp on the Stanislaus, however, Smith was gone.

*　*　*

The drumbeat of the Indian "telegraph" system was swifter than a horse could travel. Soon after Echeandia issued Smith's arrest warrant, a hunting party of Miwok warned him that *soldatos* were coming for him. He and two volunteers—the blacksmith Silas Gobel and the trapper Robert Evans—hurriedly loaded seven horses and two mules with sixty pounds of

---

* In the sixth episode of the *Star Wars* film series, *Return of the Jedi*, its creator George Lucas was said to have named the woodland creatures known as Ewoks after the Miwok tribe.

dried meat and set off up the Stanislaus River in search of a route through the mountains. Smith left Harrison Rogers in charge of the remaining eight men, with orders to cache the beaver pelts and cooperate in every way possible with the Mexican authorities. He would, he promised Rogers, return before the year was out with more hands to somehow haul their catch out of California.

When the Mexican detachment reached the American campsite, Rogers coolly explained that their outfit was trying its best to comply with Gov. Echeandia's orders to vacate the province. His Booshway Capt. Smith, Rogers said, was at the very moment searching for a path through the snows of the high Sierra. He and the remaining trappers, he added, wanted nothing more than to maintain a cordial relationship between the United States and Mexico. They just needed to find a safe way home. Rogers did not mention the pelts that he and his men had buried nearby.

The *teniente coronel* questioning Rogers was perplexed. The interlopers seemed sincere in their desire to return east. And there was no evidence that they had illegally poached any animals other than for sustenance, much less conspired with the rebel Miwok to abet their defection from the mission. He likely also doubted that anyone would again see this elusive Capt. Smith. It was well known that no white man had ever crossed the Sierra Nevada this far north at this time of year and lived to tell the tale. In the end, Rogers and his party were told to remain where they were while the officer returned to Monterey to report Smith's disappearance and receive further orders.

* * *

Jed Smith and his two companions had lost two horses and a mule to snow-slides during their eight-day mountain crossing. Finding a gap in the Sierra Nevada at nine thousand feet—soon to be named after the gold seeker John Ebbets—they'd journeyed atop snowpack up to eight feet deep but whose crust had in most places been hardened enough by the sun to support the weight of both men and animals. Now, descending the rain shadow slope of the range, they faced nearly 650 miles of searing sands separating them from

Utah's Bear Lake. As the three Americans took their first steps into the continent's Great Basin, they ventured into the harsh terrain as one might enter a blazing white crystal, where the form and shape of things became irregular, refracted. Mirages promised silver lakes and ponds that, upon approach, were swallowed by the granular earth. Judging distances accurately became problematic; wherever they looked, Smith wrote, an indistinct curtain of vapor trembled and swayed in the dry heat.

It took the little party over three weeks to cross the northern Nevada desert, which Smith dubbed the "Great Sand Plain." Along the way they were forced to kill three of their remaining five horses, boiling the horseflesh in water collected from the springs trickling from scattered rocky outcroppings. It was among these isolated hills where they encountered the few Native Americans who called these wastelands home, likely Washoe or Northern Paiute. "Indians," as Smith described them, "who appeared the most miserable of the human race having nothing to subsist on (nor any clothing) except grass seed, grasshoppers, &c." When the Americans could not find water, which was often, they pricked the ears of the mule and took turns catching drops of its blood in their mouths.

By the time they reached what today constitutes the Utah state line, both men and mounts were staggering beneath what some weary travelers across the Basin describe as a motionless yellow-white sun, hanging overhead as if suspended by a string. Pressing north along the eastern slope of the snow-capped Deep Creek Mountain Range, Smith was ecstatic when he managed to kill two hares—"much better than horsemeat," he crowed in his journal—comestibles he would have sneered at weeks earlier. Days later, slogging across the southern edges of the Great Salt Desert, their water horns again ran dry. Forced to kill another horse—slurping its blood and charring its flesh over a fire whipped by blowtorch winds—Smith spurred his companions on with a façade of false bravado. At one point he claimed to have caught sight of a pair of turtle doves, birds known to never venture far from water.

He was more frank in his diary, which reads as if he were writing his own epitaph. "The view ahead was almost hopeless," begins one entry. "With our best exertion we pushed forward, walking as we had been for a long time over the soft sand. That kind of traveling is verry tiresome to men in good health who can eat when and what they choose and drink as often as they desire, and to us worn down with hunger and fatigue and burning with thirst increased by the blazing sands it was almost insupportable."

On the afternoon of June 24, 1827—nearly a month to the day from their flight from the Stanislaus River—the three paused on the shade side of a small sand hill. There they scraped out shallow holes and buried themselves "for the purpose of cooling our heated bodies." As Smith drifted off to sleep the thought occurred that he and his companions may have just dug their own graves.

"Our sleep was not repose," he wrote, "for tormented nature made us dream of things we had not. It then seemed possible and even probable we might perish in the desert unheard of and unpitied. In those moments how trifling were all those things that hold such an absolute sway over the busy and prosperous world. My dreams were not of God or ambitious honors but of my distant quiet home, of murmuring brooks, of Cooling Cascades."

Smith, willing himself to his feet in the brisk hours before dawn, managed to rouse his companions. But as the sun sulled in the sky like a whipped mule, he noted, "it seemed to us that we were the most unhappy beings on which it poured its floods of light." By now their exposed faces and hands, their brimmed hats and shirts and trousers and boots, had assumed the same dull ochre pigment as the desiccated country through which they trudged.

It was close to mid-morning when Robert Evans gave out. Spotting a small cedar tree inexplicably lifting from the marl, Evans crawled beneath its gnarled branches, collapsed, and bade his compatriots to go on without him. "We could do no good by remaining to die with him," Smith wrote. "And [as] we were not able to help him along . . . we left him with feelings only known to those who have been in the same situation and with the hope that we might get relief and return in time to save his life."

Smith and Gobel stumbled on for another mile or so before Smith thought he caught a far-off movement. It seemed to him that two mounted Indians were riding into the desert. Horses. Horses meant water. He did not mention this to Gobel, aware that along with physical exhaustion traveled its shadowy cousin delirium. Gobel was already hallucinatory. Was he also? Had he truly seen what he thought he had seen? In any case, he was beyond offering false hope.

Smith, Gobel, and their animals reeled forward for several more miles, their mouths dry as chalk, the sturdy mule outpacing the faltering mustang. They made for a high, solitary peak jutting like a flying buttress from the wall of the Deep Creek Range. It was at the foot of this mountain where they found a spring. Men and beasts dived headlong into the little pool.

Smith's momentary rapture at "bathing my burning forehead" was sobered by the cracks of successive gunshots echoing from the desert. These were followed by a thin plume of gray smoke rising from the site that Evans had chosen as his final resting place.

* * *

Robert Evans had second thoughts about dying. Not long after the departure of Smith and Gobel, he plunged his skinning knife into the sand and gauged into the shallow taproots of the cedar tree. Running his tongue across the moist, fibrous tentacles convinced him that he had the strength to go on. He fired his rifle and sidearm near simultaneously in the hope of capturing his confederates' attention, then lit a fire to guide them back.

Smith reached him an hour or so later with a kettle brimming with six quarts of water strapped to the mule's saddlehorn. Evans downed the liquid in giant gulps before berating Smith for not bringing more. This was when Smith knew that the surly trapper would survive.

The three men and their two remaining animals spent the rest of that day and night camped at the spring. The humans feasted on the last of their horse meat. The animals were content with the grasses and forbs that ringed the pool of water. The following morning, their horns and kettles full, they again moved north. They soon came upon a temporary lodge occupied by five Indians: two men, a woman, and two children.* The little clan shared their small store of antelope meat and indicated through sign that they were but a few days' travel from buffalo country. The following morning, a ten-mile hike brought Smith, Gobel, and Evans within sight of the southwest corner of the Great Salt Lake. This was, Smith wrote, "indeed the most cheering view for although we were some distance from [Bear Lake], yet we knew we would soon be in a country where we would find game and water." As if to validate his good cheer, the next day Smith brought down "a fine, fat Buck."

* * *

Over the course of twelve months Jedediah Smith had become the first European American to lead a party across the Mojave Desert, over the Sierra Nevada, and through North America's Great Basin. His subsequent reports of these extraordinary travels, brimming with detailed geographic, topographic, military, cultural, and political observations, were soon being pored over by America's fledgling military-industrial complex. Particularly interested in the obscure Mountain Man's insights were men Smith had never heard of—statesmen and railroad entrepreneurs, army officers and mining magnates—already envisioning a transcontinental land bridge connecting the eastern seaboard to the golden shores of California.

Although never to know it, Smith's journal entries and subsequent letters to various eastern eminences represented a preliminary blueprint for a nation-defining territorial war between the United States and Mexico that was still two decades off. West of the Mississippi River, however, the Indigenous peoples whose ancestral lands were the subject of these nascent takeover schemes remained unimpressed.

---

* In his journal, Smith refers to these Native Americans as *Pahnakkee's* [sic], a bastardization of *Panaiti*, itself a corruption of *Nimi' Pan a'kwati*, or "Riverside People," the Indigenous name by which the Snake River–dwelling Bannock referred to themselves.

———•———

CHAPTER 22

DUELING WARPATHS

Bill Sublette and David Jackson, camped along the southern shore of Bear Lake on July 3, 1827, were anticipating the arrival of the Shoshone. Scouts had reported more than two hundred lodges of friendly "Snakes" heading for the third annual high-country Rendezvous. They were not expecting that Jed Smith, Silas Gobel, and Robert Evans would be riding among them.

Sublette and Jackson, awash in furs, had long thought their senior partner and his trappers dead. So overwhelmed were they by Smith's emergence from the Indian scrum that they commandeered a small cannon recently hauled into the mountains from St. Louis and fired off a celebratory round. The two then showed Smith the stacks of pelts accrued during their fall and spring hunts—$23,000 worth, as mentioned. Smith in turn surprised them by breaking the news of the fifteen hundred pounds of plews he had cached in California. He added that nary a hostile Indian—from Ute to Paiute to Mojave to Miwok—had he encountered. Sublette and Jackson had had no such luck.

They reported being harassed near daily by renegade bands of Bannock and Nez Perce, a few opportunistic Northern Shoshone, and, of course, the ever-raging Blackfeet. Neither of their companies had lost a man, but both had been close-run affairs. Thomas Fitzpatrick, riding with Jackson, related the story of revisiting a small bivouac of free trappers with whom he had camped days earlier. When he returned to the site, the men had mysteriously gone missing, their gear left behind. Fitzpatrick searched for blood trails. He found none. And Jim Clyman, accompanying Bill Sublette, described how he had inadvertently stumbled into the middle of a Blackfeet hunting party along the Teton River.

It was near dusk, as Clyman yarned the tale, and he and a partner were struggling through a strand of heavy timber to check their traps when they rode into the hostile campsite. Sensing no other option, Clyman headed straight for the Blackfeet headman's tipi and made the usual friendship signs. He claimed he had purposely sought out their cookfires in order to pass the night under the aegis of Blackfeet hospitality. The sullen chief, momentarily taken aback, instructed his women to feed the two white men. But Clyman—who had a few words of pidgin Blackfeet—also overheard the Indian order his braves to gather their weapons. Clyman signaled his companion to be ready to run. He attempted to put the Indians off their guard by offering them tobacco, while casually lighting his own clay pipe. Feigning the need to fetch more tobacco plugs from their saddlebags, the two trappers bolted for the river. Night had fallen, and both swam the stream and huddled under the far bank in the freezing water until their pursuers called off the search.

So incensed were the Indians at Clyman's audacious ruse that only days before Smith's arrival at Bear Lake a war party of more than one hundred Blackfeet had crept to the shores of the Rendezvous site and sprung an assault from the tall rabbitbrush. A combined force of trappers, Ute, and Shoshoni eventually drove them off, at the cost of three Shoshoni dead and one trapper wounded. Jim Clyman, Bill Sublette, and Jim Beckwourth had taken part in the fight. Contrary to Beckwourth's claim of counting 173 scalps taken, Sublette's estimate of killing perhaps a dozen hostiles seems more likely.

What particular existential or philosophical incident or incidents influenced Jim Clyman's forthcoming announcement will never be known.

It nevertheless came as a shock to Jed Smith when the veteran Virginian pulled him aside to tell him that he would not be joining the fall hunt. Clyman had decided to retire from the beaver trade. In appreciation of his years of friendship and loyalty, Smith allowed the thirty-five-year-old frontiersman to keep the pelts he had taken over the past twelve months to sell for a better price in St. Louis.* Though Smith does not mention it in his journals or letters, their parting must surely have been bittersweet.

* * *

The artillery piece that had boomed a welcome to Jed Smith was a gift from William Ashley, who had declined to personally venture upcountry that summer. The gun had been transported to the Rendezvous by his new field commander James Bruffee, a former French Fur Company engagé. The general's orders to Bruffee were succinct—trade the provisions he had supplied for pelts, but do no trapping. It is unreported whether Ashley's merger negotiations with Auguste Chouteau had collapsed on their own accord or if the menacing Bill Sublette's arrival at Ashley's door the previous March had frightened him away from launching his own hunting outfit. In any case, Ashley once again found himself bound to his exclusive supply contract with the firm of Smith, Jackson, and Sublette. It proved a profitable arrangement for all involved.

Between haggling with Bruffee over the price of his merchandise, between the passing of jugs and the telling of lies, between the card games and fistfights and horse races and carnal relations with eager Indian maidens, Smith, Jackson, and Sublette debated the matter of the nine men and cached pelts stranded in California. The Mexican secretary of state, exaggerating the size of Smith's southwest expedition, had already written to the U.S. representative Joel Poinsett in Mexico City decrying "the irruption of the twenty-five armed [Americans] into the Californias" the previ-

---

* Which is precisely what Jim Clyman did. Arriving in St. Louis in mid-October, Clyman sold his 278 pounds of "high-grade beaver fur" to the former Astorian Wilson P. Hunt at $4.50 a pound.

ous January. He warned Poinsett that should this reoccur, his government was prepared to take "necessary measures." In diplomatic language, this was a threat. Poinsett responded with affected ignorance, pointing out that although "infractions of the laws of Mexico were to be deplored," it was only natural for hunters in the field to sometimes stray across international borders without realizing they were doing so.

Even if Jed Smith had been aware of the diplomatic kerfuffle, it is doubtful he would have altered his plans. For by the time the 1827 Rendezvous concluded on July 13—ten days after Smith's arrival at Bear Lake—the three partners had set their itineraries. Bill Sublette and David Jackson would again ride out to trap the North Country, hewing close to their previous routes—Sublette north by northeast toward Henry's Fork and the heart of Blackfeet country, Jackson northwest along the Snake River tributaries. Simultaneously, Smith would retrace his southwest route, having outfitted a squad of eighteen men to return with him to California.

Given his experience with the rigors of such an expedition, Smith sought out a particular type of hardy to join his troop. He thus did not object when the veteran Canadian mountain hands John Relle and a mixed-race trapper listed on the manifest only as Robiseau insisted on bringing their Indian wives. Their experience on the trail offset any burden the *sulfureux* might prove. Among the others he recruited were a towering New England–born sharpshooter named Isaac Galbraith and the stout, muscled blacksmith Silas Gobel.* Robert Evans, however, had seen enough of the west. He opted to return to St. Louis, enlisting as a teamster with Bruffee's caravan.

Smith had learned too well the hazards of attempting another crossing of what he called the Great Sand Plain. Instead, he intended to skirt North America's Great Basin and re-enter the Mexican provinces via the

---

* Upon Isaac Galbraith's death in California several years later, he bequeathed his "herculean frame" to a Missouri physician with whom he was friends. For the next thirty years the doctor displayed the skeleton in his office as "a fine specimen of a Maine giant."

Colorado River and the slightly less daunting Mojave Desert. Once over the San Bernardino Mountains, he felt confident that he could prevail on Governor-General Echeandia to allow him to retrieve his companions and peltry. From there he would continue to hunt north through the Oregon Country until he reached the Columbia. Intimating that his mindset was focused on not only profit but also adventure, and certainly recognizing the neo-national implications of his explorations, he noted in his journal, "I of course expected to find Beaver. But I was also led on by the love of novelty common to all, which is much increased by the pursuit of its gratification."

With good fortune, he told his partners, upon reaching the Columbia he would bend east toward the Snake and track back to next summer's Rendezvous, again scheduled for Bear Lake. The phrase "with good fortune" was a lynchpin bearing a heavy load.

*　*　*

Smith's journal pages make but casual note of the hoofprints he noticed crosscutting the site of the vanished Paiute camp. If he found it odd that, unlike Indian mounts, the horses and mules that had left the telltale indentations were shod, he does not say. Nor did he speculate as to why the tribe's homely lodges had been burned to the ground. Moving on, several weeks later he and his party reached the confluence of the Virgin and Colorado Rivers at the same point as in the previous year. Fording the Colorado and traveling southwest, he made the Mojave villages in mid-August. The Indians, he wrote, "seemed as friendly as when I was there before." He gifted the tribe's headmen with presents and traded for corn, beans, dried pumpkin, and melons.

Seeking out the elderly, Spanish-speaking Indian known as Francisco—and using the trapper Gregory Ortago as a translator—Smith learned that not long after his departure last spring, an Anglo-Hispanic party of beaver hunters had passed through Mojave territory. The outfit, apparently having followed the Gila River out of New Mexico, was near starving when the Indians encountered them. Francisco added, somewhat elliptically, that the white men had quarreled and separated, with half riding east and the rest continuing up the Colorado. This accounted for the horse tracks Smith had spotted near the old Paiute village.

Had this hybrid crew for some reason burned out the Paiute dwellings? And if so, had they also made enemies of the Mojave? Francisco said no more, and it never occurred to Smith to further explore the matter. This was a mistake. For in fact the New Mexican trappers had indeed clashed with the Mojave, killing several braves. Though the tribe disguised it well, its warriors ached for vengeance.

As Smith's men and horses were in far finer fettle than during his previous layover at the villages, he paused only long enough to lash together several cane-grass rafts to float their supplies and equipage across the broad Colorado. On August 18, having spent three days among the people of the Mojave Valley, Smith loaded a small quantity of dried meat, a few packs of trade trinkets, a water kettle, five rifles, and a small store of ammunition onto a raft to test its seaworthiness. He left all the outfit's horses and the greater part of its gear and weapons on the sandy eastern bank in case the test craft floundered. Smith and seven others then plunged into the river, swimming the vessel through the current.

They had just reached a thin sandbar closer to the western bank of the watercourse when war whoops rent the air. Hundreds of hidden Mojave warriors burst from the thick brush and fell on the company left on the beach. So unexpected was the attack that the remaining trappers were still scrambling for their guns as nine of the ten fell, perforated by arrows and lances. The sole survivor was a veteran hand named Thomas Virgin, who, despite having his cheekbone and nose stove in by a war club, plunged into the river and made the bar. The two women, taken prisoner, watched as their husbands bled out. It is said that it took several braves to hold down the wounded Silas Gobel, while a third buried the flint blade of a tomahawk into his skull.

* * *

It must be granted that when Jed Smith described the Mojave ambush, the events he recounted were weeks in the past. Nonetheless, his diary pages exhibit an incredible sangfroid given his precarious position. "After weighing all the circumstances of my situation as camly as possible," he wrote, "I was yet on the sand bar in sight of My dead companions and not far off were some hundreds of Indians who might in all probability close in uppon us and with an Arrow or Club terminate all my measures for futurity." Well, yes.

Allowing the raft to drift downstream, Smith spread a few combs, razors, and hand mirrors across the bar in the faint hope that any Indians in immediate pursuit might pause to squabble over the loot. He then distributed equal amounts of buffalo meat to each of his men before all swam to the Colorado's western shore, making sure to keep dry the possible sacks holding their gunpowder. Two of the swimmers had to support Thomas Virgin. Along with the five rifles, all nine survivors still carried their skinning knives.

They had trudged but a few hundred yards from the river before they spotted war parties stalking them to either side. Retreating back to the water's edge, the trappers burrowed into a thick copse of cottonwoods and began hacking at the small trees with their knives. The thicker trunks were used to throw up a stopgap breastwork while they tied the hilts of their blades to the longer branches to fashion what Smith called "a tolerable lance." Although Mojave warriors were now in possession of at least two dozen of the company's rifles and pistols, Smith could only hope that it would take them some time to familiarize themselves with the weapons, particularly how to reload the guns.

Inside their flimsy redoubt, the river at their backs, Smith ordered the trappers to form a defensive semicircle. He then gave further instructions—no more than three rifles were to be fired at any one time, always leaving two available for a follow-up volley. Further, no man was to shoot unless he was certain of hitting his target. As they awaited what appeared the inevitable, a few men asked Smith about their chances of making it out alive. "I told them we would," he wrote. "But that was not my opinion."

There was no breeze that day, yet all about them the defenders observed the tangled bramble overgrowing the riverbank moving almost imperceptibly. The Mojave, who did not wear war bonnets like their Plains and Mountain brethren, were slinking closer. "Gradually the enemy was drawing near," Smith wrote, "but kept themselves covered from our fire. Eight men with but five guns were awaiting behind a defence made of brush.'

As the sun swept higher across the sky, several Indians, thinking themselves out of rifle range, stood and showed themselves. Hopping from foot to foot in a tribal war dance, they taunted the surrounded little troop with what the white men took to be death songs. At this Smith summoned his two best marksmen, including the "giant" Isaac Galbraith. Together the three raised and sighted their long guns. They fired simultaneously. Two warriors fell dead; another scuttled off wounded. "Upon this the indians ran off like frightened sheep and we were released from the apprehension of immediate death."

There were no more sallies that afternoon, the Indians apparently content to return to the far side of the river to divvy up the captured horses and abandoned spoils. The Americans waited until sundown before creeping off into the Mojave Desert under the cover of darkness. None had water horns; each carried a little over a pound and a half of dried meat for the two-hundred-mile journey that lay ahead.

* * *

Though Jed Smith located a spring the next morning, he lost the trail repeatedly over the following days, wandering miles off the route his Indian guides had taken a year earlier. Game was nonexistent, but Smith knew from experience that a lack of water would exterminate his outfit before starvation. "The days were extremely warm," he wrote, "and consequently we suffered much from thirst, my men more than myself, for they had not been accustomed to doing without water as much as I had."

---

* Thomas Virgin's incapacity likely accounts for Smith's numerical headcount.

The Native Americans who had pioneered this trace knew precisely where the few scattered springs burbled to the gritty surface. But Smith, try as he might, could not reconstruct his previous crossing. His first inclination was to travel only by night—laying up in the shade of the towering dunes during the day to avoid the searing sun. This plan was immediately scuttled because serving as his lodestone was the series of pointed spires called The Needles far off on the western horizon. When they disappeared after orange dusk he feared leading his company in circles. By their fourth day on the march, Smith's faltering trappers—nervously fingering the triggers of their rifles at every wisp of dust on the horizon—were barely surviving on the meager juices of prickly pear and barrel cacti.

As a last resort, Smith took to exhorting his party to continue walking in the direction of The Needles while he veered off to climb the closest mesas in multiple attempts to find his bearings. From these heights he managed to differentiate the skeins of the Mojave River—the sands of the stream he had named the "Inconstant" being a slightly darker shade than the adjacent dry gulches as white as bleach. With this he was finally able to guide the company from spring to spring. On several occasions, as he had with Robert Evans while traversing the Great Basin, he filled his lone kettle at a water hole and returned to succor men who had collapsed along the route.

On the afternoon of the company's ninth day out, the eastern peaks of the San Bernardino Mountains hove into view. Near the base of the range's foothills the trappers lurched into another dusty arroyo, surprising a small band of Paiute. Eyeing the white men's guns, the Indians struck a deal. They bartered two of their horses and a few clay demijohns of murky brown water in exchange for half the American outfit's steel knives and the remainder of its glass beads.

With the failing, semiconscious Thomas Virgin now strapped to a mount, Smith bucked his men for one last push. He pointed to a distant "Gape of the Mountain" rising in the west. This was Cajon Pass.

CHAPTER 23

BLOODY OREGON

The Mexican authorities were not as convivial this time around.

Jed Smith's second venture into California in the fall of 1827 began well enough, but there were foreboding omens. The priests at the sub-mission in the San Bernardino Valley allowed him and his forlorn company to slaughter and roast several cows to fill their empty bellies. As usual, the hosts provided jugs of wine to wash down the beefsteak. But during the meal they passed on dismaying information—Mexican president Guadalupe Victoria's government already suspected the United States of fomenting the previous year's Anglo insurgency in East Texas. As such, Victoria's California functionaries were unlikely to look kindly upon Smith yet again showing his face in the Republic's northwesternmost province at the head of another armed troop of Americans. Gov. Echeandia, they reminded him, was a close ally of the president, and they cautioned Smith to tack carefully through these political winds.

That night, forgoing a detour to Mission San Gabriel, Smith designated Isaac Galbraith to carry a letter to Father Sanchez thanking him for his friars' hospitality and detailing the circumstances surrounding his return to the territory.* He expected the head-of-mission to forward this explanatory missive to Gov. Echeandia, whom Smith planned to visit at his new seat in coastal Monterrey. That Sanchez never passed along the note would soon serve as a source of contention. Sanchez's lapse, however, was likely a mere oversight, as he did order the Americans equipped with supplies and fresh horses for their ride north. After this *gesto noble*, however, Smith's situation deteriorated rapidly.

Leaving Thomas Virgin at the *asistencia* to recover from his wounds, Smith reached Harrison Rogers's campsite on the Stanislaus River two weeks later. He found his old companions more content than he'd imagined. Though somewhat anxious as Smith's prolonged absence stretched from weeks to months, the mild weather and an abundance of game—some of which the Americans traded to local Indians for fresh fish and fruit, particularly black currants and raspberries—had made their isolated stay passably comfortable. And after their encounter with the military detachment four months earlier, Rogers told Smith, the secular authorities had been content to let them be.

Rogers sensed, however, that this peaceful respite was about to come to an end. The nearby Roman Catholic hierarchy had become increasingly hostile toward the Americans, suspicious over the band's casual friendships with the area's "gentile" tribes, as the Mexicans called the still-wild Indians. Word had recently reached Rogers that the Franciscans were exerting increasing pressure on the provincial governor to issue arrest warrants for him and his trappers, and he reported that he'd planned to linger but a few more days awaiting Smith's return before seeking his own route through the Sierra Nevada.

Smith immediately engaged a pair of Miwok guides and selected three men to accompany him to the governor's mansion in Monterrey "to try once more the hospitality of the Californias." He warned Rogers that ne-

---

* Having immediately found California to his liking, with Smith's permission the Maine-born Galbraith completed his cross-country sojourn and settled in Los Angeles, where it was said that he amused himself by shooting the heads off blackbirds at twenty paces.

gotiations with Echeandia might not go well, and should he become entangled in any sort of legal imbroglio, Rogers should unearth the buried pelts and lead the company toward the safety of the Oregon Country via the Russian settlement on Bodega Bay.

* * *

Smith's first stop was Mission San Jose, some seventy miles southwest of the camp on the Stanislaus and about midway to Monterrey. There he hoped to receive permission from the head-of-mission to pass through his lands. Instead, the Franciscans summoned soldiers who disarmed Smith and his companions, seized their horses, and tossed them in jail—"a dirty hovel which they called a guard house." Thus began a three-month odyssey of house arrests, dueling accusations of trespass and perfidy, and a military tribunal during which Smith was accused (and acquitted) of encouraging a Miwok uprising in order to claim for the United States the lands abutting the San Joaquin River.

At first Smith put his detention to good use, reconstructing from fresh memories the journals he had lost during the Mojave attack. Yet as the contentious weeks wore on and he was transferred to Monterrey, his simmering umbrage over the "Spanish cruelty" to which he felt subjected led him to suspect that Gov. Echeandia had somehow personally provoked the Mojave into their attack. His spirits sunk even further when he learned that Rogers and his trappers had also been detained before they could make their run for Oregon.

Smith, of course, was not without an agenda. Though his inherent honesty was never in doubt, he was nonetheless a product of his times. This meant he could not help but harbor sentiments of national and even cultural supremacy over the descendants of the haughty European conquistadors who now served as his jailors. Some might argue that his feelings of persecution seem a bit ripe coming from a man who had, after all, disobeyed the governor's previous order to exit California forthwith. Taking Echeandia's point of view, it did seem fairly galling that the American whose departure he had provisioned had not only ignored his pointed directive but had then the temerity to return unannounced. Smith could only stammer that he thought that Father Sanchez had passed on his letter explaining the unusual circumstances of his re-entry.

During one face-to-face inquest, Echeandia called Smith's bluff with a sly insouciance. "When you came to San Diego [last year]," the governor began, "you represented the route by which you had come to California as being a dry barren desert almost impassable."

This was correct, Smith said.

"And now you have come by the same route again?"

The question momentarily hung fire. Smith finally explained that, having barely survived his journey across the continent's Great Basin, he deemed the Mojave trace the lesser of two evils. His counterargument fell flat. It was true that the governor—and most Mexicans, for that matter— were so uninformed about the geography of their eastern holdings that they mistook the snow blanketing the Sierra Nevada's peaks, basins, and bulbous plutons for chalk. Echeandia, however, did not need a topographer's understanding of his jurisdiction to pose his next query regarding what he referred to as this "misterious business."

If Smith already knew that the Mojave Desert contained no beaver, the governor wondered, why had he yet again ventured into that quarter? Surely not just to retrieve his men on the Stanislaus. Could not his party have made their way back east just as he had?

And here the game was up. Smith had no choice but to admit to trapping and caching more than fifteen hundred pounds of beaver pelts prior to his escape. The rescue of his stranded companions was of course the paramount reason for his return, he said. But he also felt he required more men to haul his catch back to the United States. With this an indignant Echeandia, whom Smith complained of as having been "placed in power to perplex me," was on the verge of consigning the American to the brig of the next ship bound for Acapulco. At the last moment, however, Smith was again saved by a consortium of American sea captains on whom Alta California's burgeoning economy depended.

The shipmasters, predominantly Massachusetts traders, were wary of what they viewed as a trifling territorial misunderstanding blossoming into an international incident that might affect their livelihoods. They offered Echeandia an alternative—they would purchase Smith's furs for $2.50 per pound, and the nearly $4,000 that the Americans would collect would be more than ample to allow Smith and his wayward hunters to obtain horses, pack mules, Indian trade goods, and enough "Beef Corn Beans &c" to facilitate their exit from Mexican territory. The price for the peltry was of course below the going rate for plews sold in the mountains, much less on the St. Louis market. But Smith was in no position to bargain.

Gov. Echeandia saw merit to the sailors' plan, not to mention a way out of a sticky political situation. But before acceding to the proposal, he demanded several caveats. The American shipping syndicate, he insisted, must post a $30,000 bond—close to $1 million today—payable to the Mexican government should Smith and his company fail to depart the province by the end of the year. Further, Capt. Smith must personally pledge on his word of honor to refrain from trapping any animals south of the international border at the forty-second parallel. Smith dutifully signed the document.

By this point in his career, however, Jed Smith was nothing if not a resourceful businessman. California at the time was so overrun with feral horses denuding the mission farm fields, orchards, and especially the cattle pastures that the friars had taken to capturing and penning the animals to starve to death. So inexpensive was this horseflesh that Smith, already in possession of sixty-five mounts and pack mules, purchased another 250 at $10 per head—a pittance of what he could sell them for in the Rockies. If he could get them there.

So it was that on December 30, 1827, Smith gathered his company of nineteen men on the south shore of San Francisco Bay beneath a pewter sky. What had begun as a cold drizzle quickly escalated into buckshot bursts of rain coming in blinding sheets. The long train of inundated Americans included the nine trappers from Smith's first foray into California as well as the nine men who had survived the second journey, including the recovered Thomas Virgin, who had been briefly imprisoned in San Diego. The lone new hand was a former British seaman named Richard Leland whom Smith had met in Monterrey and signed on as a muleskinner. Moving several miles up the San Joaquin, they forded the river and rode north. Despite the shivering downpour, Smith was ecstatic. He was, he wrote, "returning to the woods, the river, the prairae, the Camp and the Game with a feeling somewhat like that of a prisoner escaped from his dungeon and his chains."

He was also riding into a new kind of Indian Country.

* * *

Once clear of the California settlements, it had taken Smith and his men nearly two months to reach the confluence of the American and Sacramento Rivers, a mere seventy-five miles northeast of San Francisco. It had been a hard passage. The rain had not let up since their departure, and traveling the river's soggy feeder bottoms had been a literal slog. The terrain over which Smith and his outfit had enjoyed a fruitful trapping season the previous spring was now a morass of hog-wallow swampland; the "slous" as Smith described them, "so deep as to be swimming."

Moreover, between the wear and tear on his original traps as well as the loss of their replacements during the Mojave attack on the Colorado River, his entire outfit was down to forty-seven serviceable beaver traps. Yet in spite of this and the miserable weather conditions, the outfit had taken close to 150 plews during its first month on the trail. Their fortunes, however, had turned by late January, around the same time that two of the party deserted, absconding with eleven of the meager store of traps.

The cloudbursts had only intensified from this point on, and setting traps became near impossible as the high-water marks of the California north country's sycamore-fringed creeks, streams, and ponds shifted daily. So murky were the tule marshes through which Smith's sodden riders ventured that men not assigned to wrangling the remuda resorted to constructing elk-hide bullboats and cottonwood rafts to float their supplies and equipage. This was little relief to the horses, which were constantly mired in mud up to their hocks. The downpours even appeared to have driven the local fauna to ground, and the farther afield they traveled, the more scarce became deer and elk. Smith and his men often went days without seeing a single game track.

Bears, on the other hand, were a constant menace. On two occasions Smith—scouting routes ahead of the party—narrowly escaped grizzly encounters. In the first he plunged into a deep creek just ahead of the pursuing silvertip and swam underwater as far as he could; on the second occasion a grizzly lunged at his horse from behind, its paws latching on to the frenzied animal's tail. "The Horse being strong and much frightened," Smith wrote, "exetered himself so powerfully that he gave the Bear no oppertunity to close uppon him and actually drew him 40 or 50 yards before he relinquished his hold. The Bear did not continue the pursuit but went off and [I] was quite glad to get rid of his company on any terms."

The clerk-diarist Harrison Rogers was less fortunate. In early March, while out hunting, Rogers was infelicitously inducted into the fraternity of Mountain Men when he was mauled by a brown bear. Smith was forced to halt the caravan for a week to wash and dress Rogers's multiple wounds several times daily with "cold water and a salve of Sugar and Soap."

The Indians, too, had become bolder than the diffident tribes the Americans had encountered in California's Central Valley. "The lowest intermediate link between man and the Brute creation," Smith wrote of the northern California peoples known as the Hupa, a group of salmon fishers whose animosity to outsiders, both red and white, lent them a mysterious aura of menace. Smith and his trappers caught occasional glimpses of these short and stoic braves, their thick streams of jet-black tresses falling past their deerskin tunics. They soon learned that unless they sat by their trap chains through the night, both the metal and any beaver catch would have vanished by sunup.

Though Smith and his party were only beginning to acclimate themselves to the habits of the far northwest's Indigenous forest dwellers, the Native Americans who occupied these lands were already well versed in the ways of the white intruders.

* * *

Prior to the arrival of European Americans in Western Canada and what would one day come to be known as the Oregon Territory, there existed a distinct aspect to intertribal combat found nowhere else on the continent. Unlike the mourning wars conducted by Eastern Woodlands tribes, the territorial battles fought by Plains Indians over control of buffalo migratory routes, or even the lightning raids conducted by Comanche, Apache, and Navajo horsemen across desolate southwest landscapes, Indigenous peoples from the rugged northern California coast and up through the British Columbia Plateau tended to resort to violence against one another on a personal level. A single brave, or at most a small fraternal band from his clan, might don warpaint to seek vengeance for some real or perceived slight. But it was unusual for entire villages to march against one another. Moreover, the evolution of elaborate ceremonial conclaves that included games of strength, tests of endurance, and the potlatch—gatherings at which host Indians acquired honor and prestige through the dissemination of gifts—allowed individuals to resolve disputes in nonlethal settings. As with Indigenous mores across North America, this would change with the arrival of the white man.

Though the doomed Astorians had done some trading with local tribes, it was the trappers from the Hudson's Bay Company who had fully introduced the likes of tobacco and refined sugar as well as manufactured goods such as steel knives, iron pots, and woolen blankets into the Indigenous economies. It was also the Canadians who transformed the culture of martial conflict, as the Indians came to realize that individual warriors stood little chance against the long rifles wielded by the pale intruders. This new threat required strength in numbers.

Thus, as Jed Smith and his troop pushed north into the wild Klamath River country, they began to encounter large bands of curious Native Americans, likely Maidu and Modoc. The Indians would cautiously venture into the American camp toting fresh fish, salal-berry cakes, and the occasional beaver or otter pelt to exchange for the outfit's razors, tobacco plugs, and beads. The next morning, in the course of rounding up their grazing remuda, the trappers would inevitably discover a number of their horses pocked with arrows. More than a few had to be put down. "Finding the [Indians] being so numerous and the Travelling being so bad," noted Harrison Rogers, "we did not pursue them, knowing it was in vain."

Further, as Smith's company advanced closer to the Pacific corridor, it became even more difficult to read the temper of the coastal tribes whose braves were as slick as otters and used to hard water. On a given morning a band might appear at the American camp to smoke and barter; by the afternoon the trappers picking their way through deep ravines or tumbling streambeds would find themselves dodging hails of arrows flickering down from the surrounding heights. Smith—who in the final weeks of April personally shot and killed several raiding hostiles—could count himself lucky that the denizens of the wet and heavily wooded country through which he was moving had little contact with the horse-and-gun culture that had consumed their brethren to the south and east. The canoe was the preferred mode of travel over long distances, and arrows, spears, and clubs remained the principal weapons.

Adding to their miseries, even the most experienced high-country hands in Smith's outfit had never encountered terrain such as this. By the time the trappers reached the lower reaches of the cloud-shrouded Cascades, Smith's exhausted train was lucky to make a mile on a good day. Wielding axes to break trail through the thick stands of pine, spruce, hemlock, and giant cedar that studded the snowy peaks had become so daunting that often the only path forward was to follow the precipitous stream banks that wound through the mountains like coiled snakes. So impaired were the horses from bulling through tangled, thorny brambles and piling upon each other in dead-end box canyons that Smith was often forced to stop for days at a time to allow the animals to recuperate and fatten on the sparse fescues and bear grass sprouting from the occasional alpine meadow.

As he observed in his journal, "Any person apprised of the character of the country through which I was traveling might form something of an Idea of the difficulty of traveling with a Band of three hundred horses." By late June, when the Americans crossed into present-day Oregon, Smith had lost close to seventy of his half-feral herd to fatigue, drownings, falls from knife-edge ridgeline trails, and Indian attacks.

It was also in June that Smith, making for the seaboard, noticed tree stumps that bore the unmistakable marks of having been felled with steel axes. Though his party was still some three hundred miles south of the Columbia River, this was a clear indication that they were approaching Hudson's Bay Company territory. It was well known that the tribes residing along the Willamette River trafficked regularly with the Canadians, with tools such as axes making their way south via age-old Indian trade routes.

Smith also surmised that this might mean that there existed a less wearying coastal path to the mouth of the Columbia. Yet when he rode out through the rain and dense fog one morning in search of a shoreline route, he was confronted with a succession of insurmountable cliffs rising from the seething ocean like a row of sickles hanging from the wall of a dry goods store. He ordered his company turned back toward the trackless, inland labyrinth. Harrison Rogers likely spoke for the entire outfit with his journal entry: "Oh God, may it please thee, in thy divine providence, to still guide and protect us through this wilderness of doubt and fear."

His prayer went unanswered.

* * *

It began, innocuously, with a stolen tool. Camped along the Umpqua River in south-central Oregon, the Americans had only just settled into a trade session with a tribe known to whites as the Kelawatset—but who called themselves the Quuiich—when the alarm was sounded.* An ax had gone missing. The suspected thief, the son of an Indian of some distinction within the band, was immediately surrounded and seized. Jed Smith, weary and irritable from over six months of hard travel, wound a rope around the man's neck and lashed him to a tree. The brave confessed soon enough, pointing to a pile of brush under which he had hidden the pilfered ax. Fifty or so of his fellow tribesmen looked on uneasily while the little troop of white men, in Rogers's telling, "stood with our guns ready in case they made any resistance . . . but [they] did not."

The robber was banished from the campsite, and with that the bartering continued—beads, tobacco, and razors were exchanged for otter skins, lamprey eels, and wicker baskets brimming with raspberries. It was as if nothing had happened. At least, so thought the trappers.

That night the Quuiich held council. The expelled brave and his kin argued for an immediate attack in retaliation for the insult. The assault was forestalled by the tribe's principal headman. The white men, though vastly outnumbered, had guns, and the chief was wary of their firepower. He was answerable to the entirety of his people, not just the young hotheads, and perhaps he also considered the widows and orphans who would inevitably become his responsibility in the wake of a pitched battle. More pertinent, the story of how the wily Tia-o-qui-aht had bided their time before taking revenge on the crew of the American vessel the *Tonquin* nearly two decades earlier still reverberated across the Northwest. The headman counseled patience.

When the Americans broke camp the next morning under a livid sky awash with blinding neurons of white lightning, the Quuiich followed. Overnight their party had nearly doubled in size, to close to one hundred

---

* Lewis and Clark, though they never journeyed this far south in Oregon, had designated the tribe the "Kelawatset" by phonetically bastardizing what the Chinook and Salish Indians to the north called the Q'elwats, or "Tied to Narrow-Wasted" peoples. The name persisted among early pioneers although the tribe itself, the southernmost branch of a loose Umpqua confederation living along the eponymous river, referred to their nation as the Quuiich, or "Southern People."

braves. A comfortable routine—travel, camp, trade—repeated itself for the next several days as the trappers entered open country rife with deer, elk, and large swaths of purplish semaphore grasses for the horses.

On July 13, Smith and his outfit reached the confluence of the Umpqua and its most-northern tributary, known as the Upper Umpqua, over which hung a ghostly mist.* The Indians indicated via sign that if the white men followed the main branch of the watercourse to its convergence with a stream called Elk Creek, they would find themselves at the foot of a spur of the Cascades that ran perhaps sixty miles due west, known today as the Calapooya Divide. Crossing these low hills would drop them down into the great fertile river valley of the Willamette, a little more than one hundred miles from the mouth of the Columbia. Every man in Smith's outfit recognized that reaching what Rogers called the "wel Hammett" would mark the beginning of the end of their arduous journey.

The next morning dawned bright and clear, as if in salute to the welcome news, as Smith and a Quuiich guide prepared to set off by canoe to scout the route north. Joining them were a brawny trapper named John Turner and the British muleskinner Richard Leland. At the last moment, somehow intuiting bad medicine in the air, Smith advised Rogers to construct a corral of driftwood and tree branches with which to pen the horses.

He also warned him that the Indian band had grown too large to be allowed into camp. For reasons never to be known, Rogers ignored the caution.

Not long after Smith's departure, Rogers and the remaining trappers—their damp gunpowder drying in the rare morning sunlight—began spreading blankets on which to display their trade goods.† They were surprised when a Quuiich strode into their midst and jumped onto a horse belonging to the hunter Arthur Black. Black, a veteran high-country hand whose relationship with Jed Smith went back to the rescue of "Le Grand

---

* The tributary was subsequently renamed the Smith River.

† A Hudson's Bay Company diarist speculates that sex was the reason for Rogers's carelessness. "But to gratify their passion for women, the men neglected to follow [Smith's] order [and] allowed the Indians to come into camp."

Pierre" Tivanitagon's Iroquois and their subsequent ride into Montana's Flathead Post four years earlier, found this amusing. Most of the Indigenous peoples the Americans had encountered in these parts appeared frightened of the animals, although a few had tried to converse with them in sign language and even in low, singsong voices. Unknown to the white men, the Indian now cantering about their camp atop Black's mustang was the very same headman who had prevented the attack after the stolen-ax incident.

A crowd of braves had gathered by the time Black, rifle in hand, caught the reins of his animal and demanded that the Indian dismount. With this the chief, humiliated in front of his people, trilled a loud string of words. Scores of hostiles sprang at the fourteen whites. Two pinned Black's arms and tried to wrestle the rifle from his hands. A third rushed at him with a maplewood war club. Black twisted from his captors' grasp at the last second. The blow from the rounded burl of the weapon grazed his head and thudded into his back. Black dropped his gun and pitched into the surrounding woods, running for his life. Glancing over his shoulder in search of pursuers, he glimpsed an array of chaotic scenes.

A brace of Quuiich wielding hatchets were straddling the prone body of the luckless Thomas Virgin, finishing the job the Mojaves had begun on the Colorado River. Beyond Virgin, the trapper Thomas Daws, having leaped into the river, was being chased by Indians in dugouts. And not far from the streambank a bevy of warriors hacked with axes at a dismembered corpse whose bloody face Black could not make out. From the distinctive quillwork adorning the man's moccasins, however, he knew it was Harrison Rogers.

CHAPTER 24

FORT VANCOUVER

It had been over three months, and the bashed skulls and shattered bones of the eleven American trappers had bleached to an alabaster hue. Jed Smith's journal entries do not reveal his thoughts as he gazed upon the remains of his company. He may have walked among the skeletons scattered about the riverbank, attempting to determine their identities. This was impossible. Their buckskins, moccasins, and any other piece of identifying clothing had long been carried off.

It was October 28, 1828, and Smith had returned to the scene of the ambush with Arthur Black, John Turner, Richard Leland, and a troop of Hudson's Bay Company men led by the Booshway Alexander McLeod. Departing Fort Vancouver and passing through numerous Native American villages on their trek up the Willamette Valley, McLeod's Tillamook scouts had picked up rumors that three more of the white men may have survived the attack. This hearsay had so far proved as unfounded as the reports of a general uprising among the entire Umpqua confederacy in the wake of the Quuiich's surprising triumph over the Americans.

When McLeod's company crossed the Calapooya Range and dropped into the Umpqua basin, his Indian outriders induced an Upper Umpqua chief to parley. The old headman—who purported to speak for all the tribes in the valley—nervously asked whether the whites had entered his territory to make war. McLeod noted in his daybook that "we answered in the negative. [I said] our wish was to establish Peace and Quietness and recover what could be got of Mr Smiths Property, and restore the Same."

The venerable Umpqua must have been as surprised by this reply as McLeod himself had been to see Jed Smith walk through the gate of Fort Vancouver eleven weeks earlier.

*   *   *

It was a given that Jedediah Smith was dead. On August 8, a naked and barely conscious Arthur Black had been deposited at the entrance to the Hudson's Bay Company's Fort Vancouver by a friendly band of Salish. Upon Black's revival, he related to the outpost's chief factor, Dr. John McLoughlin, his recollections of the fight on the banks of the Umpqua. Although the particulars remained hazy, especially after his dash into the forest, Black was certain that he was the sole survivor. That evening, in a report to the company's North American governor George Simpson, McLoughlin specifically referred to "the late Jedediah Smith."

Word of Smith's demise spread rapidly among the Canadian trappers. Smith may have represented an existential threat to the Hudson's Bay Company's London-based directors—not to mention a burr under George Simpson's saddle, but by this point in the epoch, word of his adventures from Missouri to Montana to Utah to California had spread even farther than he had traveled. He was no longer listed merely among the pantheon of Mountain Men but—even in the distant Oregon Country—he had acquired a heroic aura equal to such legendary wilderness trailblazers as Robert Rogers, Daniel Boone, and even Canada's own Alexander Mackenzie.

So it occurred that when Smith led John Turner and Arthur Leland through the gate of Fort Vancouver moments before noon on August 10, 1828, men froze where they stood, jaws agape, as if a stage director had arranged a *tableau vivant* as a personal greeting. The first person to break the spell was the American trapper Black, recovered enough from his trials to lunge at Smith and lift him off the ground in a bear hug.

That night, having absorbed Black's tale of what westerners still refer to as the "Umpqua Massacre," Smith met with John McLoughlin and Alexander McLeod, the fort's lead trapper. He described to the Canadians how, by all reason, he should rightly have gone under. On the day of the fight, he said, he had left Turner and Leland several miles upriver and floated back down the Umpqua with his Quuiich guide. The sense that something was wrong still nagged. Just before reaching the campsite, an Indian on the riverbank yelled something. At this the guide snatched Smith's rifle and plunged into the water. Near simultaneously, half a dozen or so hostiles rose from thick brush and peppered the air about him with rifle balls. They were not good shots.

There was only one source from whom the tribe could have acquired so many rifles, Smith told McLoughlin and McLeod. His own men. The Quuiich, he said, perhaps unfamiliar with the mechanisms of weapons, took too much time to reload. Smith paddled furiously for the opposite bank and scrabbled up a rise. He could not see any of his company, nor his horses. He hied back up the river on foot, gathered Turner and Leland, and together they followed the same trail that Arthur Black had taken north—to the mouth of the Umpqua, up the Pacific coast, and then inland along the Columbia.

*   *   *

By chance, on the morning of Jed Smith's appearance at Fort Vancouver, Alexander McLeod was in the early stages of organizing a beaver hunt up the Willamette, over the Calapooya Divide, and through the Umpqua Valley. Smith and his small troop naturally volunteered to join him. In the interim Dr. McLoughlin dispatched his best wilderness hand, a French Canadian named Michel Laframboise, to gather what information he could about the bloodbath and its aftermath. The thirty-six-year-old Laframboise was accustomed to traveling alone, writes Dale Morgan, "through regions where heavily armed parties ventured with trepidation." This may have been due to his reputation as having a wife in every village.

Three weeks later, when Smith, Black, Turner, and Leland saddled up with McLeod and his party of twenty-two *engagés* and fourteen Tillamook scouts, the outfit's mission had changed. Beaver-taking was now a secondary consideration to searching for hypothetical survivors of the Quuiich ambush, retrieving what it could of Smith's stolen property, and, if possible, providing Christian burials for the fallen trappers. McLoughlin had also secretly instructed McLeod that, as his point man on the ground, he was to use his discretion whether to "make War on the Murderers of [Smith's] people to restore law and order to the British domain."

McLeod's outfit was but two days out from the fort when they met the returning Michel Laframboise. He bore bad news. Smith's horses and equipage had been traded and retraded to the point of being scattered across the sixteen hundred square miles of the Umpqua Valley. What followed was four months of hard travel through incessant rain. Riding and canoeing from village to village and sometimes from isolated lodge to lodge, Smith managed to recover thirty-five horses and mules and 650 beaver and otter skins. Backed by the Canadian guns, he further collected an assortment of rifles and rifle parts, flintlock pistols, hunting knives, traps, cooking kettles, and cotton and woolen shirts. In the end, he was also able to provide his late comrades with proper interments.

Toward the conclusion of the company's circuit through the valley, a small band of Indians arrived at McLeod's camp on the Umpqua not far from the tributary that Jed Smith christened the Defeat River.* They turned over three more horses and a few traps, a rifle barrel, a copper kettle, and—as McLeod recorded it—"some Beads, Books, journals and other Papers." Thus were the diaries of Jedediah Smith and Harrison Rogers preserved for posterity.

---

* That name did not stick, and it is still known today as the Smith River.

* * *

One month shy of his thirtieth birthday, Jed Smith had now lost twenty-four men to Indian attacks in less than twelve months. Other than dutifully recording the names of the dead, the sites of their demise, and the identities of the tribes responsible, he did not share in his journal pages whatever anguish he may have felt. What he did report was his surprise at finding the Hudson's Bay Company's governor George Simpson awaiting him when, on December 14, 1828, he again passed through the wooden plank door set into the huge gate of Fort Vancouver.

This was Simpson's first visit to the Columbia Department in four years, and when he departed Manitoba, he had no idea that it would entail a face-to-face encounter with his American bête noire. Simpson had traveled west to personally inspect the impact his reorganization of the firm's business plan after London's panic over news of the opening of South Pass. The man Simpson had selected to implement his shake-up, Dr. John McLoughlin, was a forty-two-year-old Scottish Canadian physician born Jean-Baptiste McLoughlin who had Anglicized his name upon assuming his position with the British company. Gov. Simpson's florid physical description of the six-foot, four-inch McLoughlin bears repeating if only for its menacing specificity.

The chief factor, wrote Simpson, "was such a figure as I should not like to meet in a dark Night in one of the bye lanes in the neighborhood of London, dressed in Clothes that had once been fashionable, but now covered with a thousand patches of different Colors, his hands evidently Shewing that he had not lost much time at his Toilette, loaded with arms and his own herculean dimensions forming a *tout ensemble* that would convey a good idea of the high way men of former Days."

An early lantern slide of McLoughlin does indeed depict a man with a gruff, thick-lipped grimace set below dark, somber eyes, all framed by a snowslide of white hair parted in the middle and falling to his broad shoulders. But despite his hulking demeanor, McLoughlin, who had received his medical degree at nineteen, approached any obstacle set before him with the precision of a coroner dissecting a corpse. On receiving his instructions from Simpson, McLoughlin's first order of business was to raze the company's old Fort George on the southern bank of the Columbia and begin construction on the new Fort Vancouver to the north of the river. The relocation, as well as his decision to abandon the Hudson's Bay outpost known as Spokane House in favor of a more northerly site dubbed Fort Colville, was McLoughlin's precaution against the Columbia one day becoming the international border between Canada and the States.

McLoughlin then turned his attention to Peter Skene Ogden's disastrous confrontation with the Americans near the Great Salt Lake. Poring over Ogden's reports with increasing fury, he reckoned that desertions alone during the incident had cost his organization close to two thousand beaver skins. His remedy was to decree that all freemen employed by the firm would herein receive "as much or even something more" than the Americans paid for pelts. In a further effort to eliminate defections, he reduced the price of merchandise sold at Hudson's Bay Company stores. The costs of trapping equipment were slashed, and foodstuffs such as coffee, sugar, flour, and tobacco were sold for well below what Jed Smith and his new partners charged for the same goods at Rendezvous.

These measures paid immediate dividends. Desertions abruptly ceased, with some defectors even returning to the Canadian fold. Ogden's next three expeditions produced profits of £7,500—close to $1.3 million in today's dollars—more than counterbalancing the company store price reductions. In addition. Simpson and McLoughlin put into motion a new moneymaking stream that involved cutting and shipping timber to Asia from Canada's western ports.

At Simpson's first meeting with Jed Smith, he expressed a pro forma sympathy for "the lamentable and melancholy fate of your unfortunate companions . . . at the hands of the savages." In private communiqués to his superiors in London, however, Simpson declared his true feelings toward the former colonials. They were, he wrote to his board of directors, the vanguard of "the all grasping policy of the American Government."

"Common men" such as Smith, Jackson, and Sublette, he added, "who all at once promoted themselves to the Travelling title of Captains," were in reality no more than "outcasts from Society who take all their bad qualities along with them; this 'motley crew' acknowledges no master." As such, he curtly dismissed Smith's proposal to exchange fresh mounts for the exhausted remuda of thirty-eight horses and mules Smith had recovered from the Umpqua Valley. He instead offered to purchase Smith's animals for near the same price he had paid for them in California.*

Summoning his highest dudgeon, Simpson cited the time and expense the Hudson's Bay Company—"the concern"—had sacrificed in aiding Smith and his surviving trappers in their hours of need. "You are well aware that we have already experienced much inconvenience and exposed the concern to heavy loss through our anxious desire to relieve, assist, and accommodate you," he wrote to Smith. Nor was the governor keen on Smith's plan to depart immediately with Arthur Black for Fort Nez Perces, where he would cache his furs, press on for Utah, and return sometime over the summer to retrieve them.

Simpson found this "the height of impudence." He noted that one of Smith's Americans, the burly John Turner, had already decided (with Smith's blessing) to join McLeod's next trapping foray into northern California. And the notion of only the two Americans manhandling packs of plews up the Columbia to the Snake River Country "would in our opinion be sporting with Life or courting danger to madness." Smith and Black, he observed, would be dead from exposure, starvation, or Indian attack within weeks.†

Simpson, denigrating Smith's peltry as "of very bad quality the worst

---

* At two British pounds per animal, this came to about nine U.S. dollars per head in 1828 currency exchanges.

† It is at this point where the British seaman-turned-muleskinner Richard Leland disappears from history's narrative. There is some conjecture that Leland made his way to the Oregon coast and signed on with a merchant ship. Others cite a letter from John McLoughlin to his counterpart at Fort Colville, which includes a cryptic mention of a "Richard Layland" having been arrested and remanded to Canada. Other than this, the Hudson's Bay Company's extensive annals make no mention of either name.

indeed which I ever saw," instead offered to purchase the entire lot at $3 per skin. "If these terms are not satisfactory to you," he added, "the furs may be left here until you have an opportunity of removing them." Which, Smith knew, would in all practicality be never.

Alternately, Simpson informed Smith and Black that they were welcome to accompany the governor's heavily armed company to Manitoba come spring, and from there make their way across the prairie to St. Louis. Or they could wait until autumn to ride with Alexander McLeod's next expedition toward the Snake River.

In the string of letters Simpson addressed to Smith, the governor cloaked his officiousness with professions of empathy toward Smith's plight. Yet intentionally or not, the hard snip of his words seeped through. Particularly galling was his repeated insistence—in reply to Smith's multiple overtures to repay any debt he owed Simpson's "concern"—that the assistance provided to the Americans required no "renumeration . . . or indemnification, as whatsoever we have done for you was induced by feelings of benevolence and humanity alone . . . the satisfaction we derive from these good offices, will repay the Hon Hudson's Bay Comp amply for any loss or inconvenience rendering them."

This, Simpson pointedly added, was despite the company being "in Law or Equity fully entitled to Salvage" for services rendered.

The treacly subtext of Gov. Simpson's missives must have stuck in the proud Jed Smith's craw like a shard of glass. He nonetheless held his tongue, content to bide his wintertide learning everything he could about the London-based organization's operations in the American Northwest.

CHAPTER 25

"A THRONE OF GRACE"

No one knows how or why Jed Smith chose the date. The weather may have broken early, leaving the Columbia River running ice-free. More likely, news reached Fort Vancouver of a party of American trappers wintering over near Flathead Post. Whatever the impetus, on March 12, 1829—thirteen days before George Simpson planned to set out for Manitoba—Smith and Arthur Black began the five-hundred-mile trek to Montana. In payment for his pelts, horses, and mules, Smith carried with him a Hudson's Bay Company bill of exchange for $2,369.60. To Gov. Simpson's honor, he would also advise his accounting department in Manitoba of the debt owed Smith's partners in case the American died along the journey.

Remarkably, traveling by canoe and on foot along the Columbia, the two skirted the modern-day Canadian border and reached northwestern Montana without incident sometime in midsummer. There they found David Jackson and Thomas Fitzpatrick heading a small troop of trappers encamped on Flathead Lake. The latter were naturally taken aback to see Smith alive after the two-year hiatus. Over the next few days, gorging on heaps of roasted venison, the old friends exchanged twenty-four months' worth of information.

Jackson and Sublette currently had over one hundred men in the field, hunting in various-sized groups across both slopes of the Rockies. Surely to Smith's surprise, they were the only Americans trapping the vicinity. The Indian-hating Joshua Pilcher, Smith learned, had again attempted to establish a trapping presence in the late summer of 1827, not long after Smith rode southwest. But Pilcher's four-year absence from the mountains must have left him rusty, and his effort failed spectacularly when Crow raiders made off with his entire remuda of more than one hundred horses as well as a good portion of his provisions. Notwithstanding the Hudson's Bay Company's Peter Skene Ogden peregrinations along the Snake River, this left the high-altitude beaver grounds exclusive to either outfits employed by the firm of Smith, Jackson, and Sublette or free trappers reliant on its supplies.

Jackson and Sublette had taken full advantage of this near monopoly, with Sublette packing nearly $30,000 worth of furs down to the flatlands in the fall of 1828. After the usual expenses—the largest of which was remitted to Gen. Ashley for provisioning the previous year's Rendezvous—the company had been left with a profit of $16,000. Adding the Hudson's Bay Company's bill of exchange to the total and dividing by three, Jed Smith would soon have close to what today would be worth $200,000 awaiting him in a St. Louis bank.

The windfall had been dearly earned. Over a dozen trappers in the company's employ had been killed by Indians since Smith's departure, not counting men who had succumbed to the natural hazards of the profession. The unsparing Blackfeet were responsible for the vast majority of the deaths, and though a few bands of the tribe's Piegan branch had finally been brought into the trading fold after forging a loose détente with the Shoshone in the summer of 1827—a detail that Smith, remembering the enmity between the two nations, must have found astonishing—the majority remained hostile to any intruders. This was driven home by the death of "Le Grand Pierre" Tivanitagon. As Jackson told the story, the veteran Iroquois trapper and his party had been flanking Sublette's foray into Blackfeet country in the fall of 1827 when they were ambushed and their leader shot dead and "cut into pieces" in the "Hole" on the west slope of the Tetons that now bears his name.

The Blackfeet, and at opportune moments roving parties of Cheyenne, Crow, Pawnee, Arapaho, Bannock, and Shoshone, had continued their raids on both sides of the Rockies throughout 1828. These included one gunfight the previous summer wherein a party of eighteen men under the command of Smith's old Irish mate Robert Campbell was swarmed by close to three hundred Blackfeet warriors. What made the encounter so incredible was that Campbell was only miles from the Bear Lake Rendezvous site at the time. A running battle across the broken Cache Valley floor ensued before Campbell was forced to take refuge beneath a rocky outcropping. With his outfit low on ammunition, Campbell called for volunteers to run the gauntlet of hostiles to retrieve help from the hunters at Bear Lake. Jim Beckwourth and a trapper known only as Calhoun stepped forward.

Stripping down to loincloths, and in Calhoun's case darkening his pale torso with bear grease in hopes of confusing the Indians, the two were handed the reins of the company's sturdiest mounts. For once, Beckwourth does not fetch far in his flamboyant account of their desperate ride, later affirmed by Campbell and other eyewitnesses. Mounting horses "as fleet as the wind," Beckwourth writes, "we bade the little band adieu. we dashed through the ranks of our foe before they had time to comprehend our movement. The balls and arrows flew around us like hail, but we escaped uninjured. Some of the Indians darted in pursuit of us, but seeing they could not overtake us, returned to their ranks."

Hours later, with Campbell and his men down to their final few rounds and whetting their blades for a last stand, Beckwourth and Calhoun reappeared at the head of a mounted brigade of trappers accompanied by painted Shoshone and Ute. The "astonished" Blackfeet, Beckwourth crowed, "instantly gave up the battle and commenced a retreat. We followed them about two miles."

Beckwourth, being Beckwourth, put the number of hostile scalps taken at seventeen while maintaining that his troop chasing the Indians "were satisfied they had more than a hundred slain" whose corpses had been carried away. The more circumspect Campbell estimated that it was closer to several dozen, with his outfit losing one man.

Incredibly enough, among the rescue party was the apparently indestructible Hugh Glass. Glass, who had been trapping the southern Rockies with a company out of Taos for the past several years, had somehow gotten separated from his New Mexico outfit and traveled seven hundred miles to Bear Lake with an arrowhead festering in his back. One of Jackson's hands had sliced the wound open with a razor and extracted the serrated barb.

* * *

Maimings and maulings, deaths and disappearances, intentional or incidental—Jed Smith had witnessed his share. Such were the vicissitudes of life in the high country. He undoubtedly appreciated his partner's reports from a commercial point of view. And from a personal perspective, the tale of Robert Campbell's survival was particularly gratifying. Though theirs was but a brief acquaintance, Smith intuited the same honesty and openness—the same *knowingness*—in the young Irishman that ran through his own character like veins through marble. There was a reason Campbell stood as the executor of his will. Smith even had vague aspirations of perhaps one day going into the trading business with the immigrant from County Tyrone.

In a broader sense, however, Smith was already mentally composing what he would label a series of "Brief Sketches" of his travels he intended to post to Gen. William Clark in St. Louis and to President Andrew Jackson's new secretary of war, John Eaton. Though Smith viewed the hostile Native Americans occupying the tramontane as certainly posing a hindrance to American expansion, he was also early to recognize that their belligerence would eventually prove a minor barrier given the burgeoning military muscle of the United States.

The true obstacles to the nation's dream of a transcontinental dominance, he believed, were Mexico's grip on California and the Hudson's Bay

Company's budding inroads throughout the Oregon Country. The first-hand knowledge he had gleaned regarding both, he felt, would prove invaluable to eastern legislators and statesmen. The irony, of course, was that to the men on the receiving end of these reports, Jedediah Smith himself was fast becoming the human seedbed of Manifest Destiny.

* * *

Riding south from Flathead Country with David Jackson and Thomas Fitzpatrick, Jed Smith finally reunited with Bill Sublette in early August 1829 on Henry's Fork in the shadow of the Tetons. From there the combined company dropped down into Pierre's Hole, the site of that year's Rendezvous. Close to two hundred trappers had gathered in the little vale, and here Smith's personal reunions were completed when he found Jim Bridger among the revelers.

The taut and muscular Bridger had matured into a man to be reckoned with in the seven years since Smith had first encountered the gangly teenager on the Missouri River. His fortitude, endurance, and bravery were matched by his stellar horsemanship and keen eye with a rifle—it was well known that however many balls he carried in his ammunition pouch would equal the number of buffalo he could take down. Though still so illiterate as to be completely ignorant of the letters of the alphabet, his natural facility with languages allowed him to converse with almost every tribe across the west. From the Indians he had also picked up a near sacred belief in the powers of omens and dreams to predict the future, to the point where he was quick to physically challenge anyone who doubted the potency of his premonitions.

Bridger had spent the fall hunting with Robert Campbell. When he informed Smith that Campbell had already left for St. Louis with $11,000 worth of peltry, Smith was tempted to ride after him to not only see his old friend but also personally deliver his reflections to Gen. Clark. But guilt from contributing so little to the business concern that bore his name weighed on him, and he instead decided to remain in the mountains to join Sublette's fall hunt. Clark would have to settle for a written report. A

keen and accurate observer, Smith had departed California with the lay-
outs and defenses of the San Gabriel, San Diego, San Jose, Monterrey, and
San Francisco missions and presidios committed to memory. He could
now add the design and functions of the British Fort Vancouver to the
store of knowledge he would dispatch east.

* * *

In late August, with David Jackson and Thomas Fitzpatrick already departed for the Snake River Country and Sublette's younger brother Milton,
with Jim Bridger as his pilot, leading a troop of forty trappers northeast
toward the Bighorn, Jed Smith and Bill Sublette were left with but one
viable hunting option: Blackfeet territory. As their outfit broke camp and
rode north, it must have seemed to Smith that he had traveled full circle
since his innocent days as a greenhorn hunter-trapper for William Ashley
and Andrew Henry.

Smith's touchstone tour began in October, when he crossed the Continental Divide at North Pass and reached the Madison Fork of the Missouri
River not far from where he'd earned his hivernant bona fides wintering on
the Musselshell with the late and unlamented Big Mike Fink. Pushing on,
harassed near daily by Blackfeet raiders, he and Sublette lost two men to
Indian attacks while trapping the tributaries of the Gallatin Fork through
most of November until making the Yellowstone, not far above where Maj.
Andrew Henry's old fort was now a moldering pile being slowly reclaimed
by the forest. Finally turning back southeast in early December, the outfit converged with Milton Sublette's party. Together they rode for winter
camp on the Wind River, the same site from which five years earlier the
impetuous Smith had begun his halting journey through South Pass.

After caching their substantial haul, on Christmas Day 1829, Bill Sublette
and the ever-ready Moses "Black" Harris again constructed snowshoes to
slog the thirteen hundred miles to St. Louis to secure provisions and fresh
mounts and recruit new hands for the spring hunt. This time the two had
an entire train of Indian pack dogs to haul their supplies of coffee, sugar,

and dried meat. It was doubtful they would have to eat them all. Moreover, tucked inside of Sublette's woolen capote was a packet of letters Smith had composed on the trail.

* * *

The briefest of Smith's missives was addressed to his "Mutch Slighted Parents" from "Your unworthy Son." It contained what may be the most personal emotions Jed Smith had ever allowed the world to glimpse, not least his heart-heavy homesickness. "The greatest pleasure I could enjoy," he wrote to his mother and father, "would to be in the company of my family and friends, but whether I Shall ever be allowed the privilege, God only knows." Smith waxed poetic about the green fields of his youth and begged Jedediah Sr. and Sally to pray for his continued safety. He also hinted that his time in the mountains might be nearing an end.

"It is a long time since I left home & many times I have been ready, to bring my business to a close & endeavor to come home, but have been hindered hitherto—as our business is at present, it would be the height of impolicy to set a time to come Home," he concluded. "[But] I will endeavor by the assistance of Divine Providence to come home as soon as possible. May God in his infinite mercy allow me to soon join My Parents."

The same outpouring of loneliness, freighted by his even deeper Protestant passion for personal rectitude, dominated Smith's letter to his older brother Ralph, then living in north-central Ohio. He implored Ralph to send news via Gen. Ashley in St. Louis regarding the health of his parents and their seven brothers and sisters. He then turned introspective. "Oh my Brother," he wrote, "let us render to him to whom all things belongs a proper proportion of what is his due. I entangle myself altogether too much in the things of time—I must depend entirely upon the Mercy of that Being who is abundant in Goodness & will not cast off any, who call, Sincerely, upon him; again I say, pray for me My Brother—& may he, before whomm not a Sparrow falls, without notice, bring us, in his own good time, Together again."

Finally, perhaps digging into his old mentor Dr. Titus Simon's Bible to cite Hebrews 4:16 as a plea for God's mercy, Smith added, "As it respects my Spiritual welfare, I hardly durst Speak. I find myself one of the most ungrateful; unthankful, Creatures imaginable. Oh when Shall I be under the care of a Christian Church. I have need of your Prayers, I wish our society to bear me up before a Throne of Grace."

In an appended postscript evidently scribbled on the Christmas Eve before Bill Sublette and "Black" Harris departed, Smith allowed that as "Providence had made me Steward of a Small pittance," he had arranged via Sublette to forward $2,200 to his brother as a "beneficence" to his parents "to smooth the pillow of their age." He also wished for this small fortune to provide for the educations of his younger brothers Ira, Benjamin, and Nelson, "at a good English Scool," preferably under the guidance of Ralph's father-in-law, Dr. Simons "if [still] a live." Finally, he chided Ralph, "Recollect that we are Brothers! and I Shall not forgive you if you do not let me know your own Situation—be not too modest."

Having bared his soul to his family, Smith donned again the austere mantle of pathfinder, trapper, and Indian fighter in a third-person communiqué to Gen. Clark. As he considered this an official correspondence, he signed it not by name but with the imprimatur of the firm "Smith, Jackson & Sublette." He assumed that the slew of American seamen who had passed through San Francisco had already described for Clark and his eastern cohort the geographic features surrounding "the deep and spacious Bay universally considered the most safe harbor on the Western Coast of America." He also had no doubt that U.S. Navy officers were aware that the narrow entrance to the anchorage was "defended by a fort placed on the point about ½ mile from the Precidio in a situation admirably adapted for the purpose of which it was intended."

Yet what Clark might find of interest was the fact that the fort's mounted artillery, "the 15 to 20 pieces of cannon . . . I am told, is somewhat decayed," as were the "much decayed" brick barracks "capable of accommodating 20 families and 100 soldiers."

Smith was of the opinion that such literal decadence had also affected the morale of the Mexican troops stationed at each of the missions and presidios he had visited. This, he felt, was the result of their distance from, and commensurate neglect by, the seat of power in Mexico City. President Victoria's increasing paranoia toward American incursions across all of his country's northern states was shared by the officials Victoria had appointed as provincial administrators, not least California's governor-general Echeandia. But Smith had also noticed—and certainly thought Clark should be aware of—the growing rift between the mission priests who under Spanish rule had considered Alta California their exclusive religious domain and the fledgling country's secular republicans, now determined to wrest that power for the state.

It was the English, however, for whom Smith saved his most severe vitriol. After listing the names of the men killed on the Umpqua and itemizing the value of the "Merchdz. taken" by the Quuiich, he cautioned Gen. Clark that "until British interlopers are dismissed from off our territory, Americans will never be respected or acknowledged as patrons by Indians on the west side of the Rocky Mountains. Further, the British influence is gaining ground every day, which our losses and sad disasters can easily show and account for."

What he had observed during his residence at Fort Vancouver was visceral proof of this ground gain. The Hudson's Bay outpost was on the verge of self-sufficiency in nearly every manner, boasting a bevy of blacksmiths, gunsmiths, lumberjacks, carpenters, coopers, and bakers. Its farm fields during the summer prior to his arrival had yielded over seven thousand bushels of corn, wheat, barley, peas, oats, and potatoes. Innumerable brood mares, cattle, hogs, and goats roamed the premises, which included a gristmill, a sawmill, and a small shipyard. In short, the British proto-colony, protected by twelve-pound cannons, was well on its way to becoming both a military and naval base.

Smith ended his letter to William Clark with a warning. "While the [British] pass unmolested throughout all our territories from N. to S., and Even from the Hudson's Bay to the mouth of the Columbia . . . we, for no other reasons than because we are Americans, are tormented and annoyed by Every tribes."

Soon, he promised, he would write to the secretary of war to suggest a remedy to these unfair disparities.

* * *

Bill Sublette had yet to even reach St. Louis with Jed Smith's correspondence by the time its author was again on the move. In January 1830, Smith led a party of trappers including Jim Bridger north by east toward the Powder and thence to the Tongue before turning back west for the Bighorn. Scrabbling for an ever-declining beaver yield by covering more and more territory, Smith's company reached the Yellowstone in early spring, where it lost thirty horses and several hundred traps attempting to ford the river in seasonal spate. Finally crossing the watercourse by bullboat, from the Yellowstone the outfit jumped to the Musselshell, which they trapped down to its confluence with the Missouri before turning for the Judith. Smith became more wary as he inched ever deeper into the heart of Blackfeet country, and when Bridger reported the presence of a large Indian encampment blocking their path, Smith gave the command—"which was cheerfully obeyed," recalled one trapper—to turn back south.

For the first time, that year's Rendezvous had been scheduled for east of the Continental Divide, not far from where the Popo Agie flowed into the Wind. Reaching the site in the early summer of 1830, Smith was joined by David Jackson's troop. As the two parties pressed and bundled a year's worth of beaver haul, it surely occurred to the partners that they had made the leap from financially comfortable to wealthy beyond their dreams. The intimation of professional responsibility that Smith had noted in his letter to his parents—"as our business is at present, it would be the height of impolicy to set a time to come Home"—was now eliminated. This was a major impetus in his decision to finally quit the mountains. Moreover, given the foresight he had demonstrated his entire career, there was likely another factor influencing Smith's resolve to return to his family's embrace.

Though the appetite for beaver hats and shawls in American and European markets showed no sign of abating, Smith recognized the situation on the ground for what it was. The Missouri River tributaries that he had braided the past two seasons were near trapped out, as were the Green River districts across the Divide. The same, he suspected, would soon be true of the southern Rockies, already swarming with hunters out of Taos. And both the Snake River Country and the Flathead lands were showing signs of exhaustion. With the vast territory west and southwest of the Great Salt Lake nearly devoid of life, much less beaver, and the Sierra Nevada far too distant a proposition for profit as long as Mexico controlled the Pacific ports, the richest beaver grounds remaining were the regions occupied by the Blackfeet. At this point in his life, Jed Smith was content to let younger men fight those battles. When Bill Sublette returned from the flatlands, he would inform him and David Jackson of his decision.

Sublette, meanwhile, was making history along the Oregon Trail. When he arrived at Rendezvous in mid-July he was trailed by not only eighty-one mounted men but also twelve wagons drawn by mules—the first wheeled vehicles to ever reach the Rocky Mountains from the Missouri River.* That these were not the first to traverse the Divide was a mere quirk of history and geography given that year's Rendezvous site. Noting the "ease with which the [wagon wheels] rolled" across the prairie, the journalist Charles Keemle would observe for *The St. Louis Beacon*, "The wagons did not cross the mountains; but there was nothing to prevent their crossing and going on to the mouth of the Columbia. [This] shows the folly and nonsense of those '*scientific*' characters who talk of the Rocky Mountains as the barrier which is to stop the westward march of the American people."†

*   *   *

---

* Historians discount the wheeled cannon that had been dragged to the 1827 Rendezvous at Bear Lake as a "vehicle."

† The honor of being the first man to lead a wagon train across the Continental Divide would go to the U.S. Army's Captain Benjamin Bonneville—the godson of the famous revolutionary pamphleteer Thomas Paine—who, two years later, in 1832, led a rolling expedition through South Pass.

If there was any lingering doubt in Jedediah Smith's mind about dissolving his union with Bill Sublette and David Jackson, it was put to rest by a letter Sublette delivered from St. Louis. It was from Ralph Smith and contained the news of the death of their mother, Sally Strong Smith, the previous February. She was fifty-eight. Jed Smith wrote back to his brother, "The mortifying intelligence of the Death of our much loved mother [has prevented me] from administering to the necessities of Her to whoom we owe so much. We can See her no more; therefore let us prepare against the same summons."

The termination of the four-year partnership of Smith, Jackson, and Sublette was completed with a few strokes of a pen. The three transferred all provisions on hand as well as their exclusive supply contract with William Ashley to a consortium headed by Thomas Fitzpatrick, Jim Bridger, and Milton Sublette, who christened their new enterprise the Rocky Mountain Fur Company. In exchange, Smith, Jackson, and Bill Sublette received a promissory note totaling $15,532.23, payable in beaver fur at the usual rate of $3 per pound within fifteen months. As his final act as an officer of the company, Smith volunteered to lead the wagons, now piled with pelts, back to St. Louis. With that Sublette and Jackson promptly formed a new corporation.

CHAPTER 26

THE LAST TRAILHEAD

The snow-capped Rocky Mountains at his back, Jed Smith departed the Wind River for St. Louis on August 4, 1830. Rolling through "level country . . . green with grass sufficient for the support of the horses and mules," he was astounded to find how far the "white settlements" had crept across the Plains during his five-year absence.

The venerable Fort Atkinson, abandoned by the U.S. Army three years earlier in favor of a more modern military cantonment nearly two hundred miles to the south, was already crumbling into ruin. Not far from the new army base—some 240 miles west of St. Louis and named in honor of Col. Henry Leavenworth—the boomtown of Independence had sprouted on the banks of the Missouri River along prairie that Smith remembered as home to wild plum and apple orchards shading vast herds of grazing buffalo. In recognition of the region's sudden transformation, the Missouri governor John Miller had also announced the layout of a new state capital, Jefferson City, to be constructed deeper into the interior to better reflect the nation's westward expansion. The rough-and-tumble days of life on the Big Muddy were well and truly vanishing.

When Smith's wagons rolled into St. Louis on October 10, he and his company—"These hardy and sun-burnt Mountaineers," per one newspaper—

were feted as conquering heroes. Smith was shocked to learn that Robert Campbell, having taken sick, had sailed back to Ireland. His disappointment was assuaged by the unexpected appearance of his twenty-year-old brother Peter, who had journeyed west from Ohio with ambitions of following "Diah" into the high country. Smith, however, had other plans for Peter. And after delivering his furs to William Ashley—who would sell the lot for $85,000—he began putting his accruing capital to work.

Learning from Peter of a farmstead for sale near their brother Ralph's home, Smith sent $1,500 to Ralph to purchase the house and land for his eventual retirement. He then settled into a residence in the city center to fulfill his childhood dream of literarily following in the footsteps of Lewis and Clark by beginning work on the book he had long had in mind, replete with maps detailing his myriad journeys. To that end he enlisted the assistance of James Hall, an author and founding editor of *Illinois Magazine*, as well as the help of a former trapper named Samuel Parkman. Parkman had demonstrated a keen surveyor's eye while in the field and, now, settled in St. Louis, an equally deft touch with a cartographer's graphite pencil. As Parkman began sifting through and collating Smith's haphazard journals and notes, Smith—between sitting for a series of interviews with Hall—organized the pouches of western Indian artifacts, fruit seeds, and conifer leaves and cuttings he planned to deliver to William Clark to disperse among the nation's scientific communities. Finally, his housekeeping chores complete, he composed his long-delayed report to the secretary of war John Eaton.

Not including the copious register of names of men killed by Indians across Smith's time operating in the mountains as well as the years in which they died and the tribes responsible, Smith's lengthy dispatch to Eaton—dated October 29, 1830, and again written in the third person—ran close to two thousand words. It expounded upon the subjects Smith had previously addressed to Gen. Clark. He advised Secretary Eaton that he and his partners, "having traversed every part of the country west of the Rocky mountains from the peninsula of California to the mouth of the Columbia river . . . have made observations and gained information which they think it important to communicate to the Government."

Smith began by reiterating "the ease and safety" with which rolling stock might traverse South Pass to "prove the facility of communicating over land with the Pacific ocean." Then, after briefly summarizing his California calamities, he landed with the same urgency he had communicated to William Clark regarding the perfidy of the Hudson's Bay Company's presence in the Oregon Country.

"As to the injury which must happen to the United States from the British getting control of all the Indians beyond the mountains, building and repairing ships in the tide water region of the Columbia, and having a station there for their privateers and vessels of war, it is too obvious to need a recapitulation," he wrote. Shipbuilders at Fort Vancouver, he continued, had already constructed "two coasting vessels, one of which was then on a voyage to the Sandwich Islands . . . So that every thing seemed to combine to prove that this fort was to be a permanent establishment."

He then lambasted the injustice of British goods entering the Oregon Country by sea from the empire's worldwide holdings without paying American customs duties, as well as the audacity of Hudson's Bay Company trappers roaming lands east of the Rockies ceded to the United States in the Louisiana Purchase. All this, he fumed, while Americans were barred from hunting north of the forty-ninth parallel.

"The inequity of the convention with Great Britain in 1818 is most glaring and apparent," he warranted, "and its continuance is a great and manifest injury to the United States. The interests of the United States and her fur trade requires that the convention of 1818 should be terminated, and each nation confined to its own territories. These *facts* being communicated to the Government, [as Smith, Jackson, and Sublette] consider that they have complied with their duty, and rendered an acceptable service to the administration; and respectfully request you, sir, to lay it before President Jackson."

And with that bugbear off his chest, Jed Smith turned his gaze 180 degrees, from the walled-off Northwest to the commercial prospects offered by Mexico's northern territories.

* * *

Over the half a decade since the revolutionary Republic of Mexico abrogated New Spain's trade restrictions with the United States, the residents of the mountain towns of Santa Fe and Taos had exhibited a remarkable appetite for American goods. Guns, steel knives, and textiles as diverse as calicos, flannels, linens, muslins, and silks were particularly desirable. In exchange, Missouri jobbers returning east along the Santa Fe Trail led wagons laden with furs and woolen fleeces; finely woven serapes, rugs, and tablecloths; and gold and silver, both bullion and delicate filagree jewelry.

The enterprising Jed Smith, intent on investing his trapping profits, was intrigued. By 1830 the trade along the trail was still relatively light, averaging perhaps eighty wagons a year. To Smith it appeared a simple enough proposition: outfit a train brimming with American merchandise, roll into Mexican territory across the well-trod ribbon of commerce that wound from Missouri into Nuevo Mexico, barter shrewdly for goods valued much higher in the St. Louis markets, and come away with a tidy return. Further, as Smith had never been to Santa Fe, any insights gained regarding the political, military, and topographic contours of the region would certainly lend heft to the *geographicus* he intended to publish.

Smith was but a few weeks into his planning for the expedition when, in December 1830, his nineteen-year-old brother Ira arrived in St. Louis. Jed was appalled. He had hesitantly agreed to take Peter under his wing. But the idea of the teenaged Ira's "unformed character" being subject to the temptations of the city was too much to contemplate. St. Louis may have taken on the trappings of a more cosmopolitan metropolis during his years in the mountains, with libraries, sophisticated social clubs, and even a Roman Catholic institute of higher learning, destined to become the esteemed St. Louis University, germinating a stolid middle class. But the brothels and rum shacks "Under the Hill" had not suddenly transformed into convents and tea houses. The notion of Smith's even younger brothers Benjamin, seventeen, and Nelson, sixteen, following in Ira's path was even more terrifying.

"My Brother," Jed wrote to Ralph Smith. "This is the last place to which youngsters should be sent." Jed promptly enrolled young Ira in Illinois College, just across the Mississippi River. Despite being a Presbyterian (and not Methodist) "seminary of higher learning," in the words of its founder, it would have to do.

Intent on departing for Santa Fe by early spring, Smith spent the winter months of 1830–1831 hiring teamsters and hunters, securing trade goods, and, having learned his lesson during his California misadventures, acquiring the passports that would allow his party official entry into Mexico. He had hoped to partner with Robert Campbell on the venture, but Campbell's brother, Hugh, writing from his home in Richmond, Virginia, informed Smith that Robert was still too ill to return to the States from Ireland. Ever cautious, Smith found it expedient to draw up a second will to file with William Ashley.*

During these preparations, yet another Smith sibling, the twenty-three-year-old Austin, had alighted in St. Louis hoping, like Peter, to emulate his older brother Jed's adventurous lifestyle. Jed Smith, ever the worrywart when it came to family, finally reckoned that an excursion along the eight-hundred-mile trace that old William Becknell had pioneered might prove a mild enough opportunity to give the two rawboned tyros their first taste of the continent's backcountry. He even instructed Peter, Austin, and Samuel Parkman, whom he designated the expedition's chief clerk, to begin studying Spanish.

As it happened, Bill Sublette and David Jackson also turned up in the city in late March to secure wagons to stock provisions for their new partnership. Learning of Smith's Santa Fe gambit—it was, after all, the talk of the town—Sublette decided to accompany Smith's enterprise to see if qual-

---

* In this document, Smith arranged for all his "property real and personal savings" to be divided equally between his brothers and sister after stipulating that an annuity of $200—the equivalent of $7,000 today—be set aside for his father each year (Sullivan, *The Travels of Jedediah Smith*, 157).

ity beaver pelts might be secured in the southern Rockies. Jackson would ride along a portion of the journey before veering west toward South Pass.

Two weeks later, on April 10, 1831, Smith's and Sublette's combined party of seventy-four men and twenty-two mule-drawn freighters departed St. Louis. The enormous wagons rumbled down Olive Street, the city's main thoroughfare, in single file, their canvas covers flaring in the breeze while thick-booted muleskinners tramped alongside the animals cracking their eighteen-foot whips. It was a noble sight, one not seen every day, and nearly as many residents of the Mound City as had greeted Jed Smith's arrival six months earlier flocked to the sidewalks to watch his new outfit depart.

By the first of May the caravan had made the outskirts of the new township of Independence, Missouri—soon to be the jumping-off point for the Oregon Trail. It was there that Thomas Fitzpatrick rode into camp. Fitzpatrick had been charged with informing Smith and his former partners that he, Jim Bridger, and Milton Sublette had completed several productive hunts across the mountainous Three Forks country and were on schedule to make good on the payment of their promissory note. Now Fitzpatrick decided to throw in with his old companions, confident that he could complement William Ashley's haul of provisions to next summer's Rendezvous by securing fresh horses, mules, powder and shot, and new traps in New Mexico. If he managed to enliven the festivities by also transporting jugs of the notorious Taos Lightning into Cache Valley, it would only count as a bonus.

Smith had purchased Becknell's rudimentary charts and though no one in his company had experience on the Santa Fe Trail, most were veteran Plainsmen and, Smith judged, more than capable of handling the various vicissitudes of wilderness travel. Given the size and firepower of the wagon train, which included a six-pound artillery piece, he did not expect trouble from hostile Indians. Nor, for the same reason, did he much fear the roving bands of Mexican bandits called "Comancheros," who had lately been extorting tribute from American traders along the trace. These gangs, many of their members mixed-race, had acquired their name by being the only traders the wild Comanche and Kiowa tribes would deal with; as such, the Comancheros served as hard-bitten middlemen between the merchants of Mexico's northern provinces and the most powerful tribe on the Southern Plains. Which is not to say the journey was free of misfortune.

In mid-May a hunter chasing a herd of antelope strayed too far from the train and was jumped and killed by a dozen or so Pawnee. And some three hundred miles out from Independence—just northeast of the Arkansas River near present-day Fort Dodge, Kansas—Smith spotted a dust cloud kicked up by several hundred mounted Indians. He could not make out their tribal markings, although he guessed they were likely Gross Ventres moving south to visit their Arapaho cousins. He ordered the wagons corralled around the remuda and the brass six-pounder unlashed from the axle of the freighter hauling it. The whooping Indians feinted a charge, the cannon barked, and the assailants disappeared into the pitted prairie. They were not seen again.

For days thereafter the most vexing obstacles the party faced were the biting northers carrying rainstorms that mired the draft animals along muddy creek beds. The Americans would soon recall those gullywashers with fondness.

*　*　*

In 1831, the Arkansas River, as per the twelve-year-old Adams-Onis Treaty, still constituted the Mexican border with the United States. South of the waterway's shallow flow in what is now western Kansas lay a timesaving route into eastern New Mexico known as the Cimarron Cutoff. The track, avoiding the mountains, lopped about one hundred miles off the journey. It was also the most dreaded stretch of the Santa Fe Trail.

The fifty-mile plain separating the Arkansas River from the Cimarron—a waterway, like the Mojave, that disappeared beneath the sands for most of the year—was known as "The Water Scrape." Flat, dry, and utterly devoid of landmarks, it was puzzling terrain. Along some stretches the sands were so fine that wagons sank to their wheel hubs, and mule teams had to be doubled up to pull the vehicles free. At other points the wind-swept tracts were so baked by the sun that neither horse hooves nor freighter wheels left an impression. Further, it was a landscape marked only by shimmering and shifting sand hills, thus a veritable death sentence to anyone entering without a compass. Yet even caravans carrying the most modern direction-finding instruments were known to wander aimlessly as their animals slowed, stumbled, and finally dropped from thirst.

The Water Scrape was also Comanche and Kiowa territory. At first the tribes were content to watch from distant buttes as the wagons driven by the pale interlopers passed through their country. But three years earlier, in 1828, several American traders had been ambushed and killed along the scrape. The assailants were never identified. This did not stop a posse of Kansas vigilantes from riding for vengeance. Unlike most Mountain Men, few flatlanders could distinguish one Native American tribe from another. When the self-appointed lawmen stumbled upon a small camp of Comanche who apparently had nothing to do with the attack, they proceeded to murder all but one of the Indians. They should have finished the job. The lone Comanche who escaped spread word of the white man's treachery.

The incident had a spiraling effect. Since then, roving bands of Indigenous raiders laid in wait for the American mercantile trains along the parched wasteland of the Cimmaron Cutoff, biding time to attack at the travelers' most forlorn moments. Two years before Smith's caravan set out, a combined war party of Comanche and Kiowa braves reportedly numbering in the high hundreds had swooped down on an American expedition along The Water Scrape. After the wagons circled, the assault became a siege. With the sun blistering the beleaguered whites taking cover beneath their wagons, the train's wagon master managed to send off riders. Several broke through the Indian lines and located a U.S. Army regiment patrolling the north bank of the Arkansas. The Bluecoats, marching hard into Mexican territory—and breaking international law in the process—managed to avert the looming disaster. But Comanche memory was long.

So it occurred that on the morning of May 27, 1831—as Smith's store of water jugs finally went bone dry and a blinding sandstorm pushed by south winds clogged the throats of both men and animals—Smith dispatched teams of riders east and west in search of water holes. By his calculations they were perhaps two-thirds of the way through The Water Scrape and heading south by southwest. He and Thomas Fitzpatrick spurred ahead in that direction.

Several miles out the two came upon a deep hollow. The crater was dry. But the surface sand was damp. Smith told Fitzpatrick to begin digging for an underground spring. He then mounted up and plunged onward. He had spotted a line of broken ground, perhaps another three miles off. The craggy terrain, he suspected, might indicate that the Cimarron River had resurfaced atop hard rock.

CHAPTER 27

"WHERE HIS BONES ARE BLEACHING"

They searched for Jed Smith for two days.

His distraught brothers Peter and Austin were reluctant to move on. Bill Sublette and Thomas Fitzpatrick minced no words—they would all die if they lingered any longer along The Water Scrape.

It was only when the caravan reached Santa Fe on July 4 that Peter Smith spotted a vaquero carrying a rifle with the initials "JSS" scratched into its wooden stock. The Mexican cowboy was a Comanchero, only just returned from a trade session with the Comanche and Kiowa. He produced Jed Smith's two percussion-lock, silver-mounted pistols. He told the Americans the story as the Indians had told it to him.

* * *

The broken ground that Smith had made for did indeed contain water, a surfaced section of the Cimarron frequented by migrating buffalo. A Comanche hunting party of several dozen braves had camped among the dips and hollows surrounding the wet, gravelly streambed awaiting a passing drove. They spotted the lone white man's approach long before he saw them. By the time they showed themselves, it was too late. Though Smith was still half a mile away, his mount was staggering while the Indian ponies were strong and fresh. They were astounded when the *taibo*, or pale face, spurred his horse and cantered into their midst. As William Sublette and Thomas Fitzpatrick listened to the tale, they must have understood—a bold front was, at that point, Jed Smith's only option.

Smith, his rifle resting across his saddle horn, attempted sign language, likely to indicate his peaceful intentions, or perhaps as an invitation to trade. The Indians, speaking in a pidgin Spanish he could not understand, slowly spread out, attempting to encircle him. Smith's nervous horse danced and finally wheeled, exposing Smith's back. A musket ball burrowed deep into his left shoulder.

Hunched, in obvious pain, Smith turned and fired a bullet into the Comanche leader. The ball passed through the headman and struck another Indian behind him. Both fell dead. Before Smith could reach for his pistols a flurry of steel-tipped lances pierced his torso. Again. And again.

The Comanchero either could not or would not say what became of Smith's corpse. The veteran Indian fighters taking in the account could only well imagine.

*   *   *

"Though he fell under the spears of the savages, and his body has glutted the prairie wolf, and none can tell where his bones are bleaching, he must not be forgotten."

So reads a section of the extensive eulogy for Jedediah Strong Smith, "the greatest American traveler," published in *Illinois Magazine* a year after Smith's death.* Yet one ponders. Even at the relatively young age of thirty-two, Jed Smith already appeared an autumnal figure facing an uncertain and wintry future as he ushered one grand era of our nation to a close to make way for the next.

History, as Smith had lived it, was a complicated weave of plotlines

---

* Though Smith's eulogy carried no byline, from its personal nature and outpouring of emotion, some historians suspect that it was written by the magazine's editor and publisher, James Hall, likely the last journalist to interview Smith before he departed St. Louis.

that, by the time of his lonesome demise, were either careening away from their conventional narratives or coming to an end altogether. As the fledgling nation's quintessential tramontane explorer, Smith had been born into the new America of Washington and Jefferson. Had he survived to reach even the fleeting lifespan of a man of his era, one wonders what he might have made of the bloody slave uprising labeled Nat Turner's Rebellion that signaled an awakening of the nation's abolitionist movement, or the U.S. Supreme Court's ratification of the forced removal of the southeastern Native American tribes—the epochal journey now known as the "Trail of Tears." Perhaps more viscerally, he would have witnessed the North American debut of a piece of modern technology called the steam-powered locomotive that was destined to irrevocably alter the face of his beloved West.

As if to emphasize the rapidly evolving nature of what Jed Smith had considered his sense of place, the year of his death, 1831, also welcomed a brace of foreigners to American soil to document two very distinct New World species. As the Haitian-born artist John James Audubon set out to illuminate the birds of the United States, so too did the French political scientist, diplomat, and historian Alexis de Tocqueville begin his journey to document the country's strange new system of democracy.

These auguries were far from compatible with the world in which Jed Smith had come of age. Perhaps he sensed just this, as the poignance of evanescent loss was already writ large in his epistles to family and friends. One only has to read the eerily proleptic letter Smith posted to his brother Ralph on the eve of his last great adventure along the Santa Fe Trail. The missive, typically pious and laced with a longing for home, included several lines from the Scottish poet Robert Blair's most famous work, *The Grave*.

"How shocking must the summons be, oh death," Smith quoted Blair, "To him that is at ease with his possessions." Smith, citing several more lines, had apparently memorized the poem. He made clear, however, that he was prepared for such a terminal summons by also including a stanza from the prolific British Methodist hymnist Charles Wesley.

Lord, I believe a rest remains
To all Thy people known
A rest, where pure enjoyment reigns,
And Thou art loved alone

It would take decades, but eventually the wild country that this extraordinary Mountain Man had traversed and explored would be sanded down into the monoculture of the tame American east. But, for now, somewhere along the banks of the Cimarron River, Jedediah Strong Smith finally rested in peace, where his pure enjoyment reigned.

EPILOGUE

*Walk quietly in any direction and taste
the freedom of the mountaineer.*

—John Muir

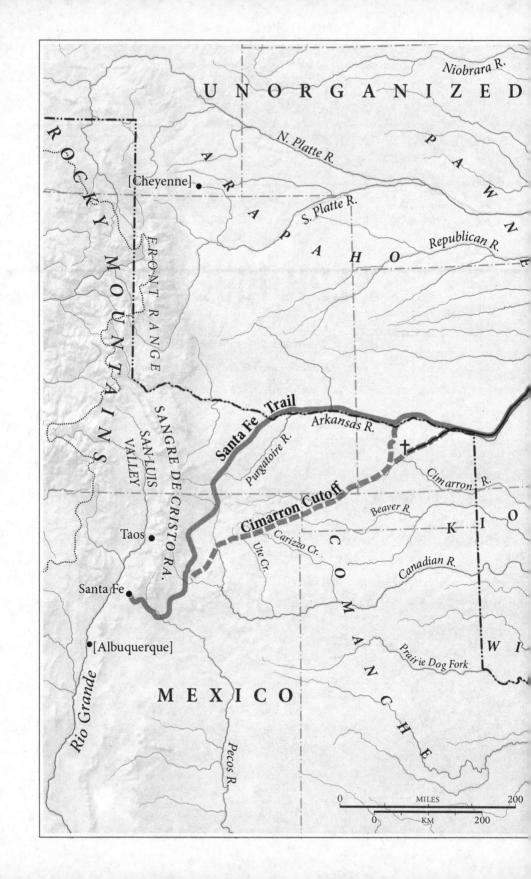

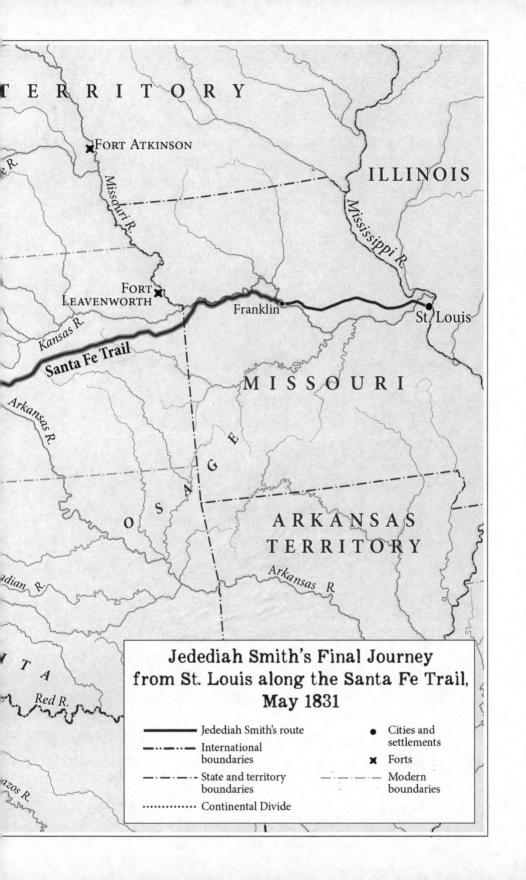

TERRITORY

✖ FORT ATKINSON

ILLINOIS

Missouri R.

Mississippi R.

FORT
LEAVENWORTH ✖

Franklin ●

● St. Louis

Kansas R.

Santa Fe Trail

MISSOURI

Arkansas R.

O S A G E

ARKANSAS
TERRITORY

Arkansas R.

dian R.

T A

Red R.

azos R.

Jedediah Smith's Final Journey
from St. Louis along the Santa Fe Trail,
May 1831

———— Jedediah Smith's route
—··—··— International
boundaries
—·—·—·· State and territory
boundaries
············ Continental Divide

● Cities and
settlements
✖ Forts
———— Modern
boundaries

EPILOGUE

Twenty years had passed since Jedediah Smith's disappearance on the Santa Fe Trail when Jim Bridger reined in his mount atop the low butte in southeastern Wyoming. Peering down at the lush grasslands bisected by the North Platte River, the old Mountain Man took in a sight that none had ever before witnessed on the Great Plains—nearly ten thousand men, women, and children from more than a dozen Indigenous nations fanned out nearly to the horizon. It was the first week of September 1851, and the tribes had convened to hear representatives of the Great White Father in Washington make the case for peace—peace not only between the Indians and the hordes of settlers, miners, and Mormons pouring through and into their lands but also peace among the Native Americans themselves.

Still hale and flinty at forty-seven, Bridger had yet to begin losing the keen eyesight for which he was justly famous. Bridger scanned the assemblage. Several miles away, hugging the left bank of the river, he could clearly make out the painted tipis of the Arikara, Mandan, Assiniboin, and Minnitaree camps. Despite the U.S. Army's pledge to police this grand treaty council—guaranteed by two hundred Bluecoats manning a phalanx of mountain howitzers ostentatiously arrayed about the assemblage—the Upper Missouri tribes had clustered together for protection from timeless enemies, their once fearsome reputations shattered by a series of smallpox epidemics that had left them as spent and hollow as an empty cartridge case.

Not far away, near the confluence of the North Platte and a fast-flowing stream called Horse Creek, Bridger watched Sioux, Cheyenne, and Arapaho braves stage manic races atop their finest war ponies, ribbons and bells streaming from the animals' manes, as tribal headmen clad in their most ornamental buckskins and full feathered headdresses looked on approvingly. The Sioux and their vassals had not even bothered to string pickets around their campsite, such was their ascendant military mastery of the northern prairie. Their might was exemplified by the absence of the Pawnee, whose mortal fear of the Sioux had led them to become the only major tribe to reject the American invitation to participate in the convocation.[*]

Closer to the American outpost of Fort Laramie rose the multicolored lodges of the Crow, lonely and cordoned off as if marooned on an island. The Crow, having completed the eight-hundred-mile trek from the buckling Yellowstone bluffs, had perhaps settled in close to the military compound to revel in their status—untold horse raids and a few, if unfortunate, lethal skirmishes notwithstanding—as never having made formal war on the white man.

But it was the site of the Blackfeet bivouac that Bridger was seeking. A year earlier he had married into the family of a Shoshone chief, and with this union came the obligation to consider the Blackfeet as ancient an adversary as did his wife's kin. This was not difficult, considering the two ugly scars creasing his back courtesy of Blackfeet arrows. At the urging of his old friend Thomas Fitzpatrick, now a respected government Indian agent, Bridger had agreed to lead a delegation of "Snakes" to the powwow in exchange for Fitzpatrick's surreptitious delivery of several cases of double-triggered Hawken rifles only recently introduced onto the Plains. Despite Fitzpatrick's vow of

---

[*] It would not be long before mystic Pawnee medicine men, anticipating the future, successfully advised the tribe's leaders to throw in their lot with the white trespassers and help the U.S. Army stand up a Pawnee Scout Corps.

enforced neutrality, Bridger had never been one to underestimate a foe, even one as diminished as the Blackfeet.

Like Indians across the continent, the Blackfeet had been ravaged by the diseases the European Americans had carried into the New World. Fourteen years earlier, in 1837, a smallpox outbreak had torn through their villages deep in the mountains, and American trappers were stunned to come upon entire communities of lodges abandoned and deserted, the branches of the surrounding conifers festooned with scores of scaffolded burial platforms. The tribe had since somewhat recovered, and its warriors never lost their lust for lifting Shoshone scalps. But though the century-long fires of defiance against white encroachment still blazed, their manpower had ebbed to the point where theirs was by now a purely defensive struggle.* A leery Bridger nevertheless made certain to raise his Shoshone lodges as far from the Blackfeet contingent as possible. This proved unnecessary.

Even the strongest of the tribes had journeyed to Fort Laramie with less interest in reigniting old feuds than gauging the strength and weapons of the Bluecoats as well as securing their portion of the promised *wakpamni*— the great distribution of gifts, $100,000 worth allocated by Congress, that Fitzpatrick planned to allot. Bridger, though sympathetic to the Irishman's intentions, had warned Fitzpatrick that his was a fool's errand. Even if the peace talks proceeded without incident, he felt, crates of beads, blankets, mirrors, and cooking pots and sacks of coffee, tobacco, and refined sugar would never keep the Indians from the warpath. Many aspects of the frontier had changed over the lifetimes of the two venerable trapping compatriots, not least the collapse of the precious beaver trade. But some violent rivalries, Bridger knew, were destined to remain ever thus.

* * *

* It would be another four years, in 1855, before the Blackfeet and their confederates the Gros Ventre agreed to a treaty with the United States ceding to the tribes much of Montana east of the northern Rockies. As was invariably the case, the terms the government had agreed to were gradually abridged and finally abandoned when gold was discovered on Indian lands in the 1860s.

Jim Bridger and Thomas Fitzpatrick had borne witness when, toward the late 1830s, a flood of cheap Asian silk exported by the British East India Company replaced the soft felt of the *Castor canadensis* as the hat material of choice in the cities of the east and all across Europe. In 1840, after half a century's heyday, the Mountain Men of the Rockies held their sixteenth, and final, Rendezvous before disappearing into the gloaming corners of the far west. What had once been a regiment of three thousand beaver hunters scouring the Douglas firs and ponderosa pines bearding the sharp granite peaks dwindled to a few score wandering diehards, unfit for any other way of life, hoping to eke out an existence above the clouds.

In the wake of this economic disruption, a few trappers, most notably Fitzpatrick, fell into government work, leveraging their knowledge of the territories and their familiarity with the tribes to carve out a niche vocation allowing them to move easily between their beloved borderlands and flatlander "civilization." And some old hands, taking advantage of the increased traffic along the Oregon, Mormon, and California Trails, hired out as wagon masters to pilot wide-eyed eastern emigrants to their respective promised lands. Others, like Bill Sublette and the Irishman Robert Campbell—recovered from his illness and returned from his home country to the States to learn of the death of his boon companion Jed Smith—intuited even more profit in staying put.

In 1834, the two founded the sleepy and isolated way station of Fort William on the North Platte at the mouth of the Laramie River. The outpost had served the earliest westering travelers' supply needs before it was sold to the army in 1849 and renamed Fort Laramie. Even Bridger constructed a ferry landing on the Green River near its confluence with the Black Forks, supplementing his income as a trail guide and army scout by conveying prairie schooners across the watercourse.

One can only wonder at the thoughts running through Bridger's and Fitzpatrick's minds on that September day in 1851 as, having escorted the Shoshone to their campsite, the two rode together toward Fort Laramie to confer with Colonel David Mitchell, the government's superintendent of Indian affairs, who had traveled from St. Louis to oversee the treaty council. Following the massive gold strike at California's Sutter's Mill three years earlier, what had once been Sublette's and Campbell's lonely and ramshackle redoubt had transformed into a lively marketplace housing a company of mounted riflemen. The old stockade's hewn cottonwood logs had been replaced with whitewashed adobe walls, and the soldiers now watched as an eclectic mélange of entrepreneurs and adventurers passed through the fort's imposing gate—Indians from across the prairie hawking buffalo robes, peddlers from St. Louis unloading barrels of rotgut whiskey at the sutler's store, and missionaries, scientists, and wealthy European sportsmen journeying west to collect souls, geological specimens, and big-game trophies.

Moreover, with the Santa Fe Trail virtually cleared of hostile Comanche and Kiowa—their populations nearly halved by successive waves of measles and cholera—the highlight of the Fort Laramie trading season was the arrival of horse wranglers like the legendary Kit Carson driving herds of Mexican mustangs north to sell at auction to both the army and the thousands of transients venturing into the mountains.

Meanwhile, in the wake of America's overwhelming triumph in its recent war with Mexico, President Millard Filmore's War Department was set on adopting a European blueprint to remake itself into an increasingly professional organization. The Indian affairs superintendent Col. Mitchell thus represented one of the final links to the gruff-and-tumble army officer corps that had matured alongside the revolutionary United States. The teenaged Mitchell had ventured into the Rockies as a trapper in the mid-1820s, and he was among the contingent of mountaineers who descended the Missouri with Henry Ashley, Jed Smith, and the grizzly-tending Jim Beckwourth in the wake of General Henry Atkinson's 1825 military excursion upriver—the first effort of the United States to consolidate treaties with the western tribes.

Gen. Atkinson never lived to see Col. Mitchell pick up his peacemaking baton, having passed at the age of sixty in 1842, four years after the death of his mentor, General William Clark. Nor was Atkinson's subordinate, Colonel Henry Leavenworth, the hero (at least to some) of the Arikara War, alive to witness Mitchell's grand gathering of the tribes on the North Platte. Following Leavenworth's abortive mission to subdue the "Rees" in retaliation for their assault on Ashley's trappers in 1823, the colonel spent the next decade overseeing the establishment of the military compound in Kansas that still bears his name. Promoted to general officer in 1833, a year later he commanded a regiment of dragoons riding southwest to lay the groundwork for the subjugation of the Comanche and Kiowa peoples. It was during this expedition that the fifty-year-old Leavenworth, already weakened by a fall from his horse during a buffalo hunt, contracted a fever and died.

However, one veteran soldier personally familiar with the early exploits of America's Mountain Men still took breath as Col. Mitchell was extending his olive branch to the tribes that autumn. This was General Jose Maria de Echeandia, by now an aging pensioner. It is not recorded if the former provincial governor of Mexico's Alta California paid any attention to the doings of his country's northern neighbor while tending to his small Mexican rancho with the help of his two widowed stepdaughters. It is safe to assume that he lost all interest in matters American upon President Lopez de Santa Anna's capitulation and the signing of 1848's humiliating Treaty of Guadalupe Hidalgo, which relinquished all Mexican claims to Texas and ceded to the United States the present-day states of New Mexico, Utah, Nevada, and California, most of Arizona and Colorado, and parts of Oklahoma, Kansas, and Wyoming—a territory nearly half as large as the existing United States—while establishing the Rio Grande as the border between the two countries.

Yet before retiring from government service, Echeandia did leave a singular, albeit short-lived mark for posterity. In 1826 he had issued a "Proclamation of Emancipation" freeing from bondage the Native Americans within the military districts of Mission San Diego, Mission Santa Barbara, and Mission Monterey. The following year the Mexican government extended Echeandia's proclamation to include all Catholic missionary servitude. These included the Miwok tribesmen who had helped the diarist Harrison Rogers and his little company to survive during the summer of 1827. That the Miwok, and hundreds of thousands of disparate West Coast Indians, subsequently fell victim to what historians call the great "California Genocide" after American settlers poured into the territory and blunted Echeandia's efforts remains but a historical footnote. Echeandia, who died in 1871, never commented on the irony.

Similarly, across what is now California's border with Oregon, the Umpqua Federation, whose Quuiich faction had all but wiped out Jed Smith's trapping party in the summer of 1828, thrived over the next several decades under the protection of the Hudson's Bay Company, which had constructed a trading post in the heart of the Umpqua Valley. With the retreat of the Canadians following the establishment of the international border at the forty-ninth parallel in 1846, however, the Indians of southwestern Oregon suffered nearly the same fate as their California brethren. Within a decade the U.S. Army had forcibly and completely depopulated the Umpqua Basin, imprisoning men, women, and children ostensibly to prevent the tribes from joining a nearby Native American uprising in the Rogue River Valley. With the fertile Umpqua lands all but crying out to be settled, American farmers and ranchers obliged.

Long departed from the former Oregon Country by then were the Hudson's Bay Company personalities and antagonists who, for good or ill, had played such major roles in Jed Smith's short life. The firm's North American governor George Simpson, for instance, had completed both the continent's longest canoe journey ever recorded—five thousand miles, in 1828—as well as his 1841 overland circumnavigation of the globe before Great Britain ceded the Oregon Country to the United States. A decade later, while Jim Bridger and Thomas Fitzpatrick were wrangling Indian tribes on the prairie abutting Fort Laramie, Simpson—a major investor in Canadian banks, railroads, shipping concerns, and mining operations— was ensconced in a palatial estate in Montreal and considered one of the country's richest men, with a net worth equal to half a billion dollars today.*

In 1860, days after entertaining the Prince of Wales on a state visit to Canada by the future King Edward VII, Simpson died of a massive stroke at the age of sixty-eight. Considered one of Canada's founding fathers, he allegedly went to his grave ruing the Crown's decision to relinquish the current states of Washington and Oregon to the upstart Americans. As for the outsized personalities Simpson had employed to such great advantage across the northwest, most merely faded into the fog of history.

The innovative Donald McKenzie—whose institution of brigade-sized trapping outfits transformed the Hudson's Bay Company's beaver-hunting template—went on to serve a thirteen-year stint as governor of Canada's Red River Colony. After retiring from politics at the age of fifty-one, McKenzie relocated to the United States in 1834 to take up life as a gentleman farmer in the Lake Erie–side town of Mayville, New York. Over the succeeding years McKenzie was frequently visited by American political luminaries such as the future secretaries of state Daniel Webster and William Seward, who sought his insights on matters ranging from the establishment of the U.S.–Canada border to the feasibility of purchasing Alaska from the Russians. McKenzie died in 1851 at the age of fifty-seven.

In contrast to McKenzie's life of leisure in his later years, the obstreperous Hudson's Bay Company Booshway Peter Skene Ogden continued his work in the field nearly to the day he died. Relishing Gov. Simpson's orders to turn the Snake River Country into a "fur desert," Ogden led multiple trapping expeditions throughout the 1820s that took eighteen thousand pelts from the area and pushed the beaver population to the brink of extinction. His job considered well done, in 1830 he was tasked with establishing new company posts throughout British Columbia and as far north as Alaska. He never lost his disdain for the United States, and he successfully

---

* Not to mention one of Canada's most profligate men; over his lifetime Simpson fathered at least eleven children by seven different women, including his Scottish wife, his several British and Canadian mistresses, and his half-Cree laundress.

countered American maritime traders attempting to establish inroads into the Pacific coast of what was still then known as Rupert's Land. He also managed to fend off several Russian trapping expeditions into what he considered sovereign Hudson's Bay territory while laying bare his opinion of the coastal tribes he encountered in a tract entitled "Notes on western Caledonia."

"A brutish, ignorant, superstitious beggarly sett of beings," Ogden called the Indians. No doubt they felt much the same toward him. In 1854, having just turned sixty-four and in ill health after a lifetime of hard wilderness living, Ogden and one of his many Native American "wives" repaired to the homestead he had purchased in Oregon's Willamette River Valley prior to the establishment of the international boundary. He died there one month later. He was interred, unironically, in the soil of the nation he despised.

Ogden's final resting place lies but paces from the grave of the man who once served as his chief factor at Fort Vancouver, Dr. John McLoughlin. McLoughlin, who resigned from the Hudson's Bay Company in 1846 in a fit of pique after the firm declined to prosecute a Canadian trapper who had killed his son in a duel, settled in the Willamette Valley village of Oregon City, renounced his Canadian heritage, became a U.S. citizen in 1849, and opened a dry goods store. Eight years later, at the age of seventy-three, he died of natural causes.

Whether the Hudson's Bay panjandrums took any pleasure over outliving their most vociferous American critics, Benjamin O'Fallon and Joshua Pilcher, is not recorded. O'Fallon never fully recovered from a mysterious illness he contracted while accompanying Gen. Atkinson's expedition up the Missouri River in 1825. He resigned his commission as Indian agent the following year and spent the rest of his life eking out a living on a small Missouri plantation hard by the banks of the Mississippi. An avid patron of the arts, O'Fallon either commissioned or purchased forty-two paintings by the then-unheralded nineteenth-century western artist George Catlin. Although O'Fallon never acquired extreme wealth in his forty-nine years on earth, a century and a half after his death in 1842 his heirs collected

$17.4 million when thirty-one of Catlin's portraits and landscapes were purchased at auction by an anonymous bidder.

Less than six months after O'Fallon was laid to rest, he was followed to the grave by the fifty-three-year-old Pilcher. After several fitful and unsuccessful attempts to revive his Missouri Fur Company, in 1838 Pilcher was appointed the U.S. superintendent of Indian affairs for the western territories by President Martin Van Buren. Befitting a man whose loathing of all things British was equaled only by his delight in burning Indian villages to the ground, Pilcher's tenure in office produced no great gains in America's relationships with its Indigenous population. It did, however, so alienate the Sioux as to set them on the warpath against the white man for the next four decades. Pilcher, whose vast Missouri real estate holdings were maintained by a "workforce" of 150 slaves, served in his government position until his death in 1843.

* * *

If any man could be said to wear the mantle of the proto–Jedediah Smith, the honor would fall to John Colter. When Colter finally descended from the Rocky Mountains and reached St. Louis in 1810, he was the first American with not only the fullest understanding to date of western geography, particularly the contours of the Bighorn and Yellowstone watersheds, but an eagerness to disseminate that knowledge. The store of information that Colter gathered during his six years in the wilderness as both a member of the Corps of Discovery and as an independent trapper proved so valuable that his former captain, William Clark—then working on his groundbreaking journals—retained him as an adviser of sorts. Colter's insights eventually made their way into Clark's seminal map of the mountainous borderlands, published in 1814. Although Clark's cartographic depictions contained several errors, the inaccuracies are generally considered to rise from the author's misinterpretation of what various Indians had related to him and the late Meriwether Lewis, and not to Colter's contributions.

With the commencement of the War of 1812, Colter enlisted and rode for a time with Nathan Boone's Missouri Rangers before purchasing and clearing a small plot of land near the Boone's Lick section of Missouri. There he erected a cabin and settled into the life of a yeoman farmer. He subsequently married a woman known to history only as Sally, sired a son, and passed his evenings trading yarns with the aging Daniel Boone before succumbing to an attack of jaundice in 1813. He was not yet forty years old.

It was perhaps to John Colter's financial misfortune that he was born too soon to take advantage of the windfalls to be earned at the height of the beaver-fur trade. John Henry Weber had better timing. The Danish former seafarer-turned-Booshway under William Ashley quit the trapping business in either 1826 or 1827 with a grubstake of close to $20,000, well over $600,000 today. Vague reports claim that Weber may have been swindled out of the bulk of his assets, forcing him—like Thomas Fitzpatrick—to find government work. In Weber's case he hired on as a superintendent for the Federal Land Office overseeing leasing contracts for the lead mines in Galena, Illinois. Following his retirement in 1840, Weber recrossed the Mississippi and settled in the riverside Iowa village of Bellevue, where he became a leading advocate for the territory's statehood. In 1859, suffering from a debilitating case of neuralgia, he took his own life at the age of eighty. Weber's legacy echoes to this day in the Utah river, canyon, county, and university that bear his name.

Weber's Utah renown is nearly equaled by the wily Quebecois trapper Etienne Provost, with the Gallic pronunciation of his name today gracing a river, a canyon, and a city in the Beehive State. Provost retired from active beaver hunting in 1830, signing on with John Jacob Astor's American Fur Company as a recruiter and wilderness guide. He also hired out to pilot private expeditions into the borderlands, including John James Audubon's groundbreaking natural history expedition of 1843. Although Provost married in 1830, his reputation as a drinker and carouser expanded with his waistline, with one portrait artist captioning his depiction of the aging raconteur, "Monsieur Proveau, with a corpus round as a porpoise." Provost spent his final years as a tale-telling fixture in the hotel saloons of St. Louis, where he died in 1850 at the age of sixty-five.

Given that the average American lifespan hovered around forty years of age in the mid-nineteenth century, hard-living men like John Henry Weber and Etienne Provost could count themselves blessed to have escaped an early and violent death. Many of their former trapping compatriots were not as fortunate. Such was the case with the legendarily charmed Hugh Glass, whose stockpile of luck finally ran dry early in the winter of 1833. Glass had by then teamed up with the mixed-race translator Edward Rose, with both employed as scouts for the U.S. Army. Sometime in January or February of that year, the two were making their way from the mouth of the Bighorn to North Dakota's Fort Union when they were surrounded on the frozen Yellowstone River by an Arikara hunting party. The Indians, recognizing their old antagonists, made short work of them. As neither man's birthdate was ever definitively established, both were thought to be somewhere around fifty years old when they met their maker.

The renowned "gaudy liar" Jim Beckwourth may or may not have also died at the hands of Indians, albeit much later in life. Beckwourth left William Ashley's employ in 1825 when he married the daughter of a Crow headman and was adopted into the tribe. He later claimed to have ascended to the chieftaincy of the entire Crow Nation, and when not leading buffalo hunts or war parties he—like Glass and Rose—also found work as an army scout. Though American military officers suspected there was more rooster than Crow to the voluble Beckwourth, he is nonetheless credited with "discovering" an eponymous pass while leading a company of Bluecoats through the Sierra Nevada. Beckwourth later opened a horse ranch and rustic inn on the California Trail, where, sometime in the 1850s, he narrated his life story to an itinerant justice of the peace. This ghostwritten autobiography, *The Life and Adventures of James P. Beckwourth: Mountaineer, Scout and Pioneer, and Chief of the Crow Nation of Indians*, was published in 1856.

Beckwourth returned east three years later, settling near Denver and again signing on with the army as a dispatch rider. In that capacity he took part in one of the most contemptible episodes in American history when, in 1864, he helped guide the Third Colorado Cavalry Regiment to a combined Arapaho-Cheyenne campsite at Sand Creek. It was there that the militiamen under the command of Colonel John Chivington slaughtered and mutilated close to two hundred Indians, most of them women and children huddling under a white flag of truce. Three years later and well into his late sixties, Beckwourth returned to his Crow village in Montana. There, in 1867, he either died of natural causes or, as some claimed, was poisoned by a rival tribesman.

Jim Clyman did not come down from the mountains in 1827 with anywhere near the nest egg accumulated by John Henry Weber. However, the 278 pounds of peltry that Jed Smith had gifted Clyman upon his departure was, when sold on the St. Louis market, enough to allow the soft-spoken Virginian to purchase a small homestead along the Big Vermillion River in Danville, Illinois. There the thirty-five-year-old opened a general store and worked part-time as a deputy sheriff. What initially portended to be a sedate and well-earned semiretirement, however, became anything but.

When a confederation of Sauk, Fox, and Kickapoo tribesmen under the leadership of the Sauk warrior-chieftain Black Hawk rose to reclaim their ancestral lands along the Illinois-Wisconsin border in 1832, Clyman enlisted in a local militia. During the short-lived campaign in what came to be known as the Black Hawk War, he served in the same company as twenty-three-year-old Private Abraham Lincoln. Upon Black Hawk's surrender, Clyman expanded his storefront establishment into an overland trading company, shuttling provision-laden wagon trains between Danville and the burgeoning Wisconsin town that its former Algonquian residents called *millioke*—"pleasant land by the river." Emigrating settlers bastardized the name into Milwaukee. During one of these forays Clyman was shot and wounded in the arm and leg by hostile Winnebago; in a scene reminiscent of his escape from the Blackfeet camp five years earlier, he hid all night in a hollow trunk of a downed tree to avoid his pursuers.

Not content with decades of derring-do, in 1844 the fifty-two-year-old Clyman sold his business, saddled his horse, and signed on as a scout for a wagon master leading a train into the Oregon Country. After lingering for several months in the northwest to survey the Willamette Valley and environs for future settlers, Clyman turned back east, reaching what was to become Fort Laramie in July 1846. There he crossed paths with a California-bound caravan of prairie schooners out of Springfield, Illinois, led by James Frazier Reed, another former militiaman with whom he had served in the Black Hawk War.

Clyman warned Reed that it was already late in the year to be westering onward. But Reed was determined to make up time by leaving the established California Trail in favor of an alternative route through the Great Salt Lake Desert called the Hastings Cutoff. Clyman was aghast. The alleged shortcut, he told Reed, was unsuited for wagon travel and would only slow him more. Reed—goaded by George Donner, the outfit's chief organizer—ignored him. The following spring Clyman, like the rest of the nation, learned that George Donner, his brother Jacob, both of their wives, four of their children, and twenty-eight other unfortunates had not survived what came to be known as the Donner Party's snowbound winter of 1846–1847 in the High Sierra. The dire demise of the Donner Party has of course since been incorporated into America's origin myth.

The following year, Clyman again led a wagon train west, this time to California. There he married one of his fellow travelers, the widowed Hannah McCombs, and settled in Napa County. The still spry fifty-six-year-old and his bride adopted three daughters, only one of whom lived long enough to attend her eighty-nine-year-old father's funeral when he died from natural causes in 1881.

Given the remarkable longevity of the likes of Jim Clyman, John Henry Weber, Jim Beckwourth, and even the sybaritic Etienne Provost, one might think that the gods of chance might follow suit and balance Jed Smith's untimely death by granting similar long lives to the various men with whom Smith had partnered through his career in the fur trade. Hardly. Neither

David Jackson nor Bill Sublette lived to celebrate their fiftieth birthdays. And the little general William Henry Ashley, the entrepreneur whose newspaper advertisement set Smith's adventurous explorations in motion, passed at the age of fifty-nine.

Jackson had seemingly appeared from nowhere at the Cache Valley Rendezvous of 1826 to form a triumvirate with Smith and Sublette. Perhaps fittingly, after the three disbanded their partnership four years later, he faded into history's obscurity much as he had entered it. Jackson spent one more trapping season in the mountains before returning to Missouri, where he may have briefly tried his hand in the Ozark lead mining business. From there he apparently drifted west, first to Santa Fe and then on to California, likely as a hand on trading expeditions to what was then still Mexican territory. His adventures in Mexico, if any, remain unrecorded. What is known is that Jackson returned to St. Louis sometime before 1837, the same year he set off for Tennessee to collect a debt of some kind. It was during this trip that he contracted typhus and, on Christmas Eve, died at the age of forty-nine.

William "Bill" Sublette's later-life peregrinations, on the other hand, are well documented. Following Jed Smith's disappearance along the Cimarron Cutoff, Sublette tarried briefly in Santa Fe before leading his supply train back into the mountains. There he reunited with the Irishman Robert Campbell. Perhaps recalling how, decades earlier, Jed Smith had sensed in the penniless, tubercular young immigrant the makings of a successful businessman, Sublette suggested a partnership. A year later, as the two led a party of trappers away from the Rendezvous of 1832, they were ambushed by a large force of Gros Ventre and Blackfeet. Sublette was severely wounded during the fight, and it took him nearly a year to recover from his injuries. Whether he was too debilitated to continue riding the high country or intuiting the beginning of the end of the beaver trade—or perhaps a combination of the two—this marked the end of Sublette's trapping days.

In 1835, Sublette and Campbell successfully lobbied Gen. William Clark for a license to import whiskey into what technically remained Indian

Country. With 450 barrels of the liquor on hand, the two constructed the cottonwood stockade on the Oregon Trail at the confluence of the North Platte and the Laramie and christened it Fort William. A year later they sold the way station to Thomas Fitzpatrick. Fitzpatrick in turn resold it to the American Fur Company, whose seventy-two-year-old owner John Jacob Astor had long been seeking a base of operations in what was to become the Wyoming Territory. Astor's representatives on the ground re-named the redoubt Fort John, perhaps feeling that a second Fort Astoria might be tempting fate.

Meanwhile, the firm of Sublette and Campbell thrived for another de-cade with the latter deducing, correctly, that the trade in buffalo robes was destined to outpace beaver pelts as a profit-making proposition. As the two men accrued capital literally off the backs of the diminishing buffalo droves, they opened a large dry goods store in downtown St. Louis, pur-chased considerable tracts of land in what was to become Kansas City, and invested in several banks and insurance companies.

In 1837, Bill Sublette buried his younger brother Milton, who suc-cumbed at the age of thirty-six to a long-festering arrow wound. Five years later Sublette and Campbell ended their partnership; it was an amicable dissolution, with the two remaining friendly and even retaining their downtown St. Louis emporium, albeit now divided down the center by a newly built wall. In the spring of 1845, the recently married Sublette, hop-ing to be appointed to the vacant St. Louis–based post of superintendent of Indian affairs, departed St. Louis for Washington, DC, to lobby for the position. That July, having traveled only as far as Pittsburgh, he fell ill and died suddenly. He was forty-six years old.[*]

As for William Henry Ashley, he never did realize his grand political ambitions nor his desire to be remembered as the man who paved the road

---

[*] In a quirky sidebar to Sublette's passing, his will stipulated that his wife, the former Frances Hereford, would forfeit the small fortune she inherited should she ever relinquish her married name. Four years after her husband's death, Frances Sublette remarried—to Bill Sublette's youngest brother Solomon Sublette, thus adhering to the codicil.

for America's march toward Manifest Destiny. Outside of Missouri he is, in fact, largely forgotten today.

Upon Ashley's withdrawal from the fur business, he plowed a part of the considerable fortune he had amassed into an 1830 campaign for a seat in the U.S. Senate. He was soundly defeated by his Jacksonian opponent. A year later, however, he won the first of three successive terms in Congress, where he served until 1837. A reliable proslavery voice, Ashley was also a pork barrel advocate to his core, regularly introducing appropriation bills for new roads, harbor improvements, river lighthouses, and increased federal representation for his Missouri constituents. As a member of the House Committee on Indian Affairs, he argued that the red and white races could never successfully coexist and advocated for the creation of great swaths of no-man's lands to separate all white settlements from tribal communities.

While serving his third congressional term, Ashley simultaneously challenged Missouri's sitting Democratic governor in the election of 1836. Running as an independent candidate, he was again trounced. He retired from public life a year later. Not long after, in failing health, he vacated his magnificent St. Louis mansion overlooking the Mississippi River in hopes that country life in the west-central part of the state would improve his constitution. It did not. In March 1838, he was felled by a sudden attack of pneumonia. He died within days, six months shy of his sixtieth birthday. He had outlived his old partner, Andrew Henry, by six years.

Thus, in September 1851, as Thomas Fitzpatrick and Jim Bridger made camp near Fort Laramie, they may well have considered themselves the last Mountain Men standing.

*   *   *

Though Fitzpatrick and Bridger certainly forged a high-country bond during their adventures and explorations, by this point in their lives the two old trappers made for an odd couple. The well-educated Irishman had made it his goal to convince government and army officials that the continent's

Indigenous population could be integrated into American society. The illiterate Missourian, in contrast, foresaw nothing but tribal exploitation and degradation, if not extermination, under the "civilized" boot heel of the burgeoning United States. Perhaps the idealist Fitzpatrick was too close to his own politics of the situation to see what the practical Bridger took as a given.

Since turning over the former Fort William to John Jacob Astor's organization, Fitzpatrick had divided his time between private and public enterprises. In the 1830s, he'd guided the first two wagon trains to ever complete the journey from Independence, Missouri, to the Oregon Country and subsequently served as a scout for Captain John Charles Fremont's fabled two-year, three-thousand-mile western mapping expedition. Under the guidance of Fitzpatrick and Kit Carson, Fremont plotted and surveyed much of the area making up today's Rocky Mountain states before moving on to chart great swaths of California, Nevada, and Utah. These of course constituted nearly all the lands that Jed Smith had previously reconnoitered—as well as the territories that farsighted Washington politicians were already plotting to steal from Mexico. As it was, Fremont's reports to his benefactor and father-in-law, the powerful Missouri senator Thomas Hart Benton, merely added an official gloss to Smith's informal dispatches.

In 1845, with President James K. Polk having secured the White House on a campaign promising American expansion, Fitzpatrick continued his army work, at one point guiding an expedition to survey the unchartered districts of eastern New Mexico, northern Texas, and western Arkansas. He then signed on with Col. Philip Watts Kearny's heavily armed march across the Santa Fe Trail. With Kearny's dragoons hauling a battery of howitzers, the mission's initial objective was to cow the still restive southwestern tribes with a show of American might. But when the United States declared war against Mexico the following April, Fitzpatrick remained at the newly promoted general's side as Kearny's 2,500-man Army of the West captured Santa Fe and drove on toward California.

In the wake of the Treaty of Guadalupe Hidalgo that ended the conflict, Fitzpatrick was appointed as the U.S. Indian agent for the Upper Platte and Arkansas Rivers. It was during this period that he negotiated so-called treaties of friendship with tribes ranging from the Cheyenne to the Arapaho, fathered two children with his Native American wife, and came to know better the mores of the people with whom he had done almost constant battle as a fur trapper. As his attitude toward the disparate sovereign nations softened, so in turn did Fitzpatrick personally earn a grudging respect from the Indians as an honest broker, though they remained highly suspect of his government's intentions. It was not for nothing that his superior, the Indian affairs superintendent Col. Mitchell, selected Fitzpatrick to spend the summer of 1851 crisscrossing the Plains from the Arkansas to the Yellowstone coaxing the tribes to attend the gathering at Fort Laramie.

At it happened, Mitchell's grand peace negotiations went for naught. In fairness, it was not an easy sell. The western tribes had spent millennia raiding and battling each other, and their running fights and blood feuds were not likely to be thrown aside in exchange for a few trinkets and a virtual pat on the head from some faraway Great White Father. Nonetheless, the Indians were sly. They had ridden hundreds of miles and delayed their fall buffalo hunts to receive the gifts Fitzpatrick promised, and they were not about to depart empty-handed. When Mitchell assembled the tribal elders and asked if they had chosen representative "chiefs" to sign his treaty, they grunted various affirmations.

Mitchell's delighted government delegation took these cryptic comments as acquiescence to all the American demands. Though a savvy frontiersman such as Fitzpatrick surely knew better, he stood mute while "headmen" that the Indians had designated as cruel jokes—the infirm, the alcoholic, the mentally challenged—queued up to "touch the pen." The tribes then collected their *wakpamni* and departed Fort Laramie with no intention of altering their lifestyles. It is said that Jim Bridger watched this entire charade with a look of bemusement.

Yet Fitzpatrick remained undeterred in his naïve belief that the United States owed the Indians a greater form of justice for their stolen lands than a few razors, sewing needles, and tobacco plugs. He also persisted in the notion that the Native Americans could be taught skills such as farming and ranching that would enable them to survive and assimilate. When the U.S. Senate refused to endorse a series of annual cash payments that Col. Mitchell had promised the Indians, Fitzpatrick took it upon himself to travel to Washington to convince Congress of its shortsightedness. He arrived in the nation's capital in early 1854 intending to plead his case. But his journey had been hard, and the bloody cough he had picked up along the way quickly bloomed into pneumonia. He died from the infection in his hotel room hard by the Potomac River in February of that year. He was fifty-five years old.

* * *

News of Thomas Fitzpatrick's death only exacerbated the deep ambivalence Jim Bridger felt toward white civilization slowly encroaching onto the Plains, into the mountains, and beyond to the western ocean. He, more than most Mountain Men, personally felt the Indians' pain. Before marrying into the Shoshone nation and fathering a boy and a girl, Bridger had lived with a Ute "wife" who died bearing him a daughter and subsequently remarried a Flathead woman who bore him three more girls but also died delivering their third child. A year later his eldest girl was killed by a raiding party of Nez Perce. Yet even this did not affect his comity toward the tribes, and he often angered white traders by warning Indians away from blankets he suspected were infected with smallpox. Which is not to say he completely turned his back on his own race.

A year before journeying to Wyoming for Mitchell's and Fitzpatrick's great treaty council, an army patrol led by a topographical engineer visited Bridger at his ferry landing on the Green River. The American officer was seeking a more direct route to Utah from the Missouri River and had specifically sought out Bridger for his advice. Bridger is reported to have yanked a burnt stick from his cook fire and scraped it along a slab of slate rock, etching a near-thousand-mile trail, from west to east, that climbed and descended the Rockies and crossed four major rivers and countless creeks. The next morning Bridger packed his mules and led the engineer along this trace. The Union Pacific Railroad was soon to follow this precise route, including through what is still called Bridger's Pass, which bisects the Continental Divide.

Moreover, following the Fort Laramie assembly, Bridger continued to hire out as a guide and scout on various scientific, military, and commercial expeditions that took him to Oregon, California, and present-day Mexico. But his by now legendary intimacy with the Indians also marked him as an enemy to the Mormons. The mountain tribes that he championed stood directly in the path of expanding Mormon settlements across the Great Salt Lake Valley spearheaded by Brigham Young, the self-proclaimed governor of the semiautonomous fiefdom he named Deseret. In July 1853, a full-scale war broke out between the Utes and the Latter-day Saints. Both sides committed the usual atrocities. Young, suspicious of Bridger's loyalties and jealous of his real estate holdings, used the bloodletting as an excuse to issue a proclamation forbidding all trade with any Indians.

The following month, at a Mormon Town Hall meeting, Bridger was accused of plotting attacks with the Utes and supplying the Shoshones with powder and lead—the weapons Fitzpatrick had smuggled to him before the Fort Laramie council. "Old Gabe" was tried and found guilty in absentia at a secret Mormon hearing, and a posse of 150 "avenging angels" was dispatched from Provo to arrest him. Forewarned by friendly Indians, he eluded the riders and got his family to Fort Laramie. When the Mormons reached his Green River ferry landing they burned his copious stocks of whiskey and rum and seized his livestock.

From Wyoming, Bridger meandered farther east until finally, after thirty years, he arrived back in St. Louis. His fame preceded him, and he was mobbed by reporters and well-wishers wherever he went. Though he purchased a substantial farmstead on the outskirts of the city, plowing, planting, and reaping were not in James Felix Bridger's blood. Through the remainder of the decade he found steady employment, at $5 a day, guiding every conceivable manner of expedition. He took part in a congressional scientific survey seeking the source of the Yellowstone and discovered a mountain pass that shortened the route between Denver and Salt Lake City for the overland mail coach—today's U.S. Route 40. He achieved some measure of revenge on the Latter-day Saints by guiding 2,500 federal troops into Salt Lake City during the "Mormon War" over Brigham Young's theocratic rebellion of 1857–1858. And in one of the more bizarre chapters of his life, he contracted with the wealthy and dissolute Irish peer Sir St. George Gore as a scout for the eccentric nobleman's hunting safari. Bridger spent the better part of two years wandering the High Plains with Gore, the Eighth Baronet of Manor Gore near Sligo, most of the time trying to prevent the self-indulgent Irishman and his retinue of beaters, skinners, wranglers, chefs, and sommeliers from wandering into hostile Lakota territory.

In 1866, with the government gearing up its campaign against the rebelling Lakota led by the master military strategist and tactician Red Cloud, Bridger was lured from his Missouri homestead to become the frontier army's chief scout by the promise of $10 per day, more than most officers were paid. It did not hurt that for all his affection for Indians, Bridger had never really cared much for the Sioux. Some soldiers thought that the sixty-two-year-old Bridger was finally showing his age. His renowned eyesight was finally flickering, and on cold winter days his arthritis barely allowed him to walk, much less mount and ride for any length of time. Moreover, when he was young an entire side of buffalo ribs would have constituted a passable meal. Now he was content to make do with a jackrabbit and an eighteen-inch trout roasted over a spit, albeit with a quart of coffee to wash down his meal. Yet despite Bridger's infirmities, officers and enlisted men alike could not help but be in awe of the veteran Mountain Man's eccentric skills. He could still find fresh water on the driest of alkaline flats, build and stoke a fire in a hellish winter whiteout, and safely guide a wagon team across a quicksand-laden river.

With the conclusion in 1868 of what was by then already known as Red Cloud's War—the only conflict in the history of the United States in which the government capitulated to each and every one of the Indian demands—Bridger returned to his Missouri farm.* There he lived with his daughter Virginia, his only surviving child. Gradually growing completely blind, Bridger died in 1881 at the age of seventy-seven.

* * *

Just as individuals edit and embroider their histories to serve their own interests, so also do nations. Thus did the myths and parables surrounding the conquest of the American West become embedded in our national ethos. Not the least of these allegories blossomed years, decades, and even centuries after the events themselves took place, blazoned across our national consciousness by sources as disparate as the politician Theodore Roosevelt, the historian Frederick Jackson Turner, the novelists Zane Grey and Larry McMurtry, and the two giant Johns of Hollywood, Ford and Wayne. All of these men realized that if life is theater, Americans were hungry to attend.

The oddity is what none of them grasped—that as perhaps the most crucial epoch in the history of the United States unspooled, it was Jedediah Strong Smith who stood center stage.

From his arrival in St. Louis in 1822, Jed Smith experienced a lifelong sunrise of sorts, witnessing the dawn of the American West in all its beauty and all its savagery. As his explorations progressed, however, he transformed from observer to driving engine—grouping the foreign exotica he observed into taxonomies of class, of geography, of fauna and flora, and even cataloging the racial and physical attributes of the peoples he encountered. His reports of his travels were key, for better or worse, to impelling the military, economic, and political reach of Colonial America's inexorable march to the Pacific. This, as it turns out, had been his plan all along.

---

* Within half a decade the United States had also reneged on each and every capitulation it had made to Red Cloud and his followers, precipitating yet another conflict with the Sioux that included General George Armstrong Custer's foolish cavalry charge into the valley of the Little Bighorn.

In the year 2000, the researcher James Hutchins found himself, like a modern-day Mountain Man, scaling the soaring piles of paperwork housed in the vaults of Washington's National Archives and Records Center. There he discovered a letter, lost for 168 years, that Smith had posted to President Andrew Jackson's secretary of war, John Eaton, only two months before his death on the Cimarron Cutoff. Unlike his previous third-person communiqués to Eaton written under the aegis of the firm of Smith, Jackson, and Sublette, this message was personal. Smith wrote that he had recently been approached by the U.S. Army lieutenant Reuben Holmes to gauge his interest in serving as a guide to an expedition into the Rocky Mountains. As Lt. Holmes explained it, the mission was a follow-up to the explorations Meriwether Lewis and William Clark's Corps of Discovery had initiated twenty-seven years earlier. Smith was interested. With a caveat.

"I cannot consent to take a subordinate post in a business that several years experience had qualified me to control," Smith wrote to Eaton. However, he added, he was more than eager to serve with Lt. Holmes as co-leader of the journey as—he reminded Eaton—"[my] knowledge of our Western Territory is equal if not superior to that of any man in the country." This was no bargaining ploy. Smith emphasized that he was not seeking financial renumeration for his services—"I would look on the most liberal pay as no inducement to again encounter the hardships and dangers incident to the life of an explorer."

Instead, he told Eaton, his would be a labor of love to share with an expanding nation his "dearly purchased" knowledge of the west. He had no desire "to lock up [this] information," he wrote. Rather, he wished to "aid in the laudable design of bringing to light the resources of the country."

There is no record of Secretary Eaton ever replying to Smith's offer. Thus was the world deprived of a Smith and Holmes Corps of Discovery redux.* Yet in Smith's lifelong passion to emulate the journeys of his

---

* Like Jed Smith, Lt. Reuben Holmes—who never did helm his exploratory mission—died young. The West Point graduate, who had been a member of General Henry Atkinson's foray up the Missouri River in 1825, succumbed to cholera in 1833 at the age of thirty-five.

heroes Lewis and Clark, the venerable high-country pilgrim was already more than successful. For in reality it is Jed Smith's geographic discoveries and cartographic instincts and talent that stands equal to his outsize adventures.

True to William Henry Ashley's first impressions in his St. Louis parlor lo those years ago, in the brief space of a decade Smith, observant and ravenous for information, had blazed trails northwest through the Upper Missouri Country, south to the Platte, across the Rockies from the Snake to the Columbia, and southwest from the Colorado to the Pacific Coast. He returned from each expedition with more than a superficial acquaintance of previously unknown territories, and the maps he produced from his journeys serve as an outline to nearly all of the 522 million acres of landmass that the United States was to acquire by the mid-nineteenth century.

In his lifetime, Jedediah Smith was feted far and wide for surviving the three worst Indian-fueled calamities of the American fur trade—at the hands of the Arikara in 1823, the Mojave in 1827, and the Umpqua in 1828. That he seemingly disappeared from the nation's history books in his afterlife is passing curious. Perhaps this stems from his death at such an early age. Unlike the Boones, Clarks, Crocketts, and Carsons of the epoch, he did not live to publish his journals nor be interviewed by myth-making hagiographers.

This absence does not change the basic facts of his narrative. When Smith took his first tentative steps into the unknown, the interior of the North American continent was a blank slate for most if not all of his countrymen. Nine years later the mountain ranges and rivers, the deserts and forests and lakes that constituted that slate had been filled in. One might say that Jedediah Smith made America whole.

ACKNOWLEDGMENTS

We could not possibly have written this book without the assistance and courtesy of archivists, curators, librarians, historians, and park rangers at multiple organizations and institutions devoted to nineteenth-century explorations west of the Mississippi and Missouri Rivers and the men and women who played significant roles in it.

We want to recognize the help provided by the unsung curators and catalogers at the Library of Congress, particularly its Prints and Photographs Division; the Crow-Indigenous Relations and Northern Affairs Canada; New York Public Library; John Jermain Memorial Library; the archivists of *True West* and *Wild West* magazines; and everyone else at institutions and organizations who proved to be invaluable to our research and reporting. A special thank-you goes to the National and State Park Service Rangers for their expertise and insights.

We are especially grateful for the courtesy shown us by Clint Gilchrist and Jim Hardee at the Museum of the Mountain Man, Michael Wurtz at the University of the Pacific, Milton von Damm at the Jedediah Smith Society, Sean Rost at the State Historical Society of Missouri, Sarah Walker at the North Dakota State Archives, Ryan Brubacher at the Library of Congress, and especially Kellen Cutsforth at the Denver Public Library.

We would be remiss if we did not highlight the work of the late historian Dale Morgan. His 1953 book, *Jedediah Smith and the Opening of the West*, was, like its subject, a trailblazer in the expansion of knowledge about the exploits of Smith and his fellow Mountain Men.

And yet again, we cannot express enough thanks for the insights and suggestions of the underground editors David Hughes, Bobby Kelly, and Denise McDonald. We are also in debt to Valerie Hanley, who came to our rescue with expert editorial assistance, as well as Bobby Crines, who still knows how to read between the lines. Needless to say, despite the trails blazed by those who before us trod the western paths of this story as well as all those mentioned above who helped to shape and sharpen this narrative, we take full responsibility for any and all errors that found their way into our text.

From the onset of this project and through its completion we have benefited from the enthusiastic support of our editor, Marc Resnick. Others we are happy to thank at St. Martin's Press are Sally Richardson, Andy Martin, Rebecca Lang, Mac Nicholas, Lily Cronig, Rob Grom, Laurie Henderson, David Lindroth, Steve Wagner, and Jennifer Crane. And as always, we survive to write another day thanks to Nat Sobel and his merry band of elves at Sobel-Weber Associates, particularly Adia Wright and Jenny Lewis. Kudos, too, to the efforts on our behalf by Joe Veltre of the Gersh Agency.

As with any long writing project, we depended on the ongoing support and encouragement of family and friends. You know who you are, but let us single out the inestimable Leslie Reingold, Kathryn and James VunKannon, Vivienne May VunKannon, Liam-Antoine DeBusschere-Drury, David Drury, and the Divine Ms. D.

BIBLIOGRAPHY

BOOKS

Allen, John Logan. *Jedediah Smith and the Mountain Men of the American West*. New York: Chelsea House, 1991.

Alter, J. Cecil. *Jim Bridger*. Norman: University of Oklahoma Press, 1986.

Ambrose, Stephen. *Undaunted Courage: Meriwether Lewis, Thomas Jefferson, and the Opening of the American West*. New York: Simon & Schuster, 1996.

Anglin, Ronald M., and Larry E. Morris. *Gloomy Terrors and Hidden Fires: The Mystery of John Colter and Yellowstone*. Lanham, MD: Rowman & Littlefield, 2014.

Baldwin, Leland D. *The Keelboat Age on Western Waters*. Pittsburgh, PA: University of Pittsburgh Press, 1941.

Barbour, Barton H. *Jedediah Smith: No Ordinary Mountain Man*. Norman: University of Oklahoma Press, 2009.

Bartlett, R. A. *The New Country*. New York: Oxford University Press, 1974.

Beckwourth, James P. *The Life and Adventures of James P. Beckwourth: Mountaineer, Scout, and Pioneer and Chief of the Crow Nation of Indians*. Mount Pleasant, SC: Arcadia Press, 2017.

Begg, Alexander. *History of British Columbia: From Its Earliest Discovery to the Present Time*. Toronto: William Briggs, 1894.

Berry, Dan. *A Majority of Scoundrels*. New York: Ballantine Books, 1971.

Blevins, Win, and Linda M. Hasselstrom, eds. *Journal of a Mountain Man: The Incredible Story of James Clyman*. Portland, OR: Champoeg Press, 2013.

Bown, Stephen R. *The Company: The Rise and Fall of the Hudson's Bay Empire*. Toronto: Penguin Random House Canada, 2020.

Brennan, Steven. *The Adventures of the Mountain Men: True Tales of Hunting, Trapping, Fighting, Adventure, and Survival*. New York: Skyhorse, 2017.

Brooks, George R., ed. *The Southwest Expedition of Jedediah S. Smith His Personal Account of the Journey to California, 1826–1827*. Lincoln: University of Nebraska Press, 1977.

Brown, Dee. *The American West*. New York: Touchstone, 1994.

———. *Bury My Heart at Wounded Knee*. New York: Holt, Rhinehart and Winston, 1971.

Butler, Samuel. *The Note Books of Samuel Butler*. London: The Floating Press, 2014.

Carlos, Ann M., and Frank D. Lewis. *Commerce by a Frozen Sea: Native Americans and the European Fur Trade*. Philadelphia: University of Pennsylvania Press, 2010.

Chambers, John Whiteclay, ed. *The Oxford Companion to American Military History*. New York: Oxford University Press, 2000.

Chittenden, Hiram Martin. *The American Fur Trade of the Far West*. Lincoln: University of Nebraska Press, 1986.

Cline, Gloria Griffin. *Exploring the Great Basin*. Norman: University of Oklahoma Press, 1963.

Clokey, Richard M. *William H. Ashley: Enterprise and Politics in the Trans-Mississippi West*. Norman: University of Oklahoma Press, 1980.

Dale, Harrison C. *The Ashley-Smith Explorations and the Discovery of a Central Route to the Pacific, 1822–1829*. Lincoln: University of Nebraska Press, 1991.

Dary, David. *The Oregon Trail: An American Saga*. New York: Knopf, 2004.

Denig, Edwin Thompson. *Five Indian Tribes of the Upper Missouri: Sioux, Arickaras, Assiniboines, Crees, Crows*. Norman: University of Oklahoma Press, 1989.

DeVoto, Bernard. *Across the Wide Missouri*. Boston: Houghton Mifflin, 1947.

Dodge, Grenville. *Biographical Sketch of Jim Bridger*. Kansas City, MO: R. M. Rigby, 1904.

Drury, Bob, and Tom Clavin. *Blood and Treasure: Daniel Boone and the Fight for America's First Frontier*. New York: St. Martin's Press, 2021.

———. *The Heart of Everything That Is: The Untold Story of Red Cloud, An American Legend*. New York: Simon & Schuster, 2013.

Edling, Max M. *A Hercules in the Cradle: War, Money, and the American State, 1783—1867*. Chicago: University of Chicago Press, 2023.

Enzler, Jerry. *Jim Bridger: Trailblazer of the American West*. Norman: University of Oklahoma Press, 2021.

Ewers, John C. *The Blackfeet: Raiders on the Northwestern Plains*. Norman: University of Oklahoma Press, 1958.

Flores, Dan L. *Jefferson and Southwest Exploration*. Norman: University of Oklahoma Press, 1984.

Goetzman, William H. *Exploration and Empire*. New York: W.W. Norton, 1978.

Gwynne, S.C. *Empire of the Summer Moon: Quanah Parker and the Rise and Fall of the Comanches, the Most Powerful Indian Tribe in American History*. New York: Scribner, 2010.

Hafen, Leroy, ed. *The Mountain Men and Fur Traders of the Far West*. Lincoln: University of Nebraska Press, 1982.

Hafen, Leroy R., and Francis Marion Young. *Fort Laramie and the Pageant of the West*. Lincoln, NE: Bison Books, 1984.

Harris, Burton. *John Colter: His Years in the Rocky Mountains*. Casper, WY: Big Horn, 1983.

Hasselstrom, Linda M., ed. *James Clyman: Journal of a Mountain Man*. Missoula, MT: Mountain Press Publishing, 1984.

Jackson, Donald. *Thomas Jefferson & the Stony Mountains: Exploring the West from Monticello*. Norman: University of Oklahoma Press, 1981.

Kay, Betty Carlson, and Gary Jack Barwick. *Jacksonville, Illinois: The Traditions Continue*. Charleston, SC: Arcadia Publishing, 1999.

Mackenzie, Alexander. *The Journals of Alexander Mackenzie: Exploring Across Canada in 1789 and 1793*. Torrington, WY: Narrative Press, 2001.

Meyer, Roy. *The Village Indians of the Upper Missouri: The Mandans, Hidatsas, and Arikara*. Lincoln: University of Nebraska Press, 1977.

Moore, Shirley Ann Wilson. *Freedom's Plains: African Americans on the Overland Trails, 1841–1869* (Volume 12, Race and Culture in the American West Series). Norman: University of Oklahoma Press, 2016.

Morgan, Dale L. *Jedediah Smith and the Opening of the American West*. Lincoln, NE: Bison Books, 1964.

Muir, John. *Our National Parks*. Layton, UT: Gibbs-Smith, 2018.

Nester, William R. *The Arikara War: The First Plains Indians War, 1823*. Missoula, MT: Mountain Plains Publishing, 2001.

Newman, Peter C. *Company of Adventurers*. New York: Viking, 1985.

———. *General Henry Atkinson: A Western Military Career*. Norman: University of Oklahoma Press, 1965.

O'Fallon, Benjamin. *Benjamin O'Fallon Letterbook and Related Materials, 1783–1859*. Yale University Archives.

Oglesby, Richard E. *Manuel Lisa and the Opening of the Missouri Fur Trade*. Norman: University of Oklahoma Press, 1963.

O'Neil, Paul. *The Old West: The Rivermen*. New York: Time-Life Books, 1975.

Parkman, Francis. *The Oregon Trail: Sketches of Prairie and Rocky-Mountain Life*. New York: Oxford University Press, 2008.

Paul, R. Eli. *Autobiography of Red Cloud*. Helena: Montana Historical Society Press, 1997.

Philip, Leila. *Beaverland: How One Weird Rodent Made America*. New York: Twelve, 2022.

Quaife, Milo, M., ed. *The Journals of Captain Meriwether Lewis and Sergeant John Ordway, Kept on the Expedition of Western Exploration, 1803–1806, Vol. 22 of Wisconsin Historical Publication Collections*. Madison: State Historical Society of Wisconsin, 1916.

Rich, Edwin E. *The Hudson's Bay Company, 1670–1870*. New York: Macmillan, 1961.

Ronda, James P. *Astoria and Empire*. Lincoln: University of Nebraska Press, 1990.

Ross, Alexander. *The Fur Hunters of the Far West*. Norman: University of Oklahoma Press, 1956.

Russell, Carl P. *Firearms, Traps and Tools of the Mountain Men*. Albuquerque: University of New Mexico Press, 1967.

Sandoz, Marie. *The Beaver Men*. Lincoln: University of Nebraska Pres, 1978.

Sides, Hampton. *Blood and Thunder: An Epic of the American West*. New York: Doubleday, 2006.

Smith, Jedidiah. *A Manuscript Journal of the Travels of Jedediah S. Smith Thro' the Rocky Mountains and West of the Same Together with a Description of the Country and the Customs and Manners of the Different Tribes of Indians Thro' Which He Travelled*. Jedediah Strong Smith Estate, 1831.

Smith, Page. *Tragic Encounters: The People's History of Native Americans*. Berkeley, CA: Counterpoint, 2015.

Sprague, Marshall. *The Great Gates: The Story of the Rocky Mountain Passes*. Boston: Little, Brown, 1964.

Stark, Peter. *Astoria: John Jacob Astor and Thomas Jefferson's Lost Pacific Empire: A Story of Wealth, Ambition, and Survival*. New York: Ecco Books, 2014.

Sullivan, Maurice S. *The Travels of Jedediah Smith—A Documentary Outline, Including His Journals*. Lincoln: University of Nebraska Press, 1992.

———. *The Travels of Jedediah Smith—A Documentary Outline, Including His Journals*. Lincoln: University of Nebraska Press, 1934.

Sunder, John E. *Bill Sublette: Mountain Man*. Norman: University of Oklahoma Press, 1987.

———. *Joshua Pilcher: Fur Trader and Indian Agent*. Norman: University of Oklahoma Press, 1968.

Tilly, Charles. *Coercion, Capital, and European States—AD 990–1992*. Oxford, UK: Basil Blackwell Press, 1990.

Turner, Frederick Jackson. *The Significance of the Frontier in American History*. Madison: State Historical Society of Wisconsin, 1894.

Tykal, Jack B. *Etienne Provost: Man of the Mountains*. Liberty, UT: Eagle's View, 1989.

Utley, Robert M. *A Life Wild and Perilous: Mountain Men and the Paths to the Pacific*. New York: Henry Holt and Company, 1997.

Vestal, Stanley. *Kit Carson: The Happy Warrior of the Old West*. Boston: Houghton Mifflin, 1928.

Winship, George Parker. *The Coronado Expedition, 1540–1542*. Whitefish, MT: Kessinger, 2006.

Wishart, David J. *The Fur Trade of the American West, 1807–1840*. Lincoln: University of Nebraska Press, 1992.

JOURNALS

"Captain Jedediah Strong Smith: A Eulogy of That Most Romantic and Pious of Mountain Men, First American by Land into California." *Castor Canadensis*, Newsletter of the Jedediah Smith Society, University of the Pacific, Stockton, California (Summer 2013): 1–3. http://jedediahsmithsociety.org/wp-content/uploads/2015/07/JSS-Summer-2013.pdf. Originally published in *Illinois Magazine*, June 1832.

Carpenter, Roger. "Making War More Lethal: Iroquois vs. Huron in the Great Lakes Region, 1609 to 1650." *Michigan Historical Review* 27, no. 2 (Fall 2001): 33–51. https://doi.org/10.2307/20173927.

Weiss, Megan. "An Imaginary River: The Legend of the Rio Buenaventura." *Utah Stories from the Beehive Archive*, Utah Humanities © 2022, accessed October 3, 2023. https://www.utahhumanities.org/stories/items/show/418.

ARTICLES

Alford, T. L. "The West as a Desert in American Thought Prior to Long's 1819–20 Expedition." *Journal of the West* 8 (1969): 515–525.

Alwin, John A. "Pelts, Provisions, and Perceptions: The Hudson's Bay Company Mandan Indian Trade, 1795–1812." *Montana: The Magazine of Western History* 29 (July 1979): 16–27.

Belue, Ted Franklin. "Daniel Boone's Yellowstone Hunt." *True West Magazine*, May 2022.

Camp, C. L. "Jedediah Smith's First Far Western Exploration." *Western Historical Quarterly* 4 (1973): 151–170.

Carpenter, Roger. "Making War More Lethal: Iroquois vs. Huron in the Great Lakes Region, 1609 to 1650." *Michigan Historical Review* 27, no. 2 (Fall 2001): 33–51. https://doi.org/10.2307/20173927.

Crampton, C. Gregory, and Gloria G. Griffen. "The San Buenaventura, Mythical River of the West." *Pacific Historical Review* 25 (May 1956): 163–171.

Del Bene, Terry A. "James P. Beckwourth and His Trail." *True West Magazine*, January 2023.

Dollar, C. D. "The High Plains Smallpox Epidemic of 1837–38." *Western Historical Quarterly* 8 (1977): 15–38.

Hafen, Leroy R. "Etienne Provost: Mountain Man and Utah Pioneer." *Utah Historical Quarterly* 36 (1968).

Nichols, Roger L. "Backdrop for Disaster: Causes of the Arikara War of 1823." South Dakota Historical Society, 1984.

Ogden, Peter Skene. "Snake Country Journals, 1824–29." Edited by T. C. Elliott. *The Quarterly of the Oregon Historical Society* 10, no. 4 (December 1909): 331–365, and 11, no. 1 (April 1910).

Ott, Jennifer. "Ruining the Rivers in the Snake Country: The Hudson's Bay Company's Fur Desert Policy." *Oregon Historical Quarterly* 4, no. 2 (2003): 166–195.

Reid, Russell, and Clell G. Gannon, eds. "Journal of the Atkinson-O'Fallon Expedition." *North Dakota Historical Quarterly* 4 (1929): 5–56.

Robinson, Doane. "The Education of Red Cloud." Collection of the South Dakota Department of History, XII (1924): 156–178.

Wesley, Edgar B. "Life at a Frontier Post: Fort Atkinson, 1823–1826." *Journal of the American Military Institute* 3 (Winter 1939): 205–206.

Worcester, Donald E., and Thomas F. Schilz. "The Spread of Firearms among the Indians on the Anglo-French Frontiers." *American Indian Quarterly* 8, no. 2 (Spring 1984).

NEWSPAPERS AND INTERNET SITES

Bagley, Will. "The Astorians Discover South Pass." WyoHistory.org, a Project of the Wyoming Historical Society, November 8, 2014. https://www.wyohistory.org/encyclopedia/astorians-south-pass-discovery.

Johnson, Kirk. "In Fraught Corner of Washington, Classroom with Forty-Foot Waves." *New York Times*, February 19, 2023, A14, New York edition.

Keemle, Charles. *Missouri Herald and St. Louis Advertiser*, November 8, 1826.

Montana.gov, May 19, 2022 (https://mt.gov/).

Williams, Glyndwr. s.v. "Ogden, Peter Skene." *Dictionary of Canadian Biography*, vol. 8, University of Toronto/Université Laval, 2003–. Accessed October 3, 2023, http://www.biographi.ca/en/bio/ogden_peter_skene_8E.html.

ARCHIVE

Hudson's Bay Company. "Snake Country Post Journal 1825–1826." Section B, Class 202, Sub-Division a, Piece 4.

LETTERS

Jedediah Smith, "To the United States Plenipotentiary at Mexico [City]," December 16, 1826.

Jedediah Smith to William Clark, July 12, 1827.

John McLoughlin to Alexander McLeod, September 12, 1828.

George Simpson to Jedediah Smith, December 26, 1828.

George Simpson to Jedediah Smith, December 29, 1828.

Jedediah Smith to Jedediah Smith Sr. and Sally Smith, December 24, 1829.

Jedediah Smith to Ralph Smith, December 24, 1829.

Jedediah Smith to William Clark, December 24, 1829.

Jedediah Smith to Ralph Smith, September 10, 1829.
Jedediah Smith to John Eaton, October 29, 1830.
Jedediah Smith to Ralph Smith, January 26, 1831.
Jedediah Smith to John Eaton, March 2, 1831.

COLLECTIONS

Dale Morgan Collection, Utah State Historical Society, Salt Lake City.
Hudson's Bay Company Archives, Winnipeg, Canada.
Missouri Historical Society, St. Louis.
William H. Ashley Papers, Missouri Historical Society, St. Louis.

NOTES

PROLOGUE

3   *"womaned up"*: "Captain Jedediah Strong Smith," *Castor Canadensis*, 1–3. Originally published in *Illinois Magazine*, June 1832.

CHAPTER 1: "ENTERPRISING YOUNG MEN"

14   *"Spanish Segars"*: Morgan, *Jedediah Smith and the Opening of the American West*, 19.

14   *TO: Enterprising Young Men*: Ibid.

15   *"jumping-off point"*: Sides, *Blood and Thunder*, 8.

15   *"had long been the portal of American expansion"*: Ibid., 60.

17   *"Lewis and Clark were"*: Dale, *The Ashley-Smith Explorations and the Discovery of a Central Route to the Pacific, 1822–1829*, 26.

18   *"We shall to the American union add a barrier"*: Thomas Jefferson to George Rogers Clark, December 25, 1780.

CHAPTER 2: ASTOR'S FOLLY

22   *"were all friendly & Glad to See us"*: Quaife, *The Journals of Captain Meriwether Lewis and Sergeant John Ordway*, 149.

22   *"varied from vicious attacks"*: Nichols, *Backdrop for Disaster*, 107.

24   *"In the spring [of 1822]"*: Sullivan, *The Travels of Jedediah Smith*, 1.

27   *"an emporium of the west"*: Begg, *History of British Columbia*, 157.

27   *"Cape Disappointment"*: Johnson, "In Fraught Corner of Washington, Classroom with Forty-Foot Waves," A14.

29   *"a thunderous roar"*: Stark, *Astoria: John Jacob Astor and Thomas Jefferson's Lost Pacific Empire*, 216.

CHAPTER 3: THE HORSE AND THE GUN

33   *"mourning wars"*: Chambers, *The Oxford Companion to American Military History*, 1.

34   *To paraphrase the sociologist Charles Tilly's*: Tilly, *Coercion, Capital, and European States*, 68.

37   *"They cut the hide open"*: Winship, *The Coronado Expedition, 1540–1542*, 111–112.

41   *"that, seeing their chiefs dead"*: Carpenter, "Making War More Lethal," 33.

42   *During his epic trans-Canadian journey*: Mackenzie, *The Journals of Alexander Mackenzie*, 89.

43   *"was one gun for twenty medium or ten large pelts"*: Worcester and Schilz, "The Spread of Fire-arms among the Indians on the Anglo-French Frontiers," 109.

44   *"the upper part of the River of the West"*: Ibid., 109.

CHAPTER 4: SHIPWRECK

47   *"No mountain man in his time"*: Utley, *A Life Wild and Perilous*, 39.

48   *"As the country was well stocked with Bees"*: Sullivan, *The Travels of Jedediah Smith*, 2.

50   *"slow, Laborious and dangerous"*: Ibid., 1.

51   *"Jedediah was not prepared to concede"*: Ibid., 32.

54   *"by one extensive prairiae"*: Ibid., 3.

54   *"Perhaps since that time"*: Ibid., 7.

55   *"above the common stature"*: Ibid., 5–6.

56   *"given to the moon"*: Paul, *Autobiography of Red Cloud*, 122.

57   *"could almost persuade a man"*: Sullivan, *The Travels of Jedediah Smith*, 5.

CHAPTER 5: *HIVERNANTS*

59   *"potato holes"*: Blevins and Hasselstrom, *Journal of a Mountain Man*, 13.

65   *"[We] moved with great care"*: Sullivan, *The Travels of Jedediah Smith*, 6–7.

67   *"a mild man and a Christian"*: Morgan, *Jedediah Smith and the Opening of the American West*, 46.

68   *"We were generally good hunters"*: Sullivan, *The Travels of Jedediah Smith*, 9–10.

68   *"to see the buffalo"*: Ibid.

69   *"to take what beaver we could conveniently"*: Ibid., 8.

70   *"out-run, out-hop, out-jump"*: O'Neil, *The Old West*, 71.

70   *"medicine"*: Blevins and Hasselstrom, *Journal of a Mountain Man*, 7.

70   *"to catch a beaver"*: Morgan, *Jedediah Smith and the Opening of the American West*, 43.

73   *"Thieving"*: Ibid., 87.

73   *"They frankly explain"*: Morgan, *Jedediah Smith and the Opening of the American West*, 87–88.

CHAPTER 6: A BLOODSTAINED BEACH

76   *"heavy beard surrounded by hair"*: Blevins and Hasselstrom, *Journal of a Mountain Man*, 66.

76   *"Falstaff's Battalion"*: Ibid., 11.

80   *"kind and agreeable manner"*: Dodge, *Biographical Sketch of Jim Bridger*, 5–6.

83   *"Some of them made it"*: Morgan, *Jedediah Smith and the Opening of the American West*, 54.

84   *"excitement of a scene so congenial"*: Nester, *The Arikara War*, 143.

84   *"tolerable strong swimmer"*: Blevins and Hasselstrom, *Journal of a Mountain Man*, 14.

84   *"Save yourself"*: Ibid., 15.

84   *"and made them a low bow"*: Ibid., 17.

CHAPTER 7: THE MISSOURI LEGION

90 *"to make these [Akikara] people"*: O'Fallon, *Letterbook and Related Materials, 1783–1859*, 12–44.

91 *"It is not only an individual"*: Ibid.

91 *"the Blackfeet will hear and tremble"*: Ibid.

92 *"imbecility"*: Ibid.

92 *"bleeding traders"*: Morgan, *Jedediah Smith and the Opening of the American West*, 61.

95 *"more like a swarm of bees"*: Blevins and Hasselstrom, *Journal of a Mountain Man*, 20.

96 *"the grizzle Bear medicine"*: Ibid., 21.

96 *"waling [sic] of squaws and children"*: Ibid., 21.

97 *"to save their stragglers"*: Morgan, *Jedediah Smith and the Opening of the American West*, 72.

98 *"The Rees might have been"*: Ibid., 73.

99 *"sufficiently humbled"*: Ibid., 76.

100 *"the greatest possible contempt for the American character"*: Ibid., 77.

100 *"fully convinced of our ability"*: Ibid., 76.

PART II: THE PASS

101 *I defy the annals*: Parkman, *The Oregon Trail*, 95.

CHAPTER 8: *LES MAUVAIS TERRES*

107 *"sweetish, pungent"*: Blevins and Hasselstrom, *Journal of a Mountain Man*, 23.

108 *"we ware not onley"*: Ibid., 24.

110 *"petrified timber"*: Blevins and Hasselstrom, *Journal of a Mountain Man*, 29.

111 *"a reclining female figure"*: Brown, *The American West*, 4.

112 *"none of us"*: Blevins and Hasselstrom, *Journal of a Mountain Man*, 27.

112 *"I told him I could do nothing"*: Ibid., 28.

112 *"Meat don't spoil in the mountains"*: Ibid., 48.

CHAPTER 9: GLASS

116 *"the nose of a Roman emperor"*: Morgan, *Jedediah Smith and the Opening of the American West*, 42.

116 *"self-willed and insubordinate"*: Ibid., 97.

121 *"Features sunken, arms and hands wasted"*: Ibid., 101.

122 *"Young man"*: Ibid., 102.

122 *"I swore an oath"*: Ibid., 102.

123 *"getting behind a large herd"*: Blevins and Hasselstrom, *Journal of a Mountain Man*, 31.

124 *"Squaws old men and children"*: Ibid.

124 *"Black. Dirty black"*: Ibid., 8.

126 *"Western Mississippi"*: Weiss, "An Imaginary River."

CHAPTER 10: SOUTH PASS

133 *"In American exploration"*: Morgan, *Jedediah Smith and the Opening of the American West*, 90.

134 *"a hericane direct"*: Blevins and Hasselstrom, *Journal of a Mountain Man*, 35.

135 *"talked cooked eat"*: Ibid., 36.

CHAPTER 11: THE SURVIVOR

138   *"Diggers"*: Blevins and Hasselstrom, *Journal of a Mountain Man*, 39.
138   *"His fear was so great"*: Stark, *Astoria: John Jacob Astor and Thomas Jefferson's Lost Pacific Empire*, 143.
139   *"our old acquaintances"*: Blevins and Hasselstrom, *Journal of a Mountain Man*, 39.
141   *"soon raised 4 or 5 fires"*: Ibid., 40.
141   *"disagreeable neighbors"*: Ibid.
143   *"I bearly saved my scalp"*: Ibid., 45.
143   *"horse brobly"*: Ibid., 44.
143   *"I swoned emmediately"*: Ibid., 44.

CHAPTER 12: DEAD MEN WALKING

147   *"right peart"*: Morgan, *Jedediah Smith and the Opening of the American West*, 107–108.
147   *"It was not the custom"*: Ibid., 108.
147   *"Go, false man"*: Ibid.
148   *Mourn not dear friends*: Blevins and Hasselstrom, *Journal of a Mountain Man*, 45.
148   *"In a more pitiable state"*: Ibid., 44–45.
150   *"The trappers and hunters"*: O'Fallon, *Letterbook and Related Materials, 1783–1859*, 12–44, 67.
151   *"first person perpendicular"*: Morgan, *Jedediah Smith and the Opening of the American West*, 156.

CHAPTER 13: FLATHEAD POST

156   *left to "remane"*: Morgan, *Jedediah Smith and the Opening of the American West*, 122.
157   *"Unruly, ill-tongued villains"*: *Journal of Alexander Ross*, 366–385.
158   *"the very scum of the country"*: Morgan, *Jedediah Smith and the Opening of the American West*, 126.
158   *"The men were reduced to virtual serfdom"*: Ibid.
158   *"two strong" in terms of*: Ibid., 127.
159   *"good for nothings"*: Ibid., 125.
160   *"trapless and beaverless"*: Ibid., 129.
161   *"a very intelligent person"*: Ibid.
161   *"more luck than I had"*: Ibid., 131.
163   *"empty headed"*: Ott, "Ruining the Rivers in the Snake Country," 175.
163   *"a fur desert"*: Ibid.

CHAPTER 14: "A SLY, CUNNING YANKEY"

165   *"were being managed in a way"*: Bown, *The Company*, 339.
166   *"for political reasons"*: Ott, "Ruining the Rivers in the Snake Country," 175.
167   *"a sly, cunning Yankey"*: Morgan, *Jedediah Smith and the Opening of the American West*, 138.
169   *"annoy and oppose the Americans"*: Ibid., 139.

CHAPTER 15: "SHETSKEDEE"

172   *"two large rivers"*: Morgan, *Jedediah Smith and the Opening of the American West*, 154.
172   *"Here is the dawn of South Pass"*: Ibid., 155.

173 *"perpetual friendship"*: Drury and Clavin, *The Heart of Everything That Is*, 61.
173 *"a wagon and team &c"*: Dale, *The Ashley-Smith Explorations and the Discovery of a Central Route to the Pacific, 1822–1829*, 118.
175 *"mass of snow and ice"*: Ibid., 128.
176 *"gaudy liar"*: Morgan, *Jedediah Smith and the Opening of the American West*, 156.
176 *"any fool can tell the truth"*: Butler, *The Note Books of Samuel Butler*, 377.
177 *"No jokes, no fireside stories, no fun"*: Beckwourth, *The Life and Adventures of James P. Beckwourth*, 19.
177 *"at some conspicuous point"*: Morgan, *Jedediah Smith and the Opening of the American West*, 162.
178 *"made red with vermillion"*: Ibid.

CHAPTER 16: GUNS ALONG THE BEAR

180 *"fell on a considerable river"*: Morgan, *Jedediah Smith and the Opening of the American West*, 143.
183 *"They appeared very doubtful of us"*: Ibid., 143.
183 *"a fatal blow to our expectations"*: Ibid., 144.
185 *"they would most willingly shoot us"*: Ibid., 148.
186 *"You have had these men"*: Ibid., 149.
186 *"Remain at your peril"*: Ibid.
187 *"Here I am"*: Ibid., 151.

CHAPTER 17: "RANDAVOUZE CREEK"

189 *"Eutau tribe"*: Dale, *The Ashley-Smith Explorations and the Discovery of a Central Route to the Pacific, 1822–1829*, 150.
190 *"made marks indicative"*: Morgan, *Jedediah Smith and the Opening of the American West*, 165.
191 *"hunting, fishing, target shooting"*: Beckwourth, *The Life and Adventures of James P. Beckwourth*, 34.
192 *"the comparative thralldom of civilization"*: Morgan, *Jedediah Smith and the Opening of the American West*, 192.
195 *"slay bells"*: Ibid., 172.
195 *"fofarraw"*: Ibid.
196 *"nothing remarkable"*: Dale, *The Ashley-Smith Explorations and the Discovery of a Central Route to the Pacific, 1822–1829*, 160.
197 *"hail[ing] our landing"*: Beckwourth, *The Life and Adventures of James P. Beckwourth*, 38.
197 *"he made a furious spring"*: Ibid.
198 *"God only knows"*: Letter, Jedediah Smith to Jedediah Smith Sr. and Sally Smith, December 24, 1829 (in Morgan, *Jedediah Smith and the Opening of the American West*, 350–351).
198 *"a party of men"*: Morgan, *Jedediah Smith and the Opening of the American West*, 175.
198 *"down the several rivers"*: Ibid., 174.
199 *"extreme west end"*: Ibid., 182.

CHAPTER 18: EASTERN STIRRINGS

209 *"coasted the lake"*: Blevins and Hasselstrom, *Journal of a Mountain Man*, 61.
210 *"spiritous water"*: Drury and Clavin, *The Heart of Everything That Is*, 25.

210 *"an inversion of the conventional order"*: Ibid., 98.

210 *"red heathens"*: Hafen and Young, *Fort Laramie and the Pageant of the West*, 54–56.

210 *"Captain Bridger's company"*: Ibid.

211 *"grand frolic"*: Barbour, *Jedediah Smith*, 74.

212 *"The Great Author of nature"*: St. Louis Enquirer, March 11, 1826.

212 *"the sterility of the country"*: Ibid.

213 *"Were indeed of no small interest"*: Keemle, *Missouri Herald and St. Louis Advertiser*, November 8, 1826.

213 *"to hunt as bare as possible"*: Morgan, *Jedediah Smith and the Opening of the American West*, 272.

213 *"If the American Traders"*: Ibid., 274–275.

214 *"Wagons and carriages"*: Ibid.

214 *"Needless to say"*: Barbour, *Jedediah Smith*, 57.

CHAPTER 19: "A COUNTRY OF STARVATION"

215 *"broad and handsomely striped"*: Harrison Rogers Journal, November 27, 1826.

216 *"a section of the country"*: Letter, Jedediah Smith to General William Clark, July 12, 1827.

216 *"Hercules in a cradle"*: Edling, *A Hercules in the Cradle*, 1.

217 *"no white men"*: Morgan, *Jedediah Smith and the Opening of the American West*, 195.

218 *"50 balls; 1 lb powder"*: Harrison Rogers Daybook, August 27, 1826.

219 *"a Country of Starvation"*: Letter, Jedediah Smith, "To the United States Plenipotentiary at Mexico [City]," December 16, 1826.

219 *"Pa-Utches"*: Letter, Jedediah Smith to General William Clark, July 12, 1827.

221 *"Pautch farm"*: Ibid.

221 *"remarkably barren"*: Ibid.

222 *"to draw even Jedediah Smith's eye"*: Morgan, *Jedediah Smith and the Opening of the American West*, 200.

223 *"the Californias"*: Letter, Jedediah Smith to General William Clark, July 12, 1827.

223 *"was not far from some of the [Spanish] Missions"*: Letter, Jedediah Smith "To the United States Plenipotentiary at Mexico [City]," December 16, 1826.

CHAPTER 20: A SPANISH INQUISITION

226 So *"complete"* were these *"barrens"*: Letter, Jedediah Smith to General William Clark, July 12, 1827.

226 *"handsome bottoms"*: Harrison Rogers Journal, November 29, 1826.

226 *"a British Barracks"*: Ibid.

227 Spanish *"sigars"*: Ibid.

227 Despite being a *"Catholick"*: Ibid.

228 *"disapproving eye toward the prevailing theology"*: Sullivan, *The Travels of Jedediah Smith*, 16.

229 *"tolerable good music"*: Harrison Rogers Journal, December 11, 1826.

229 *"forward" lass*: Ibid., January 8, 1827.

231 *"furnish no other company or Individual with Merchandise"*: Morgan, *Jedediah Smith and the Opening of the American West*, 221.

232 *"fair and fat"*: Dale, *The Ashley-Smith Explorations and the Discovery of a Central Route to the Pacific, 1822–1829*, 205.

232 *"juiceless" administrator*: Morgan, *Jedediah Smith and the Opening of the American West*, 204.

232 *"Very much of a Gentleman"*: Letter, Jedediah Smith "To the United States Plenipotentiary at Mexico [City]," December 16, 1826.

233 *"of the truth"*: Ibid.

CHAPTER 21: DREAMS OF COOLING CASCADES

237 *"Valley of the Bonadventure"*: Barbour, *Jedediah Smith*, 183, 185–186.

238 *"150 miles to 200 miles"*: Jedediah Smith Journal, February 28, 1828.

240 *"Great Sand Plain"*: Letter, Jedediah Smith to William Clark, July 12, 1827.

240 *"Indians," as Smith described them*: Ibid.

240 *"much better than horsemeat"*: Jedediah Smith Journal, June 22, 1827.

241 *"The view ahead was almost hopeless"*: Jedediah Smith Journal, June 24, 1827.

241 *"for the purpose of cooling"*: Ibid.

241 *"Our sleep was not repose"*: Ibid.

241 *"it seemed to us that we"*: Jedediah Smith Journal, June 25, 1827.

241 *"We could do no good"*: Ibid.

242 *"bathing my burning forehead"*: Ibid.

243 *"indeed the most cheering view"*: Jedediah Smith Journal, June 27, 1827.

243 *"a fine, fat Buck"*: Jedediah Smith Journal, June 29, 1827.

CHAPTER 22: DUELING WARPATHS

246 *"the irruption of the twenty-five armed [Americans]"*: Morgan, *Jedediah Smith and the Opening of the American West*, 229.

247 *"necessary measures"*: Ibid.

247 *"infractions of the laws of Mexico"*: Ibid., 230.

248 *"I of course expected to find Beaver"*: Sullivan, *The Travels of Jedediah Smith*, 26.

248 *"seemed as friendly"*: Ibid., 29.

250 *"After weighing all the circumstances"*: Ibid., 30.

250 *"a tolerable lance"*: Ibid., 31.

250 *"I told them we would"*: Ibid.

251 *"Gradually the enemy was drawing near"*: Ibid.

251 *"Upon this the indians [sic]"*: Ibid.

251 *"The days were extremely warm"*: Ibid., 32.

252 *"Gape of the Mountain" rising in the west*: Ibid., 34.

CHAPTER 23: BLOODY OREGON

254 *"to try once more"*: Letter, Jedediah Smith to William Clark, December 24, 1829.

255 *"a dirty hovel"*: Ibid.

255 *"Spanish cruelty"*: Ibid.

256 *"When you came to San Diego"*: Sullivan, *The Travels of Jedediah Smith*, 39.

256 *"mysterious business"*: Ibid., 39.

256 *"placed in power"*: Ibid., 40.

257 *"Beef Corn Beans & c"*: Ibid., 43.

258 *"returning to the woods"*: Ibid., 54.

258 *the "slous"*: Jedediah Smith Journal, February 23, 1828.

259 *"The Horse being strong and much frightened"*: Jedediah Smith Journal, April 7, 1828.

259 *"cold water and a salve of Sugar and Soap"*: Jedediah Smith Journal, March 10, 1828.

259 *"The lowest intermediate link"*: Jedediah Smith Journal, March 21, 1828.

261 *"Finding the [Indians]"*: Harrison Rogers Journal, June 25, 1828.

262 *"Any person apprised of the character"*: Jedediah Smith Journal, April 26, 1828.

262 *"Oh God, may it please thee"*: Harrison Rogers Journal, May 22, 1878.

263 *"stood with our guns ready"*: Harrison Rogers Journal, July 12, 1828.

264 *"wel Hammett"*: Harrison Rogers Journal, July 5, 1828.

CHAPTER 24: FORT VANCOUVER

267 *"we answered in the negative"*: Alexander McLeod Journal, September 12, 1828 (in Sullivan, *The Travels of Jedediah Smith*, 124).

267 *"the late Jedediah Smith"*: Morgan, *Jedediah Smith and the Opening of the American West*, 268.

268 *"Umpqua Massacre"*: Ibid., 256.

268 *"through regions where heavily armed parties"*: Ibid., 274.

269 *"make War on the Murderers"*: Letter, John McLoughlin to Alexander McLeod, September 12, 1828 (in Sullivan, *The Travels of Jedediah Smith*, 110).

269 *"some Beads, Books, journals and other Papers"*: Alexander McLeod Journal, November 10, 1828 (in Sullivan, *The Travels of Jedediah Smith*, 131).

270 *"was such a figure"*: Morgan, *Jedediah Smith and the Opening of the American West*, 270.

271 *"as much or even something more"*: Ibid., 271.

271 *"the lamentable and melancholy fate"*: Letter, George Simpson to Jedediah Smith, December 26, 1828 (in Sullivan, *The Travels of Jedediah Smith*, 136).

271 *"the all grasping policy"*: George Simpson Report to the Governor and Committee of the Hudson's Bay Company, London, March 1, 1829.

272 *"Common men"*: Ibid.

272 *"the concern"*: Letter, George Simpson to Jedediah Smith, December 26, 1828.

272 *"the height of impudence"*: Ibid.

272 *"would be in our opinion"*: Ibid.

272 *"of very bad quality"*: Ibid.

273 *"If these terms are not satisfactory to you"*: Ibid.

273 *Alternately, Simpson informed Smith and Black*: Ibid.

273 *"renumeration . . . or indemnification"*: Letter, George Simpson to Jedediah Smith, December 29, 1828.

273 *"in Law or Equity"*: Letter, George Simpson to Jedediah Smith, December 26, 1828.

CHAPTER 25: "A THRONE OF GRACE"

276 *"cut into pieces"*: Ogden Journal, February 17, 1828.

276 *"as fleet as the wind"*: Beckwourth, *The Life and Adventures of James P. Beckwourth*, 46.

276 *"astonished"*: Ibid., 47.

276 *"were satisfied"*: Ibid.

280 *"Mutch Slighted Parents"*: Letter, Jedediah Smith to Jedediah Smith Sr. and Sally Smith, December 24, 1829.

280 *"As it respects my Spiritual welfare"*: Letter, Jedediah Smith to Ralph Smith, December 24, 1829.

281 *"Smith, Jackson & Sublette"*: Letter, Jedediah Smith to William Clark, December 24, 1829.

281 *"the 15 to 20 pieces of cannon"*: Jedediah Smith Journal entry, December 27, 1828.

282 *itemizing the value of the "Merchdz. taken"*: Letter, Jedediah Smith to William Clark, December 24, 1829 (in Morgan, *Jedediah Smith and the Opening of the American West*, 341–342, 337).

282 *"While the [British] pass"*: Ibid., 342.

283 *"which was cheerfully obeyed"*: Morgan, *Jedediah Smith and the Opening of the American West*, 314.

284 *"ease with which the [wagon wheels] rolled"*: Morgan, *Jedediah Smith and the Opening of the American West*, 322–323.

285 *"The mortifying intelligence"*: Letter, Jedediah Smith to Ralph Smith, September 10, 1829.

CHAPTER 26: THE LAST TRAILHEAD

286 *"level country"*: Letter, Jedediah Smith to John Eaton, October 29, 1830.

286 *"These hardy and sun-burnt Mountaineers"*: *Missouri Intelligencer*, October 9, 1830.

287 *Not including the copious register*: Letter, Jedediah Smith to John Eaton, October 29, 1830.

288 *"the ease and safety"*: Ibid.

288 *"As to the injury"*: Ibid.

288 *"The inequity of the convention"*: Ibid.

289 *"unformed character"*: Morgan, *Jedediah Smith and the Opening of the American West*, 324.

290 *"my Brother"*: Letter, Jedediah Smith to Ralph Smith, January 26, 1831.

290 *"seminary of higher learning"*: Kay and Barwick, *Jacksonville, Illinois*, 13.

CHAPTER 27: "WHERE HIS BONES ARE BLEACHING"

296 *"Though he fell under the spears"*: "Captain Jedediah Strong Smith," *Castor Canadensis*, 1–3. Originally published in *Illinois Magazine*, June 1832.

296 *"the greatest American traveler"*: Ibid.

297 *"How shocking must the summons be"*: Letter Jedediah Smith to Ralph Smith, January 26, 1831.

298 *Lord, I believe a rest remains*: Ibid.

EPILOGUE

299 *Walk quietly*: Muir, *Our National Parks*, 36.

311 *"Notes on western Caledonia"*: Williams, "Ogden, Peter Skene." *Dictionary of Canadian Biography*, Volume VIII [1851–1860].

311 *"A brutish, ignorant, superstitious"*: Ibid.

314 *"Monsieur Proveau"*: Tykal, *Etienne Provost*, 238.

319 *As a member of the House Committee on Indian Affairs*: Dale, *The Ashley-Smith Explorations and the Discovery of a Central Route to the Pacific, 1822–1829*, 175.

326 *"I cannot consent"*: Letter, Jedediah Smith to John Eaton, March 2, 1831.

INDEX

ABOUT THE AUTHORS

43rd Bomb Group

Gordon M. Grant

Bob Drury and **Tom Clavin** are the #1 *New York Times* bestselling authors of, most recently, *The Last Hill,* as well as *Blood and Treasure; The Heart of Everything That Is; Lucky 666; Halsey's Typhoon; Last Men Out; Valley Forge;* and *The Last Stand of Fox Company,* which won the Marine Corps Heritage Foundation's General Wallace M. Greene, Jr. Award. They live in Manasquan, New Jersey, and Sag Harbor, New York, respectively.